Penguin Education

The Economics of Women and Work

The Economics of Women and Work

Edited by Alice H. Amsden

Penguin Books

Penguin Books Ltd, Harmondsworth,
Middlesex, England
Penguin Books, 625 Madison Avenue,
New York, New York 10022, U.S.A.
Penguin Books Australia Ltd, Ringwood,
Victoria, Australia
Penguin Books Canada Ltd, 2801 John Street,
Markham, Ontario, Canada L3R 1B4
Penguin Books (N.Z.) Ltd, 182–190 Wairau Road,
Auckland 10, New Zealand

First published 1980

Made and printed in Great Britain by
Richard Clay (The Chaucer Press) Ltd,
Bungay, Suffolk
Set in Monotype Times

Contents

Permission to reproduce the readings published in this
volume is acknowledged from the following sources:

1. National Bureau of Economic Research, Inc.
2. Cambridge University Press
3. Scientific American, Inc.
4. Cambridge University Press
5. Daedalus
6. Academic Press Inc. (London) Ltd
7. University of Chicago Press
8. American Economic Association
9. Industrial & Labor Relations Review
10. American Economic Association
11. Academic Press Inc. (London) Ltd
12. Eastern Economic Association and Dr Barbara Bergmann
13. British Journal of Industrial Relations
14. Industrial & Labor Relations Review
15. Joint Economic Committee, Congress of the United States
16. Organisation for Economic Co-operation and Development
17. American Economic Association
18. American Statistical Association

Acknowledgements

This study was financed in part by a grant from the Ford Foundation to the Center for the Social Sciences, Program in Sex Roles and Social Change, Columbia University. I would like to thank the following people for helpful criticisms: Moshe Adler, Johannah Brenner, Robert Brenner, Robert Cotterman, Duncan Foley, Cynthia Lloyd, Myra Strober, Sean Wilentz, Mary O'Neill Berry and participants in the Barnard Women's Studies Program.

Introduction

The renaissance in the 1960s of an active women's liberation movement in most of the advanced capitalist countries produced a proliferation of journal articles and books by economists on women and work. The American literature is far more voluminous than the rest but studies in English have also emerged from the U.K. and Canada. For some, women have merely provided yet another definable group on which to test their economic models. Others, however, have set out to understand the position of women under a capitalist system that is constantly in the process of transforming itself.

There has been much to write about, for there has been both movement and stasis in women's position. One of the most dramatic changes has been the increased participation in paid employment of both working- and middle-class women, and especially married women. In the U.K., only 10% of married women worked for wages in 1921. The figure rose to almost 22% in 1951 and shot up to over 42% in 1971 (U.K., Department of Employment, 1974). An almost identical pattern is observable in the U.S.: the labor force participation rate of married women was 9% in 1920 (roughly double what it was in 1890), 23% in 1950, 41% in 1970, and is still rising rapidly (U.S. Bureau of the Census, 1976). This change in the lives of married women has mirrored profound transformations in the economic and social structures of the Western world: the relative decline of agriculture and small family enterprise and the ascendance of monopoly capitalism; the penetration of capitalism into the home and the displacement of domestic labor (Berch, 1975; Cowan, 1976; Hartmann, 1974; Leibowitz, 1974); and the emergence of new patterns of social interaction as implied by changing birth, death, and divorce rates.

Co-existent with such change has been one constant: the continued reproduction of sexual inequality. It is written in the Bible that the value of a woman shall be assessed at three-fifths of the value of a man. However many years have elapsed since the Book of Leviticus was written, and whatever might have happened in the interim, women today still earn approximately 60% of what men earn. No less invariant has been occupational segregation by sex: a large number of women are still crowded into a small number of occupations (Gross, 1968). In

England, five out of 27 industries accounted for almost 70% of all women workers (Chiplin and Sloane, 1976a). In the U.S., about half of all employed women were concentrated in occupations where they represented 80% or more of total employment; only 2% of male workers were in these occupations (see the Table prepared by Zellner in Reading 15. There has been little movement of women into male-dominated fields over the past decade (Reagan, 1978; Blau and Hendricks, 1979).

The changing labor force participation rates of women (in relation to non-market activity), and the persistently lower pay they receive for their efforts, are the two major topics on which economists have concentrated their attention. Consequently, the first two sections of readings in this collection are devoted to these topics. Economists have also begun to question the implications for consumption, income distribution and unemployment of rising participation rates. The differential impact of business cycles on men and women has also been explored. Part Three, therefore, gathers together some of the work which has been done in this area.

Although economists differ among themselves on all of these major topics, they have not, for the most part, confronted each other with their disagreements. Those which have appeared in print have generally involved economists of the same theoretical persuasion. To correct partially for the absence of debate, not only were readings in this collection organized by topic, but an attempt was made to include antagonistic views on each topic. Four views are singled out: the neoclassical, the institutional, the Marxist, and the radical.

The purpose of this Introduction is to help students distinguish these different approaches to specific problems. The insights yielded by each can then be evaluated. Nevertheless, none of the paradigms is entirely homogeneous. There is also much theoretical overlap, especially between the institutional school and the others. The radical literature exhibits less of a sharply delineated body of theory and more of a reaction to a set of problems dramatized in the late 1960s and early 1970s. Consequently, it will not receive a separate presentation, but it is hoped that differences between radical and Marxist economists will become clear in the course of discussion.

While the four views have a common interest in the same broad sets of issues, each has differently defined what is problematic. Thus, it was sometimes necessary to reconstruct arguments and to provide a coherence where none existed. The shortcomings of each of the views were also singled out in the hope of stimulating further critical debate.

1. Neoclassical theory

Before launching into a discussion of the specifics of neoclassical theory and women's employment, a brief account of how the pieces of neoclassical theory fit together in the general case may be of help to students.

The primary analytical category in neoclassical theory is the individual. Individuals exercise freedom of choice and behave rationally to maximize utility. Their maximization of welfare, however, is subject to constraints. Income and prices are the major constraints and are the major determinants of individuals' behavior. Because it is believed that the essence of rational individuals' behavior can be captured by a model which utilizes a limited number of universal economic variables, it is also believed that this model can be projected over time and across social strata. The human subject of neoclassical investigation is a timeless, classless, raceless, and cultureless creature; although male, unless otherwise specified.

Changes in income are not understood as a structural phenomenon in neoclassical theory: quantitative changes in income do not give rise to qualitative changes. Rather, variations in income are conceptualized as occurring in small, imperceptible quanta and hence the technique of calculus is easily applied in research methodology and frequently used. Because human behavior changes glacially over time in response to anonymous variations in income, behavioral influences which are social, cultural, or ideological are assumed to be stable. Such extraneous influences are lumped together as 'tastes,' and left to other social scientists to ponder. Because behavioral differences among individuals at a moment in time are attributed mainly to differences in income, inexplicable behavior due to tastes is believed to be either trivial or idiosyncratic.

Recently it has been argued that even differences in tastes may be subsumed under income and price variables. It is worth citing a part of the argument before proceeding to specifics because the citation conveys the centrality of market prices and income in the neoclassical paradigm in the words of two of its most influential proponents:

... one does not argue over tastes for the same reason that one does not argue over the Rocky Mountains – both are there, will be there next year, too, and are the same to all men.

On the traditional view, an explanation of economic phenomena that reaches a difference in tastes between people or times is the terminus of the argument: the problem is abandoned *at this point* to whoever studies and explains tastes (psychologists? anthropologists? phrenologists? sociobiologists?). On our preferred interpretation, one never reaches this impasse: the economist continues to search for differences in prices or incomes to explain any differences or changes in behavior (Stigler and Becker, 1977).

How successful such reductionism is in explaining reality is what economists who hold opposing views are prepared to dispute.

Homework and market work

In 1962, Jacob Mincer proffered an answer to the question of why, beginning in 1890, wives' labor force participation had increased. His answer concentrated on the contraposed impact of income and prices on wives' behavior. The theoretical framework which Mincer developed inspired further research largely of a cross-sectional nature on the working-wife phenomenon. Mincer's article appears as Reading 1 in this collection.

Mincer was interested in resolving a contradiction in time series and cross-section findings on married women's labor force participation. Cross-section studies showed an inverse relationship between husbands' income and wives' labor force participation. Time series showed a positive relationship. Mincer argued that in addition to husband's earnings, a wife's own wage rate (price of labor) would influence how she chose to spend her time. Her choice, moreover, was not simply a dichotomous one between market work and leisure, but one involving market work, leisure, and homework. Mincer observed that the rising fortunes of married women in the twentieth century, in the form of their higher own take-home pay, attracted them into paid employment. The opportunity costs of both their leisure and homework rose (the greater the substitutability of market goods for home production and consumption, the greater the opportunity costs). The triumph of the substitution effect over the income effect thus in principle resolved the contradiction: while higher income pulled women towards indulging in more leisure time, higher wages pushed them in the opposite direction and out of the home. Women in increasing numbers entered paid employment, especially after World War II.[1]

Once the neoclassicists discovered that time has many competing uses in addition to market activities and leisure, they followed Mincer's lead and broadened the scope of their discipline to include non-market

1. Mincer sees the need for 'further elaboration' of this resolution of cross-section and time series findings but, unfortunately, he does not indicate what such elaboration might involve.

activities. Since for neoclassicists a problem qualifies as economic if scarcity is involved, and scarcity requires choice, precious time spent outside the monetary sector became a respectable subject of inquiry. Thus was born the 'new home economics' and marriage, motherhood, divorce, and death became grist for the economist's mill. Because Gary Becker's general theory of the allocation of time among any number of alternative uses laid the analytical groundwork for the 'new home economics', it appears as Reading 2.

Given the importance of the family outside the monetary sector, economists of all theoretical persuasions have invited Adam Smith into the household and have explored the division of labor within it. Neoclassical and Marxist theorists have also asked why the family exists at all.

According to neoclassical theory, people marry because in so doing they increase their utility. The gain from marriage (or co-habiting) compared to remaining single for any two persons is positively related to their incomes, the relative difference in their wage rates, and the level of non-market-productivity-augmenting variables, such as beauty. The gain from marriage is greater the more complementary are the inputs of husband and wife. Since a sperm and an egg are required to make a baby, and neither can be substituted for the other, the gain from marriage is positively related to the importance of children (Becker, 1973).

The division of labor within the family according to the 'new home economics' derives from the marriage market equilibrium and is determined by marginal productivities. Marriage is conceptualized as 'a two-person firm with either member being the "entrepreneur" who "hires" the other at ... (a) "salary" ... and receives residual "profits"' ... (Becker, 1974). Women hire men as breadwinners since men earn more than women in the market (women's earning powers are diminished by their childrearing activities). Men hire women as nursemaids since women bear children and are superior at rearing them (men's childrearing powers are diminished by their market earning activities). This division of labor is concluded to be consistent with economic maximizing principles.

One may be impressed by the ingenuity of so symmetrical a modelling of market and non-market activity by neoclassical theorists. Or one may be struck by its absurdity. But the real question, as discussed later, is not modelling but meaningfulness: does the 'new home economics' say anything new at all about women and the economics of the home?

Sex differentials in wage and unemployment rates

Just as individuals in neoclassical theory enjoy freedom of choice, so, too, they must bear responsibility for the choices they make. Thus, most neoclassical theorists do not ascribe women's lower earnings and flatter earnings profile over the life cycle to any injustice. Rather, they attribute it to women's voluntarily smaller investments in human capital and hence lower productivity. Productivity between men and women of the same age and level of education is said to differ for two reasons. First, women on average spend proportionately fewer years in the labor force then men. They interrupt their market work to bear and rear children. Second, when women are working, the jobs they choose provide them with fewer opportunities to enhance their skills. They thereby acquire less experience and on-the-job training than men; and their earnings merely reflect this. The classic formulation of this argument is found in Mincer and Polachek (Reading 7).

According to the argument of human capital theorists like Mincer and Polachek, since on-the-job training is costly in terms of foregone earnings, women who expect to drop out of the labor force maximize their earnings over their life cycle by avoiding employment which involves such training. Profit-maximizing principles also lead employers to fill skill-enhancing, remunerative job slots with men, in their belief that men's labor force attachment is more stable on average than women's. Employers may inadvertently discriminate against individual women whose labor force commitment is stable. The high costs of obtaining information about individual workers, however, makes such stereotypical judgments rational. Such rationality is termed 'statistical discrimination' and Phelps (Reading 8) provides an exact model of statistical discrimination for those 'who like exact models . . .'

One basic unresolved issue in the human capital argument is the extent to which low levels of human capital are the cause or the effect of observed labor force instability. Low wages due to discrimination (statistical and otherwise) may discourage women from investing in human capital; and low investments in human capital perpetuate women's lower earnings.

A second loose end in the human capital argument is the following: 'The human capital school's reliance on the primacy of the family in a woman's life could only explain a greater tendency of women to be in "low-skill" jobs. With this reasoning, they could not explain the concentration of women in a small number of female occupations within each skill category. To explain this concentration the school would have to rely on women's "tastes" [or discrimination]' (Blau and Jusenius, 1976).

No less definitive is the fact that Mincer and Polachek controlled for job experience in their empirical work but were still unable to account for a 20% differential in male and female earnings. Much subsequent research has been hopeful of achieving a better score since on-the-job training was not measured directly by Mincer and Polachek. As Cain (1976) explains: 'If, according to neoclassical theory, workers of equal productivity should receive equal wages, and they do not, then it is natural to expect the defenders of the theory to question whether productivity was really equal; specifically, whether the personal productivity factors are completely enumerated and accurately measured.'

Some neoclassical theorists assume that discrimination exists and proceed to explore the implications. One implication is that under competitive conditions employers who discriminate make lower profits than employers who don't (Becker, 1971; Arrow, 1972, 1973). This is quite important. If it is unprofitable for employers to discriminate, it is unlikely that they will, and the mechanism in a capitalist economy by which discrimination is perpetuated must be sought elsewhere. If employers either actively or passively discriminate without paying for it, the industrial organization which makes this possible must also be studied. Unfortunately, neoclassical theorists have as yet done neither. If employers discriminate, neoclassical theorists attribute this to 'tastes' and predict that discrimination will vanish under competitive conditions.[2]

Women, on average, not only earn lower pay than men. They also experience higher rates of unemployment. In no less than 14 out of 16 OECD countries, the secular unemployment rate of women is higher than that of men; and reported rates of unemployment generally underestimate joblessness.[3] Official statistics typically exclude people who

2. Neoclassical theorists also consider the case where employees have a 'taste' for discrimination. Under competitive conditions, the final result is total segregation between definable groups but no wage differential. Although there is much occupational segregation between men and women, there is also a large wage differential.

3. The 16 cited members of the OECD (Organisation for Economic Co-operation and Development) comprise: Australia, Austria, Canada, Denmark, Finland, France, Germany, Italy, Japan, the Netherlands, New Zealand, Norway, Spain, Sweden, the U.K., and the U.S. Unemployment was consistently higher for men than for women in the U.K. and the Netherlands, but unemployment statistics in

are too discouraged to search for work. The reported male-female unemployment differential, however, tends to *narrow* in business recessions.

A neoclassical analysis of differences in reported unemployment rates between men and women is developed by Niemi in Reading 14. She argues that women's higher propensity to move into and out of the labor force than men's is a major reason for their higher unemployment. Re-entrance into the labor market typically involves a period of frictional unemployment as women search for the best available jobs. The search process is conceived of as an income maximizing strategy in which workers weigh the returns and costs of search.

Niemi further argues that women's unemployment relative to men's falls in times of economic depression in part because women's labor force participation is 'procyclically' timed: women leave the labor market in business slumps and re-enter in prosperity.

In short, neoclassical theorists conceptualize unemployment as voluntary.

2. The institutional school

There is a long tradition of institutional economics both in the U.S. and in the U.K. American institutionalists writing about labor can trace their lineage back to the progressives of the late nineteenth and early twentieth centuries and to the liberal technocrats of the post World War II period (Doeringer, Reading 9, identifies the latter). The historical antecedents of the institutional school in the U.K. include the appeals by nineteenth-century reformers for legislation to improve the conditions of women and children in factories.[4] They also include the Webbs

---

these countries are based on registration data which may underestimate the extent of unemployment especially among women. Unemployment in all these countries is analyzed in Reading 16. Sorrentino (1976) gives a detailed account of differences in the measurement of unemployment among OECD countries. Bowers (1975) discusses the measurement procedure in the U.K.

4. The economists who supported factory legislation in the nineteenth century, however, were of many theoretical persuasions. They included some conservatives as well as Karl Marx. Stanley Jevons, for example, the progenitor of marginal utility theory, was for banning married women with young children from working in factories so that 'the wife, no longer a mere slattern factory-hand, would become a true mother and housekeeper' and 'troops of happy, chubby children would replace the "wizened little monkeys" of girls and the "little old men boys", which now form the miserable remnants of families' (1882). Marx supported factory reforms but saw them as inadequate.

and other Fabians in the twentieth century. What unites the traditions in the two countries is an anti-Marxism. Many institutionalists frequently have written in reaction against neoclassical orthodoxy and laissez-faireism but have not renounced conventional economic principles.

Institutionalists writing about the family today can trace their heritage back to Thorstein Veblen, Margaret Reid, and Hazel Kyrk. The family is viewed as an institution whose decision-making processes and structural permutations are explored. Unlike neoclassicists, who first look at individuals separately and then join them in marital equilibrium, institutionalists concentrate on the union between husband and wife. While institutionalists explore the connection between women's non-market and market work, they do not, as Marxists do, expand on the interconnections between the family and capital accumulation.

A piece by Isabel Sawhill is representative of the institutional approach and appears as Reading 5. The objections she raises against the 'new home economics' are reviewed later.

Valerie Oppenheimer's study (1970) of women's increased labor force participation can be construed as institutional insofar as its explanatory power rests on job typing and the system by which jobs are allocated. Oppenheimer associates the higher entry of women into the market with the growing availability of 'women's work'.

Institutionalism reaches its fullest expression on questions of occupational segregation by sex and women's lower pay. In this context, institutionalists are labeled segmented labor market (SLM) theorists. The article by Doeringer (Reading 9) was elected to represent the institutional view. Economists other than institutionalists also believe that labor markets are segmented rather than competitive. One may distinguish the radical interpretation of segmentation by Reich, Gordon, and Edwards (Reading 10); a contribution by Rubery which focuses on phenomena of particular concern to Marxists (Reading 11); and a model by Bergmann (Reading 12). The last is analytically neoclassical insofar as women are paid the value of their marginal product although they are occupationally segregated and they are occupationally segregated because of employers' 'tastes'.

The importance of occupational segregation by sex, both in theory and in practice, makes some general introductory remarks necessary before proceeding to particulars.

The division of labor by sex appears to be universal in human history. But it is not at all clear why this division is typically hierarchical or why the rewards of specialization are more equitably distributed between the sexes at some stages of economic development than at others. Even if men's superior physical strength has contributed to women's inferior position, to understand sexual subjugation solely in terms of biology may be as unhelpful as trying to understand class domination in terms of police power. As Engels wrote in *Anti-Duhring* with regard to capitalism, 'force cannot make money', and with regard to sexual inequality, the search continues for the systemic forces which reproduce it.

The work of anthropologists has helped to illuminate the deterioration of women's position in the transition from hunting and gathering to sedentary agriculture. Anthropologists have also explored the impact on women in pre-capitalist societies of such developments as the growth of private productive property, the evolution of states, the intensification of warfare, and the rise of foreign trade (*Critique of Anthropology*, 1978; Quinn, 1977; Rosaldo and Lamphere, 1974; Reiter, 1975).

Archaeologists have attempted to discover the early antecedents of women's oppression in what are now capitalist countries and historians have tried to document how the rise of capitalism impressed itself.

Recently economists have sought to bring this work forward in time by exploring the effects of *advanced* capitalism on the hierarchical division of labor by sex. There is, of course, abundant evidence of both division (specialization between men and women in the labor market is highly developed), and hierarchy (differences in earnings between the sexes are large).[5]

The general practice in empirical work has been to estimate the proportion of the male-female wage differential that is attributable to differences in productivity-related characteristics of male and female workers such as age, length of schooling, and experience.[6] In every study, the unexplained portion of the differential has been found to be substantial.

Neoclassical economists like Mincer and Polachek argue that the residual can be reduced if experience is controlled for fully. SLM economists, by contrast, argue that most of the residual is due to occupa-

5. Although there has been extensive research on differences in earnings between men and women workers, there has been little research on differences in the congeniality of the jobs which non-professional men and women workers typically hold. See, however, Lucas (1974).

6. Sawhill (1973) reviews seven such studies for the U.S. Oaxaca (1973) and Strober and Reagan (1978) discuss the methodological problems of such empirical work. Data shortages have impeded similar empirical work for the U.K., but see Chiplin and Sloane (1976a).

tional differences between men and women of equal qualifications.[7] Discriminatory hiring practices crowd women into sex-typed jobs. The clustering of a large number of women into a limited number of occupations exerts a downward pressure on their pay.

In arguing that sex inequality takes the form of 'job discrimination' (equally qualified groups of workers are not on average awarded equally remunerative jobs) rather than 'wage discrimination' (equally qualified groups of workers are paid differently for the same work), SLM economists add to an old body of literature which includes contributions by Millicent Fawcett (1918), Beatrice Webb (1919), and F. Y. Edgeworth (1922). This literature also argued that sex discrimination in the labor market commonly manifests itself not as unequal pay for equal work but rather as unequal job assignments.

Pivotal to the institutional analysis of segmentation are technological factors. Technological change under mature capitalism is said to make skills more firm-specific so that a worker's productivity increasingly becomes a function of on-the-job training and experience. To capture the returns to training, firms need a stable work force. To insure stability, high wages, fringe benefits, and prospects of advancement are offered. The number of 'ports of entry' are limited and promotion ladders are attached to each job. An oligopolistic product market facilitates the payment of wages above workers' opportunity costs. It is further argued, however, that not all jobs are subject to technological change of a type which makes on-the-job training and stability important. Jobs which aren't remain low paying and insecure. They constitute the secondary labor market. The primary sector harbors most of the good jobs. Only the lower ranking jobs within this sector are filled by minorities and women.

Since men's labor force attachment is steadier on average than women's, men and women workers are not always perfect substitutes. Nevertheless, the intermittency of women's labor force attachment appears to be changing far faster than are employers' stereotypical images of them. Institutional economists, therefore, demand government measures to integrate the labor force: non-discriminatory youth employment programs, an expanded program of public service jobs, and a strengthened program of affirmative action.[8] Since policies to open

7. Strober and Best (1979) draw some lessons from public schools. Blau (1977) develops this argument with empirical data on office work.

8. See Bergmann, Reading 15. Chiplin and Sloane refer to British legislation in Reading 13.

up jobs to women have a better chance of success when there is not a sizeable excess supply of male workers, these economists also demand fiscal and monetary measures to reduce slack.

Radical literature on segmentation also attaches importance to technological factors. But labor market fragmentation is primarily seen as having arisen during the transition from competitive to monopoly capitalism in response to the needs of capitalists to divide and rule the working class. Like Marxists, radicals argue that capital accumulation brought about the progressive homogenization of the labor force: 'The factory system eliminated many skilled craft occupations ... Production for a mass market and increased mechanization forged standardized work requirements. Large establishments drew greater numbers of workers into common working environments.' Radicals go on to argue that since an homogeneous work force facilitates class struggle, capitalists react. They create divisive job hierarchies within their own plants (over which top-down authority is exercised) and devise promotional incentives to give workers a false sense of upward mobility. Thus, according to Reich, Edwards, and Gordon: 'Labor market segmentation arose and is perpetuated because it is *functional* – that is, it facilitates the operation of capitalist institutions.' It follows that discrimination against definable groups like women and minorities is also perpetuated by the divide-and-rule stratagem of capitalists.

Most of the SLM literature is based on American data. Yet women in Germany, Italy, Holland, and Belgium may suffer more from unequal pay for equal work than from unfavorable job assignments (Addison, 1975). Chiplin and Sloane contend that this is also the case in the U.K.[9] Their arguments are reproduced in Reading 13.

Overcrowding and unemployment

The sex-typing of jobs also figures prominently in the institutional approach to women's higher rates of unemployment. According to Bergmann, just as occupational segregation underscores women's lower pay, it is a major contributor to their higher unemployment. The supply of women persistently outstrips the truncated demand they face in a segregated labor market. Bergmann's position is spelled out in Reading 15.

While women typically suffer higher rates of unemployment than men at all times, the recent recession appears to have been an equal

9. See also Chiplin and Sloane (1976b).

opportunity *dis*employer. Smith (1977) corrects for the underestimation in reported statistics of job opportunities lost due to the recession of 1974–5 in the U.S. He and June O'Neill apply the same methodology to gauge the differential impact of the recession on men and women workers in European countries. This study, which they prepared for the Organisation for Economic Co-operation and Development, and which incorporates some of Smith's work on the U.S., appears as Reading 16.

According to the authors, the main reason why women did not fare worse than men in most countries during the 1974–5 recession is that layoffs struck hardest in industries in which women were underrepresented. Thus, while institutionalists see job segregation as the major contributor to women's high secular unemployment, they also see it as responsible for a woeful equality between the sexes in business slumps. Job segregation also appears to have contributed to a *lower* unemployment rate for women than men during the Great Depression in the U.S.; although 1930s' statistics are unreliable (Milkman, 1976).[10]

While the inequity of policies which place a heavier weight on the costs of men's unemployment than women's unemployment have been hotly criticized, it should also be recognized that the costs of women's unemployment are not borne equally *among* them. The unemployment rate of minority women in the U.S. has averaged about 80% above that of white women over the last quarter of a century (Keyserling, 1977; Barratt and Morgenstern, 1974). There is also evidence that education and unemployment are inversely related. If education is used as a proxy for social class, the burden of unemployment has fallen more heavily on working-class women.

It is to a class analysis of women and work by Marxists that attention is now turned.

3. The Marxist conception

Marxists operate with a world view and a methodology which is self-consciously distinct from that of neoclassicists and institutionalists. While neoclassicists emphasize the operation of the market, Marxists are more interested in production. On the whole, Marxists attempt to take a broader historical view of economic processes and conceive variables such as prices and income, and supply and demand, as mere short-run quantitative reflections of more fundamental social decisions

10. Simeral (1978), notwithstanding, argues that American women have historically constituted an important portion of the reserve army of the unemployed, both cyclically and secularly.

concerning capital accumulation. Marxists reject as overly reductionist many of the categories of non-Marxist thought in the social sciences. Where the neoclassical economist tends to view society as a collection of individuals concerned with, say, 'consumption decisions', Marxists regard consumption as the outcome of a struggle between different economic classes in the process of production. Where the neoclassical economist tends to see change largely in quantitative terms, Marxists assume that changes in quantity can eventually result in a qualitative transformation. Take, for example, the neoclassical category of 'income'. Because neoclassicists conceive changes in incomes as involving no qualitative change, there is a directness and stability in the way in which individuals respond to changes in income over time. Marxists, by contrast, conceive changes in income as involving qualitative changes. The continuum of 'income' over time is broken into distinct historical phases: slavery and feudalism; competitive capitalism and monopoly capitalism. Class struggle is present in all episodes but takes a different form in each. Hence, behavior varies according to the mode of production. Behavioral variations cannot be reduced to numerical changes in market prices and GNP.

Whereas the individual is the primary unit of analysis in neoclassical theory, the class is elevated to primacy in Marxist theory. Class relations vary according to the mode of production and individuals' behavior varies according to class membership. While all individuals under capitalism respond to the prices they confront in the market, there are discrete differences in the way in which members of the working class and bourgeoisie can respond.

Customs, culture, and consciousness are also conceptualized by Marxists as varying qualitatively over the course of economic development. Marxists treat 'tastes' neither as exogenous nor as stable over time and space. Marxists see social forces and ideology as a function of the way in which income is produced and distributed. But Marxists also argue that production and distribution are in turn influenced by social forces and ideology.

An historical approach to labor force participation

The research of Scott and Tilly (Reading 4) does not employ Marxist categories but does provide an historical account of women's labor force participation in nineteenth-century Europe. It thereby lends itself to illustrating the Marxist contention that any episodic change in women's labor force participation can be understood only as a matter of history and not as a matter of logic (i.e., a vector of prices rises and women flood the job market). A somewhat lengthy review of the work of Scott and Tilly is necessary now in order to compare it later with the explanatory model developed by Mincer.

According to Scott and Tilly, the women who worked in great numbers in nineteenth-century Europe were overwhelmingly members of the working and peasant classes. They were also young and single. 'The traditional role of a married woman . . . sent her into the labor force when her earnings were needed by the household budget. When the income of her husband and children was sufficient for the family's needs, she left the labor force. Mothers of young children would sometimes leave the labor force *only* after their oldest child went out to work.' It is noteworthy that mothers today tend to *enter* the labor force rather than leave it when their children become old enough to work. This important difference can best be explained by changes in parental-child obligations over time. In the nineteenth century, daughters worked in the interest of the family economy: 'As parents sent daughters off with traditional expectations, so the daughters attempted to fulfill them. Evidence for the persistence of familial values is found in the continuing contributions made by working daughters to their families.' After 1914, however, 'more and more single girls kept more and more of their wages', signifying the emergence of a new parental-child relationship: 'The major transformation involved the replacement of familial values with individualistic ones. These stressed the notion that the individual was owner of him- or herself rather than a part of a social or moral whole.'

Scott's and Tilly's historical analysis ends here temporally, but they conclude: 'The changes that affected women's work and women's place in the family late in the nineteenth and in the twentieth centuries . . . cannot be understood . . . apart from the historical context we have presented.'

If one were to borrow the Scott and Tilly framework to explore the increase in wives' labor force participation after World War I (and especially after World War II), one might piece together the following picture: the gradual transformation of the family economy figured as an important force pulling and pushing married women into paid employment. Wives went to work in increasing numbers to replace the income with which their offspring no longer provided them. Women began to bear fewer children, perhaps in part because children increasingly took more from family revenues than they contributed to them (especially in an urban milieu). Women also lived longer and bore their last child earlier. Consequently, women were deprived of financial support not only from fewer children but also over a longer period of their lives. Under these conditions, working for wages became more practical (the child-care problem abated), more profitable (the success of the working class in raising the age of job entrants had a positive impact on the general level of wages), and at once more pressing (although less so than in the early phase of the industrial revolution when married women's labor force participation also reached high levels).

In sum, the Scott and Tilly framework for the nineteenth century points to the hypothesis that the demise of the tradition whereby children contributed to family income dramatized a series of social and economic changes which exerted a positive effect on wives' labor force participation in the twentieth century. Note that if this hypothesis is correct, it is in no way at variance with a choice theoretic model. What is debated later is which approach has greater explanatory power.

Sexism and segmentation

Perhaps no other subject bearing on women has received as much study by Marxists and radicals as the family. The family is pictured as the crucible of women's oppression and sex inequality in the market is predicated on sex inequality in the home. An article by Humphries (Reading 6) was selected to represent one (of several) Marxist interpretations. It at once punctuates the difference between the Marxist approach to the family and those of neoclassical, institutional, and radical economists.

Humphries organizes her research around the question of why the working-class family has persisted (albeit in a stronger or weaker form at different stages in economic development). Her aim is to begin where Marx and Engels left off, for both incorrectly anticipated that the working-class family would decay as capitalism and proletarianization became universal.

Radical literature stresses the material and political benefits which capitalists derive from the family. Consumerism and the cult of domesticity boost capitalists' sales. Familialism results in a docile labor force. A worker, it is argued, is more apt than otherwise to show up on the job Monday morning and stay through the week if she or he has family and financial obligations to meet.[11]

11. Ehrenreich and English (1975) quote a businessman as saying: 'Get them to invest their savings in their homes and own them. Then they won't leave and they

Humphries does not deny these gains which the family affords capitalists. But she rejects any radical interpretation which arms capitalists with unlimited power to dictate the family's fate. The theme of her paper, therefore, is that the resilience of the nineteenth-century British working-class family 'derives in part from workers' defence of an institution which affects their standard of living, class cohesion, and ability to wage the class struggle'.

Prices and income are as relevant in Humphries' analysis of the family as they are in the 'new home economics'. But neoclassicists take prices and income as given and see how they affect individual choices about remaining single or marrying. They then deduce the rationality of the division of labor by sex. Humphries, by contrast, examines how the working class uses the family as an instrument to affect the level of income and prices. This formulation then allows her to explore how a sexist division of labor became entrenched.

Humphries observes that in fighting for a family wage (a rate sufficient to allow a man to support his unemployed wife and schoolchildren), nineteenth-century British workers simultaneously advanced their class interests and protected the integrity of their family. They did so by pressuring wives to stay at home and tend the hearth in order to lessen competition for jobs in the market. The fight for higher wages, however, was waged 'from behind the women's petticoats'. The absence of married women in the labor market had the advantage of restricting the total supply of labor, and hence, of driving wages up. But it had the disadvantage of 'reinforcing sex-based relations of dominance and subordination'.

While institutional economists also locate sexism in the dynamics of the family, they do not incorporate the exigencies created by the class struggle into this dynamic.

Rubery's analysis of occupational segregation (Reading 11) complements Humphries' analysis of the family. Both are writing in part as a reaction against the theoretical error of radical economics: functionalism. Functionalism involves interpreting what exists as the outcome of what is needed by the ruling class. Thus, radical literature sees the family as surviving because it serves the interests of capitalists. Similarly, radical literature sees labor market segmentation as arising from the divisive manipulations of capitalists.

won't strike. It ties them down so they have a stake in our prosperity.' The authors proceed to argue that postwar federal financing helped home ownership expand into the American blue-collar working class.

Rubery argues that although capitalists may have wished to introduce divisions into the working class, they could not have done so free-handedly. Workers' organizations also played an important part in stratifying the work force. Rubery maintains that 'the progress of capitalism both destroys old skills and creates new ones'. But as soon as workers acquire new skills, 'management will design their techniques of production in order to de-skill these workers. Thus all workers are threatened by the obsolescence of skills, or by replacement of other equally skilled workers who are in plentiful supply. This threat may induce defensive actions on the part of the workers to stratify the labour force, control entry to occupations and maintain skill status long after these skill divisions become irrelevant.'

Thus, both for Humphries and Rubery, discrimination against women is intensified by the class struggle: in order to restrict the supply of labor, trade unions pressure women to stay at home; if this is unfeasible (if a family wage is unachievable or wives are uncontrollable), women are occupationally segregated. It follows that class exploitation and sexist oppression must be fought simultaneously.

Two elements in the Marxist analysis of segmentation are especially relevant to women and work; trade unions and the erosion of skills by technological change.

There is a long Marxist tradition which argues that skills become progressively diluted in the course of capital accumulation. Braverman (1974) argues that although the level of education in capitalist countries has risen over time, this education is as empty as the jobs for which it purportedly prepares people; and while jobs embody a higher scientific content, the purpose of science under capitalism is to de-skill the people who occupy these jobs. In the Braverman view, the amount of on-the-job training required by the mass of non-professional workers is minimal and their peak efficiency is reached within a matter of days or weeks.

If this is empirically the case, it weakens the foundations both of the human capital and institutional theories of pay differentials.[12] The

12. Duncan and Hoffman (1978) attempted to measure on-the-job training directly and found large differences in the amounts received by men and women workers. See also Corcoran (1978). Nevertheless, the authors' direct measure of on-the-job training was derived from answers provided by workers to the following question: 'On a job like yours, how long would it take the average new person to become fully trained and qualified?' Such subjective answers may give biased estimates of both the relative and absolute amounts of training which men and women receive. For example, Private Household workers reported an average of 0.52

former predicates that women's lower earnings are largely due to their lower investments in on-the-job training. The latter holds that women's lower earnings are due to their debarment from jobs which embody on-the-job training. True enough, earnings tend to rise with years of experience. But years of experience may have nothing to do with skill enhancement. They may simply reflect seniority – for which trade unions are responsible. If so, less trade union power rather than less productivity lies at the heart of women's relative penury.

Craft dominated trade union movements both in the U.K. and in the U.S. appear to have made the political choice to segregate women by occupations in order to improve the earnings of men rather than to include women in a unified fight to win higher wages for all. Trade unions both in the past and at present have also neglected to organize many female-dominated industries.[13] This neglect may currently derive either from bureaucratic torpor or from difficulties in organizing 'women's work'. 'Women's work' is typically believed to be difficult to organize due to an unfavorable set of sociological and economic variables. The former are rehearsed as including women's self-perception as temporary workers, as 'white collar' and outside the working class, and as providing essential social services (e.g., nursing). The latter are said to include small size firms, competitive product markets, and other variables absent in oligopolistic sectors. Nevertheless, many of these characteristics of 'women's work' are changing rapidly. There are also examples which indicate that historical and political elements play as important a part in determining which workers become unionized as economic variables. American teamsters, for example, work for small, competitive firms but have organized themselves into a very powerful union.

Given the potential importance of unionization for women's employment, it may be worthwhile re-examining the hypothesis that trade unions are epiphenomenal: viz., that they organize industries which are potentially high paying rather than that they are responsible for the high pay of the industries which they have organized.

---

years needed to become fully trained and qualified. Workers earning less than $2.00 an hour in 1975 reported an average of 0.95 years. These workers may have exaggerated the skill requirements of their jobs for personal reasons or out of a concern about confidentiality. The authors do not report deviations in mean responses.

13. A collection of articles in the British feminist journal *Red Rag* (1974) documents many instances of discrimination against women by trade unions. Kenneally (1973) provides an historical account of women and trade unions in the U.S.

4. An overview

In reconsidering the various points of view schematically outlined above, the main question becomes: how do they measure up on the insights they yield?

I think neoclassical theory does not provide an adequate explanation for the working-wife phenomenon and does not take into account the critical problems which are relevant to women as a group. The structure of neoclassical theory is itself responsible: it is a-historical and a-social. It also abstracts economics from power.

The choice theoretic framework which neoclassicists utilize to analyze the increase in wives' labor force participation over time at once explains everything and nothing. It explains everything insofar as it makes wives' behavior a function of two opposing forces. Since one or the other force must dominate, any behavioral configuration is theoretically admissible. Such a theory is thus irrefutable; notwithstanding the empirical measurability of income and price elasticities.

A theory is not objectionable simply because it admits of many configurations. Marxist theory of wives' labor force participation is even more flexible than neoclassical theory. But neoclassical theory explains nothing insofar as it leaves one ignorant as to why the income or the substitution effect governs at a particular time. Only an historical analysis can begin to provide an answer.

The application of the Scott and Tilly framework to the twentieth-century anchored the rise in married women's labor force participation in an altered parental-child relationship. Scott and Tilly ascribe this altered relationship to the 'replacement of familial values with individualist ones'. One could go further and attribute changes in values themselves to changes in prices and income. But even if changes in prices and income lie at the base of changes in values, the association between the two is mediated by qualitative developments. This mediation process comprises seeing changes in prices and income after the turn of the century as giving birth to a wholly new social and economic order out of which emerged the working-wife phenomenon. An historical analysis thus puts flesh on the skeleton of the income and substitution effects and provides a more penetrating picture of why women of different social classes went out to work in greater numbers after the War.

Another example, drawn from cross-section data, also illustrates that behavior is far more complex than simple economic maximizing principles would indicate. In the U.S., the labor force participation of black married women has exceeded that of white married women. According to Goldin (1977), part of the difference in rates can readily be explained by prices and income: the legacy of slavery lowered the earning power of black men and this 'harsh reality' forced other family members into paid employment. But Goldin goes on to argue that 'the slave experience also had an indirect social impact'. Black women were conditioned by slavery to laboring while many poor whites were too proud to work. Thus: '. . . only 14 percent of white women with low family labor income ($0 to $299) were in the work force in 1880, but over 44 percent of low-income married black women were'.

Stigler and Becker (1977) may choose to reduce racial attitudes about work to market variables. But even if such gymnastics succeed in their own terms, one may doubt their informative value unless the social and economic structure on which market variables are perched is introduced explicitly into the analysis.

The proliferation of job opportunities for women after World War II may be explained by prices and income as well. As income rose, income elasticities of demand for foodstuffs and manufactures rose less than for services. Shifts in the industrial structure resulted in an enlarged service sector which provided job opportunities for women. A richer explanation, however, is gained by dressing income in historical clothing. Thus, one might locate the rise of women's jobs in the ripening of monopoly capitalism: the dramatic growth in state spending and the fitfull encroachment of technological change upon the clerical and service sectors after the War. Why many service and clerical jobs became 'women's work', however, altogether defies a-historical and a-social explanation.

The 'new home economics' attempts to explain the division of labor within the family by economic maximizing principles. Sawhill, however, argues that when such principles are divorced from social reality, they become little more than justifications for sexism (Reading 5).

Sawhill points out that at one stage in the neoclassical argument, the division of labor within the household is taken as given. Women will consequently fail to acquire as much experience and training in the labor market as men. It then follows logically that they will earn less than men in the labor market. At another stage in the analysis, however, the female-male wage differential is taken as given. Since women earn less than men, it is now the division of labor within the household that appears logical. In Sawhill's words, '. . . we have come full circle . . .' and it is time to ask whether economists '. . . have done anything more than describe the status quo in a society where sex roles are "givens" –

defined by culture, biology, or other factors not specified in the economic model'.[14]

Such theoretical circularity infects the explanation provided by the 'new home economics' for the *origins* of the family. The gains from marriage are said to be greater, the greater the difference in wage rates between husband and wife. It follows 'logically' that women marry because they earn less than men and they earn less than men because they enter into marriages where sex roles are 'given'. Unless sexism is explicitly introduced into theory at the bottom line, there can be no explanation for either the division of labor within the family or for the existence of the family at all. Clearly children must be borne by women. But economic maximizing principles do not dictate that they must be reared by them in a nuclear family.

Neoclassical theory abstracts economics from power by assuming that individuals exercise freedom of choice. This is not an unreasonable assumption in a world populated by atomistic individuals with roughly equal endowments of material and human capital. But in a world in which men and women, and workers and capitalists, have unequal wealth and power, their abilities to exercise freedom of choice differ. In such a world, all women may be subject to discrimination. All may be saddled with childrearing responsibilities. Working-class wives may have little choice about whether or not to work.[15] The working class as a whole has no choice at all. If this is the kind of world which one believes to exist, then the neoclassical assumption of freedom of choice yields no insights into the realities of women's problems. It mystifies them.

By comparison with institutional and neoclassical theorists, Marxists have written the least on the three topics around which readings in this collection are organized. This may reflect the fact that gender is not a category which Marx integrated into his theory of capital. Therefore, there is an unresolved tension between the analysis of class exploitation and sexual oppression.

Much effort by Marxists has been devoted to incorporating women's unpaid homework into the value schema of *Capital*. The debate has illu-

14. Ferber and Birnbaum (1977a) also criticize the 'new home economics'; and see their exchange (1977b) with Robinson (1977) and Reid (1977). Several papers in the tradition of the 'new home economics' may be found in Schultz (1974) and Lloyd (1975).

15. Quick (1975) argues that even if working-class women have a choice over whether or not to work in the market, they work all the time to ensure the survival of their families. Leisure is a luxury largely restricted to middle-class women.

minated the relationship between capitalists' profits and the production of use values at home by women. (Himmelweit and Mohun, 1977, summarize the debate.) The literature, however, has shed little light on women themselves. It is very much in the nature of a theory in search of a problem.

There has also been much effort on the part of women who describe themselves as Marxist-Feminists (or Feminist-Marxists) to compose a fugue of class exploitation and sexual oppression. While I have described all such efforts as 'Marxist', different theoretical and political nuances distinguish them. On the one hand, some work has aimed at incorpor-ating explicitly the problems of women into classical Marxist analysis; problems which heretofore have been conspicuously ignored. On the other, it has been argued that 'Recent attempts to integrate Marxism and feminism are unsatisfactory to us as feminists because they subsume the feminist struggle into the "larger" struggle against capital... such feminists favor a methodology which under-estimates a system of relations between men (patriarchy) that serves to dominate women. The 'Marxism' in this feminist ... the form of rooting patriarchy in a material base ... psychic one, and in eradicating the sex-blindness of ... (Hartmann, 1979).

... serious lacunae in research on women and work ... Marxist scholars. Only two readings in this ... effects of women's increased labor force participa-... self. Sweet (Reading 18) examines the hypothesis that ... as more working-class women have entered the labor force, ... distribution among families may be expected to have improved. ... Sweet finds no change in inequality in the U.S. The higher pay of middle-class wives has offset the gains of working-class families with two income earners.[16] Strober (Reading 17) compares consumption patterns between working-wife and non-working-wife families. Holding income constant, she finds no difference between the two types of families in their durable goods/income ratio.[17] Working-wife families, however, have a higher average propensity to consume all goods and services; and Strober questions the implications for economic growth.

16. Income distribution among black and white families has remained unchanged for the same reason. Treas and Walther (1978) also find that countervailing forces have preserved the distribution of income among different types of income recipient units, i.e., individuals living alone (primarily younger men and older women) and families (male or female headed and husband-wife).

17. Specific durable goods are examined in Strober and Weinberg, 1977.

The different ways Marxists and neoclassicists conceptualize changes in income have been elaborated upon. The neoclassical conception points to further research on how women's increased labor force participation and lower pay affect G N P *quantitatively*. The Marxist conception points to further research on the qualitative effects of so dramatic an inflow of cheap female labor on the economy. Does a 'family' wage rate still prevail or has a 'bachelor' wage resurfaced in conjunction with the working-wife phenomenon? Is higher state spending necessary to absorb the number of women who are now pressured to work for wages? Can analyses, sector by sector, reveal anything about trends in rates of profit in association with the availability of large numbers of wom workers? Building on the research of institutional economists, M may wish to inquire into how much more (less) explosive t mic crisis has become in light of the working-wife pheno has been the effect of the phenomenon on both the pace change and productivity and on inflation and unem

Similarly, Marxists may wish to investigate the c how women themselves are faring as they spend mo market. Although statistics show that real income World War II, what has this meant qualitatively? women who work for wages continue to be resp Although they spend less time at homework workers, the length of their workweek (if n that of nineteenth-century workmen: it is ap (Reading 3). The incorporation into price indices *quality* of goods and services produced is problematic. fore inquire: has there been a deterioration in the quality services and urban conditions which do not show up in price in but which make it mandatory for more and more women to work merely to maintain their families' living standards? Although consumption has risen, are many consumption expenditures work-related so that their contribution to higher living standards is ambiguous?[18] Although family income distribution has remained stable, has the welfare of working- and middle-class women diverged given differences in the congeniality of their respective new jobs?

One almost never associates orthodox neoclassical economics with the advocacy of government policies to change the position of women in the economy. The non-interventionist position of the school follows from its assumption that individuals exercise freedom of choice. Such

18. Vickery (1979) addresses this question.

an assumption implies that women freely choose to acquire less formal education than men, to enter into lower paying jobs where experience is relatively unimportant, and to unemploy themselves. Thus, legislation to change women's self-imposed condition is deducible as unnecessary and undesirable from the internal logic of neoclassical theory itself. If, however, as suggested above, such an assumption is incorrect, the political perspective of the neoclassical paradigm defines women's problems out of existence and robs the paradigm itself of pertinence.

The basic assumptions of institutional economics are that inequities exist and can be put right through active state intervention. Since the need for change is overwhelming in the area of sex inequality, the research orientation towards the formulation of public policy of institutional economists has yielded many practical insights into the problems associated with women and work. But such research is not designed to study systematically how capitalism either produced or perpetuated these problems. Rather, the research of institutional economists is directed towards demonstrating the extent of such problems in order to reform the institutions which are discerned to embody them.

Marxists come equipped with a dynamic historical approach to these problems. Marxists also assume that a capitalist state will not and cannot accomplish what is necessary to end sex inequality, whether in the domain of the market or the family. For very basic structural changes are needed to overcome the injustices suffered by women of all classes. That may be so, but it is also true that positive change must be based on scientific inquiry. Hopefully, further scientific inquiry will be inspired by this collection of readings.

References

ADDISON, JOHN T., 1975. 'Sex Discrimination: Some Comparative Evidence', *British Journal of Industrial Relations*, Vol. 13, No. 2.

ARROW, KENNETH, 1972. 'Models of Job Discrimination' and 'Some Mathematical Models of Race Discrimination in the Labor Market', in A. H. Pascal (ed.), *Racial Discrimination in Economic Life*, Lexington Books, D. C. Heath.

ARROW, KENNETH, 1973. 'The Theory of Discrimination', in O. Ashenfelter and A. Rees (eds.), *Discrimination in Labor Markets*, Princeton University Press.

BARRETT, NANCY S., and MORGENSTERN, RICHARD D., 1974. 'Why Do Blacks and Women Have High Unemployment Rates?', *Journal of Human Resources*, Vol. 9, No. 9.

BECKER, GARY, 1971. *The Economics of Discrimination*, University of Chicago Press, 1957.

BECKER, GARY, 1973. 'A Theory of Marriage: Part I', *Journal of Political Economy*, Vol. 82, No. 2, Pt. 2.

BECKER, GARY, 1974. 'A Theory of Marriage', in Theodore W. Schultz (ed.), *Economics of the Family*, University of Chicago Press.

BERCH, BETTINA, 1975. 'Industrialization and Working Women in the 19th Century: England, France, and the United States', Ph.D. Dissertation, University of Wisconsin, Madison.

BLAU, FRANCINE, 1977. *Equal Pay in the Office*, Lexington Books, D. C. Heath.

BLAU, FRANCINE, and JUSENIUS, CAROL, 1976. 'Economists' Approaches to Sex Segregation in the Labor Market: An Appraisal', *Signs*, Vol. 1, No. 3, Pt. 2; reprinted in Martha Blaxall and Barbara Reagan (eds.), *Women and the Workplace*, University of Chicago Press.

BLAU, FRANCINE, and HENDRICKS, WALLACE E., 1979. 'Occupational Segregation by Sex: Trends and Prospects', *Journal of Human Resources*, Vol. 14, No. 2.

BOWERS, J. K., 1975. 'British Activity Rates: A Survey of Research', *Scottish Journal of Political Economy*, Vol. 22, No. 1.

BRAVERMAN, HARRY, 1974. *Labor and Monopoly Capital: The Degradation of Work in the Twentieth Century*, Monthly Review Press.

CAIN, GLEN, 1976. 'The Challenge of Segmented Labor Market Theories to Orthodox Theory: A Survey', *Journal of Economic Literature*, Vol. 14, No. 4.

CHIPLIN, BRIAN, and SLOANE, PETER J., 1976a. *Sex Discrimination in the Labour Market*, Macmillan.

CHIPLIN, BRIAN, and SLOANE, PETER J., 1976b. 'Male-Female Earnings Differences: A Further Analysis', *British Journal of Industrial Relations*, Vol. 14, No. 1.

CORCORAN, MARY, 1978. 'Work Experience, Work Interruption and Wages', in Greg Duncan and James Morgan (eds.), *Five Thousand American Families – Patterns of Economic Progress*, Vol. 6, Survey Research Center, Institute for Social Research, University of Michigan.

COWAN, RUTH SCHWARTZ, 1976. ' "The Industrial Revolution" in the Home: Household Technology and Social Change in the 20th Century', *Technology and Culture*, Vol. 17, No. 1.

Critique of Anthropology, 1977. 'Women's Issue', Vol. 3, Nos. 9–10.

DUNCAN, GREG, and HOFFMAN, SAUL, 1978. 'Training and Earnings', Greg J. Duncan and James N. Morgan (eds.), *Five Thousand American Families – Patterns of Economic Progress*, Vol. 6, Survey Research Center, Institute for Social Research, University of Michigan.

EDGEWORTH, F. Y., 1922. 'Equal Pay to Men and Women', *Economic Journal*, Vol. 32.

EHRENREICH, BARBARA, and ENGLISH, DEIDRE, 1975. 'The Manufacture of Housework', *Socialist Revolution*, No. 26.

FAWCETT, MILLICENT, 1918. 'Equal Pay for Equal Work', *Economic Journal*, Vol. 28.

FERBER, MARIANNE A., and BIRNBAUM, BONNIE G., 1977a. 'The "New Home Economics": Retrospects and Prospects', *Journal of Consumer Research*, Vol. 4, No. 1.

FERBER, MARIANNE A., and BIRNBAUM, BONNIE G., 1977b. 'Rejoinder', *Journal of Consumer Research*, Vol. 4, No. 3.

GOLDIN, CLAUDIA, 1977. 'Female Labor Force Participation: The Origin of Black and White Differences, 1870 and 1880', *Journal of Economic History*, Vol. 37, No. 1.

GROSS, EDWARD, 1968. ' "Plus Ça Change ... ? " The Sexual Structure of Occupations Over Time', *Social Problems*, Vol. 16, No. 2.

HARTMANN, HEIDI IRMGARD, 1974. 'Capitalism and Women's Work in the Home, 1900–1930', Ph.D. Dissertation, Yale University.

HARTMANN, HEIDI I., 1979. 'The Unhappy Marriage of Marxism and Feminism: towards a more progressive Union', *Capital and Class*, No. 8.

HIMMELWEIT, SUSAN, and MOHUN, SIMON, 1977. 'Domestic Labour and Capital', *Cambridge Journal of Economics*, Vol. 1.

JEVONS, STANLEY, 1822. 'Married Women in Factories', *Contemporary Review*, Vol. 41.

KENNEALLY, JAMES J., 1973. 'Women and Trade Unions 1870–1920: The Quandry of the Reformer', *Labor History*, Vol. 14, No. 1.

KEYSERLING, MARY, 1977. 'Women's Stake in Full Employment: Their Disadvantaged Role in the Economy – Challenges to Action', *American Women Workers in a full Employment Economy*, A Compendium of Papers Submitted to the Subcommittee on Economic Growth and Stabilization of the Joint Economic Committee Congress of the United States.

LEIBOWITZ, ARLENE, 1974. 'Education and Home Production', *American Economic Review*, Vol. 64, No. 2.

LLOYD, CYNTHIA B., (ed.), 1975. *Sex Discrimination and the Division of Labor*, Columbia University Press.

LUCAS, ROBERT E. B., 1974. 'The Distribution of Job Characteristics', *Review of Economics and Statistics*, Vol. 56, No. 4.

MILKMAN, RUTH, 1976. 'Women's Work and the Economic Crisis: Some Lessons from the Great Depression', *Review of Radical Political Economics*, Vol. 8, No. 1.

OAXACA, RONALD, 1973. 'Male-Female Wage Differentials in Urban Labor Markets', *International Economic Review*, Vol. 14, No. 3.

OPPENHEIMER, VALERIE, 1970. *The Female Labor Force in the United States: Demographic and Economic Factors Governing its Growth and Changing Composition*, Population Monograph Series, No. 5, Berkeley, University of California.

QUICK, PADDY, 1975. 'Rosie the Riveter: Myths and Realities', *Radical America*, Vol. 9, Nos. 4–5.

QUINN, NAOMI, 1977. 'Anthropological Studies on Women's Status', *Annual Review of Anthropology*, Vol. 6.

REAGAN, BARBARA B., 1978. 'De Facto Job Segregation', *American Women Workers in a Full Employment Economy*, A Compendium of Papers Submitted to the Subcommittee on Economic Growth and Stabilization of the Joint Economic Committee Congress of the United States.

Red Rag. 1974. Vol. 2.

REID, MARGARET G., 1977. 'How New is the "New Home Economics"?', *Journal of Consumer Research*, Vol. 4, No. 3.

REITER, RAYNA RAPP (ed.), 1975. *Towards an Anthropology of Women*, Monthly Review Press.

ROBINSON, JOHN P., 1977. 'The "New Home Economics": Sexist, Unrealistic, or Simply Irrelevant?', *Journal of Consumer Research*, Vol. 4, No. 3.

ROSALDO, MICHELLE, and LAMPHERE, LOUISE (eds.), 1974. *Woman, Culture and Society*, Stanford University Press.

SAWHILL, ISABEL V., 1973. 'The Economics of Discrimination Against Women: Some New Findings', *Journal of Human Resources*, Vol. 8, No. 3.

SCHULTZ, THEODORE W., (ed.), 1974. *Economics of the Family*, University of Chicago Press.

SIMERAL, MARGARET H., 1978. 'Women and the Reserve Army of Labor', in Olivia Clark, Jerry Lembke, and Bob Marotto, Jr., (eds.), *Essays on the Social Relations of Work and Labor: A Special Issue of the Insurgent Sociologist*, Vol. 8, Nos. 2 and 3.

SMITH, RALPH E., 1977. 'The Impact of Macroeconomic Conditions on Employment Opportunities for Women', A Study Prepared for the Use of the Joint Economic Committee Congress of the United States.

SORRENTINO, CONSTANCE, 1976. *Methodological and Conceptual Problems of Measuring Unemployment in O.E.C.D. Countries*, (mimeograph), Organisation for Economic Co-operation and Development.

STIGLER, G. J., and BECKER, G. S., 1977. 'De Gustibus Non Est Disputandum', *American Economic Review*, Vol. 67, No. 2.

STROBER, MYRA H., and WEINBERG, CHARLES B., 1977. 'Working Wives and Major Family Expenditures', *Journal of Consumer Research*, Vol. 4, No. 3.

STROBER, MYRA H., and REAGAN, BARBARA B., 1978. 'Sense and Nonsense in the Residual Method of Measuring Discrimination as Illustrated by an Analysis of Sex Differences in Economists' Incomes', Working Paper, Graduate School of Business, Stanford University.

STROBER, MYRA H., and BEST, LAURA, 1979. 'The Female-Male Salary Differential in Public Schools: Some Lessons from San Francisco, 1879', *Economic Inquiry*, Vol. 17, No. 2.

TREAS, JUDITH, and WALTHER, ROBIN JANE, 1978. 'Family Structure and the Distribution of Family Income', *Social Forces*, Vol. 56, No. 3.

U.K. Department of Employment, 1974. *Women and Work: A Statistical View*, Manpower Paper No. 9.

U.S. Bureau of the Census, 1976. *Historical Statistics of the United States: Colonial Times to 1970*.

VICKERY, CLAIR, (1979). 'The Work of Married Women and the Living Standards of Their Families', in Ralph E. Smith, (ed.), *The Subtle Revolution: Women at Work*, Urban Institute.

WEBB, BEATRICE, 1919. *The Wages of Men and Women: Should They Be Equal?*, George Allen and Unwin.

Part One
Market Work, Homework and The Family

1 Labor Force Participation of Married Women: A Study of Labor Supply*

Jacob Mincer

Columbia University and National Bureau of Economic Research

From: 'Aspects of Labor Economics', A Report of the National Bureau of Economic Research, Princeton, Princeton University Press, 1962, pp. 63–73 (abridged).

Introductory: Statement of the Problem

On assumption that leisure time is a normal good, the standard analysis of work-leisure choices implies a positive substitution effect and a negative income effect on the response of hours of work supplied to variations in the wage rate. An increase in the real wage rate makes leisure time more expensive and tends to elicit an increase in hours of work. However, for a given amount of hours worked, an increase in the wage rate constitutes an increase in income, which leads to an increase in purchases of various goods, including leisure time. Thus, on account of the income effect, hours of work tend to decrease. In which direction hours of work change on balance, given a change in the wage rate, cannot be determined a priori. It depends on the relative strengths of the income and substitution effects in the relevant range. The single assumption of a positive income elasticity of demand for leisure time is not sufficient to yield empirical implications on this matter.

An empirical generalization which fills this theoretical void is the 'backward-bending' supply curve of labor. This is the notion that on the average the income effect is stronger than the substitution effect, so that an increase in the wage rate normally results in a decreased amount (hours) of work offered by suppliers of labor. Extreme examples of such behavior have been repeatedly observed in underdeveloped countries. On the American scene, several kinds of empirical

*Research reported in this paper was supported, in part, by a grant from the Social Science Research Council. Data from the 1950 Survey of Consumer Expenditures were made available on punch cards by the Bureau of Labor Statistics. For encouragement and helpful comments I am indebted to Dorothy S. Brady, Gary S. Becker, Zvi Griliches, Mark Leiserson, Philip J. Nelson, Elliott Zupnick, and to members of the Columbia University Workshop in Labor Economics.

evidence apparently point to the same relationship:[1] the historically declining work week in industry; historically declining labor force participation rates of young and old males; an inverse relation between wages of adult males and labor force participation rates of females by cities in cross sections; an inverse relation between incomes of husbands and labor force participation of wives, by husbands' incomes, in budget studies. Similar phenomena have been reported from the experience of other modern economies.

The secular negative association between the length of the work week, participation rates of males, and rising real incomes is clearly consistent with the backward-bending supply curve.[2] Whether this is also true of cross-sectional data on males is a question which has as yet received little attention. Superficially, the cross-sectional behavior of females seems similarly capable of being rationalized in terms of a backward-bending supply response, or at least in terms of a positive income elasticity of demand for leisure. Such views, however, are immediately challenged by contradictory evidence in time series. One of the most striking phenomena in the history of the American labor force is the continuing secular increase in participation rates of females, particularly of married women, despite the growth in real income. Between 1890 and 1960 labor force rates of all females fourteen years old and over rose from about 18 per cent to 36 per cent. In the same period rates of married women rose from 5 per cent to 30 per cent, while real income per worker tripled.[3]

The apparent contradiction between time series and cross sections has already stimulated a substantial amount of research. The investigation reported in this paper is yet another attempt to uncover the basic economic structure which is, in part, responsible for the observed relations.

The study starts from the recognition that the concepts of work, income, and substitution need clarification and elaboration before they can be applied to labor force choices of particular population groups, in

1. The pioneering works of research and interpretation in this area are well known. See: Paul H. Douglas, *The Theory of Wages*, Macmillan, 1934; John D. Durand, *The Labor Force in the U.S.*, Social Science Research Council, 1948; Clarence D. Long, *The Labor Force under Changing Income and Employment*, Princeton University Press for National Bureau of Economic Research, 1958.

2. For a rigorous statement, see H. Gregg Lewis, 'Hours of Work and Hours of Leisure,' *Proceedings of the Industrial Relations Research Association*, 1957.

3. Based on Long, *The Labor Force*, Table A-6; and *Employment and Earnings*, Bureau of Labor Statistics, 1960.

this instance married women. The resulting analytical model, even though restricted to two basic economic factors, seems capable of explaining a variety of apparently diverse cross-sectional behavior patterns. It also, in principle, reconciles times series with cross-section behavior, though further elaboration is needed for a proper explanation of the former. The empirical focus of the paper is a reinterpretation of old cross-section materials, and an investigation of newly available data generated by the 1950 BLS Survey of Consumer Expenditures.

Conceptual framework

Work

The analysis of labor supply to the market by way of the theory of demand for leisure time viewed as a consumption good is strictly appropriate whenever leisure time and hours of work in the market in fact constitute an exhaustive dichotomy. This is, of course, never true even in the case of adult males. The logical complement to leisure time is work broadly construed, whether it includes remunerative production in the market or work that is currently 'not paid for'. The latter includes various forms of investment in oneself, and the production of goods and services for the home and the family. Educational activity is an essential and, indeed, the most important element in the productive life of young boys and girls. Work at home is still an activity to which women, on the average, devote the larger part of their married life. It is an exclusive occupation of many women, and of a vast majority when young children are present.

It is, therefore, not sufficient to analyze labor force behavior of married women in terms of the demand for leisure. A predicted change in hours of leisure may imply different changes in hours of work in the market depending on the effects of the causal factors on hours of work at home. Technically speaking, if we are to derive the market supply function in a residual fashion, not only the demand for hours of leisure but also the demand for hours of work at home must be taken into account. The latter is a demand for a productive service derived from the demand by the family for home goods and services. A full application of the theory of demand for a productive service to the home sector has implications for a variety of socioeconomic phenomena beyond the scope of this paper.

Family context

The analysis of market labor supply in terms of consumption theory carries a strong connotation about the appropriate decision-making unit. We take it as self-evident that in studying consumption behavior the family is the unit of analysis. Income is assumed to be pooled, and total family consumption is positively related to it. The distribution of consumption among family members depends on tastes. It is equally important to recognize that the decisions about the production of goods and services at home and about leisure are largely family decisions. The relevant income variable in the demand for home services and for leisure of any family member is total family income. A change in income of some family member will, in general, result in a changed consumption of leisure for the family as a whole. An increase in one individual's income may not result in a decrease in *his* hours of work, but in those of other family members. The total amount of work performed at home is, even more clearly, an outcome of family demand for home goods and for leisure, given the production function at home. However, unlike the general consumption case, the distribution of leisure, market work, and home work for each family member as well as among family members is determined not only by tastes and by biological or cultural specialization of functions, but by relative prices which are specific to individual members of the family. This is so, because earning powers in the market and marginal productivities in alternative pursuits differ among individual family members. Other things equal (including family income), an increase in the market wage rate for some family member makes both the consumption of leisure and the production of home services by that individual more costly to the family, and will as a matter of rational family decision encourage greater market labor input by him (her). Even the assumption of a backward-bending supply curve would not justify a prediction of a decrease in total hours of work *for the particular earner*, if wages of other family members are fixed.

Recognition of the family context of leisure and work choices, and of the home-market dichotomy within the world of work, is essential for any analysis of labor force behavior of married women, and perhaps quite important for the analysis of behavior of other family members, including male family heads. For the present purpose of constructing a simple model of labor force behavior of married women it will be sufficient to utilize these concepts only insofar as they help to select and elucidate a few empirically manageable variables to represent the major forces of income and substitution contained in the market supply function.

Work choices

Let us consider the relevant choices of married women as between leisure, work at home, and work in the market. Income is assumed to have a positive effect on the demand for leisure, hence a negative effect on total amount of work. With the relevant prices fixed, increased family income will decrease total hours of work. Since the income effect on the demand for home goods and services is not likely to be negative,[4] it might seem that the increased leisure means exclusively a decrease in hours of work in the market. Such a conclusion, however, would require a complete absence of substitutability between the wife and other (mechanical, or human) factors of production at home, as well as an absence of substitution in consumption between home goods and market-produced goods. Domestic servants, laborsaving appliances, and frozen foods contradict such assumptions. Substitutability is, of course, a matter of degree. It may be concluded therefore that, given the income elasticity of demand for home goods and for leisure, the extent to which income differentially affects hours of work in the two sectors depends on the ease with which substitution in home production or consumption can be carried out. The lesser the substitutability the weaker the negative income effect on hours of work at home, and the stronger the income effect on hours of work in the market.

Change in this degree of substitutability may have played a part in the historical development. At a given moment of time, the degree of substitutability is likely to differ depending on the content of home production. Thus substitutes for a mother's care of small children are much more difficult to come by than those for food preparation or for physical maintenance of the household. It is likely, therefore, that the same change in income will affect hours of market work of the mother more strongly when small children are present than at other times in the life-cycle.

While family income affects the total amount of work, the market wage rate affects the allocation of hours between leisure, the home, and the market. An increase in the real wage rate, given productivity in the

4. Fragmentary cross-sectional data on food preparation at home indicate a negligible income elasticity. The demand for other home goods and services (including care of children, and their number) may be more income elastic.

home, is an increase in prices (alternative costs) of home production as well as of leisure in terms of prices of wage goods. To the extent of an existing substitution between home goods and wage goods such a change will lead to an increase in work supplied to the market. Again, the strength of the effect is a matter of the degree of substitution between wage goods and home production.

Temporal distribution of work

In a broad view, the quantity of labor supplied to the market by a wife is the fraction of her married life during which she participates in the labor force. Abstracting from the temporal distribution of labor force activities over a woman's life, this fraction could be translated into a probability of being in the labor force in a given period of time for an individual, hence into a labor force rate for a large group of women.

If leisure and work preferences, long-run family incomes, and earning power were the same for all women, the total amount of market work would, according to the theory, be the same for all women. Even if that were true, however, the *timing* of market activities during the working life may differ from one individual to another. The life cycle introduces changes in demands for and marginal costs of home work and leisure. Such changes are reflected in the relation between labor force rates and age of woman, presence, number and ages of children. There are life-cycle variations in family incomes and assets which may affect the timing of labor force participation, given a limited income horizon and a less than perfect capital market. Cyclical and random variations in wage rates, employment opportunities, income and employment of other family members, particularly of the head, are also likely to induce temporal variations in the allocation of time between home, market, and leisure. It is not surprising, therefore, that over short periods of observation, variation in labor force participation, or turnover, is the outstanding characteristic of labor force behavior of married women.

To the extent that the temporal distribution of labor force participation can be viewed as a consequence of 'transitory' variation in variables favoring particular timing, the distinction between 'permanent' and current levels of the independent variables becomes imperative in order to adapt our model to family surveys in which the period of observation is quite short.

An economic model for cross sections

Permanent levels of variables and area regressions

The simplest specification of a labor-market supply function of married women to which the theoretical considerations lead is:

$$m > \beta_p \cdot y + \gamma w + u \tag{1}$$

where m is the quantity of labor supplied to the market, y is a 'potential permanent level' of family income[5] computed at a zero rate of leisure and of home production, w is the wife's full-time market wage or market earning power, and u reflects other factors or 'tastes'. Since family income so computed is a sum of market earning powers of family members plus property income, we may write $y = x_p + w$, where x_p stands for the permanent level of income of the family which does not include earnings of the wife. For empirical convenience we shall identify x_p with income of the husband. This creates some inaccuracy, to the extent that contribution to family income of family members other than head and wife is important.

It is useful to rewrite equation (1) in terms of income of the husband since most data relate labor force behavior of wives to incomes of husbands. Indeed, the use of observed family income in empirical study of the supply relation would be inappropriate. Instead of serving as a determinant of labor force behavior, it already reflects such decisions. Substituting for y into (1):

$$m = \beta_p (x_p + w) + \gamma w + u = \beta_p x_p + aw + u \tag{2}$$

Since $a = \beta_p + \gamma$, equation (1) can be estimated by means of equation (2).

In equation (1) parameter β_p represents the effect of 'permanent' family income on the wife's market labor input, keeping her market earning power constant; γ represents the effect of the wife's market earning power, keeping family income constant. The theoretical expectation is that $\beta_p < 0$ and $\gamma > 0$.

The statement of the hypothesis $\beta_p < 0$ in equation (2), when applied to cross sections is: Given a group of women with the same market

5. The definition of 'permanent' and 'transitory' components of income follows that stated by Friedman in his consumption theory. Permanent income is income in the long-run sense, measuring income status or normal income position. Transitory income is the difference between current and permanent income. See Milton Friedman, *A Theory of the Consumption Function*, Princeton for NBER, 1957.

earning power, and tastes for leisure assumed independent of husbands' earning power, there will be, on the average, a negative relation between husbands' income and hours of market work of wives.[6] This is so because, in this statement, a higher income of husband means a higher family income and, on the assumption that leisure is a normal good, this implies a lesser total amount of work of the wife, at home and in the market.

On the assumption that, in cross sections, productivities of women in the market are unrelated to their productivities in the home, w measures the relative price of labor in the two sectors. In equation (1) γ is therefore a pure substitution effect, hence a positive number reflecting the attractive power of the wage rate in pulling women into the labor market. Parameter a in equation (2) is a relative price effect not compensated by a change in income. The question of its sign can be stated as follows: Given a group of women whose husbands have the same earning power, what is the effect of a difference in the female wage rate on hours of work on the market? Clearly, a higher wage rate will shift women from the home sector and from leisure to the market sector. However, since in this case family income increases as a result of the increase in the wives' earning power, *total* hours of work will tend to decrease. Whether hours of work in the market will increase or decrease depends on whether the job shift from home to market adds more hours of work to the market sector than is subtracted from it by a possibly increased consumption of leisure. Whether the net outcome is a positive or negative sign of a is, therefore, an empirical question. It is certainly incorrect to predict that the income effect of the wage rate on market work exceeds the substitution effect by analogy to the backward-bending supply curve. The two substitution effects involved in this comparison are quite different; the strength of substitution between wage goods and leisure time has no bearing on the strength of substitution between home production and wage goods. If anything, one would intuitively expect the latter to exceed the former.

Equation (2) was specified in terms of long-run magnitudes, such as earning power of husband and wife which also implies a long-run concept of hours of work on the left-hand side. Such specification is inappropriate for most empirical data in which individual families report current annual income and labor force participation of the wife

6. To the extent that women with strong tastes for leisure tend to seek out rich husbands, the true income effect (keeping tastes fixed) is overestimated in cross sections.

during a survey week, or her work experience during a year. One set of data, however, is usable without adapting the model to the distinction between 'permanent' and current magnitudes: These are area statistics which were heavily utilized by Douglas and Long mainly because of the absence of more detailed disaggregations. Even with such data currently available, which are much richer on the individual level, the area averages have special advantages for the purpose of estimating the coefficients of equation (2). First, the data provide information on average earning power of employed females, which can be used as a proxy for w. The second and basic merit of the community averages is that they can be interpreted as approximations to the long-run or permanent levels of the relevant variables.[7] Given that the age and family-type mix in different communities is rather similar at a given time,[8] average income and labor force figures could be considered equivalent to average magnitudes over the life-cycle, when secular trends in population and income are disregarded. At any rate, these averages are free from short-run 'transitory' deviations of individual incomes from their normal levels. However, the community averages contain a transitory deviation common to the whole group. In other words, some areas may at a given time be below or above their normal levels of economic activity. The labor force response to such a transitory deviation should be clearly distinguished from the response to an individual difference in a group. Abnormally low or high levels of economic activity in a community create different employment opportunities, and, broadly speaking, cyclical variations in wage rates. On that account, rational timing of market work would be pro-cyclical. On the other hand, a cyclical decline means a loss in husbands' incomes and employment which may induce an opposite labor force response of wives. The controversy centering around the 'added worker hypothesis'[9] is a debate about the net outcome of these two different forces for groups over the business cycle. Responses to individual short-run

7. This strategy has been employed with some success in the analyses of consumption behavior. See Margaret G. Reid, 'Consumption and the Income Effect' (unpublished manuscript); also R. Eisner, 'The Permanent Income Hypothesis: Comment,' *American Economic Review*, Dec. 1958, pp. 972–980.

8. Labor force rates by cities, standardized for age, differ negligibly from unstandardized ones.

9. According to that hypothesis, the labor force increases in depressions because unemployment of the main breadwinner induces other family members to seek employment. See W. S. Woytinsky, *Additional Workers and the Volume of Unemployment in the Depression*, S.S.R.C., 1940. For a critical analysis see Long, *The Labor Force*, Chapter 10.

income variations *within* a group at a given time are motivated by only one of the forces, since the cyclical level is fixed for the whole group. Knowledge of this response to transitory income of the family provides, by itself, no answer to the question posed by the 'added worker' controversy.

Table 1.1 provides estimates of the coefficients of equation (2) as well as coefficients for the equation expanded to include 5 independent

Table 1.1 Area regressions of labor force rates of married women, all Northern standard Metropolitan areas of 250,000 or more population in 1950

| | Independent variables | | | | | |
	X_1 (thousands of dollars)	X_2	X_3 (per cent)	X_4	X_5	R^2
Regression coefficients	−0.62	+1.33	+0.12	−0.41	−0.24	0.62
and standard errors	(0.21)	(0.11)	(0.27)	(0.53)	(0.61)	
Regression coefficients	−0.53	+1.52				0.51
Elasticities at means	−0.83	+1.50				

Note: See text for description of independent variables.

Source: *U.S. Census of Population 1950*, Vol. II, *Characteristics of the Population*, Tables, 86, 88, 183; Special Report, *General Characteristics of Families*, Table 41; and Gertrude Bancroft, *The American Labor Force, Its Growth and Changing Composition*, New York, Wiley, 1958. Table D-11.

variables. The regression analysis was restricted to 57 largest Standard Metropolitan Areas (population, 250,000 and over) in the North. It was felt that the SMA approximate labor markets more properly than cities. Southern areas were excluded because of the desire to exclude color differentials, which need to be studied separately. The dependent variable is the labor force participation rate (in per cent) of married women with husband present during the census week early in 1950. X_1 is the median income in 1949 of male family heads, wife present; X_2 is the median income of females who worked 50 to 52 weeks in 1949. These are the empirical proxies for x_p and w in equation (2). Three independent variables were added to help in the interpretation. Since areas differ by educational composition, which may affect as well as reflect tastes for market work or for its continuity, this variable was represented by the per cent of population age 25 and over with completed high school education or more (X_3). The position of the community relative to its normal levels of economic activity (group transitory) was represented by the male unemployment rate (X_4). Finally, to take care of the more important differences in demand for work at home, the per cent of families with children under 6 years of age was represented by (X_5).

The coefficients in Table 1 are informative: Judging by the coefficient of determination (R^2), the male income (X_1) and female wage rate (X_2) variables alone explain a half of the observed variation in labor force participation rates among areas in 1950. The effect of husbands' incomes is negative,[10] as theoretically expected. The effect of wives' earning power is positive, and indeed stronger than the effect of income. This result is quite suggestive with regard to time series, though not directly applicable. The introduction of a measure of educational level (X_3) into the equation attenuates the wage rate effect somewhat, though not significantly in a statistical sense. Unemployment (X_4) is seen to have a discouraging effect on labor force participation. This appears to be a contradiction of the added worker hypothesis, though the information is not sufficient to yield statistical significance. Finally, the presence of small children (X_5) has an effect in the expected direction, though again statistical significance is lacking.

Adaptation of the model to analysis of family surveys

When labor force behavior (reported for a week or for the preceding year) of wives is related to current income of husbands in family surveys, the observed relation is a compound of two effects which it is important to distinguish: the responsiveness of labor force behavior (a) to husbands' long-run income positions, and (b) to current deviations of that income from its normal level.[11]

10. This stands in contrast to Long's finding that the negative relation between earnings of males and labor force rates of females, by areas, which was observed by Douglas and Long in other census periods, seems to have vanished in 1950. Such an impression, however, is based on a gross regression between the two variables and is not confirmed, when the other relevant variable, the female wage rate, is included in the equation. Table 1 indicates no basic change in the structure of the labor force relation between 1940 and 1950: A comparable two-variable regression in 1940 showed an income elasticity of -0.91 and a wage rate elasticity of $+1.26$. The change in the *gross* regression from negative to positive is due to a larger positive intercorrelation between male and female earnings in 1950 $(r = +0.8)$ than in 1940 $(r = +0.4)$.

11. For present purposes, a similar distinction between current and 'permanent' levels of the female wage rate is not formally introduced. Short-run variations in it, or rather in employment opportunities, are largely a matter of industry differences among communities. We may assume that such differences are much less important in family surveys than in area comparisons.

2 A Theory of the Allocation of Time

Gary Becker
Columbia University

From: *The Economic Journal*, Vol. LXXX, No. 200, September 1965, pp.
493–517.

1. Introduction

Throughout history the amount of time spent at work has never consistently been much greater than that spent at other activities. Even a
work week of fourteen hours a day for six days still leaves half the total
time for sleeping, eating and other activities. Economic development
has led to a large secular decline in the work week, so that whatever
may have been true of the past, to-day it is below fifty hours in most
countries, less than a third of the total time available. Consequently the
allocation and efficiency of non-working time may now be more important to economic welfare than that of working time; yet the attention
paid by economists to the latter dwarfs any paid to the former.

Fortunately, there is a movement under way to redress the balance.
The time spent at work declined secularly, partly because young persons
increasingly delayed entering the labour market by lengthening their
period of schooling. In recent years many economists have stressed that
the time of students is one of the inputs into the educational process,
that this time could be used to participate more fully in the labour market
and therefore that one of the costs of education is the forgone earnings
of students. Indeed, various estimates clearly indicate that forgone
earnings is the dominant private and an important social cost of both
high-school and college education in the United States.[1] The increased
awareness of the importance of forgone earnings has resulted in several
attempts to economise on students' time, as manifested, say, by the
spread of the quarterly and tri-mester systems.[2]

1. See T. W. Schultz, 'The Formation of Human Capital by Education,' *Journal
of Political Economy* (December 1960), and my *Human Capital* (Columbia University Press for the N.B.E.R., 1964), Chapter IV. I argue there that the importance
of forgone earnings can be directly seen, e.g., from the failure of free tuition to
eliminate impediments to college attendance or the increased enrolments that sometimes occur in depressed areas or time periods.

2. On the cause of the secular trend towards an increased school year see my
comments, ibid., p. 103.

Most economists have now fully grasped the importance of forgone earnings in the educational process and, more generally, in all investments in human capital, and criticise educationalists and others for neglecting them. In the light of this it is perhaps surprising that economists have not been equally sophisticated about other non-working uses of time. For example, the cost of a service like the theatre or a good like meat is generally simply said to equal their market prices, yet everyone would agree that the theatre and even dining take time, just as schooling does, time that often could have been used productively. If so, the full costs of these activities would equal the sum of market prices and the forgone value of the time used up. In other words, indirect costs should be treated on the same footing when discussing all non-work uses of time, as they are now in discussions of schooling.

In the last few years a group of us at Columbia University have been occupied, perhaps initially independently but then increasingly less so, with introducing the cost of time systematically into decisions about non-work activities. J. Mincer has shown with several empirical examples how estimates of the income elasticity of demand for different commodities are biased when the cost of time is ignored;[3] J. Owen has analysed how the demand for leisure can be affected;[4] E. Dean has considered the allocation of time between subsistence work and market participation in some African economies;[5] while, as already mentioned, I have been concerned with the use of time in education, training and other kinds of human capital. Here I attempt to develop a general treatment of the allocation of time in all other non-work activities. Although under my name alone, much of any credit it merits belongs to the stimulus received from Mincer, Owen, Dean and other past and present participants in the Labor Workshop at Columbia.[6]

3. See his 'Market Prices, Opportunity Costs, and Income Effects,' in *Measurement in Economics; Studies in Mathematical Economics and Econometrics in Memory of Yehuda Grunfeld* (Stanford University Press, 1963). In his well-known earlier study Mincer considered the allocation of married women between 'housework' and labour force participation. (See 'Labor Force Participation of Married Women,' above, p. 41.

4. See his *The Supply of Labor and the Demand for Recreation* (unpublished Ph.D. dissertation, Columbia University, 1964).

5. See his *Economic Analysis and African Response to Price* (unpublished Ph.D. dissertation, Columbia University, 1963).

6. Let me emphasise, however, that I alone am responsible for any errors.

I would also like to express my appreciation for the comments received when presenting these ideas to seminars at the Universities of California (Los Angeles), Chicago, Pittsburgh, Rochester and Yale, and to a session at the 1963 Meetings of

The plan of the discussion is as follows. The first section sets out a basic theoretical analysis of choice that includes the cost of time on the same footing as the cost of market goods, while the remaining sections treat various empirical implications of the theory. These include a new approach to changes in hours of work and 'leisure', the full integration of so-called 'productive' consumption into economic analysis, a new analysis of the effect of income on the quantity and 'quality' of commodities consumed, some suggestions on the measurement of productivity, an economic analysis of queues and a few others as well. Although I refer to relevant empirical work that has come to my attention, little systematic testing of the theory has been attempted.

2. A revised theory of choice

According to traditional theory, households maximise utility functions of the form

$$U = U(y_1, y_2, \ldots, y_n) \tag{1}$$

subject to the resource constraint

$$\Sigma p_i' y_i = I = W + V \tag{2}$$

where y_i are goods purchased on the market, p'_i are their prices, I is money income, W is earnings and V is other income. As the introduction suggests, the point of departure here is the systematic incorporation of non-working time. Households will be assumed to combine time and market goods to produce more basic commodities that directly enter their utility functions. One such commodity is the seeing of a play, which depends on the input of actors, script, theatre and the playgoer's time; another is sleeping, which depends on the input of a bed, house (pills?) and time. These commodities will be called Z_i and written as

$$Z_i = f_i(x_i, T_i) \tag{3}$$

where x_i is a vector of market goods and T_i a vector of time inputs used in producing the ith commodity.[7] Note that, when capital goods such as

the Econometric Society. Extremely helpful comments on an earlier draft were provided by Milton Friedman and by Gregory C. Chow; the latter also assisted in the mathematical formulation. Linda Kee provided useful research assistance. My research was partially supported by the IBM Corporation.

7. There are several empirical as well as conceptual advantages in assuming that households combine goods and time to produce commodities instead of simply assuming that the amount of time used at an activity is a direct function of the amount of goods consumed. For example, a change in the cost of goods relative to time could cause a significant substitution away from the one rising in relative cost. This, as well as other applications, are treated in the following sections.

refrigerators or automobiles are used, x refers to the services yielded by the goods. Also note that T_i is a vector because, e.g., the hours used during the day or on weekdays may be distinguished from those used at night or on week-ends. Each dimension of T_i refers to a different aspect of time. Generally, the partial derivatives of Z_i with respect to both x_i and T_i are non-negative.[8]

In the formulation households are both producing units and utility maximisers. They combine time and market goods via the 'production functions' f_i to produce the basic commodities Z_i, and they choose the best combination of these commodities in the conventional way by maximising a utility function

$$U = U(Z_i, \ldots Z_m) \equiv U(f_1, \ldots f_m) \equiv U(x_1, \ldots x_m; T_1, \ldots T_m) \qquad (4)$$

subject to a budget constraint

$$g(Z_i, \ldots Z_m) = Z \qquad (5)$$

where g is an expenditure function of Z_i and Z is the bound on resources. The integration of production and consumption is at odds with the tendency for economists to separate them sharply, production occurring in firms and consumption in households. It should be pointed out, however, that in recent years economists increasingly recognise that a household is truly a 'small factory':[9] it combines capital goods, raw materials and labour to clean, feed, procreate and otherwise produce useful commodities. Undoubtedly the fundamental reason for the traditional separation is that firms are usually given control over working time in exchange for market goods, while 'discretionary' control over market goods and consumption time is retained by households as they create their own utility. If (presumably different) firms were also given control over market goods and consumption time in exchange for providing utility the separation would quickly fade away in analysis as well as in fact.

The basic goal of the analysis is to find measures of g and Z which facilitate the development of empirical implications. The most direct approach is to assume that the utility function in equation (4) is maximised subject to separate constraints on the expenditure of market

8. If a good or time period was used in producing several commodities I assume that these 'joint costs' could be fully and uniquely allocated among the commodities. The problems here are no different from those usually arising in the analysis of multi-product firms.

9. See e.g., A. K. Cairncross, 'Economic Schizophrenia,' *Scottish Journal of Political Economy* (February 1958).

goods and time, and to the production functions in equation (3). The goods constraint can be written as

$$\sum_1^m p_i x_i = I = V + T_w\,\bar{w} \tag{6}$$

where p_i is a vector giving the unit prices of x_i, T_w is a vector giving the hours spent at work and $\bar{w}$ is a vector giving the earnings per unit of T_w. The time constraints can be written as

$$\sum_1^m T_i = T_c = T - T_w \tag{7}$$

where T_c is a vector giving the total time spent at consumption and T is a vector giving the total time available. The production functions (3) can be written in the equivalent form

$$\left.\begin{array}{l} T_i \equiv t_i Z_i \\ x_i \equiv b_i Z_i \end{array}\right\} \tag{8}$$

where t_i is a vector giving the input of time per unit of Z_i and b_i is a similar vector for market goods.

The problem would appear to be to maximise the utility function (4) subject to the multiple constraints (6) and (7) and to the production relations (8). There is, however, really only one basic constraint: (6) is not independent of (7) because time can be converted into goods by using less time at consumption and more at work. Thus, substituting for T_w in (6) its equivalent in (7) gives the single constraint[10]

$$\Sigma p_i x_i + \Sigma T_i \bar{w} = V + T\bar{w} \tag{9}$$

By using (8), (9) can be written as

$$\Sigma(p_i b_i + t_i \bar{w})Z_i = V + T\bar{w} \tag{10}$$

with

$$\left.\begin{array}{l} \pi_i \equiv p_i b_i + t_i \bar{w} \\ S' \equiv V + T\bar{w} \end{array}\right\} \tag{11}$$

The full price of a unit of Z_i (π_i) is the sum of the prices of the goods and of the time used per unit of Z_i. That is, the full price of consump-

10. The dependency among constraints distinguishes this problem from many other multiple-constraint situations in economic analysis, such as those arising in the usual theory of rationing (see J. Tobin, 'A Survey of the Theory of Rationing,' *Econometrica* (October 1952)). Rationing would reduce to a formally identical single-constraint situation if rations were saleable and fully convertible into money income.

tion is the sum of direct and indirect prices in the same way that the full cost of investing in human capital is the sum of direct and indirect costs.[11] These direct and indirect prices are symmetrical determinants of total price, and there is no analytical reason to stress one rather than the other.

The resource constraint on the right side of equation (10), S', is easy to interpret if $\bar{w}$ were a constant, independent of the Z_i. For then S' gives the money income achieved if all the time available were devoted to work. This achievable income is 'spent' on the commodities Z_i either directly through expenditures on goods, $\Sigma p_i b_i Z_i$, or indirectly through the forgoing of income, $\Sigma t_i \bar{w} Z_i$, i.e., by using time at consumption rather than at work. As long as $\bar{w}$ were constant, and if there were constant returns in producing Z_i so that b_i and t_i were fixed for given p_i and $\bar{w}$ the equilibrium condition resulting from maximising (4) subject to (10) takes a very simple form:

$$U_i = \frac{\partial U_i}{\partial Z} = \lambda \pi_i \qquad i = 1, \ldots m \tag{12}$$

where λ is the marginal utility of money income. If $\bar{w}$ were not constant the resource constraint in equation (10) would not have any particularly useful interpretation: $S' = V + T\bar{w}$ would overstate the money income achievable as long as marginal wage-rates were below average ones. Moreover, the equilibrium conditions would become more complicated than (12) because marginal would have to replace average prices.

The total resource constraint could be given the sensible interpretation of the maximum money income achievable only in the special and unlikely case when average earnings were constant. This suggests dropping the approach based on explicitly considering separate goods and time constraints and substituting one in which the total resource constraint necessarily equalled the maximum money income achievable, which will be simply called 'full income.'[12] This income could in general be obtained by devoting all the time and other resources of a household to earning income, with no regard for consumption. Of course, all the time would not usually be spent 'at' a job: sleep, food, even leisure are required for efficiency, and some time (and other resources) would have to be spent on these activities in order to maximise money income. The amount spent would, however, be determined solely by the effect on income and not by any effect on utility. Slaves, for example, might

11. See my *Human Capital*, op. cit.
12. This term emerged from a conversation with Milton Friedman.

be permitted time 'off' from work only in so far as that maximised their output, or free persons in poor environments might have to maximise money income simply to survive.[13]

Households in richer countries do, however, forfeit money income in order to obtain additional utility, i.e., they exchange money income for a greater amount of psychic income. For example, they might increase their leisure time, take a pleasant job in preference to a better-paying unpleasant one, employ unproductive nephews or eat more than is warranted by considerations of productivity. In these and other situations the amount of money income forfeited measures the cost of obtaining additional utility.

Thus the full income approach provides a meaningful resource constraint and one firmly based on the fact that goods and time can be combined into a single overall constraint because time can be converted into goods through money income. It also incorporates a unified treatment of all substitutions of non-pecuniary for pecuniary income, regardless of their nature or whether they occur on the job or in the household. The advantages of this will become clear as the analysis proceeds.

If full income is denoted by S, and if the total earnings forgone or 'lost' by the interest in utility is denoted by L, the identity relating L to S and I is simply

$$L(Z_i, \ldots, Z_m) \equiv S - I(Z_1, \ldots, Z_m) \tag{13}$$

I and L are functions of the Z_i because how much is earned or forgone depends on the consumption set chosen; for example, up to a point, the less leisure chosen the larger the money income and the smaller the amount forgone.[14] Using equations (6) and (8), equation (13) can be written as

$$\Sigma p_i b_i Z_i + L(Z_1, \ldots, Z_m) \equiv S \tag{14}$$

13. Any utility received would only be an incidental by-product of the pursuit of money income. Perhaps this explains why utility analysis was not clearly formulated and accepted until economic development had raised incomes well above the subsistence level.

14. Full income is achieved by maximising the earnings function

$$W = W(Z_1, \ldots Z_m) \tag{1'}$$

subject to the expenditure constraint in equation (6), to the inequality

$$\overset{m}{\underset{1}{\Sigma}} T_1 \leq T \tag{2'}$$

and to the restrictions in (8). I assume for simplicity that the amount of each dimension of time used in producing commodities is less than the total available, so that

This basic resource constraint states that full income is spent either directly on market goods or indirectly through the forgoing of money income. Unfortunately, there is no simple expression for the average price of Z_i as there is in equation (10). However, marginal, not average, prices are relevant for behaviour, and these would be identical for the constraint in (10) only when average earnings, $\bar{w}$, was constant. But, if so, the expression for the loss function simplifies to

$$L = \bar{w} T_c = \bar{w} \Sigma t_i Z_i \tag{15}$$

and (14) reduces to (10). Moreover, even in the general case the total marginal prices resulting from (14) can always be divided into direct and indirect components: the equilibrium conditions resulting from maximising the utility function subject to (14)[15] are

$$U_i = T(p_i b_i + L_i), \qquad i = 1, \ldots, m \tag{16}$$

where $p_i b_i$ is the direct and L_i the indirect component of the total marginal price $p_i b_i + L_i$.[16]

Behind the division into direct and indirect costs is the allocation of time and goods between work-orientated and consumption-orientated activities. This suggests an alternative division of costs; namely, into those resulting from the allocation of goods and those resulting from the allocation of time. Write $L_i = \partial L / \partial Z_i$ as

$$L_i = \frac{\partial T_i}{\partial L} \frac{\partial T_i}{\partial Z_i} + \frac{\partial L}{\partial x_i} \frac{\partial Z_i}{\partial x_i} \tag{17}$$

$$= l_i t_i + c_i b_i \tag{18}$$

(2′) can be ignored; it is not difficult to incorporate this constraint. Maximising (1′) subject to (6) and (8) yields the following conditions

$$\frac{\partial W}{\partial Z_i} \quad \frac{p_i b_i \sigma}{1 + \sigma} \tag{3′}$$

where σ is the marginal productivity of money income. Since the loss function $L = (S - V) - W$, the equilibrium conditions to minimise the loss is the same as (3′) except for a change in sign.

15. Households maximise their utility subject only to the single total resource constraint given by (14), for once the full income constraint is satisfied, there is no other restriction on the set of Z_i that can be chosen. By introducing the concept of full income the problem of maximising utility subject to the time and goods constraints is solved in two stages: first, full income is determined from the goods and time constraints, and then utility is maximised subject only to the constraint imposed by full income.

16. It can easily be shown that the equilibrium conditions of (16) are in fact precisely the same as those following in general from equation (10).

where $l_i = \frac{\partial L}{\partial T_i}$ and $c_i = \frac{\partial L}{\partial x_i}$ are the marginal forgone earnings of using more time and goods respectively on Z_i. Equation (16) can then be written as

$$U_i = T[b_i(p_i + c_i) + t_i l_i] \tag{19}$$

The total marginal cost of Z_i is the sum of $b_i(p_i + c_i)$, the marginal cost of using goods in producing Z_i, and $t_i l_i$, the marginal cost of using time. This division would be equivalent to that between direct and indirect costs only if $c_i = 0$ or if there were no indirect costs of using goods.

The accompanying Figure 2.1 shows the equilibrium given by equation (16) for a two-commodity world. In equilibrium the slope of the full income opportunity curve, which equals the ratio of marginal prices, would equal the slope of an indifference curve, which equals the ratio of marginal utilities. Equilibrium occurs at p and p' for the opportunity curves S and S' respectively.

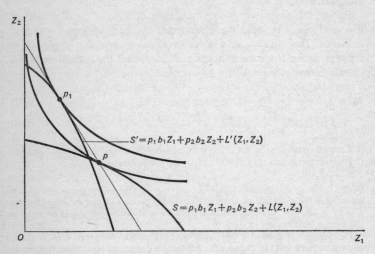

Figure 2.1.

The rest of the paper is concerned with developing numerous empirical implications of this theory, starting with determinants of hours worked and concluding with an economic interpretation of various queueing systems. To simplify the presentation, it is assumed that the distinction between direct and indirect costs is equivalent to that between goods and time costs; in other words, the marginal forgone cost of the use of goods, c_i, is set equal to zero. The discussion would not be much changed, but would be more cumbersome were this not assumed.[17] Finally, until Section IV goods and time are assumed to be used in fixed proportions in producing commodities; that is, the coefficients b_i and t_i in equation (8) are treated as constants.

3. Applications

(a) Hours of work

If the effects of various changes on the time used on consumption, T_c, could be determined their effects on hours worked, T_w, could be found residually from equation (7). This section considers, among other things, the effects of changes in income, earnings and market prices on T_c, and thus on T_w, using as the major tool of analysis differences among commodities in the importance of forgone earnings.

The relative marginal importance of forgone earnings is defined as

$$a_i = \frac{l_i t_i}{p_i b_i + l_i t_i} \tag{20}$$

The importance of forgone earnings would be greater the larger l_i and t_i, the forgone earnings per hour of time and the number of hours used per unit of Z_i respectively, while it would be smaller the larger p_i and b_i, the market price of goods and the number of goods used per unit of Z_i respectively. Similarly, the relative marginal importance of time is defined as

$$\gamma_i = \frac{t_i}{p_i b_i + l_i t_i} \tag{21}$$

If full income increased solely because of an increase in V (other money income) there would simply be a parallel shift of the opportunity curve to the right with no change in relative commodity prices. The consumption of most commodities would have to increase; if all did, hours worked would decrease, for the total time spent on consumption must increase if the output of all commodities did, and by equation (7) the time spent at work is inversely related to that spent on consumption.

17. Elsewhere I have discussed some effects of the allocation of goods on productivity (see my 'Investment in Human Capital: A Theoretical Analysis,' *Journal of Political Economy*, special supplement (October 1962), Section 2); essentially the same discussion can be found in *Human Capital*, op. cit., Chapter II.

Hours worked could increase only if relatively time intensive commodities, those with large γ, were sufficiently inferior.[18]

A uniform percentage increase in earnings for all allocations of time would increase the cost per hour used in consumption by the same percentage for all commodities.[19] The relative prices of different commodities would, however, change as long as forgone earnings were not equally important for all; in particular, the prices of commodities having relatively important forgone earnings would rise more. Now the fundamental theorem of demand theory states that a compensated change in relative prices would induce households to consume less of commodities rising in price. The figure shows the effect of a rise in earnings fully compensated by a decline in other income: the opportunity curve would be rotated clockwise through the initial position p if Z_1 were the more earnings-intensive commodity. In the figure the new equilibrium p' must be to the left and above p, or less Z_1 and more Z_2 would be consumed.

Therefore a compensated uniform rise in earnings would lead to a shift away from earnings-intensive commodities and towards goods-intensive ones. Since earnings and time intensiveness tend to be posi-

18. The problem is: under what conditions would

$$-\frac{\partial T_w}{\partial V} = \frac{\partial T_c}{\partial V} = \Sigma t_i \frac{\partial Z_i}{\partial V} < 0 \tag{1'}$$

when

$$\Sigma(p_i b_i + l_i t_i) \frac{\partial Z_i}{\partial V} = 1 \tag{2'}$$

If the analysis were limited to a two-commodity world where Z_1 was more time intensive, then it can easily be shown that (1') would hold if, and only if,

$$\frac{\partial Z_1}{\partial V} < \frac{-\gamma_2}{(\gamma_1 - \gamma_2)(p_1 b_1 + l_1 t_1)} < 0 \tag{3'}$$

19. By a uniform change of β is meant

$$W_1 = (1 + \beta)W_0(Z_1, \ldots Z_n)$$

where W_0 represents the earnings function before the change and W_1 represents it afterwards. Since the loss function is defined as

$$L = S - W - V$$
$$= W(\hat{Z}) - W(Z),$$

then

$$L_1 = W_1(\hat{Z}) - W_1(Z)$$
$$= (1 + \beta)[W_0(\hat{Z}) - W_0(Z)] = (1 + \beta)L_0$$

Consequently, all opportunities costs also change by β.

tively correlated,[20] consumption would be shifted from time-intensive commodities. A shift away from such commodities would, however, result in a reduction in the total time spent in consumption, and thus an increase in the time spent at work.[21]

The effect of an uncompensated increase in earnings on hours worked would depend on the relative strength of the substitution and income effects. The former would increase hours, the latter reduce them; which dominates cannot be determined *a priori*.

The conclusion that a pure rise in earnings increases and a pure rise in income reduces hours of work must sound very familiar, for they are traditional results of the well-known labour–leisure analysis. What, then, is the relation between our analysis, which treats all commodities symmetrically and stresses only their differences in relative time and earning intensities, and the usual analysis, which distinguishes a commodity having special properties called 'leisure' from other more commonplace commodities? It is easily shown that the usual labour–leisure analysis can be looked upon as a special case of ours in which the cost of the commodity called leisure consists entirely of forgone earnings and the cost of other commodities entirely of goods.[22]

As a description of reality such an approach, of course, is not tenable,

20. According to the definition of earning and time intensity in equations (20) and (21), they would be positively correlated unless l_i and t_i were sufficiently negatively correlated. See the further discussion later on.

21. Let it be stressed that this conclusion usually holds, even when households are irrational; sophisticated calculations about the value of time at work or in consumption, or substantial knowledge about the amount of time used by different commodities is not required. Changes in the hours of work, even of non-maximising, impulsive, habitual, etc., households would tend to be positively related to compensated changes in earnings because demand curves tend to be negatively inclined even for such households (see G. S. Becker, 'Irrational Behavior and Economic Theory,' *Journal of Political Economy* (February 1962)).

22. Suppose there were two commodities Z_1 and Z_2, where the cost of Z_1 depended only on the cost of market goods, while the cost of Z_2 depended only on the cost of time. The goods-budget constraint would then simply be

$$p_1 b_1 Z_1 = I = V + T_w \bar{w}$$

and the constraint on time would be

$$t_2 Z_2 = T - T_w$$

This is essentially the algebra of the analysis presented by Henderson and Quandt, and their treatment is representative. They call Z_2 'leisure,' and Z_1 an average of different commodities. Their equilibrium condition that the rate of substitution between goods and leisure equals the real wage-rate is just a special case of our equation (19) (see *Microeconomic Theory* (McGraw-Hill, 1958), p. 23).

since virtually all activities use both time and goods. Perhaps it would be defended either as an analytically necessary or extremely insightful approximation to reality. Yet the usual substitution and income effects of a change in resources on hours worked have easily been derived from a more general analysis which stresses only that the relative importance of time varies among commodities. The rest of the paper tries to go further and demonstrate that the traditional approach, with its stress on the demand for 'leisure', apparently has seriously impeded the development of insights about the economy, since the more direct and general approach presented here naturally leads to a variety of implications never yet obtained.

The two determinants of the importance of forgone earnings are the amount of time used per dollar of goods and the cost per unit of time. Reading a book, taking a haircut or commuting use more time per dollar of goods than eating dinner, frequenting a night-club or sending children to private summer camps. Other things the same, forgone earnings would be more important for the former set of commodities than the latter.

The importance of forgone earnings would be determined solely by time intensity only if the cost of time was the same for all commodities. Presumably, however, it varies considerably among commodities and at different periods. For example, the cost of time is often less on week-ends and in the evenings because many firms are closed then,[23] which explains why a famous liner intentionally includes a week-end in each voyage between the United States and Europe.[24] The cost of time would also tend to be less for commodities that contribute to productive effort, traditionally called 'productive consumption.' A considerable amount of sleep, food and even 'play' fall under this heading. The opportunity cost of the time is less because these commodities indirectly contribute to earnings. Productive consumption has had a long but bandit-like existence in economic thought; our analysis does systematically incorporate it into household decision-making.

Although the formal specification of leisure in economic models has ignored expenditures on goods, cannot one argue that a more correct specification would simply associate leisure with relatively important

23. For workers receiving premium pay on the week-ends and in the evenings, however, the cost of time may be considerably greater then.

24. See the advertisement by United States Lines in various issues of the *New Yorker* magazine: 'The S.S. *United States* regularly includes a week-end in its 5 days to Europe, saving [economic] time for businessmen' (my insertion).

forgone earnings? Most conceptions of leisure do imply that it is time intensive and does not indirectly contribute to earnings,[25] two of the important characteristics of earnings-intensive commodities. On the other hand, not all of what are usually considered leisure activities do have relatively important forgone earnings: night-clubbing is generally considered leisure, and yet, at least in its more expensive forms, has a large expenditure component. Conversely, some activities have relatively large forgone earnings and are not considered leisure: haircuts or child care are examples. Consequently, the distinction between earnings-intensive and other commodities corresponds only partly to the usual distinction between leisure and other commodities. Since it has been shown that the relative importance of forgone earnings rather than any concept of leisure is more relevant for economic analysis, less attention should be paid to the latter. Indeed, although the social philosopher might have to define precisely the concept of leisure,[26] the economist can reach all his traditional results as well as many more without introducing it at all!

Not only is it difficult to distinguish leisure from other non-work[27] but also even work from non-work. Is commuting work, non-work or both? How about a business lunch, a good diet or relaxation? Indeed, the notion of productive consumption was introduced precisely to cover those commodities that contribute to work as well as to consumption. Cannot pure work then be considered simply as a limiting com-

25. For example, *Webster's Collegiate Dictionary* defines leisurely as 'characterized by leisure, taking *abundant time*' (my italics); or S. de Grazia, in his recent *Of Time, Work and Leisure*, says, 'Leisure is a state of being in which activity is performed for its own sake or as its own end' (New York: The Twentieth Century Fund, 1962, p. 15).

26. S. de Grazia has recently entertainingly shown the many difficulties in even reaching a reliable definition, and *a fortiori*, in quantitatively estimating the amount of leisure. See ibid., Chapters III and IV; also see W. Moore, *Man, Time and Society* (New York: Wiley, 1963), Chapter II; J. N. Morgan, M. H. David, W. J. Cohen and H. E. Brazer, *Income and Welfare in the United States* (New York: McGraw-Hill, 1962), p. 322, and Owen, op. cit., Chapter II.

27. Sometimes true leisure is defined as the amount of discretionary time available (see Moore, op. cit., p. 18). It is always difficult to attach a rigorous meaning to the word 'discretionary' when referring to economic resources. One might say that in the short run consumption time is and working time is not discretionary because the latter is partially subject to the authoritarian control of employers. (Even this distinction would vanish if households gave certain firms authoritarian control over their consumption time; see the discussion in Section II.) In the long run this definition of discretionary time is suspect too because the availability of alternative sources of employment would make working time also discretionary.

modity of such joint commodities in which the contribution to consumption was nil? Similarly, pure consumption would be a limiting commodity in the opposite direction in which the contribution to work was nil, and intermediate commodities would contribute to both consumption and work. The more important the contribution to work relative to consumption, the smaller would tend to be the relative importance of forgone earnings. Consequently, the effects of changes in earnings, other income, etc., on hours worked then become assimilated to and essentially a special case of their effects on the consumption of less earnings-intensive commodities. For example, a pure rise in earnings would reduce the relative price, and thus increase the time spent on these commodities, *including the time spent at work*; similarly, for changes in income and other variables. The generalisation wrought by our approach is even greater than may have appeared at first.

Before concluding this section a few other relevant implications of our theory might be briefly mentioned. Just as a (compensated) rise in earnings would increase the prices of commodities with relatively large forgone earnings, induce a substitution away from them and increase the hours worked, so a (compensated) fall in market prices would also induce a substitution away from them and increase the hours worked: the effects of changes in direct and indirect costs are symmetrical. Indeed, Owen presents some evidence indicating that hours of work in the United States fell somewhat more in the first thirty years of this century than in the second thirty years, not because wages rose more during the first period, but because the market prices of recreation commodities fell more then.[28]

A well-known result of the traditional labour–leisure approach is that a rise in the income tax induces at least a substitution effect away from work and towards 'leisure'. Our approach reaches the same result only via a substitution towards time-intensive consumption rather than leisure. A simple additional implication of our approach, however, is that if a rise in the income tax were combined with an appropriate excise on the goods used in time-intensive commodities or subsidy to the goods used in other commodities there need be no change in full relative prices, and thus no substitution away from work. The traditional approach has recently reached the same conclusion, although in a much more involved way.[29]

28. See op. cit., Chapter VIII. Recreation commodities presumably have relatively large forgone earnings.
29. See W. J. Corbett and D. C. Hague, 'Complementarity and the Excess Bur-

There is no exception in the traditional approach to the rule that a pure rise in earnings would not induce a decrease in hours worked. An exception does occur in ours, for if the time and earnings intensities (i.e., $l_i t_i$ and t_i) were negatively correlated a pure rise in earnings would induce a substitution towards time-intensive commodities, and thus away from work.[30] Although this exception does illustrate the greater power of our approach, there is no reason to believe that it is any more important empirically than the exception to the rule on income effects.

(b) The productivity of time

Most of the large secular increase in earnings, which stimulated the development of the labour–leisure analysis, resulted from an increase in the productivity of working time due to the growth in human and physical capital, technological progress and other factors. Since a rise in earnings resulting from an increase in productivity has both income and substitution effects, the secular decline in hours worked appeared to be evidence that the income effect was sufficiently strong to swamp the substitution effect.

The secular growth in capital and technology also improved the productivity of consumption time: supermarkets, automobiles, sleeping pills, safety and electric razors, and telephones are a few familiar and important examples of such developments. An improvement in the productivity of consumption time would change relative commodity prices and increase full income, which in turn would produce substitution and income effects. The interesting point is that a very different interpretation of the observed decline in hours of work is suggested because these effects are precisely the opposite of those produced by improvements in the productivity of working time.

Assume a uniform increase only in the productivity of consumption time, which is taken to mean a decline in all t_i. time required to produce a unit of Z_i, by a common percentage. The relative prices of commodi-

---

den of Taxation,' *Review of Economic Studies*, Vol. XXI (1953–4); also A. C. Harberger, 'Taxation, Resource Allocation and Welfare,' in the *Role of Direct and Indirect Taxes in the Federal Revenue System* (Princeton University Press, 1964).

30. The effect on earnings is more difficult to determine because, by assumption, time-intensive commodities have smaller costs per unit time than other commodities. A shift towards the former would, therefore, raise hourly earnings, which would partially and perhaps more than entirely offset the reduction in hours worked. Incidentally, this illustrates how the productivity of hours worked is influenced by the consumption set chosen.

ties with large forgone earnings would fall, and substitution would be induced towards these and away from other commodities, causing hours of work also to fall. Since the increase in productivity would also produce an income effect,[31] the demand for commodities would increase, which, in turn, would induce an increased demand for goods. But since the productivity of working time is assumed not to change, more goods could be obtained only by an increase in work. That is, the higher real income resulting from an advance in the productivity of consumption time would cause hours of work to *increase*.

Consequently, an emphasis on the secular increase in the productivity of consumption time would lead to a very different interpretation of the secular decline in hours worked. Instead of claiming that a powerful income effect swamped a weaker substitution effect, the claim would have to be that a powerful substitution effect swamped a weaker income effect.

Of course, the productivity of both working and consumption time increased secularly, and the true interpretation is somewhere between these extremes. If both increased at the same rate there would be no change in relative prices, and thus no substitution effect, because the rise in l_i induced by one would exactly offset the decline in t_i induced by the other, marginal forgone earnings $(i_i t_i)$ remaining unchanged. Although the income effects would tend to offset each other too, they would do so completely only if the income elasticity of demand for time-intensive commodities was equal to unity. Hours worked would decline if it was above and increase if it was below unity.[32] Since these commodities have probably on the whole been luxuries, such an increase in income would tend to reduce hours worked.

The productivity of working time has probably advanced more than that of consumption time, if only because of familiar reasons associated with the division of labour and economies of scale.[33] Consequently,

31. Full money income would be unaffected if it were achieved by using all time at pure work activities. If other uses of time were also required it would tend to increase. Even if full money income were unaffected, however, full real income would increase because prices of the Z_i would fall.

32. So the 'Knight' view that an increase in income would increase 'leisure' is not necessarily true, even if leisure were a superior good and even aside from Robbins' emphasis on the substitution effect (see L. Robbins, 'On the Elasticity of Demand for Income in Terms of Effort,' *Economica* (June 1930)).

33. Wesley Mitchell's justly famous essay 'The Backward Art of Spending Money' spells out some of these reasons (see the first essay in the collection, *The Backward Art of Spending Money and Other Essays* (New York: McGraw-Hill, 1932)).

there probably has been the traditional substitution effect towards and income effect away from work, as well as an income effect away from work because time-intensive commodities were luxuries. The secular decline in hours worked would only imply therefore that the combined income effects swamped the substitution effect, not that the income effect of an advance in the productivity of working time alone swamped its substitution effect.

Cross-sectionally, the hours worked of males have generally declined less as incomes increased than they have over time. Some of the difference between these relations is explained by the distinction between relevant and reported incomes, or by interdependencies among the hours worked by different employees;[34] some is probably also explained by the distinction between working and consumption productivity. There is a presumption that persons distinguished cross-sectionally by money incomes or earnings differ more in working than consumption productivity because they are essentially distinguished by the former. This argument does not apply to time series because persons are distinguished there by calendar time, which in principle is neutral between these productivities. Consequently, the traditional substitution effect towards work is apt to be greater cross-sectionally, which would help to explain why the relation between the income and hours worked of men is less negatively sloped there, and be additional evidence that the substitution effect for men is not weak.[35]

Productivity in the service sector in the United States appears to have advanced more slowly, at least since 1929, than productivity in the goods sector.[36] Service industries like retailing, transportation, education and health, use a good deal of the time of households that never enter into input, output and price series, or therefore into measures of productivity. Incorporation of such time into the series and consideration of changes in its productivity would contribute, I believe, to an understanding of the apparent differences in productivity advance between these sectors.

An excellent example can be found in a recent study of productivity

34. A. Finnegan does find steeper cross-sectional relations when the average incomes and hours of different occupations are used (see his 'A Cross-Sectional Analysis of Hours of Work,' *Journal of Political Economy* (October, 1962)).

35. Note that Mincer has found a very strong substitution effect for women (see his 'Labor Force Participation of Married Women').

36. See the essay by Victor Fuchs, 'Productivity Trends in the Goods and Service Sectors, 1929–61: A Preliminary Survey,' N.B.E.R. Occasional Paper, October 1964.

A Theory of the Allocation of Time 69

trends in the barbering industry in the United States.[37] Conventional productivity measures show relatively little advance in barbers' shops since 1929, yet a revolution has occurred in the activities performed by these shops. In the 1920s shaves still accounted for an important part of their sales, but declined to a negligible part by the 1950s because of the spread of home safety and electric razors. Instead of travelling to a shop, waiting in line, receiving a shave and continuing to another destination, men now shave themselves at home, saving travelling, waiting and even some shaving time. This considerable advance in the productivity of shaving nowhere enters measures for barbers' shops. If, however, a productivity measure for general barbering activities, including shaving, was constructed, I suspect that it would show an advance since 1929 comparable to most goods.[38]

(c) Income elasticities

Income elasticities of demand are often estimated cross-sectionally from the behaviour of families or other units with different incomes. When these units buy in the same market-place it is natural to assume that they face the same prices of goods. If, however, incomes differ because earnings do, and cross-sectional income differences are usually dominated by earnings differences, commodities prices would differ systematically. All commodities prices would be higher to higher-income units because their forgone earnings would be higher (which means, incidentally, that differences in real income would be less than those in money income), and the prices of earnings-intensive commodities would be unusually so.

Cross-sectional relations between consumption and income would not therefore measure the effect of income alone, because they would be affected by differences in relative prices as well as in incomes.[39] The effect of income would be underestimated for earnings-intensive and overestimated for other commodities, because the higher relative prices of the former would cause a substitution away from them and towards the latter. Accordingly, the income elasticities of demand for 'leisure,'

37. See J. Wilburn, 'Productivity Trends in Barber and Beauty Shops,' mimeographed report, N.B.E.R., September 1964.

38. The movement of shaving from barbers' shops to households illustrates how and why even in urban areas households have become 'small factories.' Under the impetus of a general growth in the value of time they have been encouraged to find ways of saving on travelling and waiting time by performing more activities themselves.

39. More appropriate income elasticities for several commodities are estimated in Mincer, 'Market Prices . . .,' op. cit.

unproductive and time-intensive commodities would be under-stated, and for 'work,' productive and other goods-intensive commodities over-stated by cross-sectional estimates. Low apparent income elasticities of earnings-intensive commodities and high apparent elasticities of other commodities may simply be illusions resulting from substitution effects.[40]

Moreover, according to our theory demand depends also on the importance of earnings as a source of income. For if total income were held constant an increase in earnings would create only substitution effects: away from earnings-intensive and towards goods-intensive commodities. So one unusual implication of the analysis that can and should be tested with available budget data is that the source of income may have a significant effect on consumption patterns. An important special case is found in comparisons of the consumption of employed and unemployed workers. Unemployed workers not only have lower incomes but also lower forgone costs, and thus lower relative prices of time and other earnings-intensive commodities. The propensity of unemployed workers to go fishing, watch television, attend school and so on are simply vivid illustrations of the incentives they have to substitute such commodities for others.

One interesting application of the analysis is to the relation between family size and income.[41] The traditional view, based usually on simple correlations, has been that an increase in income leads to a reduction in the number of children per family. If, however, birth control knowledge and other variables were held constant economic theory suggests a positive relation between family size and income, and therefore that the traditional negative correlation resulted from positive correlations between income, knowledge and some other variables. The data I put together supported this interpretation, as did those found in several subsequent studies.[42]

Although positive, the elasticity of family size with respect to income

40. In this connection note that cross-sectional data are often preferred to time series data in estimating income elasticities precisely because they are supposed to be largely free of co-linearity between prices and incomes (see, e.g., J. Tobin, 'A Statistical Demand Function for Food in the U.S.A.,' *Journal of the Royal Statistical Society*, Series A (1950)).

41. Biases in cross-sectional estimates of the demand for work and leisure were considered in the last section.

42. See G. S. Becker, 'An Economic Analysis of Fertility,' *Demographic and Economic Change in Developed Countries* (N.B.E.R. Conference Volume, 1960); R. A. Easterlin, 'The American Baby Boom in Historical Perspective,' *American*

is apparently quite low, even when birth-control knowledge is held constant. Some persons have interpreted this (and other evidence) to indicate that family-size formation cannot usefully be fitted into traditional economic analysis.[43] It was pointed out, however, that the small elasticity found for children is not so inconsistent with what is found for goods as soon as quantity and quality income elasticities are distinguished.[44] Increased expenditures on many goods largely take the form of increased quality–expenditure per pound, per car, etc. – and the increase in quantity is modest. Similarly, increased expenditures on children largely take the form of increased expenditures per child, while the increase in number of children is very modest.

Nevertheless, the elasticity of demand for number of children does seem somewhat smaller than the quantity elasticities found for many goods. Perhaps the explanation is simply the shape of indifference curves; one other factor that may be more important, however, is the increase in forgone costs with income.[45] Child care would seem to be a time-intensive activity that is not 'productive' (in terms of earnings) and uses many hours that could be used at work. Consequently, it would be an earnings-intensive activity, and our analysis predicts that its relative price would be higher to higher-income families.[46] There is already some evidence suggesting that the positive relation between forgone costs and income explains why the apparent quantity income elasticity of demand for children is relatively small. Mincer found that cross-sectional differences in the forgone price of children have an important effect on the number of children.[47]

Economic Review (December 1961); I. Adelman, 'An Econometric Analysis of Population Growth,' *American Economic Review* (June 1963); R. Weintraub, 'The Birth Rate and Economic Development: An Empirical Study,' *Econometrica* (October 1962); Morris Silver, *Birth Rates, Marriages, and Business Cycles* (unpublished Ph.D. dissertation, Columbia University, 1964); and several other studies; for an apparent exception, see the note by D. Freedman, 'The Relation of Economic Status to Fertility,' *American Economic Review* (June 1963).

43. See, for example, Duesenberry's comment on Becker, op. cit.

44. See Becker, op. cit.

45. In Ibid., p. 214 fn. 8, the relation between forgone costs and income was mentioned but not elaborated.

46. Other arguments suggesting that higher-income families face a higher price of children have generally confused price with quality (see ibid., pp. 214–15).

47. See Mincer, 'Market Prices . . .,' op. cit. He measures the price of children by the wife's potential wage-rate, and fits regressions to various cross-sectional data, where number of children is the dependent variable, and family income and the wife's potential wage-rate are among the independent variables.

(d) Transportation

Transportation is one of the few activities where the cost of time has been explicitly incorporated into economic discussions. In most benefit-cost evaluations of new transportation networks the value of the savings in transportation time has tended to overshadow other benefits.[48] The importance of the value placed on time has encouraged experiment with different methods of determination: from the simple view that the value of an hour equals average hourly earnings to sophisticated considerations of the distinction between standard and overtime hours, the internal and external margins, etc.

The transport field offers considerable opportunity to estimate the marginal productivity or value of time from actual behaviour. One could, for example, relate the ratio of the number of persons travelling by aeroplane to those travelling by slower mediums to the distance travelled (and, of course, also to market prices and incomes). Since relatively more people use faster mediums for longer distances, presumably largely because of the greater importance of the saving in time, one should be able to estimate a marginal value of time from the relation between medium and distance travelled.[49]

Another transportation problem extensively studied is the length and mode of commuting to work.[50] It is usually assumed that direct commuting costs, such as train fare, vary positively and that living costs, such as space, vary negatively with the distance commuted. These assumptions alone would imply that a rise in incomes would result in longer commutes as long as space ('housing') were a superior good.[51]

A rise in income resulting at least in part from a rise in earnings would, however, increase the cost of commuting a given distance because the

48. See, for example, H. Mohring, 'Land Values and the Measurement of Highway Benefits,' *Journal of Political Economy* (June 1961).

49. The only quantitative estimate of the marginal value of time that I am familiar with uses the relation between the value of land and its commuting distance from employment (see ibid.). With many assumptions I have estimated the marginal value of time of those commuting at about 40% of their average hourly earnings. It is not clear whether this value is so low because of errors in these assumptions or because of severe kinks in the supply and demand functions for hours of work.

50. See L. N. Moses and H. F. Williamson, 'Value of Time, Choice of Mode, and the Subsidy Issue in Urban Transportation,' *Journal of Political Economy* (June 1963), R. Muth, 'Economic Change and Rural–Urban Conversion,' *Econometrica* (January 1961), and J. F. Kain, *Commuting and the Residential Decisions of Chicago and Detroit Central Business District Workers* (April 1963).

51. See Muth, op. cit.

forgone value of the time involved would increase. This increase in commuting costs would discourage commuting in the same way that the increased demand for space would encourage it. The outcome depends on the relative strengths of these conflicting forces: one can show with a few assumptions that the distance commuted would increase as income increased if, and only if, space had an income elasticity greater than unity.

For let Z_1 refer to the commuting commodity, Z_2 to other commodities, and let

$$Z_1 = f_1(x, t) \tag{22}$$

where t is the time spent commuting and x is the quantity of space used. Commuting costs are assumed to have the simple form $a + l_1 t$, where a is a constant and l_1 is the marginal forgone cost per hour spent commuting. In other words, the cost of time is the only variable commuting cost. The cost per unit of space is $p(t)$, where by assumption $p' < 0$. The problem is to maximise the utility function

$$U = U(x, t, Z_2) \tag{23}$$

subject to the resource constraint

$$a + l_1 t + px + h(Z_2) = S \tag{24}$$

If it were assumed that $U_t = 0$ – commuting was neither enjoyable nor irksome – the main equilibrium condition would reduce to

$$l_1 + p'x = 0^{[52]} \tag{25}$$

which would be the equilibrium condition if households simply attempt to minimise the sum of transportation and space costs.[53] If $l_1 = kS$, where k is a constant, the effect of change in full income on the time spent commuting can be found by differentiating equation (25) to be

$$\frac{\partial t}{\partial S} = \frac{k(\varepsilon_x - 1)}{p''x} \tag{26}$$

where ε_x is the income elasticity of demand for space. Since stability requires that $p'' > 0$, an increase in income increases the time spent commuting if, and only if, $\varepsilon_x > 1$.

52. If $U_t \neq 0$, the main equilibrium condition would be
$$\frac{U_t}{U_x} = \frac{l_1 + p'x}{p}$$
Probably the most plausible assumption is that $U_t < 0$, which would imply that $l_1 + p'x < 0$.

53. See Kain, op. cit., pp. 6–12.

In metropolitan areas of the United States higher-income families tend to live further from the central city,[54] which contradicts our analysis if one accepts the traditional view that the income elasticity of demand for housing is less than unity. In a definitive study of the demand for housing in the United States, however, Margaret Reid found income elasticities greater than unity.[55] Moreover, the analysis of distance commuted incorporates only a few dimensions of the demand for housing; principally the demand for outdoor space. The evidence on distances commuted would then only imply that outdoor space is a 'luxury,' which is rather plausible[56] and not even inconsistent with the traditional view about the total elasticity of demand for housing.

(e) The division of labour within families

Space is too limited to do more than summarise the main implications of the theory concerning the division of labour among members of the same household. Instead of simply allocating time efficiently among commodities, multi-person households also allocate the time of different members. Members who are relatively more efficient at market activities would use less of their time at consumption activities than would other members. Moreover, an increase in the relative market efficiency of any member would effect a reallocation of the time of all other members towards consumption activities in order to permit the former to spend more time at market activities. In short, the allocation of the time of any member is greatly influenced by the opportunities open to other members.

4. Substitution between time and goods

Although time and goods have been assumed to be used in fixed proportions in producing commodities, substitution could take place because different commodities used them in different proportions. The assumption of fixed proportions is now dropped in order to include many additional implications of the theory.

It is well known from the theory of variable proportions that house-

54. For a discussion, including many qualifications, of this proposition see L. F. Schnore, 'The Socio-Economic Status of Cities and Suburbs,' *American Sociological Review* (February 1963).

55. See her *Housing and Income* (University of Chicago Press, 1962), p. 6 and *passim*.

56. According to Reid, the elasticity of demand for indoor space is less than unity (ibid., Chapter 12). If her total elasticity is accepted this suggests that outdoor space has an elasticity exceeding unity.

holds would minimise costs by setting the ratio of the marginal product of goods to that of time equal to the ratio of their marginal costs.[57] A rise in the cost of time relative to goods would induce a reduction in the amount of time and an increase in the amount of goods used per unit of each commodity. Thus, not only would a rise in earnings induce a substitution away from earnings-intensive commodities but also a substitution away from time and towards goods in the production of each commodity. Only the first is (implicitly) recognised in the labour–leisure analysis, although the second may well be of considerable importance. It increases one's confidence that the substitution effect of a rise in earnings is more important than is commonly believed.

The change in the input coefficients of time and goods resulting from a change in their relative costs is defined by the elasticity of substitution between them, which presumably varies from commodity to commodity. The only empirical study of this elasticity assumes that recreation goods and 'leisure' time are used to produce a recreation commodity.[58] Definite evidence of substitution is found, since the ratio of leisure time to recreation goods is negatively related to the ratio of their prices. The elasticity of substitution appears to be less than unity, however, since the share of leisure in total factor costs is apparently positively related to its relative price.

The incentive to economise on time as its relative cost increases goes a long way towards explaining certain broad aspects of behaviour that have puzzled and often disturbed observers of contemporary life. Since hours worked have declined secularly in most advanced countries, and so-called 'leisure' has presumably increased, a natural expectation has

57. The cost of producing a given amount of commodity Z_i would be minimised if

$$\frac{\partial f_i/\partial x_i}{\partial f_i/\partial T_i} = \frac{P_i}{\partial L/\partial T_i}$$

If utility were considered an indirect function of goods and time rather than simply a direct function of commodities the following conditions, among others, would be required to maximise utility:

$$\frac{\partial U/\partial x_i}{\partial U/\partial T_i} = \frac{\partial Z_i/\partial x_i}{\partial Z_i/\partial T_i} = \frac{p_i}{\partial L/\partial T}$$

which are exactly the same conditions as above. The ratio of the marginal utility of x_i to that of T_i depends only on f_i, x_i and T_i, and is thus independent of other production functions, goods and time. In other words, the indirect utility function is what has been called 'weakly separable' (see R. Muth, 'Household Production and Consumer Demand Functions,' unpublished manuscript).

58. See Owen, op. cit., Chapter X.

been that 'free' time would become more abundant, and be used more 'leisurely' and 'luxuriously.' Yet, if anything, time is used more carefully to-day than a century ago.[59] If there was a secular increase in the productivity of working time relative to consumption time (see Section 3 (b)) there would be an increasing incentive to economise on the latter because of its greater expense (our theory emphatically cautions against calling such time 'free'). Not surprisingly, therefore, it is now kept track of and used more carefully than in the past.

Americans are supposed to be much more wasteful of food and other goods than persons in poorer countries, and much more conscious of time: they keep track of it continuously, make (and keep) appointments for specilic minutes, rush about more, cook steaks and chops rather than time-consuming stews and so forth.[60] They are simultaneously supposed to be wasteful – of material goods – and overly economical – of immaterial time. Yet both allegations may be correct and not simply indicative of a strange American temperament because the market value of time is higher relative to the price of goods there than elsewhere. That is, the tendency to be economical about time and lavish about goods may be no paradox, but in part simply a reaction to a difference in relative costs.

The substitution towards goods induced by an increase in the relative cost of time would often include a substitution towards more expensive goods. For example, an increase in the value of a mother's time may induce her to enter the labour force and spend less time cooking by using pre-cooked foods and less time on child-care by using nurseries, camps or baby-sitters. Or barbers' shops in wealthier sections of town charge more and provide quicker service than those in poorer sections, because waiting by barbers is substituted for waiting by customers. These examples illustrate that a change in the quality of goods[61] resulting from a change in the relative cost of goods may simply reflect a change in the methods used to produce given commodities, and not any corresponding change in *their quality*.

Consequently, a rise in income due to a rise in earnings would increase the quality of goods purchased not only because of the effect of income

59. See, for example, de Grazia, op. cit., Chapter IV.
60. For a comparison of the American concept of time with others see Edward T. Hall, *The Silent Language* (New York: Doubleday, 1959), Chapter 9.
61. Quality is usually defined empirically by the amount spent per physical unit, such as pound of food, car or child. See especially S. J. Prais and H. Houthakker, *The Analysis of Family Budgets* (Cambridge, 1955); also my 'An Economic Analysis of Fertility,' op. cit.

on quality but also because of a substitution of goods for time; a rise in income due to a rise in property income would not cause any substitution, and should have less effect on the quality of goods. Put more dramatically, with total income held constant, a rise in earnings should increase while a rise in property income should decrease the quality chosen. Once again, the composition of income is important and provides testable implications of the theory.

One analytically interesting application of these conclusions is to the recent study by Margaret Reid of the substitution between store-bought and home-delivered milk.[62] According to our approach, the cost of inputs into the commodity 'milk consumption at home' is either the sum of the price of milk in the store and the forgone value of the time used to carry it home or simply the price of delivered milk. A reduction in the price of store relative to delivered milk, the value of time remaining constant, would reduce the cost of the first method relatively to the second, and shift production towards the first. For the same reason a reduction in the value of time, market prices of milk remaining constant, would also shift production towards the first method.

Reid's finding of a very large negative relation between the ratio of store to delivered milk and the ratio of their prices, income and some other variables held constant, would be evidence both that milk costs are a large part of total production costs and that there is easy substitution between these alternative methods of production. The large, but not quite as large, negative relation with income simply confirms the easy substitution between methods, and indicates that the cost of time is less important than the cost of milk. In other words, instead of conveying separate information, her price and income elasticities both measure substitution between the two methods of producing the same commodity, and are consistent and plausible.

The importance of forgone earnings and the substitution between time and goods may be quite relevant in interpreting observed price elasticities. A given percentage increase in the price of goods would be less of an increase in commodity prices the more important forgone earnings are. Consequently, even if all commodities had the same true price elasticity, those having relatively important forgone earnings would show lower apparent elasticities in the typical analysis that relates quantities and prices of goods alone.

The importance of forgone earnings differs not only among commodi-

62. See her 'Consumer Response to the Relative Price of Store versus Delivered Milk,' *Journal of Political Economy* (April 1963).

ties but also among households for a given commodity because of differences in income. Its importance would change in the same or opposite direction as income, depending on whether the elasticity of substitution between time and goods was less or greater than unity. Thus, even when the true price elasticity of a commodity did not vary with income, the observed price elasticity of goods would be negatively or positively related to income as the elasticity of substitution was less or greater than unity.

The importance of substitution between time and goods can be illustrated in a still different way. Suppose, for simplicity, that only good x and no time was initially required to produce commodity Z. A price ceiling is placed on x, it nominally becomes a free good, and the production of x is subsidised sufficiently to maintain the same output. The increased quantity of x and Z demanded due to the decline in the price of x has to be rationed because the output of x has not increased. Suppose that the system of rationing made the quantity obtained a positive function of the time and effort expended. For example, the quantity of price-controlled bread or medical attention obtained might depend on the time spent in a queue outside a bakery or in a physician's office. Or if an appointment system were used a literal queue would be replaced by a figurative one, in which the waiting was done at 'home,' as in the Broadway theatre, admissions to hospitals or air travel during peak seasons. Again, even in depressed times the likelihood of obtaining a job is positively related to the time put into job hunting.

Although x became nominally a free good, Z would not be free, because the time now required as an input into Z is not free. The demand for Z would be greater than the supply (fixed by assumption) if the cost of this time was less than the equilibrium price of Z before the price control. The scrambling by households for the limited supply would increase the time required to get a unit of Z, and thus its cost. Both would continue to increase until the average cost of time tended to the equilibrium price before price control. At that point equilibrium would be achieved because the supply and demand for Z would be equal.

Equilibrium would take different forms depending on the method of rationing. With a literal 'first come first served' system the size of the queue (say outside the bakery or in the doctor's office) would grow until the expected cost of standing in line discouraged any excess demand;[63]

63. In queueing language the cost of waiting in line is a 'discouragement' factor that stabilises the queueing scheme (see, for example, D. R. Cox and W. L. Smith, *Queues* (New York: Wiley 1961)).

with the figurative queues of appointment systems, the 'waiting' time (say to see a play) would grow until demand was sufficiently curtailed. If the system of rationing was less formal, as in the labour market during recessions, the expected time required to ferret out a scarce job would grow until the demand for jobs was curtailed to the limited supply.

Therefore, price control of x combined with a subsidy that kept its amount constant would not change the average private equilibrium price of Z,[64] but would substitute indirect time costs for direct goods costs.[65] Since, however, indirect costs are positively related to income, the price of Z would be raised to higher-income persons and reduced to lower-income ones, thereby redistributing consumption from the former to the latter. That is, women, the poor, children, the unemployed, etc., would be more willing to spend their time in a queue or otherwise ferreting out rationed goods than would high-earning males.

5. Summary and conclusions

This paper has presented a theory of the allocation of time between different activities. At the heart of the theory is an assumption that households are producers as well as consumers; they produce commodities by combining inputs of goods and time according to the cost-minimisation rules of the traditional theory of the firm. Commodities are produced in quantities determined by maximising a utility function of the commodity set subject to prices and a constraint on resources. Resources are measured by what is called full income, which is the sum of money income and that forgone or 'lost' by the use of time and goods to obtain utility, while commodity prices are measured by the sum of the costs of their goods and time inputs.

The effect of changes in earnings, other income, goods prices and the productivity of working and consumption time on the allocation of time and the commodity set produced has been analysed. For example, a rise in earnings, compensated by a decline in other income so that full income would be unchanged, would induce a decline in the amount of time used at consumption activities, because time would become more expensive. Partly goods would be substituted for the more expensive

64. The social price, on the other hand, would double, for it is the sum of private indirect costs and subsidised direct costs.

65. Time costs can be criticised from a Pareto optimality point of view because they often result in external diseconomies: e.g., a person joining a queue would impose costs on subsequent joiners. The diseconomies are real, not simply pecuniary, because time is a cost to demanders, but is not revenue to suppliers.

time in the production of each commodity, and partly goods-intensive commodities would be substituted for the more expensive time-intensive ones. Both substitutions require less time to be used at consumption, and permit more to be used at work. Since the reallocation of time involves simultaneously a reallocation of goods and commodities, all three decisions become intimately related.

The theory has many interesting and even novel interpretations of, and implications about, empirical phenomena. A few will be summarised here.

A traditional 'economic' interpretation of the secular decline in hours worked has stressed the growth in productivity of working time and the resulting income and substitution effects, with the former supposedly dominating. Ours stresses that the substitution effects of the growth in productivity of working and consumption time tended to offset each other, and that hours worked declined secularly primarily because time-intensive commodities have been luxuries. A contributing influence has been the secular decline in the relative prices of goods used in time-intensive commodities.

Since an increase in income partly due to an increase in earnings would raise the relative cost of time and of time-intensive commodities, traditional cross-sectional estimates of income elasticities do not hold either factor or commodity prices constant. Consequently, they would, among other things, be biased downward for time-intensive commodities, and give a misleading impression of the effect of income on the quality of commodities consumed. The composition of income also affects demand, for an increase in earnings, total income held constant, would shift demand away from time-intensive commodities and input combinations.

Rough estimates suggest that forgone earnings are quantitatively important and therefore that full income is substantially above money income. Since forgone earnings are primarily determined by the use of time, considerably more attention should be paid to its efficiency and allocation. In particular, agencies that collect information on the expenditure of money income might simultaneously collect information on the 'expenditure' of time. The resulting time budgets, which have not been seriously investigated in most countries, including the United States and Great Britain, should be integrated with the money budgets in order to give a more accurate picture of the size and allocation of full income.

3 Time Spent in Housework

Joann Vanek

From: *Scientific American*, Vol. 231, November 1974, pp. 116–20.

One would suppose, in view of all the household appliances that have been introduced over the past 50 years, that American women must spend considerably less time in housework now than their mothers and grandmothers did in the 1920's. I have investigated the matter and found that the generalization is not altogether true. Nonemployed women, meaning women who are not in the labor force, in fact devote as much time to housework as their forebears did. The expectation of spending less time in housework applies only to employed women.

Certainly the reasons for thinking that the time spent doing housework must have diminished are abundant. Most of the household appliances that have come on the market since the 1920's have been marketed as (and have generally been regarded as) laborsaving devices. Many other products and services designed to ease the homemaker's task have been put on the market during the past 50 years. In addition to these techno- logical changes one can cite several other factors that would seem to indicate a shorter work week in the household. They include the move- ment of families from the farm; the decline in boarding; changes in the birth rate that cause women to spend fewer years in the direct care of children; the fact that fewer members of the family come home for lunch, and the pronounced increase in the number of married women in the labor force.

Fortunately information is available about time spent in housework. It is not as complete as an investigator might wish or as readily com- parable from one period of time to another, but it does provide data on how women budget time for their daily activities.

In 1925 the Federal Government made money available (under the Purnell Act) for research in home economics. One of the results was a series of studies of how women budgeted their time. My analysis is based on about 20 of these studies. They are reasonably comparable because they were conducted under a set of guidelines developed by the

U.S. Bureau of Home Economics. Although most of the studies were made in the 1920's and 1930's, the guidelines were also applied to a few studies conducted in the 1940's, 1950's and 1960's. For detailed analysis of the contemporary period I have employed the *United States Time Use Survey*, a study made in 1965 and 1966 by John P. Robinson and Philip E. Converse of the Survey Research Center at the University of Michigan. In this study women were asked to keep a diary of activities at 15-minute intervals for a full day. In the earlier studies women kept a diary of activities at five-minute intervals for at least a week.

Only the Robinson–Converse survey is based on a national sample. The studies made under the aegis of the Bureau of Home Economics involved certain localities and tabulated primarily the activities of rural women. To infer national averages from such limited studies is open to question. It is significant, however, that the findings of the earlier studies were much the same, which lends support to the supposition that they reflect national patterns.

At first the primarily rural composition of the early samples appears to be a limitation. Actually it is an advantage. During the 50 years under consideration the scene of household activity – in terms of the preponderance of women – shifted from the farm to the city. Thus one comparison I want to make is between time spent in homemaking by rural homemakers 50 years ago and time spent by urban homemakers today. Several of the early studies included town and city samples, so that it is possible to make comparisons between rural and urban women in the 1920's.

Let us turn first to nonemployed women. In 1924 such women spent about 52 hours per week in housework. The figure differs little (and in an unexpected direction) from the 55 hours per week for nonemployed women in the 1960's. It is remarkable that the amount of time devoted to household work by such women has been so stable, varying only within the range from 51 to 56 hours. It is also noteworthy that the work week of homemakers is longer than the work week of the average person in the labor force.

A comparison of rural and urban women yields another unexpected finding: Rural homemakers spend no more time in household work than urban ones. At least in part this consistency may be due to the way the early researchers distinguished between housework and farm work. Farm work included all tasks connected with the home that were not commonly carried on by both rural and urban women. Among the tasks defined as farm work were gardening, dairy activity and the care of poultry. In this way rural and urban women were compared on the same set of tasks.

Notwithstanding the distinction between household work and farm work, one would suppose that at least in the early period urban women would have spent less time on the job than rural women, inasmuch as a number of differences in working conditions remained between them. For example, urban homes were more likely than rural ones to have electricity, running water and laborsaving machines. In addition urban women could make more use of markets and commercial services, simply because they lived closer to them. Another factor was that the farm household produced a larger proportion of the family's material needs than the urban household. (A study in 1924 showed that rural families produced about 70 percent of their own food, compared with 2 percent for urban families.) In spite of all these differences urban and rural women have spent about the same amount of time in household work throughout the 50-year period. Urbanization reduced women's work only by eliminating the 10 hours per week spent in farm tasks.

Perhaps trends affecting the household have created as much work as they have saved. If less time is required for producing food and clothing, time must be added for shopping. It is not difficult to think of a number of other time-consuming household tasks that must be done now but that were non-existent or rare 50 years ago. Therefore the figure for time spent on housework probably conceals a shift in the amount of time devoted to various tasks.

The data do show that the nature of household work has changed (see Figure 3.1). The time spent in the tasks classified as shopping and managerial has increased. So has time devoted to family care. Less time is spent preparing food and cleaning up after meals, although together these activities continue to be the most time-consuming aspect of housework. No change has occurred in general tasks of home care such as cleaning.

Probably no aspect of housework has been lightened so much by technological change as laundry. In the 1920's a great many houses lacked hot and cold running water. A large variety of soaps and detergents and automatic appliances have come on the scene, and the once burdensome requirement of ironing has been greatly reduced by wash-and-wear fabrics. Nonetheless, the amount of time spent doing laundry has increased (see Fig. 3.2). Presumably people have more clothes now than they did in the past and they wash them more often.

Time spent on child care has also increased. The change reflects post-war modifications in standards of child care. Today's mother is cautioned to care for the child's social and mental development in addition to the traditional concerns of health, discipline and cleanliness.

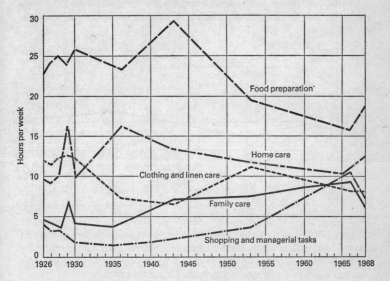

Figure 3.1. Distribution of time among various kinds of household work is traced from 1926 to 1968. The data relate only to nonemployed women, meaning women who did not have full-time jobs outside the household. Top curve includes cleaning up after meals.

More time is spent today in the tasks associated with consumption. They include shopping, household management and travel connected with the household. Contemporary women spend about one full working day per week on the road and in stores compared with less than two hours per week for women in the 1920's.

Although technological change has created new time demands in homemaking, this factor alone does not explain the consistently large amount of time devoted to housework. If it did, all women would spend long hours in housework. The data I have analyzed show that they do not. Employed women spend considerably less time in housework than nonemployed women.

In contrast to the 55 hours per week that nonemployed women spend in housework, employed women spend only 26 hours. In other words, employed women devote about half as much time to household tasks as nonemployed women. Technological change has in fact liberated some women from a certain amount of household work.

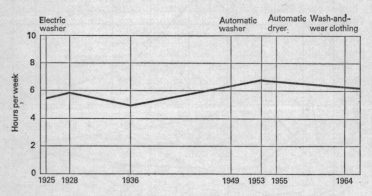

Figure 3.2. Time devoted to laundry has actually increased over the past 50 years, apparently because people have more clothes now and wash them more often. The dates shown for the various appliances and fabrics indicate about when they began to be sold widely.

The time patterns of employed women become more significant when trends in the employment of women are taken into account. During the past 50 years women have entered the labor force in increasing numbers. Moreover, since World War II the increase has been caused primarily by the dramatic rise in the employment of married women. In 1920 it was rare to find married women working outside the home; today about 40 percent of them are in the labor force. Proportionately fewer women are full-time homemakers. Notwithstanding the stability of housework time for nonemployed women, therefore, the shift in the proportion of women employed signifies a reduction over the years in the amount of time women spend in housework.

Although the impact of social change on time spent in housework is thus clarified, the question remains of why nonemployed women spend so much time in homemaking. It is possible that this finding can also be explained in a fairly straightforward way. Perhaps nonemployed women have larger families and younger children and therefore more work than employed women. In addition the nonemployed women may have less household assistance.

It has been shown by other investigators that a woman's decision to work is limited by the presence of children, particularly young children. In other words, women are less likely to work when the burden of household tasks is greatest. I tested this argument with an analysis drawing on employment, marital status, socioeconomic status (family income and woman's education) and family composition (number and age of children) as points of comparison.

The technique enables one to see whether or not a difference between employed and nonemployed women remains if the distribution of women is the same on the other points of comparison. Assuming that the distribution of women according to social class, family composition and marital status is the same, nonemployed women would still spend considerably more time in housework than employed women. Although these adjustments somewhat reduce the time differences between the two groups of women, the major amount of difference remains.

Another explanation is a reflection of the amount of assistance the homemaker receives. The employed wife may be able with her earnings to buy laborsaving devices and the services of others. In addition she may have another, perhaps subtler resource: help from other members of the family. The fact that she works outside the home may give her leverage to call on them for help.

However plausible this explanation appears to be, information from the Robinson–Converse study shows that differences in help with housework do not explain the time differences between employed and nonemployed women. Employed women made no greater use of paid help than nonemployed women. Furthermore, husbands of employed women gave no more help than husbands of nonemployed women. Contrary to popular belief, American husbands do not share the responsibilities of household work. They spend only a few hours a week at it, and most of what they do is shopping.

Other factors could explain the puzzle. Perhaps employed women receive more help from children, live in smaller dwelling units or rely more on commercial services and laborsaving devices. Unfortunately the Robinson–Converse survey did not cover these matters. Other studies, however, contain little evidence that such factors would explain the time differences between the two categories of women.

Apparently one must look deeper for the explanation. One clear contrast between employed and nonemployed women is that work in the labor market earns a paycheck whereas housework does not. In the families of nonemployed women this contrast underscores an imbalance in the economic roles of husband and wife.

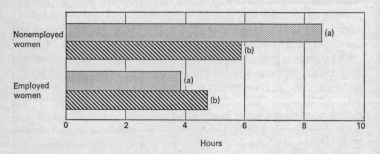

Figure 3.3. Employed and nonemployed women are compared as to the amount of time they spend in housework on weekdays (a) and weekend days (b). On weekend days both groups of women presumably have about the same amount of time available for housework.

This kind of imbalance was not always embedded in marriage. In the farm household of earlier decades there was little separation of domestic and productive roles. Both the husband and the wife contributed to the family's production, and their contributions were probably regarded as being equal. It seems unlikely that anyone would regard the bread, butter and clothing made by the woman as any less valuable than the man's work in the fields.

In modern society the homemaker's contribution to the family economy is less clear. Although cooking, cleaning and shopping for bargains are important to the family, one cannot find much evidence that they are regarded as contributions equal to the wage earner's. As S. Ferge of the Sociological Research Institute in Budapest has written: 'The results of housework do not serve this [economic] justification in a satisfactory manner because they are accepted as natural and are only noticed when they are absent. It is therefore the work itself whose existence must be felt and acknowledged; working long hours and working on Sunday can serve to demonstrate this. (These considerations are not conscious to those who are doing it; on the contrary, they are convinced of the functional necessity of this work.)'

Ferge suggests comparing women's housework schedules for weekdays and weekend days. I have done this and found that nonemployed women outdo employed women in housework on both types of day. Employed women 'catch up' on housework on weekends. Nonetheless, they spend less time at it then than full-time homemakers who have all week to accomplish their work.

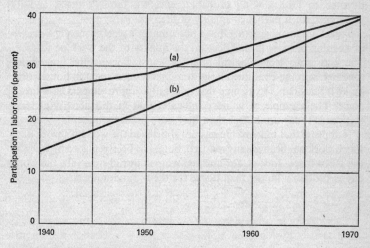

Figure 3.4. Participation in labor force is charted for all women (a) and married women (b). It was once unusual for married women to work, but now 40 percent of them do.

Perhaps the composition of the family has something to do with this finding; the presence of children, particularly young children, creates time demands that do not fit into a five-day week. I examined weekend time expenditures for women without children. Again nonemployed women spent about half an hour more per weekend day than employed women. The pattern is consistent with the view that nonemployed women schedule work so that it is visible to others as well as to themselves.

Since the value of household work is not clear, nonemployed women feel pressure to spend long hours at it. Time spent in work, rather than the results of the work, serves to express to the homemaker and others that an equal contribution is being made. Women who work in the labor force contribute income to the family and so do not feel the same pressure.

There are, to be sure, additional factors that give rise to such high expenditures of time in housework. For example, in a consumption-oriented society the time involved in obtaining and taking care of household goods is far from negligible, although it is often assumed to be. Such tasks fall to the homemaker. Moreover, a large amount of time devoted to homemaking probably reflects a family's tastes and its preference for a particular quality of life.

Thus I am not suggesting that a homemaker's work is merely a matter of keeping busy, with no effect on the quality of the work performed. The enormous technological improvements affecting the household, together with the continued large amounts of time spent in housework, make it reasonable to assume that qualitative improvements have taken place. The example of laundry indicates that in this activity at least standards today are higher than they were in an earlier era.

It appears that modern life has not shortened the woman's work day. Farm work has been greatly reduced, but it has been replaced by work in the labor force. Indeed, for married women in full-time jobs the work day is probably longer than it was for their grandmothers.

4 Women's Work and the Family in Nineteenth-Century Europe*

Joan W. Scott
University of North Carolina, Chapel Hill

Louise A. Tilly
Michigan State University

From: *Comparative Studies in Society and History*, Vol. 17, No. 1, January
1975, pp. 36–64.

I

There is a great deal of confusion about the history of women's work
outside the home and about the origin and meaning of women's traditional place within the home. Most interpretations of either of these
questions depend on assumptions about the other. Usually, women at
home in any time period are assumed to be non-productive, the antithesis of women at work. In addition, most general works on women
and the family assume that the history of women's employment, like
the history of women's legal and political rights, can be understood as a
gradual evolution from a traditional place at home to a modern position
in the world of work. Some historians cite changes in employment opportunities created by industrialization as the precursors of legal
emancipation. Others stress political rights as the source of improved
economic status. In both cases, legal-political and economic 'emancipation' usually are linked to changes in cultural values. Thus William
Goode, whose *World Revolution and Family Patterns* makes temporal
and geographic comparisons of family patterns, remarks on what he
calls 'the statistically unusual status of western women today, that is
their high participation in work outside of the home'. He maintains

*Many people have helped us with comments on earlier drafts of this essay. We
especially wish to thank Susan Rogers, Ellen Sewell, William Sewell, Jr., Charles
Tilly, Marilyn Young, Richard Sennett, Natalie Davis, Sally Brown, Robert
Brown, Lynn Hunt, Lynn Lees, and Maurine Greenwald for their critical readings
of this paper.

A version of this paper was co-recipient of the Stephen Allen Kaplan Prize, University of Pennsylvania, 1973, and will appear in a forthcoming volume incorporating the Kaplan Lectures on the Family.

that previous civilizations did not use female labor because of restrictive cultural definitions. 'I believe', Goode writes, 'that the crucial crystallizing variable – i.e., the necessary but not sufficient cause of the betterment of the western woman's position – was ideological: the gradual logical philosophical extension to women of originally Protestant notions about the rights and responsibilities of the individual undermined the traditional idea of "women's proper place".'[1]

Yet Goode makes no systematic effort to validate his statements with historical data. If, however, notions about individual rights did transform cultural values and lead to the extension of rights to women, and if opportunities for women to work stemmed from the same source, we should be able to trace an increase in the number of women working as they gained political rights. The only long period for which there are any reliable labor force statistics for any populations (whether of cities or countries) is the nineteenth and twentieth centuries. These should serve our purpose, however, since women gained political rights in most European countries only in the twentieth century. If we examine the figures for three European countries during the nineteenth and twentieth centuries, we find no confirmation of Goode's belief. In Great Britain, a Protestant country, the civil status of women was reformed through the married women's property acts of the late nineteenth century, and political emancipation in the form of suffrage came in 1918. In 1851 and 1861, about 25 percent of British women worked; in 1921, the figure was still about 25 percent. In both Catholic France and Italy, women's legal rights within the family were severely limited until after World War II. Immediately after the war, constitutional changes granted women the right to vote. In France, in 1866, 25 percent of women worked; in 1896, 33 percent worked and in 1954, 30 percent worked, down from a high of 42 percent in 1921. In Italy, the highest percentage for women's employment outside the home (before 1964) was in 1901.[2]

1. William Goode, *World Revolution and Family Patterns* (New York, 1963), p. 56. Ivy Pinchbeck makes the opposite point – that occupational changes played a large part in women's emancipation – in the preface to the reprinted edition of her book, *Women Workers and the Industrial Revolution, 1750–1850* (New York, 1969), p. v.

2. T. Deldycke, H. Gelders and J. M. Limbor, *La Population active et sa structure*, under the supervision of P. Bairoch (Brussels, 1969), pp. 29–31. The figures given for Italy indicate that 1881 had even higher proportion of women working. The 1901 census, however, has been shown to be more reliable, especially in designating occupation. In 1881, census categories tended to overestimate the numbers of women working. In 1901, about 32.5 percent of Italian women worked.

There are several conclusions to be drawn from these figures. First, there was little relationship between women's political rights and women's work. The right to vote did not increase the size of the female labor force, neither did the numbers of women in the labor force dramatically increase just prior to their gaining the vote. Moreover, great numbers of women worked outside the home during most of the nineteenth century, long before they enjoyed civil and political rights. Finally, rather than a steady increase in the size of the female labor force, the pattern was one of increase followed by decline.

What then is the source of Goode's inaccurate conception? It stems above all from a model that projects middle-class experience and middle-class values as representative of all experience and all values. It generalizes a particular class experience into one which represents 'western civilization'. And it projects backward in linear fashion, twentieth-century values and experiences. As a result, Goode fails to make important distinctions about women, work and values, and he therefore misrepresents their history. Middle-class women formed an insignificant part of the female labor force in nineteenth- and early twentieth-century Europe, although their numbers began to increase in that period.[3] If we ask: 'which women worked?' and 'what kind of work did they do?',

---

3. The percentage of women in 'middle-class' (white collar) occupations – teachers, nurses, shop assistants, secretaries and civil servants – increased in England between 1881 and 1911, while the percentage of women employed in working-class occupations fell.

	1881	1911
Middle-class occupations	12.6%	23.7
Working-class occupations	87.4	76.3

Lee Holcombe, *Victorian Ladies at Work* (Hamden, Conn., 1973), p. 216. Holcombe shows that although mid-Victorian ideologies about women's place and women's dependent position in the patriarchal family were still being publicized, middle-class women were increasingly entering the labor force. The reasons lie in demographic and economic realities, not ideology. The first of these was the surplus of unmarried or 'redundant women', in Harriet Martineau's phrase. These women, to whom the sex ratio denied husbands and for whom male mortality denied fathers and brothers, had to work. Furthermore, the expansion of the tertiary sector in England provided jobs for these women and for working-class women who could take advantage of increased educational opportunities. In Holcombe's analysis, the development of feminist ideology about women's work accompanied change and justified it. It did not precede it or cause it in any sense.

In France, there was a similar move into 'middle-class' occupations in the twentieth century. Francis Clark, *The Position of Women in Contemporary France* we discover that not only are Goode's facts wrong, but his model of social change is inappropriate as well.

The women who worked in great numbers in the nineteenth century were overwhelmingly members of the working and peasant classes. Most held jobs in domestic service, garment making or the textile industry. In England in 1841 and still in 1911 most working women were engaged in domestic or other personal service occupations. In 1911, 35 percent were servants (including laundresses), 19.5 percent were textile workers and 15.6 percent were engaged in the dressmaking trades.[4] In Milan, according to the censuses of 1881, 1901 and 1911, a similar concentration of women in domestic service existed, with garment making ranking second and textiles much less important than in England.[5] Similarly, in France, excluding agriculture, textiles, garment making and domestic service were the chief areas of female employment. In France, 69 percent of working women outside agriculture were employed in these three fields in 1866: domestic service, 28 percent; garment making, 21 percent; textiles, 20 percent. In 1896, the proportions were altered, but the total was 59 percent: domestic service, 19 percent; garment making, 26 percent; textiles, 14 percent.[6]

Despite very different rates of industrialization in England, France and Italy, the evidence strongly suggests that women in all three cases did not participate in factory work (except in textiles) in large numbers.

(London, 1937), pp. 74–5, gives the following figures for the percent female in selected occupations:

	1906	1926
Typists, copyists, accountants	22.8	54.8
Workers in hospitals, convalescent homes, etc.	73.2	76.1
Postal service	22.4	30.5
Teachers (state)	48.5	59.2
Teachers (private)	68.7	71.4

4. Pinchbeck, p. 315; E. L. Hutchins, *Women in Modern Industry* (London, 1915), p. 84.

5. Louise A. Tilly, 'Women at Work in Milan, Italy – 1880–World War I', paper presented to the American Historical Association annual meeting, 28 December 1972. The national distribution of women workers, in Italy as a whole, showed textiles more important than domestic service as an employer of women. Domestic servants were disproportionately concentrated in cities, textile production outside cities.

6. Calculated from data in Deldycke *et al.*, p. 174. Agricultural activity was unimportant in England and in the city of Milan, so French figures are made comparable by excluding agriculture.

Rather, economic and social changes associated with urban and industrial development seem to have generated employment opportunities in a few traditional sectors in which women worked at jobs similar to household tasks. The economic changes leading to high employment of women included the early industrialization of textiles [7] and the nineteenth-century pattern of urbanization, with cities acting as producers of and markets for consumer goods and as places of employment for domestic servants. The expansion of production of consumer goods involved the growth of a large piece-work garment industry. Production moved from the workshops of craftsmen to the homes of people who sewed together pre-cut garments. This change in the process of production generated employment opportunities for large numbers of women. The subsequent decline of this method of producing ready-made goods and its replacement by factory production, as well as the decline of textiles and the growth of heavy industry, led to lower female participation in the work forces of all three countries we have examined.

The kinds of jobs available to women were not only limited in number and kind; they also were segregated – that is, they were held almost exclusively by women. [8] The women who held these jobs were usually young and single. In Milan, about 75 percent of women aged 15 to 20 worked in 1881 and 1901. In female age groups over 20, employment in textile manufacture and garment making declined sharply, presumably as women stopped work after marriage. The only female occupation with appreciable proportions (50 percent or more) of workers aged over 30 was domestic service, in which celibacy prevailed. [9] In Great Britain, similar age patterns are evident in the scattered available data. Most women operatives in the Lancashire cotton mills in 1833 were between 16 and 21 years old. Only 25 percent of female cotton workers were married in the Lancashire districts in 1841. Hewitt argues for an increase in proportions either married or widowed among cotton operatives peaking sometime in the 1890s and declining thereafter. The highest percentage of married women in this occupation was about one-

7. By industrialization we mean the process in which, over time, secondary and tertiary economic activity gain in importance in an economy. This is accompanied by an increased scale of these activities and consequent increasing productivity per capita.

8. See Edward Gross, 'Plus ça change . . . ? The Sexual Structure of Occupations over Time', *Social Problems*, 16 (Fall, 1968), pp. 198–206.

9. Census data from 1871 to 1901 analyzed in Louise A. Tilly, 'The Working Class of Milan, 1881–1911', unpublished doctoral dissertation, University of Toronto, 1974.

third.[10] The much less specialized labor force of London in the 1880s was primarily aged between 15 and 25 years.[11]

When census figures finally provide marital status, some big national differences can be noted. In 1911, while 69 percent of all single women in Britain worked, only 9.6 percent of married women did.[12] In France in 1896, 52 percent of all single women were in the labor force, and 38 percent of married women.[13] Although our evidence is impressionistic and scattered, it looks as though as industrialization advanced (at least in the pre-1914 period), fewer married women worked. Thus Britain, the more advanced industrial country in 1911, had the lower proportion of married women workers; on the other hand, in France, in which both agriculture and manufacturing were organized on a smaller scale than in Britain, more married women were in the labor force.

Why did women work in the nineteenth century and why was the female labor force predominantly young and single? To answer these questions we must first examine the relationship of these women to their families of origin (the families into which they were born), not to their families of procreation (the family launched at marriage). We must ask not only how husbands regarded their wives' roles, but what prompted families to send their *daughters* out into the job market as garment workers or domestic servants.

The parents of these young women workers during industrialization were mostly peasants and, to a lesser extent, urban workers. When we examine the geographic and social origins of domestic servants, one of the largest groups of women workers, their rural origins are clear. Two-thirds of all the domestic servants in England in 1851 were daughters of rural laborers. For France, we have no aggregate numbers, but local studies suggest similar patterns. In his study of Melun, for example, Chatelain found that in 1872, 54 percent of female domestic servants were either migrants from rural areas or foreigners.[14] Theresa McBride

10. Miriam Cohen, 'The Liberation of Working Class Women in England?', unpublished paper, History Department, University of Michigan, p. 15; Hutchins pp. 81–2; Edward Cadbury, M. Cecile Matheson and George Shann, *Woman's Work and Wages. A Phase of Life in An Industrial City* (Chicago, 1907), p. 219; Margaret Hewitt, *Wives and Mothers in Victorian Industry* (London, 1958), p. 17.

11. Pinchbeck, pp. 197–8.

12. Deldycke *et al.*, p. 169.

13. Ibid., p. 185.

14. Abel Chatelain, 'Migrations et domesticité feminine urbaine en France, XVIII siècle–XX siècle', *Revue historique économique et sociale*, 47 (1969), p. 521; E. Royston Pyke, *Golden Times* (New York, 1970), p. 156.

calculated that in Versailles from 1825 to 1853, 57.7 percent of female domestic servants were daughters of peasants. In Bordeaux, a similar proportion obtained: 52.8 percent. In Milan, at the end of the nineteenth century, servants were less likely to be city-born than any other category of workers.[15]

If cultural values were involved in the decisions of rural and lower-class families to send their daughters to work, we must ask what values they were. Goode's loose references to 'values' obscure an important distinction between modern middle-class values and pre-industrial lower-class values. Goode assumes that the idea of 'woman's proper place', with its connotations of complete economic dependency and idealized femininity is a traditional value. In fact, it is a rather recently accepted middle-class value not at all inconsistent with notions of 'the rights and responsibilities of the individual'. The hierarchical division of labor within the family which assigned the husband the role of bread-winner and the wife the role of domestic manager and moral guardian emerged clearly only in the nineteenth century and was associated with the growth of the middle class and the diffusion of its values.[16] On the other hand, as we will demonstrate at length below, traditional ideas about women held by peasant and laboring families did not find feminine and economic functions incompatible. In the pre-industrial Europe described by Peter Laslett and in contemporary pre-modern societies studied by anthropologists,[17] the household or the family is the crucial

15. Theresa McBride, 'Rural Tradition and the Process of Modernization. Domestic Servants in Nineteenth Century France', unpublished doctoral dissertation, Rutgers University, 1973, p. 85; Tilly (1974), pp. 129–30. McBride found that in Versailles in the same period only 19.5 percent of female domestic servants were from urban working-class families.

16. Philippe Aries, *Centuries of Childhood: A Social History of Family Life*, translated by Robert Baldick (London, 1962); J. A. Banks, *Prosperity and Parenthood. A Study of Family Planning Among the Victorian Middle Classes* (London, 1954); J. A. and Olive Banks, *Feminism and Family Planning in Victorian England* (New York, 1964) all associate the idea of these separate feminine characteristics with the middle class. John Stuart Mill made a compelling argument for granting political equality to women while recognizing feminine preferences and qualities which distinguish women from men. See J. S. and H. T. Mill, *Essays on Sex Equality*, Alice Rossi, ed. (Chicago, 1971). For analysis of hierarchical patterns see Susan Rogers, 'Woman's Place: Sexual Differentiation as Related to the Distribution of Power', unpublished paper, Northwestern University, April 1974.

17. Peter Laslett, *The World We Have Lost* (New York, 1965). Among the many anthropological and historical studies of pre-industrial societies are George Foster 'Peasant Society and the Image of the Limited Good', *American Anthropologist*, 67 (April 1965), pp. 293–315; Conrad Arensberg and Solon Kimball, *Family and*

economic unit. Whether or not all work is done at home, all family members are expected to work. It is simply assumed that women will work, for their contribution is valued as necessary for the survival of the family unit. The poor, the illiterate, the economically and politically powerless of the past operated according to values which fully justified the employment of women outside the home.

We are arguing then, contrary to Goode, that pre-industrial values, rather than a new individualistic ideology, justified the work of working-class women in the nineteenth century. In so doing, we are not merely disputing his analysis, we are rejecting the model of social change on which he bases that analysis. Goode's model (a standard one for theorists of development) assumes a one-to-one connection between cultural values and social change. He argues, in effect, that ideological changes led directly and immediately to structural and behavioral changes. We also reject the antithesis of Goode's argument which says that material changes in economic, political or social structures led directly and immediately to changes in values and behavior. It, too, is based on a model which assumes that change in one realm necessarily and directly leads to change in another. Thus Engels tells us that the coming of capitalism excluded women from 'participation in social production' and reduced their role and status to that of servants in the home. Proletarian women are exceptions to this description because in industrial society they are engaged in social production. Nonetheless, in both instances, Engels makes a direct connection between economic change and changes in values and status.[18]

Our examination of the evidence on women's work in the nineteenth century has led us to a different understanding of the process which led to the relatively high employment of women outside the home in nineteenth-century Europe. The model we use posits a continuity of traditional values and behavior in changing circumstances. Old values coexist with and are used by people to adapt to extensive structural changes. This assumes that people perceive and act on the changes they experience in terms of ideas and attitudes they already hold. These ideas

---

Community in Ireland (Cambridge, Mass., 1968); Ronald Blythe, *Akenfield, Portrait of an English Village* (New York, 1968); Edgar Morin, *The Red and the White: Report from a French Village* (New York, 1970); Mack Walker, *German Home Towns: Community, State and General Estates, 1648–1871* (Ithaca, New York, 1971).

18. Frederick Engels, *The Origins of the Family, Private Property and the State* (New York, 1972), p. 81.

eventually change, but not as directly or immediately as Goode and Engels would have us believe. Behavior is less the product of new ideas than of the effects of old ideas operating in new or changing contexts.[19]

Traditional families then, operating on long-held values, sent their daughters to take advantage of increased opportunities generated by industrialization and urbanization. Industrial development did not affect all areas of a given country at the same time. Rather, the process can best be illustrated by an image of 'islands of development' within an underdeveloped sea, islands which drew population to them from the less developed areas.[20] The values of the less developed sector were imported into the developing sector and there were extended, adapted and only gradually transformed.

As peasant values were imported, so was the behavior they directed. And work for the wives and daughters of the poor was a familiar experience in pre-industrial societies. No change in values, then, was necessary to permit lower-class women to work outside the home during the nineteenth century. Neither did industrialization 'emancipate' these women by permitting more of them to work outside the home. And, given the fluctuations in the size of the female labor force especially, it is difficult to see any direct connection between the work of peasant and working-class women and the political enfranchisement of all women.

II

Let us now attempt to reconstruct the historical experience of women workers during the early stages of industrialization. Since most were of rural origin, we will begin by examining the peasant or family economy whose values and economic needs sent them into the job market.

Commentators on many different areas of Europe offer strikingly similar descriptions of peasant social organization. Anthropologists and social historians seem to agree that regardless of country 'the peasantry is a pre-industrial social entity which carries over into contemporary society specific elements of a different, older, social structure, economy

19. Our notion is a variation of the one presented by Bert Hoselitz: 'On the whole, the persistence of traditions in social behavior ... may be an important factor mitigating the many dislocations and disorganizations which tend to accompany rapid industrialization and technical change'. Bert Hoselitz and Wilbert Moore, *Industrialization and Society* (New York, 1966), p. 15.

20. W. Arthur Lewis, 'Economic Development with Unlimited Supplies of Labour', in A. N. Agarwala and S. P. Singh, eds., *The Economics of Underdevelopment* (New York, 1963), p. 408.

and culture'. The crucial unit of organization is the family 'whose solidarity provides the basic framework for mutual aid, control and socialization'. The family's work is usually directed to the family farm, property considered to belong to the group rather than to a single individual. 'The individual, the family and the farm appear as an indivisible whole'. 'Peasant property is, at least *de facto*, family property. The head of the family appears as the manager rather than the proprietor of family land'.[21]

These descriptions of Eastern European peasants are echoed by Michael Anderson in his comparison of rural Lancashire and rural Ireland early in the nineteenth century. He suggests that in both cases the basis of 'functional family solidarity . . . was the absolute *interdependence* of family members such that neither fathers nor sons had any scope for alternatives to the family as a source of provision for a number of crucially important needs'.[22] Italian evidence confirms the pattern. Although in late nineteenth-century Lombardy a kind of *frérèche* (brothers and their families living together and working the land together) was a frequent alternative to the nuclear family, the household was the basic unit of production. All members of the family contributed what they could either by work on the farm, or, in the case of women and the young, by work in nearby urban areas or in rural textile mills. Their earnings were turned over to the head of the household; in the case of brothers joined in one household, the elder usually acted as head. He took care of financial matters and contractual relationships in the interests of all.[23] For Normandy in the eighteenth century, Gouesse's recent study has described the gradual evolution of reasons given for marriage when an ecclesiastical dispensation had to be applied for. At the end of that century, reasons such as 'seeking well-being', or 'desire

21. Teodor Shanin, 'The Peasantry as a Political Factor', in T. Shanin, ed., *Peasants and Peasant Societies; Selected Readings* (Penguin Books, 1971), pp. 241–4. A similar analysis of the peasant family in mid-twentieth century can be found in Henri Mendras, *The Vanishing Peasant: Innovation and Change in French Agriculture*, translated by Jean Lerner (Cambridge, Mass., 1970), p. 76: 'The family and the enterprise coincide: the head of the family is at the same time the head of the enterprise. Indeed, he is the one because he is the other . . . he lives his professional and his family life as an indivisible entity. The members of his family are also his fellow workers'.

22. Michael Anderson, *Family Structure in Nineteenth Century Lancashire* (Cambridge, 1971), p. 96.

23. 'Giunta per la Inchiesta Agraria e sulle condizioni della Classe agricola *Atti*', Rome, 1882, Vol. VI, Fasc. II, pp. 552, 559, Fasc. III, pp. 87, 175–6, 373, 504, 575.

to live happily' became more common. Gouesse considers these differences of expression rather superficial; what all these declarations meant, although few stated this explicitly, was that one had to be married in order to live. 'The married couple was the simple community of work, the elementary unit'. In nineteenth-century Brittany, 'all the inhabitants of the farm formed a working community . . . linked one to the other like the crew of a ship'.[24]

Despite differences in systems of inheritance and differences in the amount of land available, the theory of the peasant economy developed by Chayanov for nineteenth-century Russia applies elsewhere. The basis of this system is the family, or more precisely the household – in Russia, all those 'having eaten from one pot'. It has a dual role as a unit of production and consumption. The motivations of its members, unlike capitalist aims, involve 'securing the needs of the family rather than . . . making a profit'. The family's basic problem is organizing the work of its members to meet its annual budget and 'a single wish to save or invest capital if economic conditions allow'.[25]

Members of the family or household have clearly defined duties, based in part on their age and their position in the family and in part on their sex. Sex role differentiation clearly existed in these societies. Men and women not only performed different tasks, but they occupied different space.[26] Most often, although by no means always, men worked the fields while women managed the house, raised and cared for animals,

24. Y. Brekilien, *La vie quotidienne des paysans en Bretagne au XIXe siècle* (Paris, 1966), p. 37. Jean-Marie Gouesse, 'Parenté, famille et marriage en Normandie aux XVIIe et XVIII siècles', *Annales, Economies, Sociétés, Civilisations*, 27e Année (July–October, 1972), pp. 1146–7.

25. Basile Kerblay, 'Chayanov and the Theory of Peasantry as a Specific Type of Economy', in Teodor Shanin, ed., *Peasants and Peasant Societies*, op. cit., 151, and *A. V. Chayanov on the Theory of Peasant Economy*, Daniel Thorner, Basile Kerblay and R. E. F. Smith, eds. (Homewood, Ill., 1966), pp. 21, 60. See also Henriette Dussourd, *Au meme pot et au meme feu: étude sur les communautés familiales agricoles du centre de la France* (Moulins, 1962).

26. For the most part, men worked outside the home. They performed public functions for the family and the farm. Women, on the other hand, presided over the interior of the household and over the private affairs of family life. Separate spheres and separate roles did not, however, imply discrimination or hierarchy. It appears, on the contrary, that neither sphere was subordinated to the other. This interpretation is, however, still a matter of dispute among anthropologists. See Lucienne A. Roubin, 'Espace masculin, espace feminin en communauté provençale', *Annales, E.S.C.* 26 (March–April, 1970), p. 540; Rogers (1974), op. cit., and Rayna Reiter, 'Men and Women in the South of France: Public and Private Domains', unpublished paper, 1973, New School for Social Research.

tended a garden and marketed surplus dairy products, poultry and vegetables. There was also seasonal work in the fields at planting and harvest times.[27] Martin Nadaud, a mason from the Creuse, expressed a husband's expectation for his wife this way:

We know there are countries where women marry with the oft-realized hope of having to work only in the house; in France, there is nothing of the sort, precisely the contrary happens; my wife, like all other women of this country was raised to work in the fields from morning until night and she worked no less ... after our marriage ...[28]

Of course the wives of masons from the Creuse were in a peculiar position. Their husbands were gone for long periods of time building houses in Lyon or Paris. They had to do all agricultural chores since the division of labor in the Creuse was between women who handled most of the agricultural tasks and men whose primary work was as artisans in the cities. Women's work on the farm was so important there that at one point Nadaud's family tried to arrange a marriage for him with a girl whose mother was widowed. That way, the Nadaud family farm would acquire two female hands instead of one.

Despite the peculiarity of the Creuse, however, Nadaud's expectation that women would work seems typical of peasant economies. Eilert Sundt's reports on the Norwegian peasantry in the mid-nineteenth century show that women were needed as workers, so experienced and often older women were the choice of young men as wives. Sundt wrote, 'the material progress of a family depended as much upon the wife as upon the husband'.[29] And Frederick Le Play, describing marriage customs of Slavic peasants, noted that 'the peasant takes a wife to augment the number of hands in his family'.[30]

Women labored not only on the farm, but at all sorts of other work, depending in part on what was available to them. In most areas their activity was an extension of their household functions of food provision, animal husbandry and clothing making. Documentation of this

27. Pinchbeck, Part I, *passim*; Alain Girard et Henri Bastide, 'Le budget-temps de la femme mariée à la campagne', *Population*, 14 (1959), pp. 253–84.

28. Martin Nadaud, *Mémoirs de Leonard, ancien garçon* (Paris, 1895, reissued 1948), p. 130. Agricole Perdiguier recalled that his father made his daughters work in the fields: 'Madeleine and Babet worked with us, like men'. *Mémoires d'un compagnon* (Paris, 1964), p. 33.

29. Quoted in Michael Drake, *Population and Society in Norway, 1735–1865* (Cambridge, 1969), pp. 145, 139–40.

30. Frederick Le Play, *Les ouvriers européens,* 6 vols. (Paris, 1855–78), Vol. 5, p. 45.

can be found in almost every family monograph in the six volumes of Le Play's *Les ouvriers européens*. There was the wife of a French vineyard worker, for example, whose principal activity involved the care of a cow. 'She gathers hay for it, cares for it and carries its milk to town to sell.' Another wife worked with her husband during harvest seasons and 'washed laundry and did other work . . . for farmers and landowners in the neighborhood'. She also wove linen 'for her family and for sale'. Other women sewed gloves or clothing; some took in infants to nurse as well.[31] In the regions surrounding the silk-weaving city of Lyon, the wives and daughters of farmers tended worms and reeled silk.[32] Similarly, in Lombardy, seasonal pre-occupation with the care of the hungry worms filled the time of women and children in the household.[33]

Work of this type was a traditional way of supplementing the family income. Indeed, Le Play insisted on including all activities of family members in his budgets because, he argued, 'the small activities undertaken by the family are a significant supplement to the earning of the principal worker'. In fact, he often noted that not only did women work harder than men, but they contributed more to 'the well-being of the family'.[34] Often women's work meant the difference between subsistence and near starvation. Pinchbeck cites a parish report on rural women who, in a time of economic crisis, could find no work: 'In a kind of general despondency she sits down, unable to contribute anything to the general fund of the family and conscious of rendering no other service to her husband except that of the mere care of his family.'[35]

In non-farming and some urban families a similar situation seems to have prevailed. In fact, Chayanov's description of the peasant economy seems a fitting characterization of pre-industrial working-class social arrangements. In *The World We Have Lost* Peter Laslett describes the household as the center of production. The workshop was not separated from the home, and everyone's place was at home. In the weaver's household, for example, children did carding and combing, older daughters and wives spun, while the father wove. In the urban worker's home a

31. Ibid., Vol. 6, pp. 145, 127, and Vol. 5, p. 261, respectively.
32. Arthur Dunham, *The Industrial Revolution in France* (New York, 1935), p. 170.
33. Marie Hall Ets, *Rosa, The Life of an Italian Immigrant* (Minneapolis, 1970).
34. Le Play, Vol. 3, p. 8 and Vol. 6, p. 109, respectively.
35. Pinchbeck, p. 59. See also R. H. Hubscher, 'Une contribution à la connaissance des milieux populaires ruraux au XIXe siècle: Le livre de compte de la famille Flahaut, 1811–1877', *Revue d'histoire économique et sociale*, 47 (1969), pp. 361–403.

similar division of labor often existed. Among Parisian laundry workers, for example, the entire family was expected to work, although women were uniquely responsible for soaping and ironing. This kind of business, in fact, was as well run by women as by men. And parents willed their shops and their clientele to their daughters as frequently as to their sons.[36] Wives of craftsmen sometimes assisted their husbands at their work of tailoring, shoemaking and baking. Sometimes they kept shop, selling the goods and keeping accounts. The wives of skilled cutlery workers served as intermediaries between their husbands and their masters. They not only picked up materials for their husbands to work on at home and transported finished products back to the employer, but they also negotiated work loads and wages.[37]

When the husband worked away from home, women engaged in enterprises of their own. Like their rural counterparts, urban working-class women contributed to the family economy by tending vegetable gardens and raising animals – usually some pigs and hens – and marketing the surplus. Some women set up cafés in their homes, others sold the food and beverages they had prepared outside. A Sheffield knife-maker's wife prepared a 'fermented drink called "pop", which she bottled and sold in the summer to the inhabitants of the city'.[38] These are early-nineteenth-century examples, but Alice Clark refers to gardening and the garment trades in seventeenth-century England. She cites another expedient of poor women, 'selling perishable articles of food from door to door'.[39] This practice continued in the nineteenth century. Le Play details the work of a German miner's wife who 'transported foodstuffs on her back. Two times a week she goes to [the city] where she buys wheat, potatoes, etc. which she carries [10 kilometers] . . . Some of this food is for her household, some is delivered to wealthy persons in town, the rest is sold [for a small profit] at the market'.[40] In eighteenth-century Paris and Bordeaux, among the popular classes, 'it was generally accepted that womenfolk had an important part to play in the domestic economy. Most took a job to bring in an additional in-

36. Le Play, Vol. 5, p. 386.

37. Ibid., Vol. 3, p. 281. Le Play adds that 'For each day of work . . . the women transport twice, a weight of about 210 kilograms a distance of one kilometer'. Vol. 3, p. 161.

38. Ibid., Vol. 3, 325.

39. Alice Clark, The Working Life of Women in the Seventeenth Century (London, 1919), pp. 150, 209.

40. Le Play, Vol. 3, pp. 106–7.

come'.[41] They worked as domestics, laundresses, seamstresses, innkeepers, and beasts of burden – hauling heavy loads many times a day. They also begged and smuggled if they had to. 'The importance of the mother within the family economy was immense; her death or incapacity could cause a family to cross the narrow but extremely meaningful barrier between poverty and destitution'.[42] The popular culture which valued the work of women existed in France during much of the nineteenth century.[43]

The indispensable role of women was demonstrated, too, by the fact that in many communities, widows could manage a farm alone (with the assistance of a few hired hands) whereas widowers found the task almost impossible.[44] It is also demonstrated vividly in times of financial hardship. Hufton insists that women were the first to feel the physical effects of deprivation, in part, because they denied themselves food in order to feed the rest of the family. Other observers describe a similar situation. The report Anderson cites from Lancashire is representative of conditions in Italy, England and France: 'an observation made by medical men, that the parents have lost their health much more generally than the children and particularly, that the mothers who most of all starve themselves, have got pale and emaciated'.[45]

The role women played in the family economy usually gave them a great deal of power within the family. Scattered historical sources complement the more systematic work of contemporary anthropologists

41. Alan Forrest, 'The Condition of the Poor in Revolutionary Bordeaux', *Past and Present*, No. 59 (1973), pp. 151–2.

42. Olwen Hufton, 'Women in Revolution, 1789–1796', *Past and Present*, No. 53 (1971), p. 92.

43. Edith Thomas, *Les Petroleuses* (Paris, 1963), p. 73–9. The fleeting history of social concern and legislation during the Paris Commune of 1871 shows these values reflected in popular radicalism. Although women were not granted political equality by the Communards, illegitimate children were granted legal claims parallel to those of legitimate children. Among the institutions set up by the women of the Commune themselves were day nurseries for working mothers.

44. Susan Rogers, 'The Acceptance of Female Roles in Rural France', unpublished paper, 1972, pp. 95–6; Anderson, p. 95; Leonard Covello, *The Social Background of the Italo-American School Child* (Leiden, 1967), quotes a Sicilian proverb: 'If the father is dead, the family suffers; if the mother dies, the family cannot exist', pp. 208–9. A French version of this is, 'Tant vaut la femme, tant vaut la ferme', quoted in Plan de Travail, 1946–47, *La Role de la femme dans la vie rurale* (Paris, 1946).

45. Hufton, pp. 91–3, Tilly (1974), p. 259, Anderson, p. 77, Laura Oren, 'The Welfare of Women in Laboring Families: England, 1860–1950', *Feminist Studies*, I (Winter–Spring, 1973), pp. 107–25.

on this point. All indicate that while men assume primacy in public roles, it is women who prevail in the domestic sphere. Hufton even suggests they enjoyed 'social supremacy' within the family.[46] Her suggestion echoes Le Play's first-hand observation. In the course of his extensive study of European working-class urban and rural families (carried out from the 1840–70s), he was struck by the woman's role. 'Women are treated with deference, they often . . . exercise a preponderant influence on the affairs of the family (*la communauté*).' He found that they worked harder and in a more sustained fashion than their husbands and concluded that their work, their energy and their intelligence 'makes them more fit . . . to direct the family'.[47]

The key to the woman's power, limited almost exclusively, of course, to the family arena, lay in her management of the household. In some areas, wives of craftsmen kept business accounts, as did the wives or daughters of farmers.[48] Their familiarity with figures was a function of their role as keeper of the household's accounts, for the woman was usually the chief buyer for the household in the market place and often the chief trader as well. Primitive as was the accounting these women could do, it was a tool for dealing with the outside world. Working-class women also often held the purse strings, making financial decisions, and even determining the weekly allowance their husbands received for wine and tobacco. Le Play's description of the Parisian carpenter's wife was typical not only of France:

46. Hufton, p. 93; Susan Rogers, 'Female Forms of Power and the Myth of Male Dominance: A Model of Female/Male Interaction', unpublished paper, 1973; Rémi Clignet, *Many Wives, Many Powers; Authority and Power in Polygynous Families* (Evanston, 1970); Ernestine Friedl, 'The Position of Women: Appearance and Reality', *Anthropological Quarterly*, 40 (1967), pp. 97–108; Evelyn Michaelson and Walter Goldschmidt, 'Female Roles and Male Dominance Among Peasants', *Southwestern Journal of Anthropology*, 27 (1971), pp. 330–52; Rayna Reiter, 'Modernization in the South of France: The Village and Beyond', *Anthropological Quarterly*, 45 (1972), pp. 35–53; Joyce Riegelhaupt, 'Salaoio Women: An Analysis of Informal and Formal Political and Economic Roles of Portuguese Peasant Women', *Anthropological Quarterly*, 40 (1967), pp. 127–38. See also Olwen Hufton, 'Women and the Family Economy in Nineteenth Century France', unpublished paper, University of Reading, 1973.

47. Le Play, Vol. 5, p. 404 and Vol. 6, p. 110, respectively.

48. That sometimes management roles implied literacy as well is indicated in a manuscript communicated to us by Judith Silver Frandzel, University of New Hampshire. It is the account book of a farm in Besse-sur-Barge, Sarthe, undated but from the 1840s, kept exclusively by the daughter of the family. She lists everything, from sale of animals and land to purchase of handkerchiefs, kitchen utensils or jewelry, for which money was spent or received.

She immediately receives his monthly wage; it is she who each morning gives her husband the money necessary to buy the meals he takes outside the house. To her alone . . . in conformity with the custom which prevails among French workers, are confined the administration of the interior of the home and the entire disposition of the family resources.[49]

Indeed, this practice was so linked to the wife's role that when factories replaced the home as the location of work for craftsmen, factory owners sometimes paid directly 'to the wives the wages earned by their husbands'.[50] Whether in Lorraine, Brittany or Lancashire, among Northern English miners, peasants, or London workers, women seem to have dominated family finances and some areas of family decision making. 'The man struts, presides at the table, gives orders, but important decisions – buying a field, selling a cow, a lawsuit against a neighbor, choice of a future son-in-law – are made by *la patronne*'.[51] Or, as a retired farmer from a French village remarked to a visiting anthropologist: 'The husband is always the *chef d'exploitation* . . . Well, that's what the law says. What really happens is another matter, but you won't find that registered in the *Code Civil*'.[52]

It is important here to stress that we speak here of married women. Whatever power these women enjoyed was a function of their participation in a mutual endeavor, and of the particular role they played as a function of their sex and marital status. Their influence was confined to the domestic sphere, but that sphere bulked large in the economic and social life of the family. In this situation, women were working partners in the family enterprise.

Daughters were socialized early, in lower-class families, to assume family and work responsibilities. 'Daughters . . . begin as soon as their strength permits to help their mother in all her work'.[53] Frequently they were sent out of the household to work as agricultural laborers or domestic servants. Others were apprenticed to women who taught them to weave or sew. In areas of rural Switzerland where cottage industry was also practiced, daughters were a most desirable asset. It was they who

49. Le Play, Vol. V, p. 427; see also, IV, p. 198 for the life history of the tinsmith of Savoy and his wife.

50. Le Play, Vol. 6, pp. 110–11. See also Marie José Chombart de Lauwe and Paul-Henry Chombart de Lauwe, *La Femme dans la société* (Paris, 1963), p. 158.

51. Brekelien, p. 69. See also Anderson, p. 77; Peter Stearns, 'Working Class Women in Britain, 1890–1914', in Martha Vicinus, ed., *Suffer and Be Still* (Bloomington, Indiana, 1972), pp. 104, 108; Rogers (1973), p. 28.

52. Rogers (1973), p. 21.

53. Le Play, Vol. 3, p. 111.

could be spared to spin and weave while their mothers worked at home; and they gave their earnings 'as a matter of course to the economic unit, the maintenance of whose property had priority over individual happiness'.[54] Whatever her specific job a young girl early learned the meaning of the saying, 'woman's work is never done'. And she was prepared to work hard for most of her life. Many a parent's advice must have echoed these words to a young girl, written in 1743: 'You cannot expect to marry in such a manner as neither of you shall have occasion to work, and only a fool would take a wife whose bread must be earned solely by his own labor, and who will contribute nothing towards it herself.'[55] Women were expected to work, and the family was the unit of social as well as economic relationships; these were the cultural values held by families who sent their daughters out to work in the early stages of industrialization.

III

Women's work was in the interest of the family economy. Their roles, like those of their husbands, brothers and fathers, could be modified and adjusted to meet difficult times or changing circumstances. Here Chayanov's discussion of the limits of self-exploitation is instructive:

When our peasant as worker entrepreneur is not in a position to develop an adequate sale of his labor on his own farm and to get for himself what he considers sufficient earnings, he temporarily abandons his undertaking and simply converts himself into a worker who resorts to someone else's undertaking, thus saving himself from unemployment in his own.[56]

This means that traditional families employed a variety of strategies to promote the well-being of the family unit. Sometimes the whole family hired itself out as farm hands, sometimes this was done only by men, at other times by one or more children. Supplemental work in domestic industry was frequently resorted to by mothers of families in time of greater need or economic crises. That is why such work was so often seasonal or undertaken sporadically. The custom of sending children of both sexes out to serve on other farms, or to work in nearby cities was yet another expedient – a way of temporarily extending the family beyond its own limited resources in order to increase those resources and thereby guarantee economic survival.

54. Rudolf Braun, 'The Impact of Cottage Industry on an Agricultural Population', in David Landes, ed., *The Rise of Capitalism* (New York, 1966), p. 63.
55. Pinchbeck, pp. 1–2.
56. Chayanov, p. 40.

As major structural changes affected the countries of Europe (in the late eighteenth century in England, much later in France and Italy) these strategies were adapted and new ones were developed (in the face of new pressures and opportunities) to attain the traditional goals of the family economy. In Western Europe in the nineteenth century population growth was causing land-shortage in some areas. In addition rationalized large-scale agriculture was putting marginally productive lands under great competitive pressure. New forms and methods of industrial production also transformed the location and nature of the work of rural and urban craftsmen. In this situation, it became increasingly necessary for family members, but particularly for children, to work away from home. The development of domestic industry, of rurally located textile mills and the expansion of urban populations (with their increased demand for consumer goods and domestic services) provided opportunities for these people to work.

In Lombardy, for example, the northern Italian province of which Milan is the capital, peasants had long practiced labor intensive farming on small holdings. During the nineteenth century, peasants were increasingly unable to support their growing families on these holdings. They seized options similar to the temporary expedients they had customarily employed. Women and girls, whose work on the farm was less productive than that of men, went to work in nearby rural silk mills. Others went to Milan as domestic servants or garment workers, into what were essentially self-exploitative, low-paying, marginally productive jobs. The point was to make enough money to send home.[57]

In the hinterland of Zürich, described by Rudolf Braun, another sort of strategy developed. Originally among landed peasants all family members worked to make ends meet – as domestics, as soldiers, or as quasi-servants in the households of their siblings who had inherited land. Everyone turned his money over to the family. 'The maintenance of the property had priority over individual happiness . . . the question of who got married and at what age, was less an individualistic decision than a family agreement'. Demographic and economic pressures made some families landless, others had to supplement their farming with work in rural industry, particularly textiles. In these areas the system of *Rastgeben* arose. This was the practice of children paying their parents a set amount for room and board. If they did not work at home, but

57. Tilly (1972); this pattern of behavior also confirmed for pre-World War I Piedmont, another province of northern Italy, by interviews with several women who went, as young as age 10, to the city of Turin as domestic servants.

spun at another house, the children paid the landlady the *rast*. Once such money or work had been given as a matter of course. The practice became formalized and the size of the contribution specified as work relations among family members changed. Braun tells us that modifications of this sort eventually broke down family solidarity.[58] He is undoubtedly right. The important point of the Zürich example for our argument, however, is that in the process of transformation old values and practices informed strategic adaptations to new conditions.

Similar examples can be drawn from non-farming families as well. The first industrial revolution in England broke the locational unity of home and workshop by transferring first spinning and then weaving into factories. Neil Smelser's study of *Social Change in the Industrial Revolution* shows, however, that in the first British textile factories the family as a work unit was imported into the mills. 'Masters allowed the operative spinners to hire their own assistants ... the spinners chose their wives, children, near relatives or relatives of the proprietors. Many children, especially the youngest, entered the mill at the express request of their parents'.[59] This extension of the family economy into factories in early industrialization declined after the 1820s, of course, with the increased differentiation and specialization of work. But the initial adjustment to a changed economic structure involved old values operating in new settings.

This is eminently demonstrable in the case of women workers, the single ones who constituted the bulk of the female labor force and the less numerous married women as well. Long before the nineteenth century, lower-class families had sent their daughters out to work. The continuation of this practice and of the values and assumptions underlying it is evident not only in the fact of large numbers of single women but also in the age structure of the female labor force, the kinds of work these women did and in their personal behavior.

The fact that European female labor forces consisted primarily of young, single women – girls, in the language of their contemporaries – is itself an indication of the persistence of familial values. Daughters were expendable in rural and urban households, certainly more expendable than their mothers and, depending on the work of the family, their brothers. When work had to be done away from home and when its duration was uncertain, the family interest was best served by sending

58. Braun, in Landes, ed., pp. 61–3.

59. Neil Smelser, *Social Change in the Industrial Revolution: An Application of Theory to the British Cotton Industry* (Chicago, 1959), pp. 188–9.

forth its daughters. Domestic service, the chief resort of most rural girls, was a traditional area of employment. It was often a secure form of migration since a young girl was assured a place to live, food and a family. There were risks involved also; servant unemployment and servant exploitation were real. Nevertheless, during the nineteenth century, though many more girls were sent into service and moved farther from home than had traditionally been the case, the move itself was not unprecedented. Domestic service was an acceptable employment partly because it afforded the protection of a family and membership in a household.[60]

This was true not only of domestic service, but of other forms of female employment. In Italy and France, textile factory owners attempted to provide 'family' conditions for their girls. Rules of conduct limited their activity, and nuns supervised the establishments, acting as substitute parents. *In loco parentis* for some factory owners sometimes even meant arranging suitable marriages for their female operatives.[61] These factory practices served the owner's interests too, by keeping his work force under control and limiting its mobility. They also served the interests of the girls' families more than those of the girls as individuals, for the girls' wages sometimes went directly to their parents. We do not wish to argue that the factory dormitory was a beneficent institution. The fact that it used the family as model for work and social relationships, and the fact that the practice did serve the *family* interest to some degree, is, however, important.

In the needle trades, which flourished in urban centers, similar practices developed. The rise of ready-made clothing production involved a twofold transformation of garment-making. First, piece-work at home replaced workshop organization. Only later (in England by 1850, in France by the 1870s depending on the city and the industry, in Italy, still later) did new machinery permit the reorganization of the garment

60. Chatelain, p. 508.

61. Ets, p. 87–115; Italy, Ufficio del Lavoro, *Rapporti sulla ispezione del lavoro* (*1 dicembre 1906–30 giugno* (*1908*)), pubblicazione del Ufficio del Lavoro, Serie C, 1909, pp. 64, 93–4, describes the dormitories and work arrangements in north Italian textile mills; Evelyne Sullerot, *Histoire et sociologie du travail féminin* (Paris, 1968), pp. 91–4; Michelle Perrot, *Les Ouvriers en Grève, France 1871–1890* (Paris, 1974), pp. 213, 328. Recent interpretations of similar American cases are to be found in John Kasson, 'The Factory as Republican Community: The Early History of Lowell, Mass.', unpublished paper read at American Studies Convention, October 1973, and Alice Kessler Harris, 'Stratifying by Sex: Notes on the History of Working Women', working paper, Hofstra University, 1974.

industry in factories. In the period when piece-work expanded women found ample opportunity for work. Those who already lived in cities customarily took their work home. Migrants, however, needed homes. So, enterprising women with a little capital turned their homes into lodging houses for piece-workers in their employ. While these often provided exploitative and miserable living conditions, they nonetheless offered a household for a young girl – a household in which she could do work similar to what she or her mother had done at home.[62]

Domestic service, garment-making and even textile manufacturing, the three areas in which female labor was overwhelmingly concentrated, were all traditional areas of women's work. The kind of work parents sent their daughters to do, in other words, did not involve a radical departure from the past. Many a wife had spent her girlhood in service at someone else's house. Piece-work and spinning and weaving were also common in traditional households. The *location* of work did change and that change eventually led to a whole series of other differences; but, initially, there must have been some comfort for a family sending a daughter to a far-off city in the fact that they were sending her to do familiar, woman's work.

As parents sent daughters off with traditional expectations, so the daughters attempted to fulfill them. Evidence for the persistence of familial values is found in the continuing contributions made by working daughters to their families. If in some cases factories sent the girls' wages to their parents, in others, girls simply sent most of their money home themselves. In England, it was not until the 1890s that single working girls living at home kept some of their own money.[63] Earlier, on the continent, their counterparts 'normally turned over all their pay to the family fund'. The daughter of a Belgian locksmith first served her family by tailoring. She habitually gave her family all her earnings 'and thus had no savings at the time of her marriage'.[64] Irish migrants sent money back from as far away as London and Boston.[65] And, even when they no

62. Eileen Yeo and E. P. Thompson, *The Unknown Mayhew* (New York, 1972), pp. 116–80. See also, Henry Mayhew, *London Labour and the London Poor*, 4 vols. (London, 1861), reprinted (London, 1967). Sullerot, p. 100, describes the household-like organization of seamstresses in small shops, in which the *patronne* and workers ate *en famille*, the less skilled workers dismissed, like children, before dessert.

63. Stearns, p. 110.   64. Le Play, Vol. 5, p. 122.

65. Anderson, p. 22; Lynn Lees, personal communication: 'The sending back of money seems to have been a standard practice for Irish migrants everywhere. Rural Ireland has been living on the proceeds for several generations'.

longer expected to return home to marry and live in their natal villages, French and Italian servant girls continued to send money back home. The servant girls working for the Flahaut family during the period 1811 to 1877 in rural France sent money home to their parents. There were regular arrangements by which Monsieur Flahaut sent foodstuffs instead of money or paid the rent on the father's farm or sent clothing and coal directly to the parents of his servant girls. Sometimes, too, younger or unemployed brothers and sisters received these payments which were deducted from the domestic's wages. Hubscher tells us that for certain farmers who rented their lands, their daughters' contributions were 'indispensable, without them it would have been impossible to cultivate the fields they rented'. He adds that the 'financial support' of the daughters for their parents 'seemed absolutely normal to both' parties. It represented a 'strong family solidarity which required a mature and economically independent child to contribute to the support of its relatives'.[66] Mill girls in Lombardy also made contributions to their families and, if they lived close enough, the families sent regular baskets of food. According to one autobiographical report, the employer actually sent a man and wagon around to the girls' villages weekly to pick up their families' food baskets.[67]

In Lancashire 'considerable contact was maintained' between migrants and their families. Money was sent home, members of the family were brought to the city to live by family members who had 'travelled' and sometimes even 'reverse migration' occurred.[68] The children of married daughters working in Norwegian cities as domestics were sent home to be raised by grandparents. In this case, the young husband and wife continued to work separately as domestics to save to set up their own household.[69] Even when whole families migrated to the United States, they carried these traditional practices with them. Willa Cather notes in *My Antonia* that immigrant girls' work as domestics or farm hands 'contributed to the prosperous, mortgage free farms' their parents built in Nebraska.[70]

66. Hubscher, pp. 395–6.   67. Ets, pp. 138–40.
68. Anderson, p. 153.   69. Drake, p. 138.
70. Robert Smuts, *Women and Work in America* (New York, 1971), p. 9. See also Virginia Yans McLaughlin, 'Patterns of Work and Family Organization: Buffalo's Italians', *Journal of Interdisciplinary History*, II (Autumn, 1971), pp. 299–314. The predominance of the family interest over that of individuals and the importance of the family as a model for social relationships can be glimpsed in the lives of young working men as well as in those of young girls. The Irish custom of sending money to parents was followed by boys as well as girls. In Italian immigrant families in the

The cultural values which sent young girls out to work for their families also informed their personal behavior. The increase, noted by historians and demographers, in illegitimate birth rates in many European cities from about 1750 to 1850 can be seen, paradoxically, as yet another demonstration of the persistence of old attitudes in new settings.[71] Alliances with young men may have begun in the city as at home,

U.S., boys and girls turned over their salaries to parents. In French working-class families, likewise. The compagnonnage system offered boys sponsored migration and houses in which to live, complete with a substitute family of mère, père and frères. These houses seemed to offer this kind of family setting without the authoritarian aspects of the factory dormitories.

71. Cf. Edward Shorter, 'Illegitimacy, Sexual Revolution and Social Change in Europe, 1750–1900', *Journal of Interdisciplinary History*, 2 (1971), pp. 237–72; 'Capitalism, Culture and Sexuality: Some Competing Models', *Social Science Quarterly* (1972), pp. 338–56, and, most recently, 'Female Emancipation, Birth Control and Fertility in European History', *American Historical Review*, 78 (1973), pp. 605–40. Shorter has argued that the increase in illegitimate fertility which began in the mid-eighteenth to late nineteenth centuries in Europe was preceded by a dramatic change in values. This change, he says, was stimulated by rebellion against parental authority and by exposure to 'market values' when young women broke with 'old traditions' and went out to work. The change was expressed in a new sexual 'liberation' of young working girls. They sought self-fulfillment and self-expression in sexual encounters. In the absence of contraception, they became pregnant and bore illegitimate children. We find Shorter's speculations imaginative but incorrect. He makes unfounded assumptions about pre-industrial family relationships and about patterns of work in these families. The actual historical experience of young women working in the nineteenth century was not what Shorter assumes it was. When one examines their history and finds that peasant values and family interests sent them to work, and when one examines the kinds of work they did and the pay they received, it is impossible to agree with Shorter that their experience was either radically different from that of women in the past, or was in any sense 'emancipating'.

Shorter cannot demonstrate that attitudes changed; he deduces that they did. We show that the behavior from which Shorter deduced changed values was consonant with older values operating in changed circumstances. Illegitimacy rose at least partly as a consequence of a compositional change in population – i.e., the increasing presence of many more young women in sexually vulnerable situations as workers in cities, removed from family protection and assistance. Under these circumstances, illicit liaisons can be seen as alternate families and illegitimate children the consequence of an attempt to constitute the family work unit in a situation in which legal marriage sometimes could not be afforded, other times, was not felt necessary. Far from their own parents and the community which could have enforced compliance with an agreement to marriage which preceded sexual relations, women were more likely to bear illegitimate children. This is discussed more fully in the text below. See J. DePauw, 'Amour illégitime et société à Nantes au XVIIIe siècle', *Annales, Economies, Sociétés, Civilisations*, 27e Année (July–

the girls seeking potential husbands in the hope of establishing a family of their own. The difference, of course, was that social customs that could be enforced at home, could not be in the city.

When a girl was far from home, her family had little control over whom she married, or when. The pressure that kept a Swiss daughter spinning at home until she was forty could not affect the choices of a daughter who had migrated to the city. In fact, her migration implied that she was not needed in the same way at home. The loneliness and isolation of the city was clearly one pressure for marriage. So was the desire to escape domestic service and become her own mistress in her own home as her mother had been. The conditions of domestic service, which usually demanded that servants be unmarried, also contributed to illicit liaisons and led many a domestic to abandon her child. This had long been true; what was different in nineteenth-century Europe was that the great increase in the proportions of women employed in domestic service outstripped increased employment in manufacturing. This meant that more women than ever before, proportionately, were employed in this sector, which was particularly liable to produce illegitimate children.

Yet another motive for marriage was economic. Girls in factories were said to be fairly well-paid, but most girls did not work in factories. Women in the needle trades and other piece-work industries barely made enough to support themselves. (Wages constantly fluctuated in these consumer product trades and declined after the 1830s in both England and France. Women in these trades were also paid half of what men received for comparable work, often because it was assumed that women's wages were part of a family wage, an assumption which did not always correspond with reality.[72]) In the rural households they came

---

October, 1972), pp. 1155–82, esp. p. 1163. De Pauw shows (p. 1166) that promises of marriage in cases of illegitimacy increased as both illegitimacy increased and the unions which produced the bastards increasingly occurred between social equals in the eighteenth century. (In each subsequent version of his argument, Shorter has become less qualified and more insistent about the logic of his argument. Logic, however, ought not to be confused with actual historical experience and Shorter has little solid evidence from the past to support his speculation.) See Louise Tilly, Joan Scott and Miriam Cohen, 'Women's Work and European Fertility Patterns', unpublished paper, 1973.

72. Charles Booth, *Life and Labour of the People of London* (London, 1902); Yeo and Thompson, pp. 116–80; France, Direction du Travail, *Les associations professionelles ouvrières*, Vol. 4 (1903), pp. 797–805; P. Leroy-Beaulieu, *Le travail des femmes au XIXe siècle* (Paris, 1873), pp. 50–145.

from, subsistence depended on multiple contributions. The logical move for a single girl whose circumstances took her far from her family and whose wages were insufficient either to support herself or to enable her to send money home, would be to find a husband; together they might be able to subsist.

It may well be that young girls became 'engaged' to their suitors and then followed what were in many rural areas customary practices: they slept with the men they intended to marry.[73] When they became pregnant, however, the men either disappeared, or continued living with them, but did not marry them. Sometimes the couple married after the child or children were born. The constraint of the traditional necessity to bring a dowry to her marriage sometimes meant that a woman worked while cohabiting with her lover until the requisite trousseau was put aside. The absence of the moral force of family, local community and church prevented the fulfillment of marital expectations. Lack of money and severe economic pressures, as well perhaps as different attitudes and expectations on the part of the men, kept them from fulfilling their promise. The testimony of abandoned women to Henry Mayhew indicates that often (a) there was no money for a proper wedding; (b) the men's jobs demanded that they move on; (c) poverty created a possible emotional stress; and (d) traditional contexts which identified and demanded proper behavior were absent.[74] Young girls, then, pursued mates and behaved with them according to traditional assumptions. The changed context yielded unanticipated (and often unhappy) results.

Even among prostitutes, many of whom were destitute or unemployed servants and piece-workers, a peculiar blend of old and new attitudes was evident. In pre-industrial society, lower-class women developed endless resources for obtaining food for their families. Begging was not unheard of and flirtations and sexual favors were an acknowledged

73. P. E. H. Hair, 'Bridal Pregnancy in Rural England in Earlier Centuries', *Population Studies*, 20 (1966–7), pp. 233–43, and 'Bridal Pregnancy in Earlier Rural England, Further Examined', ibid., 24 (1970), pp. 59–70; Thomas F. Sheppard, *Loumarin in the Eighteenth Century: A Study of a French Village* (Baltimore, 1971); E. A. Wrigley, *Population and History* (New York, 1969), pp. 61–106; K. R. V. Wikman, *Die Einleitung der Ehe: Eine vergleichgende Ethnosoziologisch euntersuchung über die Vorstufe der Ehe in den sitten des Schwedischen Volkstums* (Abo, 1937; Acta Academie Aboensis, Humaniora, 11).

74. Yeo and Thompson, pp. 167–80. For eighteenth-century Nantes, De Pauw, pp. 1166–7, shows how economic promises to find the woman work, or teach her a craft led to liaisons which ended in pregnancy; Thomas, pp. 20–22, 76–9, describes common-law marriage in the Parisian working class at the time of the Commune

way of obtaining bread or flour in time of scarcity. Similarly, in nine-teenth-century London, prostitutes interviewed by Mayhew explained their 'shame' as a way of providing food for their families. One, the mother of an illegitimate boy, explained that to keep herself and her son from starving she was 'forced to resort to prostitution'. Another described the 'glorious dinner' her solicitations had brought. And a daughter explained her prostitution to the author of *My Secret Life* as her way of enabling the rest of the family to eat: 'Well, what do you let men fuck you for? Sausage rolls?' 'Yes, meat-pies and pastry too'.[75]

Not all single working girls were abandoned with illegitimate children, nor, despite the alarm of middle-class observers, did most become prostitutes. Many got married and most left the labor force when they did. Both the predominance of young single girls in the female labor force and the absence of older married women reflect the persistence of traditional familial values. When they married, daughters were no longer expected to contribute their wages to their parents' household. Marriage meant a transfer from one family to another and the assumption of some new roles. Single girls, however, carried the values and practices of their mothers into their own marriages. The traditional role of a married woman, her vital economic function within the family economy, sent her into the labor force when her earnings were needed by the household. When the income of her husband and children was sufficient for the family's needs, she left the labor force. Mothers of young children would sometimes leave the labor force *only* after their oldest child went out to work. Over the developmental cycle of the family, this pattern is valid, but in cases of temporary need, such as sickness, or in the case of the death of a money earner, the married woman would go back to work.[76] Even without a money contribution, however, her contribution to the family economy was nevertheless substantial. In the 1890s in London, the wives of the lower classes 'had great responsibility, whether they earned a salary of their own or not, they handled most of the family's money and were responsible not only for food shopping, but for paying

75. Yeo and Thompson, pp. 141, 148, 169; E. M. Sigsworth and J. J. Wylie, 'A Study of Victorian Prostitution and Venereal Disease', in Vicinus, cited above, p. 81.

76. Chayanov and other economic studies of peasantry remark on the concept of 'target income'. On the demographic reflections of the development cycle see Lutz Berkner, 'The Stem Family and the Development Cycle of the Peasant House-hold: An Eighteenth-Century Austrian Example', *American Historical Review*, 77 (April 1972), pp. 398–418. Lynn Lees is working on urban applications of the developmental cycle concept with English and Irish workers' families.

the rent, buying clothes, keeping up insurance payments and overseeing school expenses for their children'.[77]

Although increasingly the location of work in factories or shops outside the home made such work more feasible for single women, some married women continued to find jobs. Industrialization only gradually transformed occupational opportunities. Old jobs persisted for many years alongside the new. Women who married industrial workers and who lived in cities imported old styles of behavior into new contexts. Much of the work performed by married women was temporary. Anderson describes varieties of domestic employment for married women in Preston in 1851. Many helped their husbands, others ran 'a little provision shop or beer house'. Well over a third of those who worked, he continues, 'were employed in non-factory occupations. Many others also worked irregularly or part time' and often were not even listed in official records as having an occupation. Indeed, Anderson's formulation for Lancashire that 'patterns of family structure in towns can only be explained as hangovers from rural patterns' has much wider application.[78] Whether in the cities and towns of Europe or in America, the patterns of work of married women resembled older, pre-industrial practices. Immigrant women in New England textile mills, for example, were 'the only large group of regularly employed married women' other than blacks. Smuts explains that they were attracted by the familiar work of spinning and weaving and, more important, by the opportunity of working with their children. 'A mother whose children worked could look after them better if she worked in the same mill'.[79] Depending, of course, on their past experience, immigrant women adapted their skills to American conditions. Thus Italian mothers with their children picked fruit and vegetables around Buffalo, New York, an activity reminiscent of southern Italy.[80] Italian women on New York's lower East Side sewed pants or made paper flowers with their daughters at home. Their husbands, lacking these skills, dug ditches and swept the streets. When these same women followed their work into factories and sweatshops, the husbands sometimes kept house and cared for the children. Married Irish women with only agricultural

77. Stearns, p. 106.
78. Anderson, pp. 71, 79 respectively.
79. Smuts, p. 57.
80. Virginia Yans McLaughlin, 'A Flexible Tradition: South Italian Immigrants Confront a New York Experience', unpublished paper, 1973, pp. 8, 11, and McLaughlin, 1972, op. cit.

experience became domestics. But many cleaned New York office buildings at night so they could care for their families during the day.[81]

Whether they worked outside the home or not, married women defined their role within the framework of the family economy. Married working-class women, in fact, seem almost an internal backwater of pre-industrial values within the working-class family. Long after their husbands and children had begun to adopt some of the individualistic values associated with industrialization, these women continued the self-sacrificing, self-exploitative work that so impressed Le Play and that was characteristic of the peasant or household economy. Surely this (and not the fact that 'husbands gave purpose to married women among the poor') is the meaning of the testimony of a woman from York cited by Peter Stearns: 'If there's anything extra to buy such as a pair of boots for one of the children, me and the children goes without dinner – or mebbe only 'as a cop o' tea and a bit o' bread, but Him allers takes 'is dinner to work, and I never tell 'im'.[82] As long as her role is economically functional for her family, familial values make sense for the lower-class woman. And the role of provider and financial manager, of seamstress and occasional wage earner was economically functional for a long time in working-class families.

Perhaps most illustrative is this case history which embodies the collective portrait we have just presented. Francesca F. was born in about 1817 in a rural area of Moravia and remained at home until she was 11.[83] She had a typical childhood for a girl of her class. She learned from her mother how to keep house and help on the farm, and she learned at school how to read, write, figure and, most important of all, sew. At eleven, she was sent into domestic service in a neighboring town. She worked successively in several different houses, increasing her earnings as she changed jobs. At one house she acquired a speciality as a seamstress. She saved some money, but sent most of it home, and

81. Louise Odencrantz, *Italian Women in Industry: A Study of Conditions in New York City* (New York, 1919), p. 19. Odencrantz also describes the concept of the family income – the sum of earnings of fathers, mothers, sons and daughters, other relatives, and returns from lodgers – as typical of Italian immigrants in New York. Covello, p. 295, describes the resistance of Italian immigrants to school requirements, and their haste to send boys out to work. One mother exclaimed, 'The law [for school attendance] was made against the family'. The father of Louise Tilly, as an Italian immigrant schoolboy in New York before World War I, and the only member of his family not employed, did the cooking and kept house.

82. Stearns, p. 104.

83. Le Play, Vol. V, pp. 9, 16–17, 45, 50–54.

she returned home (to visit and renew her passport) at least once a year.

Until her eighteenth year, Francesca's experience was not unlike young girls' of earlier generations. Her decision to 'seek her fortune in Vienna', though, began a new phase of her life. With the good wishes of her parents, she paid her coach passage out of her savings and three days after she arrived she found a job as a maid. She lived with the bourgeois family she worked for for six months. Then she left for a better position which she held until her master died (six months). Yet another job as a domestic lasted a year.

At twenty, attracted by the opportunities for work available in a big city and tired of domestic service, she apprenticed herself to a wool weaver. He went bankrupt after a year and she found yet another job. That one she quit because the work was unsteady and she began sewing gloves for a small manufacturer. Glove-making was a prospering piece-work industry and Francesca had to work 'at home'. Home was a boarding house where she shared her bed with another working girl of 'dubious character'. Unhappy with these arrangements, Francesca fortunately met a young cabinet-maker, himself of rural origin with whom she began living. (The practice of sleeping with one's fiancé was not uncommon in rural Moravia according to Le Play.) She soon had a child whom she cared for while she sewed gloves, all the while saving money for her marriage. (Viennese authorities at this time required that workers show they could support a family before they were permitted to marry. The task of accumulating savings usually fell to the future bride.)

Three years after she met the cabinet-maker, they were married. Francesca paid all the expenses of the wedding and provided what was essentially her own dowry – all the linens and household furnishings they needed. The daughter of rural peasants, Francesca was now the mother of an urban working-class family. Although the care of her children and the management of her household consumed much of her time, she still managed to earn wages in 1853, by doing the equivalent of 125 full days of work, making gloves. (Although it amounted in Le Play's calculation to 125 days, Francesca sewed gloves part of the day during most of the year.)

As long as piece-work was available to her, Francesca F. could supplement her husband's wage with her own work. With the decline of such domestic work, however, and the rise of factories, it would become increasingly difficult for the mother of five young children to leave her household responsibilities in order to earn a wage. Economic conditions in Vienna in the 1850s still made it possible for Francesca to fulfill the role expected of a woman of the popular classes.

IV

Traditional values did not persist indefinitely in modern or modernizing contexts. As families adapted customary strategies to deal with new situations they became involved in new experiences which altered relationships within the family and the perceptions of those relationships. As the process of change involved retention of old values and practices, it also transformed them, but in a more gradual and complex manner than either Goode or Engels implied.

The major transformation involved the replacement of familial values with individualistic ones. These stressed the notion that the individual was owner of him- or herself rather than a part of a social or moral whole.[84] They involved what Anderson calls 'an instrumental orientation' of family members to their families 'requiring reciprocation for their contribution in the very short run'.[85] These attitudes developed differently in different places depending in part on specific circumstances. Nonetheless, the evidence indicates an underlying similarity in the process and the final outcome. Sons first, and only later daughters, were permitted to keep some of their earnings. They were granted allowances by their parents in some cases; in others a specified family contribution was set, in still others the child decided what portion of her pay she would send home (and it diminished and became increasingly irregular over time). Anderson points out that in Preston, high factory wages of children reversed normal dependencies and made parents dependent on their children. The tensions created by the different priorities of parents and children led to feuds. And in these situations children often left home voluntarily and gladly and 'became unrestrained masters of their destiny'.[86]

Long distance and permanent migration also ultimately undermined family ties. And the pressures of low wages and permanent urban living, the forced independence of large numbers of young girls, clearly fostered calculating, self-seeking attitudes among them. They began to look upon certain jobs as avenues of social and occupational mobility, rather than as a temporary means to earn some money for the family. Domestic

84. C. B. MacPherson, *The Political Theory of Possessive Individualism, Hobbes to Locke* (Oxford paperback, 1964), p. 3.
85. Anderson, pp. 131–2.
86. Ibid.

service remained a major occupation for women until the twentieth century in most of Europe. (In fact, in the mid-nineteenth century the number of women employed as domestics increased tremendously.) Nonetheless, as it embodied traditional female employment, a position as a servant also began to mean an opportunity for geographic and occupational mobility. Once the trip to the city and the period of adjustment to urban life had been accomplished under the auspices of service, a young girl could seek better and more remunerative work.[87] Her prospects for marrying someone who made better money in the city also increased immeasurably.

Their new experiences and the difficulties and disillusionment they experienced clearly developed in young women a more individualistic and instrumental orientation. They lived and worked with peers increasingly. They wanted to save their money for clothes and amusements. They learned to look out for their own advantage, to value every penny they earned, to place their own desires and interests above those of their families.

Decreased infant mortality and increased educational opportunity also modified family work strategies. And instead of sending all their children out to work for the family welfare, parents began to invest in their children's futures by keeping them out of the work force and sending them to school. (Clearly this strategy was adopted earlier for sons than daughters – the exact history of the process remains to be described.) The family ethic at once sponsored intergenerational mobility and a new individualistic attitude as well.[88]

A number of factors, then, were involved in the waning of the family economy. They included the location of job opportunities, increased standards of living and higher wages, proximity to economic change, increased exposure to and adherence to bourgeois standards as chances for mobility into the bourgeoisie increased, ethnic variations in work patterns and family organization, and different rates of development in different regions and different countries. All of these factors contributed to the decline of the family as a productive unit and to the modification of the values associated with it. The decline can be dated variously for various places, classes and ethnic groups. It reached the European peasant and working classes only during the nineteenth century, and in

87. McBride, op. cit.; Chatelain makes a similar point.

88. For an important discussion of changes in family strategies, see Charles Tilly, 'Population and Pedagogy in France', *History of Education Quarterly* (Summer, 1973), pp. 113–28.

some areas, like Southern Italy, rural Ireland and rural France, not until the twentieth century. The usefulness of the family model as a unit of analysis for social relationships and economic decision making, however, has not disappeared.[89]

A great deal more work is needed on the redefinition of family relationships and on the changes in the definition of women's work and women's place that accompanied it. Clearly many things changed. The rising standard of living and increased wages for men, which enabled them to support their families, made it less necessary for married women to work outside the home. (In early industrialization, such work also exacted great costs in terms of infant and child mortality.)[90] Even for single women, economic change reduced traditional work opportunities, while new jobs opened up for those with more education. After World War I, for example, domestic service was much less important as an area of employment for young women. A smaller number of permanent servants who followed that occupation as a profession replaced the steady stream of young women who had constituted the domestic servant population.[91] The rise of factory garment production seems to have limited work available for women in Milan and elsewhere.[92] On the other hand, the growth of new jobs in expanding government services, in support services for business, in commerce, in health services and in teaching provided work opportunities, primarily for single women, especially for those with at least a basic education.[93]

There is evidence also that women's role in the household, whether as wives or as daughters, was modified with time. In Britain, women in working-class families began to lose control over finances early in the twentieth century, but the process was not complete until World War II. Working girls began to receive spending money of their own only at the end of the nineteenth century. After about 1914, more and more single girls kept more and more of their wages, and wives began to receive a household allowance from their husbands, who kept the rest and deter-

89. See for example Marc Nerlove, 'Economic Growth and Population: Perspectives on the "New Home Economics"', unpublished draft, Northwestern University, 1973.

90. Hewitt, pp. 99–122 and Appendix I. For France, see the debate surrounding the passage of the Loi Roussel in 1874, regulating wet nursing.

91. Chatelain; McBride, p. 20. Domestic service continued, at the same time, to be the channel of geographic mobility of small rural population groups, sometimes in international migration streams.

92. Tilly (1972).

93. Holcombe, op. cit.

mined how it was spent.[94] The rhetoric of some working-class organizations also suggests a change in ideas about family roles. Labor unions demanded higher wages for men so that they could support families and keep their wives at home. Some socialist newspapers described the ideal society as one in which 'good socialist wives' would stay at home and care for the health and education of 'good socialist children'.[95]

The changes that affected women's work and women's place in the family late in the nineteenth and in the twentieth centuries are subjects which are virtually unexplored by historians. They cannot be understood, however, apart from the historical context we have presented. It was European peasant and working-class families which experienced at first hand the structural changes of the nineteenth century. These experiences were anything but uniform. They were differentiated geographically, ethnically and temporally and they involved complex patterns of family dynamics and family decision making. The first contacts with structural change in all cases, however, involved adjustments of traditional strategies and were informed by values rooted in the family economy. It is only in these terms that we can begin to understand the work of the vast majority of women during the nineteenth century. We must examine *their* experience in the light of *their* familial values and not our individualistic ones. The families whose wives and daughters constituted the bulk of the female labor force in western Europe during most of the nineteenth century simply did not value the 'rights and responsibilities of the individual' which Goode invokes. Their values cannot be logically or historically tied to the political enfranchisement of women. The confusion about women's work and women's place begins to be resolved when assumptions are tested against historical data. The evolutionary model which assumes a single and similar experience for all women, an experience in which political and economic factors move together, must be discarded in the light of historical evidence.

94. Stearns, p. 116.

95. These particular attitudes were expressed in *Le Reveil des Verriers* in an article published in 1893, entitled 'La Femme socialiste', but they are representative of many such attitudes expressed in the working-class press. See M. Guilbert, 'La Presence des femmes dans les professions: incidences sur l'action syndicale avant 1914', *Le Mouvement Social*, No. 63 (1968), p. 129. For Italy, see *La Difesa delle Lavoratrici* (a socialist newspaper for women) 11 May 1912, for a socialist view of women's role as mothers. See also Theodore Zeldin, *France, 1848–1945*. Vol. I. *Ambition, Love and Politics* (Oxford, 1973), p. 346.

5 Economic Perspectives on the Family

Isabel V. Sawhill

From: *Daedalus* (*Journal of the American Academy of Arts and Sciences*), Vol. 106, No. 2, Spring 1977, pp. 115–25.

Introduction

Back in the fifties, a colleague of mine in the economics department of a small college was sitting in his office preparing a class in 'money and banking.' He was interrupted by a call from an anxious housewife who thought she had been referred to the department of home economics. She wanted to bake bread and was seeking advice on the amount of yeast to use. Partly in amusement and partly in irritation at having been interrupted, he responded: 'Madam, I know something about how one raises money but nothing about how one raises dough.'[1] Today, even though economists have not gone so far as to study the art of bread-making, there is a whole new literature within the discipline labeled the 'new home economics' and devoted to examining such topics as marriage, fertility, and decisions about the use of both time and goods within the household or family.[2] These interests are quite new – dating perhaps from the early or mid sixties and heavily influenced by the development of human capital theory and the theory of the allocation of time.[3] Before their appearance, economists had concentrated almost exclusively on markets and exchange; in such a context, the household or family was only relevant as a final consumer of market-produced goods and services or as a supplier of productive inputs, chiefly labor. What went on *within* the household was largely ignored.

There are several reasons for the economist's newly discovered in-

1. An incident reported by Professor Frederick Reuss, now retired from the department of economics at Goucher College in Baltimore, Maryland.

2. Several recent publications illustrate the direction of research in this area. One is *Economics of the Family: Marriage, Children, and Human Capital*, ed. Theodore W. Schultz (Chicago, 1974); another is *Sex, Discrimination, and the Division of Labor*, ed. Cynthia B. Lloyd (New York, 1975).

3. Gary Becker, 'A Theory of the Allocation of Time,' (see above, p. 52) and *Human Capital: A Theoretical and Empirical Analysis with Special Reference to Education* (New York, 1964).

terest in the family. One stems from the common views of most economists and their own definition of the scope of their discipline, the core of
which is that an economic problem exists whenever resources that have
multiple and competing uses are scarce. Scarcity requires *choice*, and
choices are best guided by comparing the costs and benefits of all the
possible alternatives. Once one has defined 'resources' and 'costs and
benefits' broadly enough, there is almost no area of human behavior
to which the economic paradigm cannot be applied. More specifically:

– Resources include not only the physical environment (land, other
natural resources) and the finiteness of earthly space, but also human
resources and the finiteness of human time. Increases in the quantity
or quality of either natural or human resources are called 'investments'
and lead to an accumulation of either physical or human 'capital.' A
major activity which takes place within the family is investment in
human capital – e.g., the rearing of children – while the ultimate scarcity
for this purpose is parental time.

– It is assumed in economic theory that individuals are rational, that
they attempt to maximize their own welfare, and that they have information with which to evaluate and choose among alternative courses of
action.

– Individuals begin by deciding whether to marry, and when, and
whom to pick from among all possible mates. Once formed, households face a number of additional decisions about how much work to
do, by whom (husband or wife), and where (in the home or in the
market). They must also choose which set of market goods and home
produced goods to consume, and whether to have children (one type
of home-produced good).

All the above decisions are influenced by the costs and benefits associated with the various alternatives. Costs are measured in both time
and money and include psychic elements as well as opportunities foregone (e.g., one of the costs of marrying individual A is not marrying
individual B). Similarly, benefits may be monetary or nonmonetary in
character (e.g., if a woman quits her job to keep house, it is because her
time at home is valued more than the income she would have earned).
Thus, the broad applicability of economic theory to a wide range of
nonmarket phenomena is one reason for the economist's emerging
interest in the family.

A second reason is the realization that differences in earnings and in
family economic well-being cannot be explained solely in terms of the
operation of labor markets. Two of the critical determinants of indi-

vidual earnings are education and experience, but a great deal of that education either goes on within the home or else is successful because of its interaction with family influences. As for experience, the problem is that those (for example, married women) who devote a great deal of their time to family activities will be handicapped in the labor market as a result of an insufficient investment in marketable skills.[4] Finally, family economic well-being may depend as much on the ratio of earners to non-earners within the household as it does on individual earnings, but this ratio is determined by decisions about marriage, childbearing, and labor force participation (especially by wives).[5]

Specific contributions

To date, what has the economist's foray into these new areas produced? Most of the literature has been devoted to analyses of (a) fertility, (b) marriage and divorce, and (c) the division of labor within the home and its concomitant effects on labor-force participation and the earnings of men and women. What follows is a brief review of the findings of, and the insights emerging from, this literature. Throughout this review, I shall attempt to reproduce the flavor of the economic writing on these subjects as accurately as possible without commenting on its merits. Later, I shall try to provide an evaluation of the economist's contribution.

(a) Fertility, childbearing, and child rearing

In the 'old' economics, the size of the population was occasionally viewed as either a cause or a consequence of the rate of economic growth, but at a microeconomic level, no attempt was made to explain why people had children and why some people had more than others. Children either arrived with the stork (i.e., exogenously) or as the unintended outcome of sexual activity (i.e., almost randomly). In the new home economics all of this has changed.[6] Children are viewed as either 'producer durables' (i.e., producing a stream of future income for their parents – perhaps when the latter are old and retired, if not sooner) or as 'consumer durables' (i.e., producing a stream of future satisfactions

4. Jacob Mincer, *Schooling, Experience, and Earnings* (New York, 1974).

5. *Five Thousand American Families: Patterns of Economic Progress*, I–IV, ed. Greg J. Duncan and James N. Morgan (Ann Arbor, 1973–6).

6. See Part Two, 'Economics of Family Fertility,' in T. W. Schultz (cited above, note 2).

for their parents in the same fashion as does an automobile or a house).[7] In a modern, industrialized country with a well-developed system of social insurance and little or no child labor, children are most clearly analogous to consumer goods. In the rural areas of industrialized nations or in the less developed parts of the world, their value as workers is greater, and this is undoubtedly one explanation for the higher fertility in these areas.

Because of children's value – whether as producer or as consumer goods – parents are willing to invest both time and money in child-bearing and child-rearing. They make decisions not only about how many children to have, but also about how much time and money to devote to each child. In other words, the demand for, and supply of, children has both a quantity and quality component, with various trade-offs between the two being possible. In either case, children tend to be extremely time-consuming. Not only is the basic care of children demanding of adult (especially the mother's) time, but the enjoyment that parents are presumed to derive from their companionship, growth, and development also takes many hours, and it must compete with alternative uses of such time, including other leisure-time activities. In a past era, spending time with one's children did not so often have to compete with trips to Europe, Sunday golf games, or evenings at the theater. Nor were women's wages high enough or their employment opportunities sufficient to cause many families to consider a mother's foregone income as an important cost of having children.

In poor societies, alternative uses of time are neither as attractive nor as available. In fact, as Steffan Linder has noted, there may even be 'idle time,' that is, time which is truly a surplus in that it is not devoted to productive work, to the active enjoyment of leisure pursuits, or to personal maintenance (sleep, etc.).[8] In any case, the time costs of children are low and the (producer) benefits are high relative to what they become in a more affluent and industrialized society. Thus, it is not surprising that fertility declines with economic growth.

In an industrialized economy, the much greater productivity of human resources increases the value of time relative to the value of goods, and it changes people's behavior in subtle but important ways. Rather than bake our own bread, we buy it in the store. Even if valued at the minimum wage, the 'time cost' of baking bread is about four

7. For a critique, see Judith Blake, 'Are Babies Consumer Durables?,' *Population Studies*, 22 (March 1968), pp. 5–25.

8. Steffan B. Linder, *The Harried Leisure Class* (New York, 1970).

dollars while the same product is available for less than one dollar in a commercial bakery or a local supermarket. It will be protested that the quality of the latter is inferior, but it may not be inferior to the tune of the other three dollars or so. Most people, then, bake bread only because they regard it as an enjoyable activity. Even at this level, however, it must still compete with riding a bicycle and playing the piano. In the past, more people baked their own bread not only because the store-bought variety was relatively more expensive, but also because they could less easily afford bicycles, pianos, television sets, and cameras to fill their leisure hours.

In a somewhat similar fashion, the amount of time needed to raise and enjoy one's children has led to a reduction in the size of families. Where possible, there has been a substitution of market goods and services (analogous to the store-bought bread) for parental time, as when we send children to a day-care center or sit them in front of the television set or buy them records and books instead of talking, singing, or reading to them.[9] The point is that what some have labelled the 'dehumanization' of family life or the neglect of children may simply be a matter of the economics of time. As the price of time increases, those commodities the production or consumption of which are time-intensive (e.g., children) will be less in demand than those which are more goods-intensive. Thus, as the parent's (usually the mother's) actual or expected wage rate rises, the demand for children tends to decline. On the other hand, holding the price of time constant, we would expect the demand for children to increase with family income, as is the case with other consumer goods.

Turning to the empirical evidence,[10] the economic literature on fertility has established quite unequivocally that childbearing is negatively related to the price of the mother's time. The effects of income on fertility are much weaker, once the possible confounding influences of education and of the price of time have been removed. One likely possibility is that there is a substitution of quality for quantity at higher income levels – that is, more affluent families may devote more time and money *per child* than their less affluent counterparts in the same way that they buy higher quality food or more expensive clothes. These in-

9. Some young couples I know view their household pets as partial and inexpensive substitutes for children.

10. The empirical literature for the United States is summarized in an appendix to an article by T. Paul Schultz which appears in T. W. Schultz (cited above, note 2).

vestments in children, in turn, have important implications for the transmission of inequality to succeeding generations. To date, we have had little success in using extra-family institutions or programs to compensate for these inequalities in family investment.

Finally, it has been found that better-educated parents have fewer children, even after controlling for income. This could be because they have a different set of preferences, because they are relatively more adept at producing high-quality children and thus inclined to make still further substitutions of quality for quantity, or because they are better contraceptors. There is growing empirical support for the last-mentioned possibility. The better educated use more effective contraceptive techniques and also use a given set of techniques with a higher degree of success.[11]

If further improvements in contraceptive efficiency and additional increases in the cost of children contribute to a continuing decline in fertility, what are the implications for marriage?

(b) Marriage and divorce

The economic theory of marriage has been developed by Gary Becker.[12] In his view, a major motivation for marriage is the desire to have one's own children. In addition, the frequent contact and sharing of resources which people who love one another find desirable can occur more efficiently if the individuals share the same household on a relatively permanent basis. Still a third motivation stems from the efficiency associated with the specialization of male and female time within marriage. If women's market productivity and wages are lower than men's, but women are at least as productive within the household as men, then marriage permits a substitution of the wife's less expensive time for the husband's more expensive time in household activities and a corresponding substitution of the husband's time for the wife's time in the labor market. As Becker puts it, 'Each marriage can be considered a two-person firm with either member being the "entrepreneur" who "hires" the other at ... [a] salary ... and receives residual "profits" ...'[13] Men 'hire' women to bear and rear children and to do housework because they are physically incapable of the first and because their time is too valuable to devote to the second and third. Women 'hire'

11. See Robert T. Michael, 'Education and the Derived Demand for Children,' ibid.
12. See Gary Becker, 'A Theory of Marriage,' ibid.
13. Ibid., p. 310.

men to be breadwinners and to earn the wages which they are generally not able to command. Thus, each marriage partner gains by teaming up with the other.[14] On most traits, other than wage rates, husbands' and wives' activities are seen as complementing, rather than substituting for, one another, and in these cases positive assortive mating is predicted to occur, i.e., likes marrying likes. Finally, if spouses love one another sufficiently – if there is what Becker calls 'full caring' within the marriage – then each individual will take pleasure in the 'consumption' or well-being of the other, effectively doubling the potential gains from the marriage.[15]

The gains from marriage have to be compared with the costs, which include not only such things as wedding ceremonies or license fees, but, more importantly, the costs of searching further for an appropriate mate (or learning more about the present candidate). The net gain, then, will be positively related to a potential spouse's unearned income, to relative *differences* in the earnings (and household productivity) of the two partners, to the desire for children, and to the degree of caring. A general increase (equal for both men and women) in real wages will have uncertain effects, because the cost of time-intensive activities may or may not loom larger in the lives of married than of single individuals.

What kinds of empirically testable implications emerge from this analysis, and where does the evidence support the theory?

Love and caring are not readily observable, and the (ex ante) desire for children is also difficult to measure. Hypotheses about the effects of income on marriage should be a good deal easier to test, although past studies of marriage and divorce have not distinguished earned from un-earned income or the wife's earnings from the husband's.[16] However, as a result of the theoretical developments described here and the availa-

14. However, as I have suggested elsewhere, it seems clear that the monetary gain generally accrues to the wife and all the compensating non-monetary gains – including greater power and authority within the marriage – generally accrue to the husband. See Heather L. Ross and Isabel V. Sawhill, *Time of Transition: The Growth of Families Headed by Women* (Washington, D.C., 1975), ch. 3.

15. Another potential gain would come from 'economies of scale' which occur when two can live together more cheaply than either can live alone. However, economies of scale also exist in nonmarried communal households. Both male and female time are viewed as necessary to married living in Becker's model, since it takes both to produce a child and since love and sexual attraction are more com-mon between members of the opposite sex.

16. For a review of this literature, see Isabel Sawhill, Gerald Peabody, Carol Jones, and Steven Caldwell, *Income Transfers and Family Structure* (Washington, D.C., 1975).

bility of new data, some evidence is beginning to appear which suggests that the level of earned income within the family is not as important a determinant of marital stability as differences in the earnings of husbands and wives and the level of unearned income. It is also fairly well established that husbands and wives tend to be similar with respect to age, race, IQ, education, and religion and that homogeny along most of these dimensions increases marital stability.[17] All these findings are consistent with the predictions of the theory.[18]

One of the most dramatic and consistent findings has been the greater prevalence of marriage and the lower probability of divorce where women's wages or labor-market participation are relatively low. To understand marital behavior, then, we must pursue these topics further and inquire why women's wages are lower than men's. This exercise will reveal a certain circularity of reasoning, which is an important element in understanding and evaluating the new home economics.

(c) Sex roles

As we have seen, in the economic theory of marriage, differences in the wages of men and women determine the gains from marriage along with love, the desire for children, and some other factors. And if we refer back to our earlier discussion of fertility, it will be recalled that one of the more important determinants of the demand for children is the price of time which is largely captured by the mother's wage rate. In both cases, female earnings are a key explanatory variable, but one which is treated as essentially 'given' for the purpose of these analyses. What happens if we now ask why women earn so little relative to men? The answer, which is derived from human capital theory, is that *because* women marry and bear and rear children, they fail to participate in the labor force as continuously or at the same level as men. As a result they fail to acquire valuable on-the-job experience (a type of human capital) and this lowers their market productivity and their earnings.[19] In this

17. See, for example, Larry L. Bumpass and James A. Sweet, 'Differentials in Marital Instability: 1970,' *American Sociological Review*, 37 (December 1972), p. 754.

18. See Sawhill *et al.* (cited above, note 16); Mary Jo Bane, 'Economic Influences on Divorce and Remarriage' (Wellesley College, unpublished paper); Andrew Cherlin, 'Social and Economic Determinants of Marital Separation' (dissertation in progress, University of California. Los Angeles), Thomas Kneiser, 'On the Economics of Marital Instability (unpublished paper, University of North Carolina, Chapel Hill).

19. Jacob Mincer and Solomon Polacheck, 'Family Investments in Human Capital; Earnings of Women.' See below, p. 169.

case, it is marriage, fertility, and the division of labor within the household that are treated as the 'givens' in the analysis. So we have come full circle. We have seen that women earn less than men because of their special role within the family, but that their special role within the family – and indeed the desirability of marriage and children – are importantly related to the economic status of women.

One place, then, to begin an assessment of what economists have contributed to the study of the family is to ask whether they have done anything more than describe the status quo in a society where sex roles are 'givens' – defined by culture, biology, or other factors not specified in the economic model. But this would be only one of many observations which one might wish to make in the broader assessment to which I now turn.

An assessment

The secret to understanding the family, and particularly variations in family life over time and across cultures, may not be within the grasp of the economist, but then it is not clear that other disciplines have done much better. The difference between economists and other social scientists is that the latter are much more modest. Paul Samuelson has called economics 'the queen of the social sciences,'[20] while Gary Becker has argued that 'economic theory may well be on its way to providing a unified framework for *all* behavior involving scarce resources, nonmarket as well as market, nonmonetary as well as monetary, small group as well as competitive.'[21] Certainly his own work has been extraordinarily influential in moving economics in that direction. The question is, Would some other line of inquiry have been more fruitful? To anyone who has been trained as an economist, the charms of economic analysis are nearly irresistible. It is intellectually clean, challenging, and rigorously deductive. In addition, the methodological sophistication of most economists, although not essential to good theory, gives them a competitive edge in empirical work. Most importantly, the economic paradigm does have a certain 'unifying power' because it is highly general and highly abstract. This power, however, has been purchased at the price of obliterating most of the trees from the forest. Many of the variables found in sociological literature, for example, are included in the economist's household-production function in a formal sense, but they are only occasionally illuminated by being

20. Paul A. Samuelson, *Economics*, (9th ed., New York, 1973), p. 6.
21. Gary Becker, 'A Theory of Marriage' (cited above, note 2), p. 299.

viewed in this context. It might be argued that the trees can easily enough be put back into the forest as extensions of the basic analysis, but the danger is that the forest will turn into a Procrustean bed – the variables and observed relationships from empirical work being forced to fit the received microeconomic doctrine.

Second, many of the assumptions underlying the economic theory of the household could be questioned. Are scarce resources the only constraint on people's freedom to choose from among alternative courses of action? As Duesenberry has put it, economics is all about why people make choices, while sociology is all about why they don't have any choices to make.[22] Preferences are shaped by social norms and by individual psychology, and we must look at both. It is not particularly instructive simply to assume that people do what they want to do. Kenneth Boulding's statement that the economist's indifference curve (representing individual preferences) was 'immaculately conceived' gets at the heart of the matter.[23] Finally, the people marching through the economist's household are an enviable group: they are motivated by love and caring and rarely by hate or fear. Very little attention is given to the nature of conflict or to the use of power within the family. In fact, everyone's preferences are swept into one household utility function because different family members are assumed to care enough about one another to weigh each other's preferences in arriving at family decisions. Under these circumstances, it is surprising that divorce ever occurs. Stories of abused children and battered wives together with the statistics that show a large proportion of murders being perpetrated by one family member on another need to be explained. Why is it that marriage sometimes leads to positive and sometimes to negative caring among family members? The economist has no answers.

A third problem with the economist's view of the family is that it is not particularly dynamic. Divorce, for example, is probably best viewed as reflecting a disequilibrium in a relationship, a point at which costs and benefits are out of line and recontracting occurs. In general, many changes in family relationships and behavior occur over the life cycle, and these changes are difficult to explain with existing models.

On the other hand, theory, by its very nature, can never illuminate all reality, so perhaps what has been said thus far should be given less weight

22. James Duesenberry, 'Comment on "An Economic Analysis of Fertility," by Gary S. Becker,' in *Demographic and Economic Change in Developed Countries* (*Universities-National Bureau Conference Series*, 11 (Princeton, 1960)).

23. Kenneth E. Boulding, *Economics as a Science* (New York, 1970), p. 118.

than some additional considerations. There will always be (in the social sciences at least) more than one theory or conceptual framework consistent with observed behavior, and there will always be facts that even the best of theories cannot explain. There are, then, other criteria by which we can judge the usefulness of abstract ideas. One of these criteria is the extent to which the ideas, or the additional questions or empirical work they generate, are ultimately a force for positive change. Has the development of an economic theory of the family provided us with new information or insights that give us greater control over our own destinies and the wisdom to make enlightened individual or collective decisions? Much of science, especially the policy sciences, is devoted to this end. The policy analyst begins with the normatively based question, 'What do we need to know in order to control and thus improve our lives?,' while the more academically oriented social scientist asks, 'What are our lives like?' Although the latter may draw out the policy implications of the analysis, these are a by-product rather than a stimulus to work. Let me, then, try to suggest some of the research issues in the area of family life which the more policy-oriented scientist might wish to address.

First, there are questions about the various consequences of individual decisions which often have implications for both personal and social well-being. In economic theory, it is generally assumed that people have sufficient information about alternatives to make reasonably intelligent choices. In some areas, it is easy to obtain such information either before one acts or through experience, and mistakes are not very costly. For example, if one chooses a restaurant and it serves a poor meal, one need not go there again. On the other hand, if one marries or has a child and either decision turns out badly, the situation is not so easily corrected. Furthermore, one's own reactions to it have serious ramifications for the lives of others. Unfrequented restaurants will, and should, go out of business; unloved spouses and children are not so easily written off. Moreover, the costs of these mistakes are often shifted onto the state, as when a mother and children are deserted and forced to seek public assistance, or when an abused child must be institutionalized or a neglected child grows up to be a delinquent.

The mistakes occur, first, because some alternatives are never considered or because current benefits tend to loom large in people's thinking relative to future costs of which they may be only dimly aware. They also occur because, even where the future costs are known, individuals can conveniently ignore the social, as opposed to the private, consequences of their own behavior and will usually act accordingly. Finally, they occur through imitating the behavior of a previous generation which is often codified in a set of social norms. These may once have served as a reasonably inexpensive surrogate for the accumulation of individual wisdom, but they may be inappropriate in a more modern context. Thus, there are essentially three reasons for poor choices: insufficient knowledge of private consequences, failure to consider social consequences, and the obsolescence of social guidelines and mores in a rapidly changing world. Each of these reasons for what I shall call 'the failure of individual choice' gives rise to a new set of research issues.

The first is to scrutinize the consequences of individual decisions in the areas of marriage, childbearing, and child-rearing. For example, does having a first child at age 17 rather than at age 21 reduce the probability that one or both parents will finish school and embark on a successful career? What is the 'cost' of such early childbearing (if any) in terms of foregone income at, say, age 35? Or, to take another example, does the amount of time one's children spend watching television affect their school achievement or the likelihood that they will enter a life of crime? The number of examples could be greatly expanded, but the point is that decisions are continually being made in the face of great uncertainty about the probable outcomes. Ironically, the objective of research on such questions is to make all human beings more like 'economic man' – that is, possessing sufficient knowledge about the consequences of alternative behavior patterns to be able to act rationally and wisely.

The second need is for more information about *social* consequences. Early childbearing, for example, may have no long-term impact on the well-being of parents, but it may impose costs on the child, on the child's grandparents, or on society generally – all of whom may have to compensate in one way or another for the relative immaturity or lack of financial resources of the parents. Such costs (or benefits) need to be estimated in each instance. Then, if the findings suggest an overwhelming public interest in encouraging or discouraging various types of behavior, the appropriateness of providing incentives or disincentives to promote the public good might be considered. This idea will not be popular because the privacy of family life has traditionally been viewed as inviolable. But the time has come at least to examine the implications of a laissez-faire family policy and to consider where decisions not to intervene may be doing more harm than good. Nor should we be lulled into believing that existing policies fail to influence family behavior, even though the effects they elicit may not have been those foreseen or intended. Some effort has recently been made to analyze these effects. For example, the feasibility of developing 'family impact statements' is being investigated by Sidney Johnson,[24] while the Urban Institute has given some attention to the effects of existing and proposed welfare programs on family composition, and it has studied the impact of liberalized abortion laws on out-of-wedlock fertility and subsequent public dependency.[25] Still another example is the extent to which rigidities in the work schedules of most employees affect the ability of parents to combine job and family life. These rigidities stem, in part, from government policies that require extra compensation for hours worked in excess of 8 per day or 40 per week, making flexible schedules more costly for employers. They are also related to the structure of social security and unemployment compensation laws, which increase the costs of hiring part-time workers.[26]

A third area of research growing out of 'the failure of individual choice' centers on the need to know how the future will differ from the past. In stable societies, the wisdom of prior generations guides the choices of the young and the rules by which they live. In an unstable one, changing attitudes and new technology may quickly make such wisdom obsolete. Perhaps nowhere are public policies and individual decisions as much in danger of being guided by obsolete norms as they are in the area of sex roles. Yet changing sex roles have profound implications for home and family life.[27] These changes need to be understood, so that we can begin to plan for a set of policies that can replace those appropriate only to some earlier time.

This overview of policy-oriented research on the family contrasts quite sharply with the new home economics and suggests that the latter has not yet moved directly into the policy arena. However, as John Maynard Keynes once noted:

... the ideas of economists and political philosophers, both when they are right and when they are wrong, are more powerful than is commonly under-

24. A grant has recently been made to the Institute for Education Leadership at George Washington University for this purpose.

25. Sawhill *et al.* (cited above, note 16); and Kristin A. Moore and Steven B. Caldwell, *Out-of-Wedlock Pregnancy and Childbearing* (Washington, D.C., 1976).

26. Testimony of Isabel V. Sawhill and Ralph E. Smith before the Subcommittee on Employment, Poverty, and Migratory Labor, 8 April, 1976.

27. Implications that I have discussed elsewhere; See Kristin A. Moore and Isabel V. Sawhill, 'Implications of Women's Employment for Home and Family Life,' August 1975.

stood. Indeed the world is ruled by little else. Practical men, who believe themselves to be quite exempt from any intellectual influences, are usually the slaves of some defunct economist. Madmen in authority, who hear voices in the air, are distilling their frenzy from some academic scribbler of a few years back. I am sure that the power of vested interests is vastly exaggerated compared with the gradual encroachment of ideas.[28]

Similarly, the intellectual influence of this new school of home economists is likely to be considerable. Their ideas will find their way into the more practically and empirically oriented work of the policy analyst and eventually into the political domain. Of all the ideas that have emerged from this body of work perhaps the most central and potentially the most influential is the emphasis on the value of human time. In the past, economists believed that the ultimate scarcity was the finiteness of nature. As the population increased relative to land and other natural resources, standards of living would eventually fall to a subsistence level (although the decline might temporarily be offset by the benefits of technology). Thus, economics was labeled 'the dismal science.' The popularity of such books as *The Limits to Growth* and *Small Is Beautiful* attest to the modern-day appeal of this Malthusian view.[29] But T. W. Schultz has now given us a more optimistic future to ponder.[30] The ultimate scarcity in his vision of the future is not natural resources but human time. Investment in human capital (e.g., education, health) keeps occurring so that each generation is more productive, and the value of what they can accomplish in an hour or a year increases.[31] But as the value of human time rises, fertility will fall and standards of living will continuously improve. The process will come to a halt when there is no time left to consume the products of an affluent society and thus no reason to seek further increases in per-capita income. There will, in short, be a sufficiency of goods, given the time people will have to enjoy them. It is an interesting, if not entirely credible, view.

28. John Maynard Keynes, *The General Theory of Employment, Interest and Money* (New York, 1960), p. 383.

29. Donella H. Meadow, Dennis L. Meadows, Jørgen Randers, and William B. Behrens, III, *The Limits to Growth* (New York, 1972); and E. F. Schumacher, *Small is Beautiful* (New York, 1973).

30. T. W. Schultz, 'Fertility and Economics Values,' in *Economics of the Family* (cited above, note 2).

31. These investments continue to be 'profitable' because new knowledge improves the *quality* as well as the *quantity* of education, health care, early childhood experiences, and so forth, thus preventing any diminishing returns (e.g., a declining return to higher education) from setting in over the long run.

For the nearer term, the likely prospect is an increase in the labor-market participation of women as the higher value of their time makes home-based activities, including the rearing of children, more expensive. There will not only be fewer children but also fewer marriages as the wage differential between the sexes narrows. Does this mean that the nuclear family will wither away? I suspect that in a quantitative sense it will diminish in importance, but that the quality of life for children and the relationships between husbands and wives can only improve. In the past, marriage was too often an economic necessity for women, and childbearing either the unintended outcome of sex or an insurance policy against the insecurities of old age. In the future, economics and technology are likely to ensure that the act of having a child and the decision to share life with another adult are freely and consciously chosen for the personal satisfactions they entail rather than as a means to some other end. Personal values and psychological needs met by marriage, children, and family life will be the final arbiters of choice.

6   Class Struggle and the Persistence of the Working-Class Family

Jane Humphries[*]

University of Massachusetts, Amherst

From: *Cambridge Journal of Economics*, Vol. 1, September 1977, pp. 241–58.

Marxist analyses have generally failed to explain the persistence of the working-class family as a central feature of capitalist social formations. The theoretical perspective of Marx and Engels denied that the kinship ties of the working class had any material basis, and led them to postulate the immanent decay of the traditional working-class family.

More recently certain authors have attempted to remedy this deficiency and to explain the continued existence of the working-class family by directing attention to its role in the reproduction of labour-power. They emphasize that capital derives certain benefits from the existence of family structures, in the form of both additional surplus value and of political stability. From this they deduce that the family survives because it is in the interests of capital that it should do so. This is an unbalanced approach, for it assumes the power of capital to be unlimited and fails to recognize that capital's ability to transform existing social institutions, like the family, is circumscribed by the opposition of those concerned. The theme of this paper is that the resilience of the family derives in part from workers' defence of an institution which affects their standard of living, class cohesion and ability to wage the class struggle.

The plan of the paper is as follows. The first section contains a brief critique of the perspective on the working-class family found in the writings of Marx and Engels. Marx is shown to abstract from issues crucial to an understanding of the material base of working-class kinship. The second section deals with attempts in the recent literature to develop a Marxist analysis of the role of domestic labour in the repro-

[*] I would like to thank Sam Bowles, Jean Elshtain and Michelle Naples for their comments on an earlier draft of this paper. The students and faculty of the Cambridge Social and Political Science 'Women in Society' course provided many supportive discussions and interesting suggestions. The journal editors gave much valued editorial help. Special thanks are due to Michael Best.

duction of labour-power, an issue not investigated by Marx himself. Criticism of this literature for its neglect of the possible benefits accruing to labour from kinship networks leads to the alternative hypothesis. The kinds of advantages appropriated by the working class are subsequently analysed in the specific context of early industrial capitalism in nineteenth-century England. The major conclusion is that the anti-family position of most Marxists is ill-informed, in that it ignores the connections between the material conditions of the working class and familial relationships. The theoretical ideas presented suggest a reassessment of the historic role played by the family.

Marx, Engels and the working-class family

The approach inherited from Marx and Engels explains the family as an outgrowth of property relations, and in the last analysis as itself constituting a property relation.[1] As early as 1845 Marx, arguing that the family was in decay, admitted its survival among the bourgeoisie only as a formal property relation, and among the proletariat declared the family already abolished! 'There the concept of the family does not exist at all.'[2] Although elsewhere Marx and Engels document the contemporary deterioration of working-class life, this particular conclusion was independent of observation and was derived *theoretically* from Marx's idea of the family as a property relation. Since the proletariat was by definition propertyless, the working-class family could not act as an instrument for the concentration of wealth. According to Marx there was therefore no material reason for its existence, and he concluded without empirical evidence that it had already ceased to exist. In *The Origin of the Family, Private Property and the State* Engels discusses the property relation more explicitly and argues that 'monogamy', involving fidelity for the woman only, afforded the means through which private property could be individually bequeathed.[3]

This vision of the family suffers from an ahistoric interpretation

1. The connection between property and bourgeois forms of family is made in several places in the writings of Marx and Engels, but most clearly in Engels (1972).
2. Marx and Engels (1976), p. 181; quoted in Draper (1970). This article provides a useful survey illustrating the complex perspectives on 'the woman question' found in the writings of Marx and Engels.
3. Engels (1972). This work should be treated as a collaboration, since it was drawn from Marx's as well as Engels' notes on Lewis Henry Morgan's *Ancient Society*.

of property relations. Private property exists in almost all modes of production, but its form, extent and implications differ fundamentally according to the dominant mode of production. Is it then likely to have identical implications for social relations in all social formations? The equation of the family with monogamy is also invalid. Monogamy is neither a necessary nor a sufficient condition for the existence of the family, which encompasses, but is not necessarily defined by, the man–woman relationship. The family commonly describes a network of social relationships which may be based on genealogical relationships but which also needs to be produced and sustained by social practices reinforcing reciprocal kinship relations. Most important of all, to emphasize the family as a bourgeois phenomenon, as an instrument for the concentration of wealth, diverts attention from the working-class family.[4] The latter then seems historically empty, a superficial reflection of an upper-class institution, without foundation and doomed to wither away under the strains of proletarianization and capitalist expansion.

This invisibility of the proletarian family is reflected in Marx's analyses of the determination of the working-class standard of living, class cohesion and the terms of class struggle. Specifically, the treatment of the reproduction of labour-power in *Capital* abstracts from two issues which are crucial in any investigation of the material base of working-class family life.

First, the working-class family constitutes an arena of production, the inputs being the commodities purchased with family wages, and one of the outputs being the renewed labour-power sold for wages on the market. Neither the material aspects nor the social forms of household productive activity, family relations and family activity are capitalistic. But household activity is welded to the capitalist mode of production through the reproduction cycle of labour-power.

Marx recognized the importance of the latter to capitalism, but did not investigate the process within the working-class household.

The maintenance and reproduction of the working class is, and must ever be, a necessary condition to the reproduction of capital. But the capitalist may safely leave its fulfillment to the labourer's instincts of self-preservation and of propagation (Marx, 1967, p. 572).

The working-class family in Marx is like the firm in neoclassical economics – a black box whose inner workings are simultaneously neglected and mystified.

4. For a similar criticism, see Leacock's introduction to Engels (1972).

Marx abstracts from the problem of domestic labour by dealing with a situation in which all workers are engaged in capitalist production and perform no domestic labour whatsoever. No use-values are produced within the household and the capitalist sector provides everything required to replace the labour-power used up in production. This gives the reproduction cycle of labour-power a distinctive feature in that value is neither created nor destroyed but merely recycled. Wages are used to purchase a subsistence bundle of commodities whose 'consumption' mysteriously leads to the replacement of used-up labour-power. This new labour-power is then exchanged for a new bundle of commodities, which is in its turn consumed, and so the process continues indefinitely, with labour-power being used up in capitalist production and replaced through the act of consumption.[5]

While abstraction from the problem of domestic labour is acceptable within the terms of reference of *Capital*, its analysis is crucial not only for an explanation of the continued existence of the working-class family, but also for an understanding of the relationship between women's oppression and capitalism. Thus this issue has received considerable attention in the recent literature, which is discussed below.

The second issue from which Marx abstracts in *Capital* is the sensitivity of the value of labour-power to the employment structure of the working-class family. He acknowledges this connection:

There are, besides, two other factors that enter into the determination of the value of labour-power. One, the expenses of developing that power, which expenses vary with the mode of production; the other, its natural diversity, the difference betweed the labour-power of men and women, of children and adults. The employment of these different sorts of labour-power, an employment which is, in its turn, made necessary by the mode of production, makes a great difference in the cost of maintaining the family of the labourer, *and in the value of the labour power of the adult male* (Marx, 1967, p. 519, my emphasis).

5. One consequence of Marx's neglect of domestic labour can be seen in his discussion of the value of labour-power. In the case of other commodities he determines their value by considering the way in which they are produced. In the case of labour-power, however, he adopts a quite different approach and begins not with production but with consumption. The wages of the average worker are used to purchase a given bundle of capitalistically produced commodities. To produce this subsistence bundle requires a certain amount of labour and Marx calls this amount the 'value' of labour-power. So the value of labour-power, in contrast with that of other commodities, is defined without any reference to its own conditions of production (and reproduction). Instead it is based on the conditions of production of those commodities for which it is exchanged.

It is not, however, pursued. Instead Marx assumes a situation in which the male worker is supporting a wife and children, none of whom are wage labourers. This entails a redefinition of necessary labour-time, which is no longer the labour-time necessary to secure the conditions of reproduction of the labourer, but has become that necessary to secure the conditions of reproduction of the working-class family. In the circumstances discussed by Marx this also involves a parallel change in the value of labour-power. 'The value of labour-power was determined not only by the labour-time necessary to maintain the individual adult labourer but also by that necessary to maintain his family' (Marx, 1967, p. 395). But Marx also emphasized that the widespread contemporary phenomenon of working women and children, which he saw as a long-run tendency towards universal proletarianization, would spread the value of labour-power over the whole working-class family and so reduce the value of any one member's labour-power. His assignment of a crucial role in this process to machinery introduces an element of technological determinism.

Although Marx does not develop the argument, a reduction in the value of labour-power, caused by universal proletarianization, provided the working-class with a strong motive for defending traditional family structures during certain periods of capitalist development. Within these structures the working class was better equipped to exercise some jurisdiction and control over the supply of labour. The withdrawal of certain members of the working class from the labour market, in conjunction with a campaign for 'a family wage', supported by a bourgeois ideology which emphasized the fragility of women and integrity of the family, could, by raising the real wages of the remaining workers, improve the working-class standard of living. In this case the pursuit of class interest would promote labour's defence of the family, a defence which could have been critical in the latter's resilience. This argument will be further developed below.

The working-class family in the contemporary Marxist literature

Recent Marxist writing has focused almost exclusively on extensions of value theory which abandon Marx's first abstraction and so accommodate the existence of domestic labour.[6] The latter undermines the unique correspondence between the level of wages and the historically given working-class standard of living, which now depends not only on pur-

6. For a recent review of this literature which illustrates the points to be made, see Himmelweit and Mohun (1977).

chased commodities but also on household activity. The abstract labour-time embodied in the goods purchased with the wage can no longer be regarded as equivalent to the labour-time necessary to secure the maintenance and reproduction of the working class, either from day to day or from generation to generation. Wages have to be transformed into the use-values consumed in the home, a transformation embodying not inconsiderable labour-time.

Despite the heterogeneity of the approaches (in terms of the definition of domestic labour, the particular generalization of value theory, etc.), there are significant agreements. It is usually assumed that the payment made by capital to labour is premised on the existence of a certain volume of domestic work and state services. The power of capital is such that in the presence of domestic labour the wage is lower than it would have been had the standard of living of the working class been solely dependent on purchased commodities. In this way surplus labour is extracted from the housewife and ultimately transformed into surplus value.[7]

However, even within the above analyses of the relationship between domestic labour and the capitalist mode of production, there exists at least the *possibility* that domestic labour permits the working class to enjoy a higher standard of living. The ability or inability of capital to capture the benefits of household activity surely depends on the state of the class struggle.

This possibility is ignored in the literature because labour-power is considered only from the viewpoint of capital. To understand the relationship between domestic labour and capitalism, it is necessary to begin not with capital but with the capitalist mode of production, es-

7. This idea is widespread in the literature, but it should be emphasized that the authors listed do not agree on the *precise* characterization of the transfer. See Althusser (1971), Benston (1969), Dalla Costa (1972), Gardiner (1975), Rowbotham (1973). Although John Harrison's approach is distinguished by his adherence to the concept of a domestic mode of production, it too could be included here (see Harrison, 1974). Similarly, although Gardiner, Himmelweit and Mackintosh's work is notable for its rejection of the comparability of domestic labour-time and labour-time expended in capitalist commodity production, they too postulate an ultimate and indirect effect on profits (see Gardiner, Himmelweit and Mackintosh, 1975). Even Seccombe, who argues that the housewife 'creates value embodied in the labour-power sold to capital, equal to the value she consumes in her own up-keep' and therefore that surplus value is unaffected, also believes that the pressure of capital is such that she is 'without leeway in converting the wage into renewed labour-power' (Seccombe, 1974 and 1975).

sential aspects of which are antagonistic relations of production and class struggle. To consider *only* the perspective of capital is to compound Marx's original mistake, and leads, ultimately, to a kind of technological determinism. On the one hand, the fate of the working-class family is seen as dependent upon capital's ability to produce cheap substitutes for domestic labour, and/or its need to augment the industrial reserve army. If this were solely the case the proletarian family would indeed be long gone. This is recognized, in that the quest for surplus value, through its erosion of an institution which is viewed as vital in the reproduction of the forces and relations of production, is seen as endangering the conditions under which surplus value is created and realized – and indeed the existence of the capitalist mode of production itself. Thus the persistence of the working-class family is a product of the contradiction implicit in its relationship with capital.

Capitalism's dependence on the family and inability to generate alternative institutions never seem to be adequately explained. The intrinsic contradiction does not seem to be sufficiently strong to have guaranteed the working-class family two centuries of survival in capitalism. This enigma cannot be resolved without broadening the perspective on the working-class family to encompass a materialist analysis based on a non-individualistic theory of human needs.

Marx's abstraction from the sensitivity of the value of labour-power to the employment structure of the working-class family has received much less attention in the recent literature than his neglect of domestic labour. This is surprising, since it suggests a similar reappraisal of value theory. The remainder of this paper is concerned with the integration of such an approach into the theoretical perspective described above. The intention is to complement the existing literature by beginning from the capitalist mode of production, but nevertheless looking at the proletarian family from its own perspective. From this perspective it is of secondary importance whether or not the working-class family is essential to the existence of the capitalist mode of production. What matters is that the working class has always resisted alternatives to the family, recognizing in the erosion of traditional family structures an infringement of its standard of living and a deterioration in the position from which it engages in class struggle. This position is elaborated below.

The material bases of the working-class family

An investigation of the abstract nature of traditional family forms must preface any discussion of the material benefits derived by the working class from those family forms.

Apart from Seccombe, there is some agreement in the literature discussed above on the proposition that domestic labour produces a surplus. This takes the form of labour by the domestic worker beyond that necessary for her own subsistence. The immediate beneficiaries of this surplus labour are the other members of her family; but ultimately through a reduction in the wages earned by the family, it is captured, wholly or partly, by the capitalist, who by increased exploitation of the family's wage earners adds to surplus value.

New light may be cast on this process by reference to the ambiguity in the concept of necessary labour. Is this the labour necessary to secure the conditions of existence of the individual, or the labour necessary to secure the conditions of existence of the family to which the individual belongs?

This question is emphatically resolved in Marx's writings, which contain a recurring vision of humanity as 'the ensemble of the social relations' (Marx, 1967, p. 7). This definition of human existence has the important implication that labour has to relate to the maintenance and reproduction of the individual *in certain definite relationships with his community*. This in turn requires the existence of some surplus labour over and above necessary labour, as traditionally defined, *in all modes of production*, because the conditions of reproduction of the individual labourer are not equivalent to the conditions of reproduction of the economy as a whole.[8]

It follows that surplus labour does not exist solely to provide for a class of non-labourers. While the latter may or may not exist, non-labouring *individuals* can be found in all social formations, including children, the old, the sick and those who do unproductive but socially necessary work. Social functions in which there is no allowance for these individuals are unlikely to be resilient or evolutionary. Thus in all interesting cases the appropriation of surplus labour necessary to secure the reproduction of the economy and its conditions of existence in the

8. For a careful statement of this position see Hindess and Hirst (1975), pp. 23 ff. The following discussion of the primitive communist mode of production owes much to this exposition.

totality of social relationships has to include an allowance, in some cases minimal, for these individuals.

It is instructive to remember how the surplus is appropriated in primitive communism. Here collective appropriation, manifested in the communal form of property, is achieved by denying any necessary correspondence between labour expended in a particular labour process and the share of the product received in reward. Instead the product is distributed among the producers and others according to established social relations. For redistribution to ensure the reproduction of the conditions of existence of the social formation, it has to involve a network of individuals extending beyond those engaged in the immediate labour. By the simple extension of shares in the community's product to those who have little to contribute in terms of 'the mutual exchange of activities', surplus is appropriated, and the non-labouring individuals given sustenance.

Redistribution requires a communal network defining precise reciprocal relationships between all pairs of individuals. These relationships then correspond to definite mutual responsibilities. The correspondence, when made effective by ideological conviction and commitment, maps out the flows of labour-time socially demanded from each individual and each individual's relative share in the social product. So the community simultaneously possesses and allocates the surplus.

The historical basis for such a network of definite relationships is kinship. Family ties are thus a basic element in this mode of appropriation, as the ideological interpretation of these ties constitutes the basis of the redistribution by which the surplus is appropriated.

These observations may appear unremarkable as long as they are directed towards primitive communism. Their generalization to other modes of production is more controversial. The argument is that family ties, vitalized by ideology, bind together labouring and non-labouring individuals, and secure for the latter a share in the product of the former, not only in primitive communism, but also in more developed modes of production.

According to this perspective the wage earner, while receiving the value of his labour-power, if this includes a contribution to the maintenance and reproduction of his family as well as his own, must receive some surplus over and above the value of his labour-power individualistically defined. Similarly the domestic worker engages in surplus labour if her labour is related to the abstract labour-time involved in her own subsistence. Her surplus labour is embodied in use-values which contribute to the maintenance and reproduction of her family. In total she produces use-values embodying the socially necessary labour-time to secure the conditions of reproduction of herself *in relation to her community*, which is, immediately, her family.

In pre-capitalist societies all members of the family helped to produce the family subsistence, which included the support of non-labouring members and those whose productivity was insufficient to ensure their survival. The surplus labour involved in this support was appropriated by the family members themselves in the process of family production. The analogy with primitive communism is obvious.

The conditions of existence of the capitalist mode of production made this process more difficult and less transparent, as the direct producer was now separated from the means of production and appropriation was in the form of surplus value. Proletarianization of some members of the family became a prerequisite for survival. In capitalism the family can dispose of commodities purchased by the family's wages, and use-values produced by domestic labour. But the extension of shares in their product to family members who are unproductive, or not sufficiently productive to secure their own subsistence, still ensures their survival. Both wage workers and domestic workers participate in this 'mutual exchange of activities'.

Even in primitive societies a division of labour is likely to be associated with the development of hierarchy. Under capitalism the division of labour becomes extremely marked. The domestic labour process is isolated from the dominant mode of production, and its separation from the means of exchange has the effect of rendering it invisible and 'valueless'. This stands in sharp contrast to the 'distinctness' of the wage. Thus, whatever the origins of the sexual division of labour, the resulting differential experience of men and women cumulatively reinforces the differences between the marketability of different skills. The productivity of wage labour rises relative to that of domestic work, encouraging the tendency to hierarchy among specialized workers, which is further stimulated by the personal service characteristic of domestic work. Relations of dominance and subordination relating to age, sex, and division of labour exist within the family in primitive communism, but they take on their contemporary character under capitalism. The dominant capitalist mode of production corrupts the primitively communal family relations, and simultaneously hides the primitively communal core which the family retains in the union of labouring and non-labouring individuals which secures the survival of the latter.

The family as a popular support system during early industrialization

Why is it important to expose the primitively communal aspects of the family? Are they simply grotesque remnants of a less developed mode of production, protected from disintegration by the preservative of capitalist ideology only because they make it easy to shift responsibility from capital to labour?

Non-labouring individuals among the working class have to be supported. If their sustenance is not forthcoming from labour, via the primitive communism of the family, then it must come from capital in the form of state supplied services or individual charitable impulses. The usual argument is that capital generally finds it cheaper, more convenient, and less politically unsettling to maintain the historically given working-class autonomy, allowing a sufficient element of surplus in wages to sustain the non-labouring family members. Doubts have been expressed above about capital's long-run vested interest in the family, but the question of political stability provides a clue to another explanation of the latter's resilience. Presumably this course is less politically disruptive because any concerted attempt by capital to take over these functions, and to reduce the non-labouring members of the working class to more direct and obvious dependence on capital, would encounter resistance. Labour's opposition would arise from the realization (which might be imperfect) that the traditional arrangements can operate to its advantage, in terms of the determination of the standard of living and the development of class consciousness and cohesion, at least in certain periods of capitalist development.

Bureaucratic methods of support for non-labouring members of the working class are usually alienating and demoralizing, and have been chronically so in the past. While the implications of this fact for the interests of capital are not clear, it would seem that it is not in the interests of labour. From a purely materialistic point of view, it may be that the welfare of the non-labouring members of the working class is better secured by informal mechanisms than by more formal institutional channels, especially in periods of parsimonious and primitive capitalism. The humanity of the traditional methods, in comparison with the brutal and degrading alternatives, must have had positive implications for the development of working-class consciousness.

A full investigation of this approach requires detailed research into the changing structure of support for non-labouring members of the working class, and the attitudes of capital and labour to these changes.

However, some support for such a perspective is provided by existing historical evidence.

For the working-class family in nineteenth-century England, kinship ties provided a major source of non-bureaucratic support in conditions of chronic uncertainty. Agriculture had always involved uncertainty associated with the vagaries of climate and crop, as well as seasonally related periods of dependence on stored produce. Now there were also cyclical fluctuations in industrial output and employment, which, in a mode of production where the direct producers are separated from the means of production, impose considerable insecurity. Wage dependence also aggravates other 'critical life situations', i.e., situations in which the individual is unlikely to be competent to cope without help, such as sickness, death, disaster, old age, marriage and childbirth.

The view that industrialization typically disrupts pre-existing wider kinship ties has been called into question by recent discoveries about the pre-industrial family (Laslett, 1965). A comparison of the latter with modern traditional working-class communities, characterized by well developed kinship ties, as described by Willmott and Young (1957), suggests, superficially at least, that in Britain 'modernization' did not reduce kinship cohesion. The same conclusion is reached in Michael Anderson's investigation of kinship structures during the industrial revolution, which documents the retention, indeed the strengthening, of certain kinship connections (Anderson, 1971). The picture is one of a world where despite 'migration, residential mobility, industrial employment and high mortality rates most people managed to maintain relationships with their family, both the current nuclear family and the family as a web of wider kinship ties' (Anderson, 1971, p. 66).

Anderson's study clearly illustrates the material base of such relationships, in the importance of the family to non-labouring members of the working class. The help given to orphans, widows and widowers, and those temporarily unable to secure their own livelihood as a result of one or another of life's critical situations, is amply documented. Rowntree's classic study of the working class in York at the end of the nineteenth century tells a similar story (Rowntree, 1902). Migrants into the new industrial towns provided another group of temporarily non-labouring members of the working class, who sought to turn to their own account kinship ties with established residents.

Anderson emphasizes what he calls the 'instrumentalist' attitude to family ties, i.e., that most of the kinship relations maintained were mutually advantageous within a rather short period of time. Nevertheless, he shows that the working class exhibited a fierce element of dependence on low-cost kinship relations. The kinds of family ties described are exactly what would be expected in the context of primary poverty and universal insecurity, when responsibilities cannot always be met and must always be limited. It is clear that, although blood ties constitute a basis for possible kinship ties, the latter have to be created and maintained by social practices related to a specific material base. The latter, therefore, decisively influences the nature and extent of the kinship system that results.

That kinship ties provided a structure for reciprocal relationships among the early industrial working class, just as they did in primitive society, is reflected in the way they were moulded to meet particular circumstances. For example, in the period when the family structure was integral to the capitalistic labour process, if spinners had no children they would frequently employ younger siblings, or children of neighbours and relatives, who were then taken into the family in a quasi-familial way (Anderson, 1971, p. 117; Smelser, 1959, p. 191). Similarly in mining communities, when it was common for colliers to employ their own children as 'hurriers', if an individual's family structure could not provide the labour-power needed, parish children would be employed as apprentices. It was not unusual for these children to be well treated by the standard of the times and to have obvious respect and affection for their quasi-family (Parliamentary Papers, 1842, pp. 120 and 138).

It was also common, because of housing shortages in the early industrial towns and the migration into these centres, for individuals to board with families with whom they had only distant kin connections or no such ties at all (Foster, 1974, p. 96; McGeown, 1967, p. 20; Rowntree, 1902, p. 391). Frequently these relationships would then assume fictive kin status. The lodger who lived in such close proximity was symbolically addressed as 'brother' and 'uncle'. Such quasi-kin ties ensured the development of community in the early industrial towns, binding together unrelated adults and thereby infusing such communities with conceptions of obligation which had flowed initially from family ties rooted in blood and marriage. The strength of neighbourhood ties among the nineteenth-century working class and their role in reciprocal assistance has been remarked upon by many contemporary commentators (Booth, 1902, p. 51; Rowntree, 1902, p. 43) and recent social historians (Stedman Jones, 1971, p. 87), as well as illustrated in surviving working-class autobiographies (Burnett, 1974, p. 62).

In areas where women were habitually wage workers the proportion of old women on relief was lower than elsewhere, which suggests that they were able to support themselves by childminding, laundering and so on. Anderson quotes the example of one old lady of seventy who lived with a family to which she was not related, but which supported her because she was able to contribute within their family configuration. Her explanation vividly illustrates the extension of the primitive communism of the family to include such quasi-kin, and thus the extension of mutual obligation to unrelated adults in the community. 'They cannot afford to pay me nought but aw fare as they fare'n, and they dunnot want to part wi' me' (Anderson, 1971, p. 143).

The official position in the early nineteenth century promoted family integrity and autonomy with respect to the care of the young, the old and the destitute. Legally, families were still governed by the '43 Elizabeth' which enjoined them to care for their dependents (Checkland and Checkland, 1974). But in an era of wage dependence, increased longevity and rising labour mobility, the traditional responsibilities could not be enforced. Industrialization and the concomitant changes produced a pressing need for the state to provide safety nets. At first the old Poor Law was stretched accommodatingly, but eventually, in 1834, new institutions had to be created. Capital's provision for the non-labouring members of the working class was neither magnanimous nor genial, and significantly involved a bitterly resented attack on the family (Hart, 1965, p. 208; Hobsbawm, 1964, p. 188); nevertheless it did exist.

The harshness of the 1834 Poor Law was an attempt to discourage recourse to the official channels and to make the poor 'self-sufficient'. It has been suggested above that individuals can never be 'self-sufficient'. What was promoted was 'class-sufficiency' via mutually reciprocal kinship ties. In the context of primary poverty the family could not always bear the weight of these ties. As a result they were rationalized as described above, and family members were put on relief even under conditions of 'less eligibility'.[9] But the Poor Law was a refuge of last

9. This phrase was used to describe the requirement that life in the workhouse be less pleasant than the life of the poorest independent worker. Only if this 'principle' was maintained could the workhouse provide 'a test', in the sense of screening out all those capable of earning their own living. The intention was to provide a workhouse so uncomfortable as to deter from entrance anybody who could possibly earn a bare living. It might be thought that the application of such a test is only relevant to the able-bodied poor, whereas the majority of people relieved were unable to work. But 'less eligibility' was extended to prescribe more miserable lives for aged paupers, sick paupers and orphans, lest the incentive to provide for old age,

resort, to be submitted to only in times of dire distress. This can be seen from the rise in the numbers of old and infirm on relief in the crisis years 1839–46, as families which had shouldered their responsibilities bravely enough in better times found that they could no longer cope. Because of the deprivation and degradation of the workhouse, bureaucratic forms of assistance were hated and feared by the working class, whose *class* resistance was thereby enhanced (Hanson, 1975, p. 245; Smelser, 1959; Thompson, 1963). Kinship ties were strengthened because they provided the only framework controllable by the working class, within which reciprocation could occur that was sufficiently defined to provide an adequate guarantee of assistance in crisis situations.

According to this perspective the endurance of the family reflects a struggle by the working class for popular ways of meeting the needs of non-labouring comrades within a capitalist environment. Such a struggle could not but promote social obligation, i.e., concern among workers for non-kin. Social obligation is not of course identical with class consciousness; but it is a necessary condition for the development of such consciousness.

Thus, the family, as an institution, has been shaped by the aspiration of people for personalized non-market methods of distribution and social interaction. To ignore the role that these aspirations and beliefs have played in guiding human conduct and in shaping the class struggle is to fail to understand the proletarian family and its persistence.

The value of labour-power and the family labour supply

A second important reason for the working-class preference for traditional family forms relates to their implications for the control of the labour supply. Marx's prediction of the proletarianization of all members of the working-class family was not vindicated by nineteenth-century British history. Child labour was regulated and the age of entry into the labour force rose steadily. Incomplete data suggest that married women's participation rates fell from the high levels reached in the early phase of industrialization and the Napoleonic wars and thereafter slowly recovered (Hewitt, 1958). Female participation rates remained remarkably constant throughout the late nineteenth century, at around

---

infirmity or dependent childhood be diminished. The 'principle' illustrates the obsession of the Commissioners with the able-bodied poor, and their intention of setting up institutions conducive to the unfettered workings of a free labour market. See Webb and Webb (1929).

26% of the female population. Mass proletarianization of married women never occurred (Best, 1971, p. 100; Burnett, 1974, p. 49).

Most explanations of this phenomenon have emphasized the changing needs of expansionary capitalism in terms of the quality and quantity of labour, its inability to provide substitutes for the use-values produced in the home, and the association between the maintenance of the family structure and political stability. Again the stress is on capital's restraint in its attack on the family. An alternative perspective is presented here in that the family is seen to be defended by the working class, which recognizes that it can act as an obstacle to the cheapening of labour-power.

Compare two extreme situations:

(1) There is a single wage earner who receives the historic subsistence *family* wage. The activities of the other household members remain outside the jurisdiction of the capitalist and can be directed to the production of use-values, raising the family's standard of living.
(2) All the able-bodied family members are proletarianized, including the children, and the family wage is received piecemeal.

In both cases the non-labouring family members are supported out of the family product, distribution taking place according to non-market criteria. Under the assumption that the *same* family wage is received in both situations, the standard of living of the working class must be higher in (1) and surplus value creation (per family) greater in (2).

How valid is the assumption that the same family wage would be received in both situations? First it can be argued that the wage bargain in (1) would take into account the existence of domestic labour, and so be premised on a certain level of use-value production. The value of labour, in terms of the labour-time embodied in commodities purchased by the wage, could then be reduced below family subsistence by the amount of labour-time embodied in use-value production. Capital would gain control of the level and intensity of domestic production and indirectly drain value out of the working-class household.

While this appears to be a valid *possibility* – certainly in periods of falling real wages the working-class housewife tries to defend her family's standard of living by increasing her own efforts – it is not the *only* possibility. The extent to which capital can take advantage of domestic labour in this way surely depends on the success of the working-class defence of its standard of living, as given by the level of wages *and* the domestic production of use-values.

Secondly, is it probable that the total family wage would be unrelated to the number of family wage earners? Clearly, the more members of the family undertake wage employment the lower would be the value of any one member's labour-power; but the total family wage would be larger unless the fall in the value of labour-power was so great as to offset the incremental income earned by the additional wage workers. What do nineteenth-century labour market conditions indicate in this respect? Three observations may be considered relevant.

First, during the Ten Hours Campaign it was widely believed among the working class that limitations on hours would not permanently reduce wages, but that ultimately the same earnings would be realized in ten hours as had previously required twelve hours of work (Parliamentary Papers, 1833). Generalization from the labour demand conditions implicit in this argument suggests that widespread proletarianization of married women and children, while raising the number of hours worked by each family, could not in the long run expand family earnings.

Secondly, there is evidence that in certain trades over-stocked labour markets caused wages to be reduced to family subsistence level. Under these conditions proletarianization of additional family members was futile.

The same pressure that leads to the employment of the children presently leads in a slack time to the acceptance of yet lower pay for the sake of securing work . . . Thus, by and by, mother and children come to receive no more than did the mother working alone. The employer . . . has in fact obtained the labour of the children without extra payment (Black, 1907, p. 148).

Thirdly, it must be clear that it is invalid to compare one working-class family with a single breadwinner with another family with multiple wage earners. In a situation where most families contained several wage workers, competition would have driven down the price of labour-power and each worker would receive only a fraction of the family subsistence. With labour-power so cheapened, a family with only one earner would be in an unfortunate position indeed. Poverty would force other family members into wage labour, the value of labour-power would sink even lower, and the vicious circle would be complete (Black, 1907; Mayhew, 1861, pp. 301–4).

The relevant comparison is between two general social settings, each characterized by a particular family employment structure, and an associated wage level. This approach exposes the material interest of the working class in the maintenance of a family structure and explicates the motivation for class struggle on this issue, since it seems at least possible that a retreat of certain family members from the labour force, in conjunction with an organized attempt to secure a 'family wage', would raise the standard of living of the working class. This view was expressed by a labourer in the *Trades Newspaper* of 16 October 1825.

Wages can never sink below the sum necessary to rear up the number of labourers the capitalists want. The weaver, his wife and children all labour to obtain this sum; the blacksmith and the carpenter obtain it by their single exertions . . . The labouring men of this country . . . should return to the good old plan of subsisting their wives and children on the wages of their *own* labour, and they should demand wages high enough for this purpose . . . By doing this, the capitalist will be obliged to give the same wages to men alone which they now give to men, women and children . . . I recommend my fellow labourers, in preference to every other means of limiting the number of those who work for wages, to prevent their wives and children from competing with them in the market, and beating down the price of labour (Hollis, 1973, pp. 193–4).

Working-class movements in the nineteenth century seem to be characterized by elements of this strategy, the demand for a family wage being only one example. Notions of endangered family integrity, the 'unsexing' of working-class men and women, and the adverse effects likely to become apparent in future generations of workers, were also used in the battle for factory legislation on conditions and hours; in the latter case to such an extent that Hutchins and Harrison conclude: 'the battle for the limitation of the hours of adults in general was fought from behind the women's petticoats' (Hutchins and Harrison, 1903, p. 186).

How can this working-class use of sexist ideology be judged in retrospect? It has been argued that the male-dominated trade unions selfishly sought to impede the employment of women, with whom they felt competitive in the labour market and whom they preferred to retain as dependent domestic workers. Undoubtedly the regulation of hours and occupations caused acute misery in individual cases, when women lost jobs that were vital to their survival. More important still, the opportunistic use of sexist ideology by labour must have reinforced sexism among workers and employers and so in the long run made the attainment of economic equality more difficult.

But to condemn this strategy out of hand is to be insensitive to the material conditions of nineteenth-century labour. One of the few sources of working-class control over the supply of labour lay in the levers that could be brought to bear on the labour supplied by married women. This was also one of the few tactics that could be accompanied by a supportive mobilization of bourgeois ideology. Both these points are apparent in the following contemporary description of the trade union perspective on female wage labour:

it [the trade union perspective] recognizes the danger of intolerable strain both to women themselves and to their actual and possible offspring, and it sees in the frantic efforts of the unskilled, unorganized woman to work for impossible hours, to undersell her competitors and lower both her and their standard of life, an 'offence', which, however pardonable in an individual, must in a member of society, by some means, be controlled or prevented for the general good. We cannot discuss these matters on purely individualistic lines . . . The one worker, whether man or woman, who works excessive hours sets the pace, compels others to work long hours also, and inevitably lowers the rate of pay for all (Hutchins and Harrison, 1903, p. 185).

The tragedy is that action could not be controlled on a class basis, but had to be regulated *systematically* on the basis of *female* labour, and theoretically of *married* female labour, so reinforcing sex-based relations of dominance and subordination.

Nevertheless, the strategy was not entirely disadvantageous to working women. To think so is again to misunderstand the material conditions of working-class experience. First, the argument that male workers gained from regulation at the expense of 'protected' workers (female) is not easily substantiated. Hutchins and Harrison argue that, as men were then earning higher wages and working shorter hours, they had little to gain from 'supplanting' women. Gains were mainly at the lower end of the labour hierarchy, where women themselves were concentrated. There does not seem to have been a trend to replace protected workers by unprotected workers.

Secondly, women workers as well as being female are also members of the working class. Class action which tries to raise the price of labour usually had beneficial effects, if not directly on women's wages, then indirectly through increased *family* wages. This exposes the fallacy in the argument that women workers might be subject to disabilities in the guise of protective legislation. Such misunderstanding results from conflating the social and customary disabilities encountered by women in the professions with the constraints placed by law on women's work in industry. The two are very different. Their confusion illustrates the inability of protagonists of such views to understand the material conditions of the working class, especially as manifested in the industrial labour process.

The mistake that some of them [i.e. liberal women's groups making such charges] have made is in transferring their own grievances to a class whose troubles are little known and less understood . . . in supposing that while they pined to spend themselves in some intolerable toil of thought Mary Brown or Jane Smith should also pine to spend herself in fourteen hours a day washing or tailoring (Hutchins and Harrison, 1903, p. 184).

Hutchins and Harrison's verdict on this issue may be considered relevant.

The Trade Unions, whatever the faults in their economics or the lacunae in their reasoning, have never fallen into the blank and unfruitful individualism that has blighted the women's movement in the middle class; and the working woman we would submit has a far better chance to work out her economic salvation through solidarity and co-operation with her own class than by adopting the tactics and submitting to the tutelage of middle or upper class organizations (Hutchins and Harrison, 1903, p. 198).

Class cohesion and class consciousness

All too frequently in the modern literature the family is seen as engendering false consciousness, promoting capitalist ideology, undermining class cohesion and threatening the class struggle. In short, it stands charged with being a bourgeois institution acting in collaboration with capital against the real interests of the working class.[10] But superficial plausibility and anecdotal substantiation are no substitutes for thoroughgoing investigation. Many of the scenarios depicted in this literature seem coloured by preconceived ideas of working-class existence. The prosecution's case can be confronted with equally plausible counter-arguments and comparable (if fragmentary) evidence.

Some connections have already been suggested between the existence of family ties and the growth of community and social obligation, important events in the development of class consciousness. For example, the existence of fictive kin involved an extension of family ties

10. The orthodox view is that the family promotes values and associated behaviour compatible with the capitalist mode of production: '. . . the nature of the relation is such that the performance of the respective sex-roles is seen as signs of love by the rest of the family. A good and loving husband is also a good factory worker, one who gets a large pay packet; a good and loving wife is one who spends much time on domestic work of one sort or another' (Gardiner, Himmelweit and MacKintosh, 1975, p. 6).

outwards into the community. In addition the struggles around the family, such as the resistance to 'in house relief' and the battle for a family wage, united families in *class* endeavours.

The bourgeoisie made repressive use of its provision for the working class. Poor relief was withheld during lockouts (Clements, 1961, p. 102), and denied to those who subscribed to the Chartist Fund (Hollis, 1973, p. 211). Truculent workers who lived in 'tied' cottages were evicted, and in general employers 'were suspected of the manipulation of charitable activity as yet another weapon in their disciplinary armour' (Benson, 1975, p. 402). Under these circumstances family and community-based assistance, both formal and informal, played a vital role in maintaining working-class integrity and autonomy.

Heroic family loyalties undoubtedly sustained many individuals through the turbulent period of industrialization, and engendered a feeling of comradeship in oppression. This must have been important. Class solidarity does not materialize out of a sudden recognition by isolated individuals that their situation is shared and that though weak individually they have collective power. It develops slowly over time, as a result of real-life experiences. Rather than promoting individualism, the mutual dependence of the family could well point up class community and class interest.[11]

Kinship ties are known to have been important instruments ensuring community solidarity in the eighteenth-century resistance to unpopular authorities, and legislation which redefined traditional rights in the light of the new overwhelming value placed upon property. Douglas Hay's study of poachers on Cannock Chase acknowledges that the 'virtually complete' solidarity against the keepers arose partly from 'bonds of blood and marriage, the tangled skein of alliances in small communities where degrees of kinship merged imperceptibly into those of friendship and acquaintance' (Hay, 1975, p. 200). Similarly the villagers of Hoylake on the Wirral, said to be unanimously engaged in wrecking and coastal plunder, were described as intermarried and 'nearly all related to each other' (Rule, 1975, p. 173). The reporter presumably believed this to be important for an understanding of their unity.

In contrast with the idea that the family socializes its members into

11. The author believes that there is a class difference in the relationship between the family and the promotion of individualism or class solidarity. The middle-class family undoubtedly does promote individualism. The argument pursued in the text is not true of the working-class family.

acceptance of the dominant values stands the *possibility* that the family can, and sometimes does, promote 'deviant' ideas and behaviour. Evidence supporting this perspective is easy to find; witness the maternal indoctrination additive specific to the first all-female offshoot of union societies, which listed among its objectives 'to instill into the minds of our children a deep and rooted hatred of our corrupt and tyrannical rulers' (Marlow, 1971, p. 79).

Such unconventional idealism could be preserved within the family in periods of oppression and perpetuated intergenerationally. Joseph Arch is a good example of a working-class leader influenced not only by the experiences and reactions of his father, but also by the attitudes of his mother (Arch, 1898). John Foster's analysis of Oldham's working-class leadership documents other connections. The two Cleggs listed by Foster (1974, p. 151), were cousins, John Earnshaw, active in the 1816–19 period had a nephew, John Lees, who was killed at Peterloo. Foster's summary assigns to the family a crucial role in the growth and development of working-class consciousness and struggle.

Though there were always tactical disagreements and a constant stream of new recruits, what strikes one most from the descriptive evidence is the degree to which members saw themselves as part of a continuing tradition. Radical allegiances tended to be inherited within families and associated with particular neighbourhoods. The Swires, Earnshaws and Warwicks were all families that produced at least two generations of radicals (p. 138).

Similarly, family responsibilities did not always discipline working men, but sometimes promoted their radicalization. The experience of watching the suffering and oppression of their families could instigate class action. As Richard Marsden, a hand-loom weaver from Preston, put it: 'There is something in the effects of hunger and the sight of your family suffering from it which none can judge of but those who have felt it. The equilibrium of temper and judgement is deranged' (Hollis, 1973, p. 227). Richard Pillings, another Chartist, at his trial in 1843 described how the sufferings of his family and his desire to keep them from the workhouse provided his action (Hollis, 1973, p. 293).

The working-class standard of living depends not only on the level of wages, the traditional trade union concern, but also on the cost of living, which is the primary concern of the administrator of the wage – the housewife. Attacks on the working-class situation through price increases have historically produced concerted action.

E. P. Thompson states that in the early nineteenth century the cost of bread was the most sensitive indicator of popular discontent and that, consumer consciousness was positively related to the evolution of class consciousness (Thompson, 1963). The bread riot predates the strike as an expression of workers' community of interest, and has remained in various more modern guises an important weapon in labour's arsenal down to the present day. The prominence of working-class women in these class struggles of the marketplace derives precisely from their family roles as the executors of consumption.

So, although women undoubtedly felt divided loyalties with respect to class action that incidentally imposed deprivation on their families,[12] their concern for the latter could also promote a class response, the effects of which were not inconsequential. Recent historical research has documented working women's early and widespread involvement in the class struggle (Thompson, 1963; Rowbotham, 1974). The charge that the nineteenth-century working-class mother was apathetic about, if not opposed to, class action depends crucially on the definition of the latter, and the particular historical circumstances considered. It certainly remains to be demonstrated. Similarly the case against the working-class family is not proven.

Conclusion

An analysis of the role of the family in the maintenance and reproduction of labour-power is inadequate to explain the survival of working-class kinship structures under capitalism. Alternative private or state childrearing agencies, benefiting from economies of scale, could be envisaged which would meet capital's need for a passive labour force. The centralization of support involved in the substitution of state for family services would certainly give capital greater control over the administration of resources, which could then be streamlined and modified in the interests of capitalist production.

Capitalism has a history of market relations inexorably replacing social relations, as capitalist expansion leads to the rationalization of production according to the dictates of production for profit. The working-class family has escaped the disciplinary power of the market only because it has resisted that power. A comprehensive explanation

12. Olwen Hufton's fascinating article (Hufton, 1971) illustrates the cyclical operation of these divided loyalties during the course of the French Revolution. An up-to-date example of the same phenomenon, the infamous 'wives revolt' at the Cowley complex of British Leyland in 1974, is described in Coulson, Magas and Wainwright (1975), p. 63.

of labour's opposition to a total universalization of markets requires a theoretical framework based on a non-material as well as a material theory of human needs. The purpose of this paper was more modest: it was to demonstrate that in a capitalist environment the working class has certain well-defined reasons for defending the family which have been ignored in the literature. The preservation of non-market relations within the family emerges as neither an obsolete remnant of a less developed mode of production, nor a sociological anomaly, but a result of labour's struggle.

Family life has not been idealized here; there has been recognition that patterns of dominance relating to age, sex and the division of labour existed long before capitalism, and remain characteristic of family relations today. Their existence, however, should not blind observers to the material benefits that the family imparts to the working class in its struggle for a better life.

References

ALTHUSSER, L., *Lenin and Philosophy*, Monthly Review Press, 1971.
ANDERSON, M., *Family Structure in Nineteenth Century Lancashire*, CUP, 1971.
ARCH, J., *The Life of Joseph Arch by Himself*, Hutchinson, 1898.
BENSON, J., 'English coal miners' trade union accident funds, 1850–1900', *Economic History Review*, Vol. XXVIII, No. 3, 1975.
BENSTON, M., 'The political economy of women's liberation', *Monthly Review*, September 1969.
BEST, G., *Mid-Victorian Britain, 1857–1875*, Weidenfeld and Nicolson, 1971.
BLACK, C., *Sweated Industry and the Minimum Wage*, Duckworth, 1907.
BOOTH, C., *Life and Labour of the People in London*, Macmillan, 1902.
BURNETT, J., ed., *Useful Toil: Autobiographies of Working People from the 1820's to the 1920's*, Allen Lane, 1974.
CHECKLAND, S. G., and CHECKLAND, E. O. A., eds., *The Poor Law of 1834*, Penguin, 1974.
CLEMENTS, R. V., 'British trade unions and popular political economy, 1850–1875', *Economic History Review*, Vol. XIV, No. 1, 1961.
COULSON, M., MAGAS, B., and WAINWRIGHT, H., 'The housewife and her labour under capitalism', *New Left Review*, No. 89, 1975.
DALLA COSTA, M., 'Women and the subversion of the community', in *The Power of Women and the Subversion of the Community*, Falling Wall Press, 1972.
DRAKE, B., *Women in Trade Unions*, Special Edition for the Labour Movement, Trade Union Series No. 6, 1921.
DRAPER, H., 'Marx and Engels on women's liberation', *International Socialism*, July–August 1970.
ENGELS, F., *The Origin of the Family, Private Property and the State*, International Publishers, New York, 1972.

FOSTER, J., *Class Struggle and the Industrial Revolution: Early Capitalism in Three English Towns*, Weidenfeld and Nicolson, 1974.

GARDINER, J., 'Women's domestic labour', *New Left Review*, No. 89, 1975.

GARDINER, J., HIMMELWEIT, S., and MACKINTOSH, M., 'Women's domestic labour, *Bulletin of the Conference of Socialist Economists*, Vol. IV, No. 2, 1975 (reprinted in *On the Political Economy of Women*, CSE Pamphlet No. 2, Stage One, 1976).

HANSON, C. G., 'Craft unions, welfare benefits, and the case for trade union law reform, 1867–75', *Economic History Review*, Vol. 28, No. 2, 1975.

HARRISON, J., 'Political economy of housework', *Bulletin of the Conference of Socialist Economists*, Spring, 1974.

HART, J., 'Nineteenth century social reform: a Tory interpretation of history', *Past and Present, A Journal of Historical Studies*, No. 31, 1965.

HAY, D., 'Poaching and the game laws on Cannock Chase', in *Albion's Fatal Tree: Crime and Society in Eighteenth Century England*, D. Hay, P. Linebaugh, J. G. Rule, E. P. Thompson and C. Winslow, eds., Pantheon Books, 1975.

HEWITT, M., *Wives and Mothers in Victorian Industry*, Rockliff, 1958.

HIMMELWEIT, S., and MOHUN, S., 'Domestic labour and capital', *Cambridge Journal of Economics*, Vol. 1, No. 1, 1977.

HINDESS, B., and HIRST, P. W., *Precapitalist Modes of Production*, Routledge and Kegan Paul, 1975.

HOBSBAWM, E. J., *Labouring Men: Studies in the History of Labour*, Weidenfeld and Nicolson, 1964.

HOLLIS, P., ed., *Class and Conflict in Nineteenth Century England: 1815–1850*, Routledge and Kegan Paul, 1973.

HUFTON, O., 'Women in revolution, 1789–1796', *Past and Present*, No. 53, 1971.

HUTCHINS, B. L., and HARRISON, A., *A History of Factory Legislation*, P. S. King and Son, 1903.

LASLETT, P., *The World We Have Lost*, Charles Scribners' Sons, 1965.

MARLOW, J., *The Peterloo Massacre*, Panther Books, 1971.

MARX, K., *Capital*, Vol. I, International Publishers, New York, 1967.

MARX, K., and ENGELS, F., *Collected Works*, Vol. 5, Lawrence and Wishart, 1976.

MAYHEW, H., *London Labour and the London Poor*, Griffin, Bohn and Company, 1861.

McGEOWN, P., *Heat the Furnace Seven Times More*, Hutchinson, 1967.

PARLIAMENTARY PAPERS, Vol. XX. Reports from Commissioners, Factories Inquiry Commission, His Majesty's Stationery Office, 1833.

PARLIAMENTARY PAPERS, Vol. XVII. Reports from Commissioners, Children's Employment (Mines), William Clowes and Sons, for Her Majesty's Stationery Office, 1842.

ROWBOTHAM, S., *Women's Consciousness, Man's World*, Penguin, 1973.

ROWBOTHAM, S., *Women, Resistance and Revolution*, Vintage Books, New York, 1974.

ROWNTREE, B. S., *Poverty, A Study of Town Life*, Macmillan, 1902.

RULE, J. G., 'Wrecking and coastal plunder', in *Albion's Fatal Tree: Crime and Society in Eighteenth Century England*, D. Hay, P. Linebaugh, J. G. Rule, E. P. Thompson and C. Winslow, eds., Pantheon Books, 1975.

SECCOMBE, W., 'The housewife and her labour under capitalism', *New Left Review*, No. 83, 1974.

SECCOMBE, W., 'Domestic labour – reply to critics', *New Left Review*, No. 94, 1975.

SMELSER, N. J., *Social Change in the Industrial Revolution: An Application of Theory to the British Cotton Industry*, University of Chicago Press, 1959.

STEDMAN JONES, G., *Outcast London: A Study in the Relationship between Classes in Victorian Society*, Penguin, 1971.

THOMPSON, E. P., *The Making of the English Working Class*, Vintage Books, New York, 1963.

WEBB, S., and WEBB, B., *English Poor Law History, Part II: The Last Hundred Years*, Private Subscription Edition, 1929.

WILLMOTT, P., and YOUNG, M., *Family and Kinship in East London*, Routledge and Kegan Paul, 1957.

Part Two
Job Segregation by Sex
and Women's Lower Pay

7 Family Investments in Human Capital: Earnings of Women*

Jacob Mincer
Columbia University and National Bureau of Economic Research

Solomon Polachek
University of North Carolina

From: *Journal of Political Economy*, Vol. 82, No. 2, Part 2, March–April 1974, pp. S76–S108.

1. Introduction

It has long been recognized that consumption behavior represents mainly joint household or family decisions rather than separate decisions of family members. Accordingly, the observational units in consumption surveys are 'consumer units,' that is, households in which income is largely pooled and consumption largely shared.

More recent is the recognition that an individual's use of time, and particularly the allocation of time between market and nonmarket activities, is also best understood within the context of the family as a matter of interdependence with needs, activities, and characteristics of other family members. More generally, the family is viewed as an economic unit which shares consumption and allocates production at home and in the market as well as the investments in physical and human capital of its members. In this view, the behavior of the family unit implies a division of labor within it. Broadly speaking, this division of labor or 'differentiation of roles' emerges because the attempts to promote family life are necessarily constrained by complementarity and substitution relations in the household production process and by comparative advantages due to differential skills and earning powers with which family members are endowed.

Though the levels and distribution of these endowments can be taken

*Research here reported is part of a continuing study of the distribution of income, conducted by the National Bureau of Economic Research and funded by the National Science Foundation and the Office of Economic Opportunity. This report has not undergone the usual NBER review. We are grateful to Otis Dudley Duncan, James Heckman, Melvin Reder, T. W. Schultz, and Robert Willis for useful comments, and to George Borjas for skillful research assistance.

as given in the short run, this is not true in a more complete perspective. Even if each individual's endowment were genetically determined, purposive marital selection would make its distribution in the family endogenous, along the lines suggested by Becker in this volume. Of course, individual endowments are not merely genetic; they can be augmented by processes of investment in human capital and reduced by depreciation. Indeed, a major function of the family as a social institution is the building of human capital of children – a lengthy 'gestation' process made even longer by growing demands of technology.

Optimal investment in human capital of any family member requires attention not only to the human and financial capacities in the family but also to the prospective utilization of the capital which is being accumulated. Expectations of future family and market activities of individuals are, therefore, important determinants of levels and forms of investment in human capital. Thus, family investments and time allocation are linked: while the current distribution of human capital influences the current allocation of time within the family, the prospective allocation of time influences current investments in human capital.

That the differential allocation of time and of investments in human capital is generally sex linked and subject to technological and cultural changes is a matter of fact which is outside the scope of our analysis. Given the sex linkage, we focus on the relation within the family between time allocation and investments in human capital which give rise to the observed market earnings of women. Whether these earnings, or the investments underlying them, are also influenced or reinforced by discriminatory attitudes of employers and fellow workers toward women in the labor market is a question we do not explore directly, though we briefly analyze the male-female wage differential. Our major purposes are to ascertain and to estimate the effects of human-capital accumulation on market earnings and wage rates of women, to infer the magnitudes and course of such investments over the life histories of women, and to interpret these histories in the context of past expectations and of current and prospective family life.

The data we study, the 1967 National Longitudinal Survey of Work Experience (NLS), afford a heretofore unavailable opportunity to relate family and work histories of women to their current market earning power. Accumulation of human capital is a lifetime process. In the post-school stage of the life cycle much of the continued accumulation of earning power takes place on the job. Where past work experience of men can be measured without much error in numbers of years elapsed since leaving school, such a measure of 'potential work experience' is clearly inadequate for members of the labor force among whom the length and continuity of work experience varies a great deal. Direct information on work histories of women is, therefore, a basic requirement for the analysis of their earnings. To our knowledge, the NLS is the only data set which provides this information, albeit on a retrospective basis. Eventually, the NLS panel surveys will provide the information on a current basis, showing developments as they unfold.[1]

2. The Human-Capital Earnings Function

To the extent that earnings in the labor market are a function of the human-capital stock accumulated by individuals, a sequence of positive net investments gives rise to growing earning power over the life cycle. When net investment is negative, that is, when market skills are eroded by depreciation, earning power declines. This relation between the sequence of capital accumulation and the resulting growth in earnings has been formalized in the 'human-capital earnings function.' A simple specification of this function fits the life cycle 'earnings profile' of men rather well. The approach to distribution of earnings among male workers (in the United States and elsewhere) as a distribution of individual earnings profiles appears to be promising.[2]

For the purpose of this paper, a brief development of the earnings function may suffice:

Let C_{t-1} be the dollar amount of net investment in period $t - 1$, while (gross) earnings in that period, before the investment expenditures are subtracted, are E_{t-1}. Let r be the average rate of return to the individual's human-capital investment, and assume that r is the same in each period. Then

$$E_t = E_{t-1} + rC_{t-1}. \tag{1}$$

1. For a description of the NLS survey of women's work histories, see Parnes, Shea, Spitz, and Zeller (1970). For an analysis of earnings of men, using 'potential' work-experience measures, see Mincer (1974). Though less appropriate, the same proxy variable was used in several recent studies of female earnings. Direct information from the NLS survey was first used by Suter and Miller (1971). The human-capital approach was first applied to these data by Polachek in his Columbia Ph.D. thesis, 'Work Experience and the Difference between Male and Female Wages' (1973). This paper reports a fuller development of the analysis in that thesis.

2. See, for instance, Rahm (1971), Chiswick and Mincer (1972), Chiswick (1973), Mincer (1974), and a series of unpublished research papers by George E. Johnson and Frank P. Stafford on earnings of Ph.D.s in various fields.

Let $k_t = C_t/E_t$, the ratio of investment expenditures to gross earnings, which may be viewed as investment in time-equivalent units. Then

$$E_t = E_{t-1}(1 + rk_{t-1}). \tag{2}$$

By recursion $E_t = E_0(1 + rk_0)(1 + rk_1) \ldots (1 + rk_{t-1})$. The term rk is a small fraction. Hence a logarithmic approximation of $\ln(1 + rk) \simeq rk$ yields

$$\ln E_t = \ln E_0 + r \sum_{i=0}^{t-1} k_t. \tag{3}$$

Since earnings net of investment expenditures, $Y_t = E_t(1 - k_t)$, we have also

$$\ln Y_t = \ln E_0 + r \sum_{i=0}^{t-1} k_t + \ln(1 - k_t). \tag{4}$$

Some investments are in the form of schooling; others take the form of formal and informal job training. If only these two categories of investment are analyzed, that is, schooling and postschool experience,[3] the k terms can be separated, and

$$\ln E_t = \ln E_0 + r \sum_{i=0}^{s-1} k_i + r \sum_{j=s}^{t-1} k_j \tag{5}$$

where the k_i are investment ratios during the schooling period and the k_j thereafter. With tuition added to opportunity costs and student earnings and scholarships subtracted from them, the rough assumption $k_i = 1$ may be used.[4] Hence,

$$\ln E_t = \ln E_0 + rs + r \sum_{j=s}^{t-1} k_j. \tag{6}$$

The postschool investment ratios k_j are expected to decline continuously if work experience is expected to be continuous and the purpose of investment is acquisition and maintenance of market earning power. This conclusion emerges from models of optimal distribution of investment expenditures C_t over the life cycle (see Becker 1967 and Ben-

3. The inclusion of other categories in the earnings function is an important research need, since human capital is acquired in many other ways: in the home environment, in investments in health, by mobility, information, and so forth.

4. According to T. W. Schultz, this assumption overstates k, especially at higher education levels, leading to an understatement of r.

Porath 1967). A sufficient rationale for our purposes is that as t increases, the remaining working life $(T - t)$ shortens. Since $(T - t)$ is the length of the payoff period on investments in t, the incentives to invest and the magnitudes of investment decline over the (continuous) working life. This is true for C_t and a fortiori for k_t, since with positive C_t, E_t rises, and k_t is the ratio of C_t to E_t.

In analyses of male earnings, a linearly (or geometrically) declining approximation of the working-life profile of investment ratios k_t appears to be a satisfactory statistical hypothesis.

It will be useful for our purpose of studying earnings of women to decompose net investments explicitly into gross investments and depreciation. Let C_{t-1}^* be the dollar amount of gross investment in period $t - 1$, δ_{t-1} the depreciation rate of the stock of human capital, hence of earnings E_{t-1} during that period, and $k_t^* = C_t^*/E_t$, the gross investment ratio. Hence

$$E_t = E_{t-1} + rC_{t-1}^* - \delta_{t-1}E_{t-1}$$

and

$$\frac{E_t}{E_{t-1}} = 1 + rk_{t-1}^* - \delta_{t-1} = 1 + rk_{t-1}, \qquad \text{by equation (2),} \quad \text{(1a)}$$

thus

$$rk_t = rk_t^* - \delta_t. \tag{2a}$$

The earnings function (3) can, therefore, be written as

$$\ln E_t = \ln E_0 + \sum_{i=0}^{t-1} (rk_i^* - \delta_i). \tag{3a}$$

In transferring the analysis to women, we face two basic facts: (1) After marriage, women spend less than half of their lifetime in the labor market, on average. Of course, this 'lifetime participation rate' varies by marital status, number of children, and other circumstances, and it has been growing secularly. (2) The lesser market work of married women is not only a matter of fewer years during a lifetime, and fewer weeks per year, or a shorter work week. An important aspect is discontinuity of work experience, for most of the married women surveyed in 1967 reported several entries into and exits from the labor force after leaving school.

The implications of these facts for the volume and the life-cycle distribution of human-capital investments can be stated briefly:[5]

1. Since job-related investment in human capital commands a return which is received at work,[6] the shorter the expected and actual duration of work experience, the weaker the incentives to augment job skills over the life cycle. With labor-force attachment of married women lasting, on average, about one-half that of men, labor-market activities of women are less likely to contain skill training and learning components as a result both of women's own decisions and decisions of employers who may be expected to invest in worker skills to some extent.

Table 7.1 Labor-force participation of mothers: proportion working, white married women with children, spouse present

| Age | Proportion working (%) | | | |
	In 1966	After first child	Ever	Sample size
30–34	43	64	82	925
$S < 12$	46	71	75	294
$S = 12$	43	63	84	446
$S > 12$	40	59	88	185
35–39	47	67	87	945
$S < 12$	45	66	82	336
$S = 12$	49	68	88	422
$S > 12$	47	67	92	187
40–44	53	70	88	1,078
$S < 12$	52	72	78	465
$S = 12$	54	70	91	446
$S > 12$	51	68	93	167

Source: NLS, 1967 survey.
Note: S = years of schooling.

2. Given discontinuity of work experience, the conclusion of optimization analysis to the effect that human-capital investments decline continuously over the successive years of life after leaving school is no longer valid. Even a continuous decline over the years spent in the job

5. For a mathematical statement of the optimization analysis applied to discontinuous work experience, see Polachek (1973, ch. 3).
6. For the sake of brevity, the term 'work' refers to work in the job market. We do not imply that women occupied in the household do not work.

market cannot be hypothesized if several intervals of work experience rather than one stretch represent the norm.

3. The more continuous the participation, the larger the investments on initial job experience relative to those in later jobs.

Women without children and without husbands may be expected to engage in continuous job experience. But labor-force participation of married women, especially of mothers, varies over the life cycle, depending on the demands on their time in the household as well as on their skills and preferences relative to those of other family members. The average pattern of labor-force experience is apparent in Tables 7.1–7.3, which are based on the NLS data reported by women who were 30–44 years of age at the time of the survey. According to the data:

1. Though less than 50 percent of the mothers worked in 1966, close to 90 percent worked sometime after they left school, and two-thirds returned to the labor market after the birth of the first child (Table 7.1). Lifetime labor-force participation of women without children or without husbands is, of course, greater.

2. Never-married women spent 90 percent of their years after they left school in the labor market, while married women with children spent less than 50 percent of their time in it. In each age group, childless women, those with children but without husbands (widowed, divorced, or separated), and those who married more than once spent less time in the market than never-married women, but more than mothers married once, spouse present (Table 7.2).

3. Table 7.3 shows the characteristic work histories of mothers,[7] spouse present (MSP), who represented over two-thirds of the women in the sample. We show chronologically the length of nonparticipation (h_1) during the interval between leaving school and marriage; the years of market work between school and the birth of the first child (e_1); an uninterrupted period of nonparticipation, h_2, starting just before the first child was born, followed by e_2 and h_3, which sum intermittent participation and nonparticipation, respectively; and finally e_3, the present job tenure of women working at the time of the survey.

It is clear from the tabulations that, after their schooling, the life cycle of married women features several stages which differ in the nature and degree of labor-market and home involvement. There is usually continuous market work prior to the birth of the first child. The second stage is a period of nonparticipation related to childbearing

7. The six intervals shown in Table 7.3 are aggregated from eight available ones. Both sets described in the Appendix.

Table 7.2 Work histories of women aged 30–44 by marital status (average number of years)

Group	h_1	e_1	h_2	e_2	h_3	e_3	Σe	Σh	S	N_c	Sample size
White, with children: Married once, spouse present	0.57	3.55	6.71	1.14	1.22	1.69	6.4	10.4	11.8	3.16	2,398
Remarried, spouse present	0.54	2.43	7.85	2.60	2.02	2.00	7.1	10.3	10.6	3.28	341
Widowed	1.11	4.25	9.37	1.51	1.44	2.56	8.4	11.9	12.0	2.44	45
Divorced	0.94	2.96	6.54	4.24	2.38	2.92	10.1	9.8	10.8	2.98	133
Separated	0.74	3.97	7.81	2.71	1.14	2.08	8.7	9.6	10.1	2.86	65
White, childless: Married once, spouse present	1.01	5.18	—	4.39	3.35	4.90	14.5	3.3	11.7	—	147
Never married	—	7.08	—	—	1.46	7.48	14.5	1.5	12.9	—	153
Black, with children: Married once, spouse present	1.12	3.00	7.12	2.95	2.14	3.26	9.1	10.3	10.0	4.59	563
Remarried, spouse present	0.96	2.44	7.43	4.93	2.05	3.36	10.7	11.7	9.6	4.22	170
Widowed and divorced	1.19	2.23	7.67	4.36	1.90	3.68	10.3	10.8	9.8	4.20	149
Separated	1.28	2.86	6.24	5.57	2.38	2.81	11.2	9.8	9.4	4.22	191
Black, childless: Married once, spouse present	2.33	4.75	—	3.83	4.58	4.77	13.4	6.9	10.9	—	71
Never married	—	7.15	—	—	4.74	6.45	13.6	4.7	10.9	—	47

Note: h_1 = years not worked between school and first marriage; e_1 = years worked between school and first marriage (for never-marrieds, = years worked prior to current job); h_2 = interval of nonparticipation following birth of first child; e_2 = years worked after h_2 prior to current job; h_3 = interval of nonparticipation just prior to current job; e_3 = years on current job; Σe = years worked prior to current job; Σh = years of nonparticipation since school; S = years of schooling; N_c = no. of children.

and child care, lasting between 5 and 10 years, followed by intermittent participation before the youngest child reaches school age. The third stage is a more permanent return to the labor force for some, though it may remain intermittent for others. In our data, which were obtained from women who were less than 45 years old, only the beginning of the third stage is visible.

The following conjectures about investment behavior in each of these stages are plausible in view of the described patterns which are to some extent anticipated by the women.

1. Prospective discontinuity may well influence many young women during their prematernal employment (e_1) to acquire less job training than men with comparable education, unless they do not expect to marry or have an overriding commitment to a work career.

2. During the period of childbearing and child care, prolonged non-participation may cause the skills acquired at school and at work to depreciate. Some revisions of expectations and of commitments may also take place.[8] Little investment, if any, can be expected during the episodic employment period e_2.

3. There is likely to be a stronger expectation of prospective continuity of employment after the children reach school age. To the extent that the current job (e_3) is more likely to represent this more-permanent return to the labor force than e_2 does, strong incentives to resume investments in job-related skills should reappear.

These conjectures imply that the investment profile of married women is not monotonic. There is a gap which is likely to show negative values (net depreciation) during the childbearing period and two peaks before and after. The levels of these peaks are likely to be correlated for the same woman, and their comparative size is likely to depend on the degree of continuity of work experience. The whole profile can be visualized in comparison with the investment profiles of men and of single women. For never-married women, stage 1 (e_1) extends over their whole working life, and the investment profile declines as it does for men. To the extent, however, that expectation of marriage and of childbearing are stronger at younger ages and diminish with age, investment of never-married women is likely to be initially

8. We are reminded by T. W. Schultz that erosion of market skills during periods of nonparticipation is likely to be associated with growth in nonmarket productivity. If so, the longer the time spent out of the labor force the greater the excess of the reservation of 'shadow' price over the market wage, hence the smaller the probability of subsequent labor-force participation.

Table 7.3 Work histories of married women by age, education, and current work status

Age and category	Variable									Sample size
	h_1	e_1	h_2	e_2	h_3	e_3	Σe	Σh	N_c	
30–34:										
Worked in 1966:										
$S < 12$	1.93	2.37	5.80	3.18	2.20	1.90	7.45	9.93	3.42	135
$S = 12$–15	0.90	2.84	5.41	2.21	1.39	2.31	7.36	7.70	2.89	233
$S \geq 16$	0.37	2.57	2.65	2.22	1.22	2.00	6.79	4.24	2.39	35
Did not work in 1966, but worked since birth of first child:										
$S < 12$	1.67	2.23	6.29	1.31	5.09	—	3.54	13.05	3.50	68
$S = 12$–15	0.81	2.90	4.65	1.23	4.75	—	4.13	10.21	3.49	93
$S \geq 16$	0.50	1.85	3.57	1.71	3.57	—	3.56	7.64	3.00	14
Has not worked since birth of first child:										
$S < 12$	4.54	1.42	9.64	—	—	—	1.42	14.18	3.24	85
$S = 12$–15	2.28	3.21	7.93	—	—	—	3.21	10.21	3.03	211
$S \geq 16$	1.95	1.11	7.20	—	—	—	1.11	9.15	3.14	34
35–39										
Worked in 1966:										
$S < 12$	1.94	2.78	7.98	3.47	2.78	3.40	9.65	12.70	3.37	152
$S = 12$–15	0.98	3.42	6.84	3.09	2.01	3.70	10.21	9.84	2.99	250
$S \geq 16$	1.01	2.95	4.72	2.04	1.25	5.46	10.45	6.98	2.72	43

Table 7.3 (Continued)

Did not work in 1966, but worked since birth of first child:

S < 12	2.15	2.96	9.00	1.80	6.40	—	4.76	17.55	3.70	65
S = 12–15	1.20	3.74	7.42	1.18	5.94	—	4.92	14.56	3.51	101
S ≥ 16	0.38	5.75	6.50	1.15	2.62	—	6.90	9.50	2.87	8

Has not worked since birth of first child:

S < 12	4.23	3.54	13.53	—	—	—	3.54	17.76	3.58	113
S = 12–15	2.97	3.85	11.62	—	—	—	3.85	14.59	3.16	170
S ≥ 16	1.88	2.65	10.15	—	—	—	2.65	12.03	3.50	26

40–44:

Worked in 1966:

S < 12	2.41	3.29	10.38	3.94	2.95	4.93	12.16	15.74	3.18	240
S = 12–15	1.55	4.16	8.74	3.57	2.63	4.43	12.16	12.92	2.72	297
S ≥ 16	0.93	3.20	6.89	3.06	1.86	4.89	11.15	9.68	3.65	29

Did not work in 1966, but worked since birth of first child:

S < 12	2.35	3.31	12.95	1.51	6.89	—	4.82	22.19	3.41	89
S = 12–15	1.39	3.68	10.43	1.24	8.23	—	4.92	20.05	3.36	82
S ≥ 16	3.19	1.19	9.80	1.34	4.80	—	2.53	17.79	3.59	5

Has not worked since birth of first child:

S < 12	6.23	2.63	17.66	—	—	—	2.63	23.89	3.93	130
S = 12–15	3.36	4.88	15.12	—	—	—	4.88	18.48	3.12	141
S ≥ 16	3.03	2.67	13.35	—	—	—	2.67	16.38	2.98	31

Note: See notes to Table 7.2 for explanation of variables.

lower than that of men. At the same time, given lesser expectation of marriage on the part of the never-married, their initial on-the-job investments exceed those of the women who eventually marry, while the profile of the latter shows two peaks.

The implications for comparative-earnings profiles are clear: Greater investment ratios imply a steeper growth of earnings, while declining investment profiles imply concavity of earnings profiles. Hence, earnings profiles of men are steepest and concave, those of childless women less so, and those of mothers are double peaked with least overall growth.

3. Women's wage equation

To adapt the earnings function to persons with intermittent work experience we break up the postschool investment term in equation (6) into successive segments of participation and nonparticipation as they occur chronologically. In the general case with n segments we may express the investment ratio $k_i = a_i + b_i t$, $i = 1, 2, \ldots, n$, and

$$\ln E_t = \ln E_0 + rs + r \sum_{i=1}^{n} \int_{t_i}^{t_{i+1}} (a_i + b_i t) \, dt. \tag{7}$$

Here a_i is the initial investment ratio, b_i is the rate of change of the investment ratio during the ith segment: $(t_{i+1} - t_i) = e_i =$ duration of the ith segment. Note that in (7) the initial investment ratio refers to its projected value at $t_1 = 0$, the start of working life. In a work interval m which occurs in later life there is likely to be less investment than in an earlier interval j, though more than would be observed if j continued at its gradient through the years covered by m. In this case, a_m in equation (7) will exceed a_j.

Alternatively, a_j and a_m can be compared directly in the formulation

$$\ln E_t = \ln E_0 + rs + r \sum_{i=1}^{n} \int_{0}^{e_i} (a_i + b_i t) \, dt, \tag{8}$$

since a_i is the investment ratio at the beginning of the particular segment i.

While the rate of change in investment b_i is likely to be negative in longer intervals, it may not be significant in shorter ones. Since the segments we observe in the histories of women before age 45 are relatively short, a simplified scheme is to assume a constant rate of net investment throughout a given segment, though differing among segments. The earnings function simplifies to

$$\ln E_t = \ln E_0 + rs + r \sum_i a_i e_i. \tag{9}$$

Whereas $(ra_i) > 0$ denotes positive net investment (ratios), $(ra_i) < 0$ represents net depreciation rates, likely in periods of nonparticipation.

The question whether the annual investment or depreciation rates vary with the length of the interval is ultimately an empirical one. Even if each woman were to invest diminishing amounts over a segment of work experience, those women who stay longer in the labor market are likely to invest more per unit of time, so that a_i is likely to be a positive function of the length of the interval in the cross section.

Thus, even if $k_{ij} = a_{ij} - b_{ij}t$ for a given woman j, if $a_{ij} = a_j + \beta_j t$ across women, on substitution, the coefficient b of t may become negligible or even positive in the cross section. On integrating, and using three segments of working life as an example, earnings functions (7), (8), and (9) become:

$$\ln E_t = a_0 + rs + r[a_1 t_1 + \tfrac{1}{2} b_1 t_1^2 + a_2(t_2 - t_1) \\ + \tfrac{1}{2} b_2(t_2^2 - t_1^2) + a_3(t - t_2) + \tfrac{1}{2} b_3(t^2 - t_2^2)], \tag{7a}$$

$$\ln E_t = a_0 + rs + r(a_1 e_1 + \tfrac{1}{2} b_1 e_1^2 + a_2 e_2 \\ + \tfrac{1}{2} b_2 e_2^2 + a_3 e_3 + \tfrac{1}{2} b_3 e_3^2), \tag{8a}$$

$$\ln E_t = a_0 + rs + r(a_1 e_1 + a_2 e_2 + a_3 e_3). \tag{9a}$$

In this example, t is within the last (third) segment, and the middle segment, $e_2 = h$, is a period of nonparticipation or 'home time.' The signs of b_i are ambiguous in the cross section, as already indicated; the coefficients of e_1 and of e_3 are expected to be positive, but those of e_2 (or h) negative, most clearly in (9a).

The equations for observed earnings $(\ln Y_t)$ differ from the equations shown above by a term $\ln(1 - k_t)$ – as was shown in the comparison of equations (3) and (4). With k_t relatively small, only the intercept a_0 is affected, so the same form holds for $\ln Y_t$ as for $\ln E_t$.

It will help our understanding of the estimates of depreciation rates to express earnings function (9a) in terms of gross-investment rates and depreciation rates:

$$\ln E_t = \ln E_0 + \sum_i (r k_i^* - \delta_i) \\ = \ln E_0 + (rs - \delta_s) + (r k_1^* - \delta_1) e_1 \\ + (r k_h^* - \delta_h) h + (r k_3^* - \delta_3) e_3. \tag{9b}$$

This formulation suggests that depreciation of earning power may occur not only in periods of nonparticipation (h), but at other times as well. On the other hand, market-oriented investment, such as informal study and job search, may take place during home time, so that $k_h^* > 0$. Positive coefficients of e_1 and e_3 would reflect positive net investment, while a negative coefficient of h is an estimate of net depreciation. If $k_h^* > 0$, the absolute value of the depreciation rate δ_h is underestimated.

4. Empirical findings

Tables 7.4–8 show results of regression analyses which apply our earnings function to analyze wage rates of women who worked in 1966, the year preceding the survey. The general specification is $\ln w = f(S, e, h, x) + u$, where w is the hourly wage rate; S is the years of schooling; e is a vector of work-experience segments; h is a vector of home-time segments and x is a vector of other variables, such as indexes of job training, mobility, health, number of children, and current weeks and hours of work; u is the statistical residual.

The findings described here are based on ordinary least-squares (OLS) regressions. The Tables show shorter and longer lists of variables without covering all the intermediate lists. In view of a plausible simultaneity problem we attempted also a two-stage least-squares (2SLS) estimation procedure, which we describe in the next section. Since the 2SLS estimates do not appear to contradict the findings based on OLS, we describe them first below.

1. Work history detail and equation form

When life histories are segmented into five intervals (eight is the maximum possible in the data), three of which are periods of work experience and two of nonmarket activity,[9] both nonlinear formulations (equation forms [7] and [8]) are less informative than the linear specification (9). Rates of change in investment (coefficient b) are probably not substantial within a short interval, and the intercorrelation of the linear and quadratic terms hinders the estimation. Dropping the square terms reduces the explanatory power of the regression slightly but increases the visibility of the life-cycle investment profile. Conversely, when the segments are aggregated, the quadratic term becomes negative but does not quite acquire statistical significance by conventional

9. Tables 7.2 and 7.3 show six intervals, including a very short nonparticipation interval h_1 between school and marriage. This interval is aggregated in other home time in the regressions.

standards. The quadratic term for current work experience is negative and significant. In the case of never-married women, one segment of work experience usually covers most of the potential working life. Here the nonlinear formulation over the interval is as natural and informative as it is for men.

2. Investment rates

Table 7.4 compares earnings functions of women by marital status and presence of children, Tables 7.5 and 7.6 by level of schooling, and Table 7.7 by lifetime work experience. In each Table we can compare groups of women with differential labor-force attachment. According to human-capital theory, higher investment levels should be observed in groups with stronger labor-force attachment.

We can infer these differences in investment by looking at the coefficients of experience segments, e_1 (prematernal), e_2 (intermittent, after the first child), and e_3 (current). These increase systematically from married women with children to married women without children to single women in Table 7.4, and from women who worked less than half to those who worked more than half of their lifetime in Table 7.7. An exception is the coefficient of e_3 which appears to be somewhat higher for the group who worked less (see Table 7.7). Note, however, that these coefficients are investment ratios (to gross wage rates), not dollar volumes. Since wage rates are higher in the groups with more work experience, the conclusions about increasing investment hold for dollar magnitudes, a fortiori, and the anomaly in Table 7.7 disappears.[10]

Classifications by schooling show mixed results. In Table 7.5, where schooling is stratified by <12, 12–15, and 16+, investment ratios (coefficients of e_i) are lower at higher levels of schooling (with the exception of the coefficient of e_1). Translated into dollar terms,[11] no clear pattern emerges. At the same time in Table 7.6, where the schooling strata are ≤ 8, 9–12, and 13+, a positive relation between investment volumes and levels of schooling is somewhat better indicated. Note that the sample size for the highest-schooling groups (10+) is quite small in Table 7.5, as is that for the lowest-schooling groups (≤ 8) in Table 7.6.

10. The coefficient of e_3, calculated as $\partial \ln W / \partial e$, is 15 percent higher in the right-hand group. However, the wage rate of this group is about 25 percent lower.
11. Wage rates are roughly 30 percent higher in successive schooling groups.

Table 7.4 Earnings functions, white women

Var.(1)	(1) b	(1) t	Var.(2)	(2) b	(2) t	Var.(3)	(3) b	(3) t	(4) b	(4) t	(5) b	(5) t
	With children			With children			With children		No children		Never married	
C	0.38	—	C	0.21	—	C	0.09	—	−0.42	—	0.55	—
S	0.076	11.5	S	0.063	10.5	S	0.064	12.0	0.081	4.4	0.077	4.9
$(A-S-6)$	0.04	3.8	e	0.012	1.6	e_1	0.008	2.8	0.014	1.6	0.026*	1.5
$(A-S-6)^2$	−0.001	−4.2	e^2	−0.0002	−0.5	e_2	0.001	0.3	0.011	1.3	−0.0007†	−1.1
R^2	0.16	—	e_3	0.021	2.8	e_3	0.012	2.7	0.015	2.2	0.009	1.5
			e_3^2	−0.0008	−1.9	h_1	−0.012	−2.5	−0.005‡	−1.5	−0.009‡	−0.6
			h	−0.007	−1.5	h_2	−0.003	−0.7	0.002§	0.7	—	—
			h^2	0.000	0.2	etr	0.0002	1.5	0.003	2.4	0.0003	1.7
			R^2	0.25		ect	0.010	3.2	−0.003	−1.2	−0.011	−1.8
						hlt	−0.0003	−1.3	−0.002	−1.3	−0.0008	−1.2
						res	0.001	−1.2	0.006	1.7	−0.012	−2.2
						loc	0.044	−2.7	−0.021	−0.4	−0.02	−0.3
						$\ln Hrs$	−0.11	−3.7	−0.15	−1.6	−0.43	−4.4
						$\ln Wks$	0.03	1.6	0.25	2.2	0.21	1.4
						N_c	−0.008	−1.0	—	—	—	—
						R^2	0.28		0.39		0.41	
						N	993		147		138	

Note: Var. = variable; C = intercept; S = years of schooling; A = age; e = total years of work; e_1 = years of work after first child; e_2 = years of work before first child; e_3 = current job tenure; h = total home time; h_1 = home time after first child; h_2 = other home time; etr = experience × training (months); ect = experience × certificate (dummy); hlt = duration of illness (months); res = years of residence in county; loc = size of place of residence at age 15; $\ln Hrs$ = (log of) hours of work per week on current job; $\ln Wks$ = (log of) weeks per year on current job; N_c = no. of children; b = regression coefficient; t = t-ratio; R^2 = coefficient of determination; N = sample size.

* Total work experience, e. † e^2. ‡ Total home time, h. § h^2.

Table 7.5 Earnings functions of WMSP, by schooling

Variable	$S < 12$				$S = 12\text{-}15$				$S = 16+$			
	b	t	b	t	b	t	b	t	b	t	b	t
C	−0.095	—	−0.98	—	−0.61	—	−0.03	—	0.86	—	0.36	—
S	0.046	4.7	0.039	3.8	0.105	5.1	0.086	4.0	0.038	0.4	0.107	1.1
e_1	0.016	−3.1	0.015	2.2	0.012	1.7	0.008	1.3	0.023	1.5	0.010	−0.5
e_2	0.014	2.8	0.012	1.8	0.006	1.2	0	0	−0.013	−2.3	−0.016	−3.0
e_3	0.021	4.7	0.019	3.2	0.015	3.7	0.011	1.9	0.002	1.6	0.004	2.4
h_1	−0.002	−0.6	0.001	0.2	0.013	−3.4	−0.018	−2.9	−0.023	−2.2	−0.012	−1.7
h_2	0.002	0.5	0.003	0.5	−0.001	−0.2	−0.006	−1.0	0.006	0.4	0.002	1.0
etr			0.0004	1.2			0.0004	2.0			0.0007	0.5
ect			0.016	2.4			0.008	1.9			0.032	2.1
hlt			−0.0006	−1.7			0	0			0	0
res			0.001	0.5			0.002	1.3			0.008	1.2
loc			0.06	2.4			0.036	1.6			0.05	0.8
ln Hrs			−0.044	−0.9			−0.11	−3.9			−0.16	−3.4
ln Wks			−0.45	1.5			.031	1.2			0.05	0.7
N_c			−0.004	−0.4			−0.002	−0.2			−0.05	−1.5
R^2	0.17		0.22		0.14		0.18		0.16		0.39	
N	435				622				83			

Note: WMSP = white married women, spouse present. See Table 7.4 for key to symbols.

3. Investment profiles

Another implication of the human-capital theory refers to the shape of the investment profile: it is monotonically declining in groups with continuous participation, hence earnings are parabolic in aggregated experience for men and never-married women.[12] In the groups with discontinuous participation, the profiles are not expected to be monotonic.

We can summarize the implicit profiles schematically, in terms of the coefficients of e_1, length of work experience before the first child, h_1, uninterrupted nonparticipation after the first child, and e_3, the current work interval. We find (Table 7.4, col. 3) that white married women with children (with spouse present) have current investment (ratio which exceeds the investment ratio) incurred in experience before the first child.[13] Presumably, current participation in the labor force, which takes place when most of the children have reached school age, is expected to last longer than the previous periods of work experience. This is certainly true of women over age 35, and it holds in regressions with or without standardization for age.

Looking at regressions within three education levels (Tables 7.5–7.6), we find that coefficient of prematernal experience (e_1) exceeds the coefficient of current work experience (e_3) at the highest level of schooling (in the short equations, though not in the long ones), and the opposite is true at lower levels. For women without children the coefficient of prematernal work experience equals that of current work experience. The investment profile of never-married women has a downward slope. Comparable early segments of their postschool job experience contain higher investment ratios – indeed, the fit implies a linear decline of such ratios over the life cycle. Evidently, women who intend to spend more time in the labor force invest more initially. This is true, presumably, even if their plans are later changed following marriage and childbearing.

4. Depreciation rates

The coefficient of home time is negative, indicating a net depreciation of earning power. During the home-time interval (h_1), associated with

12. In the earnings regressions, the quadratic term of aggregated experience is often negative, but not significant statistically.

13. All statements about differences in coefficients refer to point estimates. The differences are mentioned because they are suggestive, though they would not pass strict tests of statistical significance within a given equation.

Table 7.6 Earnings functions of WMSP (with children), by schooling

	S ≤ 8				S = 9-12				S = 13+			
Variable	b	t	b	t	b	t	b	t	b	t	b	t
S	0.049	1.6	0.044	1.3	0.051	3.2	0.055	3.4	0.068	2.8	0.079	2.7
e_1	0.007	0.4	-0.002	-0.4	0.013	1.7	0.012	1.5	0.021	1.4	0.018	1.2
e_2	-0.004	-2.1	-0.028	-1.8	0.009	1.6	0.003	0.6	-0.020	-1.5	-0.020	-1.4
e_3	-0.002	-0.3	-0.008	-0.5	-0.013	-0.7	0.009	0.5	0.009	2.0	0.011	2.2
h_1	-0.011	-1.5	-0.007	-1.2	-0.014	-1.8	-0.010	-1.6	-0.043	-3.1	-0.031	-2.8
h_2	-0.006	-0.4	-0.003	-0.2	-0.002	-0.4	-0.002	-0.4	-0.005	-0.4	-0.004	-0.3
hlt			-0.0007	-0.7			-0.0011	-2.3			-0.009	-0.6
ln Hrs			-0.050	-0.7			-0.090	-1.8			-0.130	-1.1
ln Wks			-0.070	-0.6			0.060	1.6			0.090	1.2
N_c			-0.008	-0.2			-0.019	-0.4			-0.010	-2.0
R^2	0.26	—	0.32	—	0.21	—	0.26	—	0.27	—	0.33	—
N	182	—	—	—	593	—	—	—	218	—	—	—

Note: WMSP = white married women, spouse present. See Table 7.4 for key to symbols.

Table 7.7 **Earnings functions of WMSP by lifetime work experience**

| Variable | Worked more than half of years | | | Worked less than half of years | | |
	b	t	M	b	t	M
C	−0.28	—	—	−0.10	—	—
S	0.073	9.4	11.8	0.059	7.9	11.0
e_1	0.009	2.1	4.9	0.003	0.4	2.2
e_2	0.006	1.4	5.6	−0.005	−0.6	1.5
e_3	0.017	2.0	4.9	0.022	3.8	1.6
e_3^2	−0.0002	−0.7	—	−0.001	−1.5	—
h_1	−0.014	−2.3	2.2	−0.010	−2.6	10.7
h_2	0.011	1.7	2.1	−0.004	−0.9	4.7
hlt	−0.0008	−2.1	10.8	−0.0001	−0.3	13.7
res	0.002	1.1	12.1	0.002	1.0	11.8
loc	0.064	2.8	0.97	0.024	1.0	0.90
ln Hrs	−0.08	−2.0	3.52	−0.13	−4.4	3.40
ln Wks	0.07	1.9	3.71	0.023	1.0	3.29
N_c	−0.015	−1.4	2.21	−0.001	−0.2	3.18
R^2	.22	—	—	.21	—	—
N	536	—	—	604	—	—

Note: WMSP = white married women, spouse present. See Table 7.4 for key to symbols.

marriage or the birth of the first child, this net depreciation amounts to, on average, 1.5 percent per year. In Table 7.5 the depreciation rate is small (−0.2 percent) and insignificant for women with less than high school education, larger (−1.3 percent) for those with 12–15 years of schooling, and largest (−2.3 percent) for those with 16+ years of schooling. In Table 7.6, the net depreciation rate is −1.1 percent for women with elementary schooling or less, −1.4 percent for women with some high school, and −4.3 percent for women with at least some college. Sampling differences probably account for the different estimates in the two Tables. The depreciation rate also appears higher in the group who worked more than half the years (Table 7.7).

It would seem that the depreciation rate is higher when the accumulated stock of human capital is larger. An exception appears in the comparison of women without children (married and single) with women with children. The former have a lower depreciation rate. Of course, these women spend much less time out of market work, and some of this time might be job-oriented (e.g., job search).

It is useful to return to the formulation (9b) of the earnings function for a closer analysis of the depreciation rates: $\ln E_t = \ln E_0 + (rs - \delta_s) + (rk_1^* - \delta_1)e_1 + (rk_h^* - \delta_h)h + (rk_3^* - \delta_3)e_3$. Our coefficient of home time measures the depreciation rate only if market-oriented investment k_h^* is negligible. This is likely to be true for the period of child caring, the period defined as h_1 in the regression (h_2 in the tabulations).

An interesting question is whether the depreciation rate (δ_h) during nonparticipation is different from the depreciation that occurs at work as well. The question is whether depreciation due to nonuse of the human capital stock (atrophy?) exceeds the depreciation due to use (strain?) or to aging (?). We are inclined to believe that depreciation through nonuse ('getting rusty') is by far more important, particularly in groups of the relatively young (below age 45). Moreover, the atrophy aspect suggests that depreciation due to nonparticipation is strongest for the market-oriented components of human capital acquired on the job, and weakest for the inborn, initial, or general components of the human-capital stock. If so, a fixed rate of 'home-time depreciation' applicable to on-the-job accumulation of human capital would appear as a varying rate in the earnings function: given the volume of other human capital, the larger the on-the-job accumulated component of human capital, the higher the observed (applied to the total earning power) depreciation rate.[14]

This may be an explanation of the observed higher depreciation rates at higher schooling and experience levels of mothers. In particular, there is a positive relation between the coefficients of h_1 (in absolute value) and of e_1 across schooling groups (Table 7.6), experience groups (Table 7.7), and race groups (compare Tables 7.4 and 7.8).

5. Effect of family size

Do family size and number of children currently present affect the accumulation of earning power beyond the effect on work experience? The answer is largely negative: when numbers of children and some measures of their age are added to work histories in the equations, the children variables are negative but usually not significant statistically.

14. Where δ is the observed depreciation rate, δ_J the rate applicable to job-accumulated capital H_J, and H_0 the volume of other human capital, $\delta = (\delta_J H_J)/(H_J + H_0) = \delta_J[1 + (H_0/H_J)]$. With a fixed rate δ_J for all individuals, the larger H_J the larger δ.

Their inclusion reduces the absolute values of the coefficients of experience and of home time and does not add perceptibly to the explanatory power of the regression. Note, however, that the children variable does approach significance in the relatively small groups of highly educated women (Tables 7.5–7.6), and more generally among women with stronger labor-force attachment (Table 7.7). Possibly, shorter hours or lesser intensity of work are, to some extent, the preferred alternatives to job discontinuity.

6. Formal postschool training

The coefficients of experience, a_i, represent estimates of rk_i, where k_i is the average investment ratio across women over the segment and r is the average rate of return. Individual variation in k_i is not available to us. We have some individual information, however, on months of formal job training received after completion of schooling as well as on possession of professional certificates by, among others, registered nurses, teachers, and beauticians. If the length of training and possession of a certificate are positive indexes of k, we may represent $a_i = a_0 + \beta \cdot tr$, where tr is the length of training. The term $a \cdot e$ in that equation becomes

$$(a_0 + \beta tr) \cdot e = a_0 \cdot e + \beta(tr \cdot e).$$

Thus, an interaction term $(tr \cdot e)$ can be added to the equation, and if the hypothesis is correct, the coefficient β should be positive. This is indeed the case in most of our equations, confirming the training interpretation of the experience coefficients in the earnings function. Both interactions with months of job training and with possession of a certificate are significant for married women. The training interaction variable is also positive in the earnings function of single women, but the certificate variable is negative. Whereas the negative coefficient of the certification-experience variable implies less than average investment behavior among persons who work continuously, the corresponding positive coefficient for intermittent workers implies more than average investment behavior.

7. Effects of mobility

Research in mobility has shown that, so long as mobility is not involuntary – resulting from layoffs – it is associated with a gain in earnings. However, geographic labor mobility of married women is often exogenous, due to job changes of the husband. In that case, it may militate against continuity of experience and slow the accumulation of earning power. We used the information on the length of current residence in a county or a Standard Metropolitan Statistical Area (SMSA) as an inverse measure of mobility. This variable has a small positive effect on wage rates of white MSP women and a significant negative effect for single women. To the extent that mobility is job oriented for single women and exogenous for married women, the differential signs provide a consistent interpretation.

8. Hours and weeks in current job

When (logs of) weeks and hours worked in the survey year are included in the regression, a negative sign appears for the weekly-hours coefficient and a positive but less significant one for the weeks-worked coefficient. The hours' coefficients are smaller for married women than for single women and smaller for white than for black women. The negative sign of weekly hours may be partly or wholly spurious since some pay periods indicated by respondents were weeks or months and the hourly wage rate was obtained by division through hours. Of course, the direction of causality is suspect: it is more likely that women with lower wage rates work longer hours than the converse. Deletion of the variables, however, has a minimal effect on the equations.

9. Other variables

Three other variables were included in the equations:

1. Twenty percent of the married women who worked in 1966 dropped out of work in 1967. We used a dummy variable with value 1 if persons working in 1966 stopped working in 1967, and 0 otherwise.[15] This variable had a negative sign, since it indicated a shorter current job experience compared with the prospective work interval of others who continued to work in 1967 – the completed interval of those dropping out was not longer than the interval of stayers. In effect, women who dropped out of the labor force in 1967 had wage rates about 5 percent lower than women who continued working, given the same characteristics and histories.[16] The proportion of dropouts is somewhat larger at lower education levels.

2. The size of community in which the respondent lived at age 15 had

15. Not shown in the Tables.
16. Without standardization, women who had dropped out had wage rates about 10 percent lower than women who continued working.

a positive effect on earning power of married women but no effect on that of single women.

3. Duration of current health problem in months was used as a measure of health levels. It is an imperfect measure for retrospective purposes and shows a very small negative effect on the wage rate.

Table 7.8 **Earnings functions of black women**

MSP with children			Never married		
Variable	b	t	Variable	b	t
C	−0.02	—	C	−0.48	—
S	0.095	11.2	S	−0.110	3.7
e_1	0.005	0.8	e	0.004	0.1
e_2	0.001	0.3	e^2	−0.0003	−0.2
e_3	0.006	1.4	e_3	0.001	0.2
h_1	−0.006	−1.2	h	−0.02	−0.05
h_2	−0.005	−0.9	h^2	0.001	1.1
etr	0.0005	1.3	etr	0.0006	1.4
ect	0.008	1.9	ect	0.003	0.4
hlt	−0.0002	−0.5	hlt	−0.001	−1.8
res	0.002	0.9	res	0.001	0.2
loc	0.11	4.0	loc	0.23	2.7
ln Hrs	−0.30	−7.2	ln Hrs	−0.13	−0.7
ln Wks	0.08	2.2	ln Wks	0.03	0.2
N_c	0.005	0.6	N_c	—	—
R^2	0.39	—	R^2	0.46	—
N	550	—	N	70	—

Note: MSP = black married women, spouse present. See Table 7.4 for key to symbols.

10. Black women

The regressions for black MSP (Table 7.8) show experience coefficients about half the size of the corresponding white population. Home time or depreciation coefficients are not significant; neither are the children variables. The implication is that there is less investment on the job, even though black women spent more time than white women in the labor market. They had more and younger children, on average. The other variables behave comparably with those in the white regressions except that hours of current work and location at age 15 show stronger effects. In contrast to white women, the size of community of residence at age 15 has a positive effect for never-married women as well. Again, the experience coefficients are smaller for black single women than for whites. Perhaps contrary to expectations, neither health problems nor rates of withdrawal from the labor force in 1966 differ for black as compared to white married women with children, spouse present. Rates of return to schooling appear, if anything, to be higher for black women.

5. Lifetime participation and the simultaneity problem

The earnings function, as we estimate it, relates wages of women to investments in schooling and on-the-job training and to a number of additional variables already discussed.

The interpretation of some of the independent variables as factors affecting earning power may be challenged on the grounds that they may just as well be viewed as effects rather than causes of earning power. Presumably, women with greater earning power have stronger job aspirations and work commitments than other women throughout their lifetimes. Hence, what we interpret as an earnings function may well be read with causality running in the opposite direction – as a labor-supply function. This argument is most telling for concurrent variables, such as last year's hours and weeks worked in relation to last year's wage rate. But these variables are of only marginal importance in the wage equation of married women. All other independent variables temporally precede the dependent variable (current wage rate), which makes the earnings function interpretation less vulnerable, though not entirely so for there is a serial correlation between current and past work experience and current and past earning power. Since lifetime work experience depends, in part, on prior wage levels and expectations, our experience variables are, in part, *determined* as well as *determining*. If so, the residual in our wage equations is correlated with the experience variables, and the estimates of coefficients which we interpreted as investment ratios are biased.

How serious this problem is for our analysis depends on the strength of individual correlations between current and past levels and expectations of earning power and on the strength of effect of these prior levels on subsequent work histories of individuals. Of course, when the data are grouped these correlations and effects are likely to be strong. Better-educated women tend to have higher wage rates than less educated women throughout their working lives, (see, for instance, Fuchs 1967) and as our Table 7.3 shows, they spend a larger fraction of their lives in the labor force. Table 7.3 also shows that married mothers who currently do not work spent, on average, less of their lifetime working than those who currently work.

One econometric approach to an estimation of the earnings function in the presence of endogeneity of 'independent' variables is the two-stage least-squares (2SLS) approach. We estimate work experience as a variable dependent on exogenous variables, some of which are in the earnings function and others outside of it. In effect, we estimate a 'lifetime labor-supply function.' The second step is to replace the work-experience variables (e) in the earnings function by the estimated work experience ($\hat{e}$) from the labor-supply function. Parameter estimates in this revised earnings function are theoretically superior to the original, simple least-squares estimates.[17]

Our application of a 2SLS procedure is far from thorough, for two reasons:

1. It is difficult to implement it on the segmented function, since each of the segments would have to be estimated by exogenous variables. For this purpose we aggregate years of work experience and compare the reestimated earnings function with the original, using aggregated experience.

2. One of the variables in our lifetime labor-supply function is the number of children, which is not exogenous. In principle, we should expand the equation system to three to include the earnings function, the labor-supply function, and the fertility function. At this exploratory level we prefer not to do it, particularly since the fertility function would be estimated by the same variables as the labor-supply function.

The supply function obtained for all white MSP women was

$$\frac{e}{e_p} = \underset{(5.1)}{.514 + .020\ S_F} - \underset{(1.8)}{.0064\ S_M} - \underset{(12.0)}{.062\ N_c,}$$

where e is total years of work, e_p is 'potential job experience,' that is, years since school, S_F is education of wife, S_M is education of husband, and N_c is number of children. The addition of earnings of husband reduced the coefficient of S_M to insignificance without changing the coefficient of determination, which was $R^2 = .14$.

Estimated values of the numerator ($\hat{e}$) are used to reestimate the earnings function. A comparison of 2SLS and OLS estimates of the earnings function is shown in Table 7.9. If anything, the reestimated function

17. Since $\hat{e}$ is a function of exogenous variables, it is not correlated with the stochastic term in the reestimated earnings function.

shows larger positive coefficients for (total) experience and stronger negative coefficients for home time. The children variable becomes even less significant (in terms of t-values) than before. The reestimation leaves our conclusions, based on the OLS regressions, largely intact.

Table 7.9 **Earnings function, WMSP women, OLS and 2SLS**

Variable	OLS		2SLS		OLS		2SLS	
	b	t	b	t	b	t	b	t
C	−0.20	—	−0.06	—	0.19	—	0.26	—
S	0.069	12.8	0.063	12.0	0.053	9.4	0.048	8.5
e	0.010	3.2	0.012	2.7	0.008	2.8	0.010	1.9
h_1	−0.008	−3.0	−0.015	−7.7	−0.007	−1.9	−0.013	−5.5
h_2	0.0006	0.2	−0.006	−2.3	0.001	0.5	−0.006	−1.9
e_3	0.009	3.2	0.009	3.5	0.009	3.4	0.010	3.7
tr	—	—	—	—	0.005	2.2	0.006	2.2
cert	—	—	—	—	0.18	5.1	0.18	5.1
hlt	—	—	—	—	−0.0003	−1.3	−0.0003	−1.4
res	—	—	—	—	0.001	1.3	0.021	1.4
loc	—	—	—	—	0.044	2.8	0.042	2.5
ln Hrs	—	—	—	—	−0.11	−5.0	−0.11	−4.9
ln Wks	—	—	—	—	0.03	1.5	0.03	1.6
N_c	—	—	—	—	−0.010	−1.3	0.003	0.3

Note: WMSP = white married women, spouse present; tr = months of training; $cert$ = certification (dummy); see Table 7.4 for key to other symbols.

6. Prediction

A test of the predictive power of the earnings function was performed on a small sample of women who did not work in 1966 but were found in the same first NLS survey to have returned to work in 1967. They were not included in our analyses, but their life histories and 1967 wage rates are available. The latter were predicted with several variants of the earnings function and compared to the reported wage rates. On average, the prediction is quite close, and the mean-square error is even smaller – relative to the variance of the observed wage rates – than the residual variance in the regressions.[18] In other words, the predictive power outside the data utilized for the regressions is no smaller than within the regressions. The test, however, is weak, because the sample

18. The (squared) correlation between predicted and actual wage rates was 0.37. The mean of actual rates was 5.196, with $\sigma = 0.335$; the mean of predicted wages was 5.187, with $\sigma = 0.204$.

is so small (45 observations). Similar tests will be performed on larger samples of women who return to the labor market in subsequent surveys.

7. Earnings inequality and the explanatory power of earnings functions

As Table 7.10 indicates, the earnings function is capable of explaining 25–30 percent of the relative (logarithmic) dispersion in wage rates of white married women and about 40 percent of the inequality in the

Table 7.10 **Earnings inequality and explanatory power of wage functions, 1966**

Group	σ^2 (ln W)	R_W^2	σ^2 (ln Y)	R_Y^2	σ^2 (ln H)	N
Married women by education (yrs):						
< 12	0.17	0.21	0.81	0.76	0.64	435
12–15	0.18	0.17	0.92	0.78	0.74	622
+ 16	0.17	0.16	0.77	0.74	0.60	83
Total	0.22	0.28	0.97	0.78	0.75	1,140
Single women	0.30	0.41	0.62	0.66	0.32	138
Married men	0.32	0.30	0.43	0.50	0.11	3,230

Note: σ_2 (ln W) = variance of (log) wages; σ_2 (ln Y) = variance of (log) annual earnings; σ_2 (ln H) = variance of (log) annual hours of work; R_W^2 = coefficient of determination in wage rate function; R_W^2 = coefficient of determination in annual earnings function.

rather small sample of wage rates of single women in the 30–44 age group who worked in 1966. The earnings function is thus no less useful in understanding the structure of women's wages than it is in the analysis of wages of males.

The dispersion of hours worked during the survey year is much greater among married women, σ^2 (ln H) > 0.75, than among men, σ^2 (ln H) > 0.11. The (relative) dispersion in annual earnings of women is, therefore, dominated by the dispersion of hours worked. This factor is also important in the inequality of annual earnings of single women and of men of comparable ages, but much less so. It is not surprising, therefore, that the inclusion of hours worked in the earnings function raises the coefficient of determination from 28 percent in the hourly-wage equation to 78 percent in the annual-earnings equation of married women, from 41 percent to 66 percent for that of single women, and from 32 to 50 percent for that of men.

The lesser inequality in the wage-rate structure of working married women than in the structure of male wages is probably due to lesser average, and correspondingly lesser variation in, job investments among individuals. At the same time, the huge variation in hours, reflecting intermittency and part-time work as forms of labor-supply adjustments, creates an annual earnings inequality among women which exceeds that of men. However, the meaning of that inequality, both in a casual and in a welfare sense, must be seen in the family context. As was shown elsewhere (Mincer 1974), the inclusion of female earnings as a component of family income narrows the relative inequality of family incomes compared with that of incomes of male family-earners.

8. Some applications

1. The wage gap

To compare wage rates of women with wage rates of men, we analyzed earnings of men from the Survey of Economic Opportunity (SEO) for the same year (1966). We find that the average wage rate of white married men, aged 30–44, was $3.18, compared with $2.09 for white married women and $2.73 for white women in our NLS data.

We inquired to what extent the larger wage ratio (152 percent) of married men to married women and the smaller one (116 percent) of married men to single women can be explained by differences in work histories and by differences in job investment and depreciation. For this purpose we estimated a single earnings function of men, aged 30–44, in SEO. The coefficients and means of the variables for these men are shown in Table 7.11, which also gives the NLS estimates for both married and single women.

Note that married men and married working women have just about the same average schooling, while never-married women are somewhat better educated (by 1 year, on average). The coefficients of schooling are somewhat lower for married women but higher for single women. The big differences are in years of work experience since completion of schooling. These are 19.4 for men, 15.6 for single women, and 9.6 for married women. The coefficients of initial experience are 0.034 for men, 0.026 for single women, and about half as much for married women.

Multiplying the coefficients by the variables (Table 7.11) and summing yields contributions of postschool investments to the (log of) wage rates as shown in Table 7.12. These differences, roughly 40 percent between husbands and wives and 10 percent between married men and single women, are about 70 percent of the observed difference in wage rates between married men and married women and a half of the difference between married men and single women.

Table 7.11 **Experience and depreciation coefficients, 1966, ages 30–44**

Variable	Married women		Single women		Married men	
	b	M	b	M	b	M
S	0.063	11.3	0.077	12.5	0.071	11.6
$\hat{e}$	0.012	9.6	—	—	—	—
e	—	—	0.026	15.6	0.034	19.4
e^2	—	—	−0.0006	258	−0.006	409
e_3	0.009	3.2	0.009	8.0	—	—
h_c	−0.015	6.7	—	—	—	—
h_0	−0.006	3.5	—	—	—	—

Sources: Women: NLS, 1967; men: SEO, 1967.

Note: S = years of schooling; h_c = home time following birth of first child; h_0 = other home time; e = years of work experience since completion of schooling; e_3 = current job tenure; $\hat{e}$ = 2SLS estimate of total work experience; b = regression coefficient; M = means.

If one prefers to be agnostic about the human-capital approach, one can treat the earnings function simply as a statistical relation and the regression coefficients as average 'effects' of work experience and of

Table 7.12 **Effects of work experience on wage rates**

	Relative contribution of		Percent of wage gap explained	
	actual experience	men's experience		
	(1)	(2)	(3)	(4)
Married women	+0.02	+0.26	45	42
Single women	+0.32	+0.33	7	40
Married men	+0.42	—	—	—

nonparticipation on wages, without reading magnitudes of investment or depreciation into them. In that case we may ask how much the sex differential in wage rates would narrow if work experience of women were as long as that of men, but the female coefficients remained as they are. A multiplication of the female coefficients by the male variables in Table 7.11 yields the following answers: for married women, 45 percent of the gap would be erased; for single women, only 7 percent of the much smaller gap (Table 7.12, col. 3). The answer is similar for married women if the converse procedure is used, that is when the work experience of women is multiplied by the male coefficients (Table 7.12, col. 4). For single women, the reduction of the gap is larger than in the first procedure.

We believe, however, that the weight of the empirical analysis of female earnings supports the view that the association of lower coefficients with lesser work experience is not fortuitous: a smaller fraction of time and energy is devoted to job advancement (training, learning, getting ahead) per unit of time by persons whose work attachment is lower. Hence, the 45 percent figure in the explanation of the gap by duration-of-work experience alone may be viewed as an understatement.

Indeed, comparing the annual earnings of year-round working women and men in the 30–40 age groups, Suter and Miller found a female-to-male earnings ratio of 46.7 percent. However, the ratio rose to 74 percent for women in this group who worked all their adult lives. The same comparison for high school educated persons yielded 40.5 as against 74.9 percent. Thus lifelong work experience reduces the wage gap by 51 or 58 percent, respectively.[19]

At this stage of research we cannot conclude that the remaining (unexplained) part of the wage gap is attributable to discrimination, nor, for that matter, that the 'explained' part is not affected by discrimination. More precisely, we should distinguish between the concepts of direct and indirect effects of discrimination. Direct market discrimination occurs when different rental prices (wage rates) are paid by employers for the same unit of human capital owned by different persons (groups). In this sense, the wage-gap residual is an upper limit of the direct effects of market discrimination. Indirect effects occur in that the existence of market discrimination discourages the degree of market orientation in the expected allocation of time and diminishes incentives to investment in market-oriented human capital. Hence, the lesser job investments and greater depreciation of female market earning power may to some extent be affected by expectations of discrimination.

19. Suter and Miller (1971, Table 1). Their figures are not quite comparable with ours: their male data come from the Current Population Survey (CPS), and ours from SEO. They compare full-time earnings rather than wage rates, and they compare men and women without regard to marital status.

Of course, if division of labor in the family is equated with discrimination, all of the gap is by definition a symptom of discrimination. Otherwise, the analyses of existing wage gaps and of their changes over time remain meaningful, not tautological.

Our data on work histories show some interesting trends which suggest a prospective narrowing of the wage differential. Table 3 shows that the uninterrupted period of nonparticipation which starts just prior to the birth of the first child has been shrinking when older women are compared with younger ones. Women aged 40–44 who had their first child in the late 1940s stayed out of the labor force about 5 years longer than women aged 30–34 whose first child was born in the late 1950s. Family size is about the same for both groups, but higher for the middle group (35–39) whose fertility marked the peak of the baby boom. Still, the home-time interval in that group is shorter (by about 2 years) than in the older group and longer than in the younger. Thus, the trend in labor-force participation of young mothers was persistent. If, by the time the 30–34-year-old women get to be 40–44 (i.e., in 1977), they will have had 4 years of work experience more than the older cohort, and their wage rates will rise by 6 percent on account of lesser depreciation and by another 2–4 percent due to longer work experience. Thus, the total observed wage gap between men and women aged 40–44 should narrow by about one-fifth, while the gap due to work experience should be reduced by one-quarter.[20]

2. The price of time and the opportunity costs of children

The loss or reduction of market earnings of mothers due to demands on their time in child rearing represents a measure of family investment in the human capital of their children. This investment cost has been measured by valuing the reduction of market time at the observed wage rate. As pointed out by Michael and Lazear (1971), this valuation is incomplete for two reasons. First, if job investments take place at work, the observed wage rate understates the true foregone wage (gross or capacity wage) by the amount usually invested during the period when earnings are foregone. Second, as is clear from earnings-function

20. Two opposing biases mar this conjecture: The shorter home-time interval for younger women is an average duration for those who already returned to work. It will lengthen with the passage of time as additional women return to the labor force. It can be shown, however, that the apparent trend is genuine. At the same time, the assumption of unchanged job-investment behavior leads to an understatement.

analysis, the reduction of market time in turn reduces future wage rates because of a depreciation in earning power during the period of non-participation. The present value of future earnings lost through depreciation is a component of the opportunity cost of time, hence of children.[21]

The data and the estimated wage functions permit a tentative, perhaps only an illustrative, empirical assessment of the opportunity cost of women's time and of children. Specifically, the marginal opportunity cost per hour of a year spent at home – rather than in the market – consists of (1) the gross wage rate (W_g), that is the observed but foregone wage (W) augmented by currently foregone investment costs, and (2) the present value of the reduction of the future gross wage through current depreciation:[22]

1. We can estimate W_g since $W = W_g(1 - k)$, and rk is estimated in the earnings function by a_1, the coefficient of work experience (e_1) preceding the interruption $k = a_1/r$, where r is the rate of return.

2. The present value of the reduction in W_g due to depreciation, using r as the discount rate, is $d/r \cdot W_g$, where d is the (depreciation) coefficient of home time in our wage equations.[23]

The estimates of marginal opportunity costs of a year (in dollars per hour) are shown in panel I of Table 7.13 for three education groups of white mothers, aged 35–39. In panel II we calculate total opportunity expenditures incurred during the nonparticipation period following the birth of the first child. This is the period for which the earnings functions show significant depreciation coefficients. The length of the period depends, in part, on the number of children. Though interpreting all of the foregone earnings in this period as an opportunity expenditure on children may be an overstatement, we impose an opposite bias by ignoring subsequent periods of nonparticipation[24] which may also be child induced. Figures in panel II are the marginal costs per hour (per year) multiplied by h, the duration of home time. Figures in panel III are average opportunity expenditures per child (N_c) in each group. Since h is in years, the dollar figures in panels II and III should be multiplied

21. As Robert Willis suggested to us, this is strictly correct for the excess of depreciation during home time over the depreciation at other times. As we stated earlier, we believe that the latter is negligible in our age groups.

22. Note that we are looking at household productivity as the return, the purpose of reducing market work, not as a negative element in costs.

23. A 10 percent discount rate was used in these calculations.

24. Inclusion would lead to a 20–25 percent increase in expenditures for the age group.

Table 7.13 Marginal price of time and opportunity costs of children, 1966, working white mothers (aged 35–39) – by years of schooling

	Price of time per hour			Total opportunity expenditure on children			Opportunity expenditures per child		
	<12 (I)	12–15	16+	<12 (II)	12–15	16+	<12 (III)	12–15	16+
1. Observed wage	1.66	2.25	3.54	14.60	16.33	18.51	4.23	5.52	6.60
2. Capacity wage	1.96	2.59	4.60	17.25	18.87	24.05	5.00	6.41	8.57
3. Depreciation	0.05	0.30	1.40	0.44	2.18	7.32	0.13	0.73	2.63
Sum (2 + 3)	2.01	2.89	6.00	17.69	21.05	31.37	5.13	7.14	11.20
Assuming 1,500 hr work per year	—	—	—				7,740	10,710	16,800
h_c	—	—	—	8.80	7.26	5.23	—	—	—
N_c	—	—	—	3.45	2.96	2.81	—	—	—
h_c/N_c	—	—	—	2.55	2.45	1.86	—	—	—

Note: h_c = duration of home time; N_c = no. of children.

by annual hours of work. For example, with 1,500 hours of work per year, the opportunity investment expenditures per child range from about $8,000 spent in 8.8 years by mothers with less than high school education to $17,000 spent in 5.2 years by mothers with college education or more.

Only panel I represents the marginal price of time. Note that the observed wage rate[25] represents 80 percent of the marginal price of an hour below college levels and only 60 percent at higher levels. The same proportions hold in the other two panels. However, figures in these panels are not prices but expenditures which depend on both the price of time and the number of children and the average home-time interval per child. Both of these variables can be viewed as responses to the marginal price of time. As the Table indicates, observed wage rates and, even more so, marginal prices of time (panel II) increase with education. Lesser fertility and closer spacing of children are the responses:[26] both numbers of children and interval of home time per child diminish. Consequently, the differences in total expenditures by education level are reduced. While the marginal price of time of the highest education group is three times as high as that of the lowest, the expenditures per child are a little over twice as high, and total expenditures are only 70 percent higher.

Since the opportunity costs of labor-force withdrawal ('home time') are not quite the same thing as the opportunity costs of children, we again caution the reader to view the estimates of Table 7.13 as largely illustrative. They clearly illustrate the point which the title of this paper intends to convey: foregone market-oriented human capital of mothers is a part of the price of acquiring human capital in children, and more generally, a price exacted by family life. Of course, the greater market specialization, longer hours, and greater intensity of work and of job training on the part of husbands and fathers can be viewed as a 'price exacted by family life' in exactly the same sense.

Implicitly, families balance such prices against perceptions of received

25. In principle, wage rates just before the period h are required. The wage at ages 35–39 represents, on average, a small overstatement: wage profiles of married women with children are relatively flat in the age span 25–39 within education groups.

26. Direct evidence on closer spacing at higher levels of education is shown in research for a Columbia Ph.D. dissertation by Sue Ross (1973). In the NLS data, there is a strong correlation between the length of home time and the birth interval from oldest to youngest child.

benefits.[27] Of course, both perceptions of net benefits and prices change. While perceptions are matters of individual psychology and of cultural climate, the marginal opportunity cost of time has risen secularly with the rise in real wages and with the growth of human capital. It is natural for economists to connect to this basic fact both upward trends in labor-force participation of women and downward trends in fertility,[28] changes in the family, and even some of the rhetoric which accompanies these developments.

Appendix

Note on the construction of work-experience intervals

The 1967 NLS survey of women aged 30–44 permits a division of time elapsed since leaving school into, at most, eight intervals. The following information was used in constructing these intervals: (a) Dates were available for school leaving (S), first marriage (M), birth of first child (C), start of first job, return to labor force after birth of first child, start of current job, and end of last job, if currently not working. (b) Number of years during which the woman worked at least 6 months between: (1) school leaving and first marriage, (2) marriage and birth of first child, (3) return to labor force after the first child, and (4) the start of current job.

On this basis, we describe the intervals in the order of their chronological placement: interval h_1 (on average, half a year) is the interval between school and first job; e_1 is the number of years of work between school and marriage. The placement and continuity of this interval checks rather closely with the data, though direct statements are absent; e_2 is years worked (similarly defined) between first marriage and birth of first child; h_2 is the residual home time, given information on the length of interval between first marriage and birth of first child. The assumption of continuity and order of placement of e_2 and h_2 are somewhat arbitrary. They are justified by evidence of frequent identity of job e_1 and e_2 and the plausibility of h_2 starting during pregnancy. Indeed, h_2 is a fraction of a year, on average; h_3 is the uninterrupted inter-

27. Some of these benefits are analyzed in the papers of Leo Benham and Arleen Leibowitz in this volume (see *Journal of Political Economy*, Vol. 82, Part 2, March–April 1974).

28 For economic analyses which bear on the upward secular trends in labor-force participation of married women, see Mincer (1962) Reading 1 of this collection and Cain (1966). For analyses bearing on fertility trends,s ee 'New Economic Approaches to Fertility,' *J.P.E.*, Vol. 81, No. 2, suppl. (March–April 1973).

val of home time following the birth of the first child. It is placed by direct information; e_3 is years of work and h_4 the residual amount of time in the interval between returning to the labor force at the end of h_3 and start of current job. However, neither e_3 nor h_4 needs to be continuous. The succession of h_4 after e_3 is more plausible than the converse. Also $(e_3 + h_4)$ is, on average, about 3 years altogether; e_4 is clearly defined and placed as the current job interval.

In Tables 7.2 and 7.3 we aggregate $(e_1 + e_2)$ and call it e_1, $(h_2 + h_3)$ is h_2, and the other intervals are correspondingly renamed.

In the regressions we added h_1 to h_3 to get h_2 other home time. Separately, or together, these intervals are quite short and show little effect in our analysis.

References

CAIN, GLEN G., *Married Women in the Labor Force: An Economic Analysis*, Chicago, Univ. Chicago Press, 1966.

CHISWICK, BARRY R., *Income Inequality: Regional Analysis within a Human Capital Framework*, New York, Nat. Bur. Econ. Res., 1973.

CHISWICK, BARRY R., and MINCER, JACOB, 'Time-Series Changes in Personal Income Inequality in the United States from 1939, with Projections to 1985,' *JPE*. 80, No. 3, suppl. (May–June 1972), S34–66.

JOHNSON, GEORGE E., and STAFFORD, FRANK P., 'Social Returns to Quantity and Quality of Schooling,' *J. Human Resources* 8 (Spring 1973): 139–55.

MINCER, JACOB, 'Labor Force Participation of Married Women,' in *Aspects of Labor Economics*, edited by H. Gregg Lewis, Universities National Bureau Conference Series No. 14, Princeton, N.J., Princeton Univ. Press, 1962.
Schooling, Experience, and Earnings, New York, Nat. Bur. Econ. Res., 1974.

PARNES, HERBERT S., SHEA, JOHN R., SPITZ, RUTH S., and ZELLER, FREDERICK A., *Dual Careers*, Vol. 1. Manpower Research Monograph No. 21, Washington: Dept. Labor, 1970.

POLACHEK, SOLOMON, 'Work Experience and the Difference between Male and Female Wages,' Ph.D. dissertation, Columbia Univ., 1973.

RAHM, M., 'The Occupational Wage Structure,' Ph.D. dissertation, Columbia Univ., 1971.

ROSS, SUE, 'The Effect of Economic Variables on the Timing and Spacing of Births,' Ph.D. research in progress, Columbia Univ., 1973.

SCHULTZ, THEODORE W., *Investment in Human Capital*, New York, Free Press, 1971. *Human Resources: Fiftieth Anniversary Colloquium 6*, New York

SUTER, LARRY E., and MILLER, HERMAN P., 'Components of Income Differences between Men and Women in the United States,' Paper presented at the American Sociological Association meetings, Denver, 1971.

WILLIS, ROBERT J., 'A New Approach to the Economic Theory of Fertility Behavior,' *JPE*. 81, pt. 2, suppl. (March–April 1973): S14–64.

8 The Statistical Theory of Racism and Sexism

Edmund S. Phelps*

Professor of Economics, Columbia University

From: *American Economic Review*, Vol. 62, No. 4, September 1972, pp. 659–61.

My recent book, *Inflation Policy and Unemployment Theory*, introduces what is called the statistical theory of racial (and sexual) discrimination in the labor market.[1] The theory fell naturally out of the non-Walrasian treatment there of the labor 'market' as operating imperfectly because of the scarcity of information about the existence and characteristics of workers and jobs.

A paradigm for the theory is the traveller in a strange town faced with choosing between dinner at the hotel and dinner somewhere in the town. If he makes it a rule to dine outside the hotel without any prior investigation, he is said to be discriminating against the hotel. Though there will be instances where the hotel cuisine would have been preferable, the rule represents rational behavior – it maximizes expected utility – if the cost of acquiring evaluations of restaurants is sufficiently high and if the hotel restaurant is believed to be inferior at least half the time.

In the same way, the employer who seeks to maximize expected profit will discriminate against blacks or women if he believes them to be less qualified, reliable, long-term, etc., on the average than whites and men, respectively, and if the cost of gaining information about the individual applicants is excessive. Skin color or sex is taken as a proxy for relevant data not sampled. The a priori belief in the probable preferability of a white or a male over a black or female candidate who is not known to differ in other respects might stem from the employer's previous statistical experience with the two groups (members from the less favored groups might have been, and continue to be, hired at less favorable terms); or it might stem from prevailing sociological beliefs

* The paper was written under a grant from the Fels Institute, University of Pennsylvania.

1. I am indebted to Edward Prescott and Karl Shell for proposing the extension of the paper to Case 2.

that blacks and women grow up disadvantaged due to racial hostility or at least prejudices toward them in the society (in which latter case the discrimination is self-perpetuating).

The theory is applicable to the class of 'liberal' employers and workers who have no distaste for hiring and working alongside black or female workers. By contrast, the theory of discrimination originated by Gary Becker is based on the factor of racial taste. The pioneering work of Gunnar Myrdal *et al.* also appears to center on racial (and, in an appendix, sexual) antagonism.

Some indications of interest in the new theory, and the independent discovery of the same statistical theory by Kenneth Arrow, convince me that it is time for a formalization of the theory in terms of an exact statistical model. Though what follows is very simple, it may be useful to those who like exact models and it may stimulate others to develop the theory further.

An employer samples from a population of job applicants. The employer is able to measure the performance of each applicant in some kind of test, y_i, which, after suitable scaling, may be said to measure the applicant's promise or degree of qualification, q_i, plus an error term, μ_i.

$$y_i = q_i + \mu_i \tag{1}$$

where μ is normally distributed with mean zero.

It is conceivable (and it sometimes occurs in practice) that the employer will have no other information about each applicant, including skin color.[2] In that special case, the employer may use q_i as a least-squares predictor of the applicant's y_i according to the regression-type relation:

$$q'_i = a_1 y'_i + u'_i$$
$$0 < a_1 = \frac{\text{var } q'_i}{\text{var } q'_i + \text{var } \mu_i} < 1, \; Eu_i = 0 \tag{2}$$

where q'_i and y'_i are deviations from their respective population means.[3]

2. The Fair Employment Practices Law forbids employers from asking for information on race in written applications. The Boston Symphony Orchestra auditions candidates from behind an opaque screen.

3. In (2), a_1 is the probability limit, as $N \to \infty$, of the regression coefficient

$$\hat{a}_1 = \frac{N}{1} \sum_{i=1}^{N} y'_i q_i \Big/ \frac{1}{N} \sum_{i=1}^{N} (y'_i)^2$$

$$= \frac{N}{1} \sum_{i=1}^{N} (q_i + \mu_i) q'_i \Big/ \frac{1}{N} \sum_{i=1}^{N} (q_i + \mu_i)^2$$

Suppose instead that skin color is observed along with the test datum, and suppose that the employer postulates a model of job qualification

$$q_i = a + x_i + \eta_i \tag{3}$$

in which

$$x_i = (-\beta + \varepsilon_i)c_i, \qquad \beta > 0, \tag{3a}$$

where $c_i = 1$ if the applicant is black and zero otherwise. Here x_i is the contribution of social factors, and these are believed to be race-related according to (3a). The random variables ε_i and η_i are normally and independently distributed with mean zero. Letting $\lambda_i = \eta_i + c_i \varepsilon_i$ and $z_i = -\beta c_i$, we may write

$$q_i = \alpha + z_i + \lambda_i \tag{4}$$
$$y_i = q_i + \mu_i = \alpha + z_i + \lambda_i + \mu_i$$

Then the test datum can be used in relation to the race (sex) factor to predict the degree of qualification net of the race factor, the latter being separately calculable:

$$q'_i - z'_i = a_1 \cdot (y'_i - z'_i) + u_i$$
$$0 < a_1 = \frac{\text{var } \lambda}{\text{var } \lambda + \text{var } \mu} < 1$$

or, equivalently

$$q'_i = \frac{\text{var } \lambda_i}{\text{var } \lambda_i + \text{var } \mu_i} \cdot y'_i \tag{5'}$$
$$+ \frac{\text{var } \mu_i}{\text{var } \lambda_i + \text{var } \mu_i} \cdot z'_i + u_i$$

The weights applied to the test information and the skin color information are inversely related to the variances of the respective disturbance terms corresponding to them.[4]

Case 1. If growing up black is believed by the employer to be socially disadvantageous, so that $z'_i < 0$ for black applicants, then one might expect to find a lower prediction of q_i for blacks than whites having equal test scores. This is generally true, however, only in the special case where $\varepsilon \equiv 0$ for all i, i.e., for all blacks as well as whites. This means

4. My attention has been called by the referee to the derivation of a generalization of equation (5'), from which can be deduced all my cases, in the extended footnote on p. 325 in Thomas Wonnacott and Ronald Wonnacott.

that there is no differential variability in promise as between blacks and whites. Then var λ_i = var η_i and hence the coefficients in (5') are independent of c. Therefore the prediction curve relating q_i to y_i for blacks lies parallel and below that for whites, as illustrated in Figure 8.1.

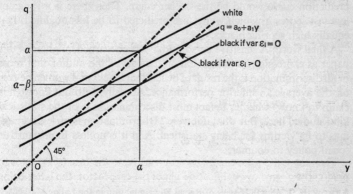

Figure 8.1. Prediction of qualification by race and test score

Case 2. In general the variance of λ depends upon skin color. The formulation in (3) ascribes to blacks the larger postulated variance, as reflected in (6):

$$\text{var } \lambda_i = \text{var } \eta_i + c_i^2 \text{ var } \varepsilon_i \tag{6}$$

It follows that the coefficient of the test score in the least-squares prediction of qualification is *greater* for blacks than for whites. (In the limit, as var $\varepsilon_i \to \infty$, the coefficient of y_i – the slope of the prediction curve for blacks – approaches one.) For any positive var ε_i it is a consequence of the race-related difference in coefficients that at some high test score and higher ones the black applicant is predicted by the employer to excel over any white applicant with the same or lower score. The employer credits an equally good test score by the white applicant as a *less credible* indication in view of the prior notions of the comparatively narrow range of white promise. Note that one can reverse these implications by replacing the dummy variable in (3) with $(1 - c_i)$ instead.

A further case. It is straightforward to make the disturbance term in (1) conditional on race in the way that λ was made conditional on skin color:

$$\mu_i = \xi_i + c_i \rho_i \tag{7}$$

The Statistical Theory of Racism and Sexism 209

Then whites' test scores are regarded by the employer as *more reliable* than the scores of blacks – that is, they measure promise with less error. In that case the greater reliability of whites' test scores might overcome any tendency for them to have less credibility, so that the white prediction curve would be the steeper curve. Then there is a range of low test scores in which whites are predicted to be less qualified than equally high scoring blacks.

A final word. A sensitive person, I have been warned, might read this paper as expressing an impression on the part of the author that most or all discrimination is the result of beliefs that blacks and women deliver on the average an inferior performance. Actually, I do not know (nor claim to know) whether in fact most discrimination is of the statistical kind studied here. But what if it were? Discrimination is no less damaging to its victims for being statistical. And it is no less important for social policy to counter.

References

ARROW, K. J., 'Some Models of Racial Discrimination in the Labor Market,' RAND Corporation research memorandum R M-6253-R C, multilith, Santa Monica, February 1971.

BECKER, G. S., *The Economics of Discrimination*, Chicago, 1959.

MYRDAL, G., *An American Dilemma*, New York, 1944.

PHELPS, E. S., *Inflation Policy and Unemployment Theory*, New York, 1972.

WONNACOTT, T. H., and WONNACOTT, R. J., *Introductory Statistics*, New York, 1969.

9 Determinants of the Structure of Industrial Type Labor Markets *

Peter B. Doeringer

Instructor of Economics, Harvard University

From: *Industrial and Labor Relations Review*, Vol. 20, No. 2, January 1967, pp. 206–20

In the classical competitive labor market model, the market for labor is perceived as a bourse, a place where the buyers and sellers of labor meet to transact their business and where every job in the economy is continuously open to all workers on the same terms and conditions. In a dynamic market environment, the work relationship between employer and employee in such a system must be, perforce, of a non-permanent nature; each worker is subject to being underbid and each employer faces the exodus of his employees if he fails to pay the current, market-determined wage. Such is the way the forces of competition are envisioned to operate in the classical model to produce the efficient allocation of labor resources and the concomitant marginal equalities required in a competitive equilibrium.

For the *cognoscenti* of labor market operation, however, the descriptive or predictive usefulness of this classical model, as characterized by (1) reliance upon wage rates to produce adjustments to changing

*The typical manufacturing establishment constitutes what Clark Kerr has described as a 'structured internal labor market,' that is, a job market where access to work opportunities is governed by institutional rules set up by management or by management and union together. This study analyzes the factors – the technology of the production process, quantitative and qualitative changes in product demand, external labor market conditions, tradition, employee pressures for equity and for wage and employment security – which determine the structure of such intrafirm labor markets.

The material in this article is based upon interviews during 1964 and 1965 with industrial engineers and industrial relations and operating executives in twenty-four manufacturing plants. This research was part of a project sponsored by the U.S. Department of Labor under the authority of Title I of the Manpower Development and Training Act of 1962, as amended. Points of view or opinions stated in the article do not necessarily represent the official position or policy of the Department of Labor.

market conditions, and (2) assumptions of frictionless mobility and 'open' job structures, is vitiated by the realities of the employment relationships and wage-setting procedures observed in the manufacturing sector. The need for a viable alternative to the classical labor market model, similar to those developed in the product market by E. H. Chamberlin[1] and Joan Robinson,[2] has been demonstrated by the assaults upon the validity of the classical model,[3] by the development of institutional models of wage determination, and by the market models and case studies dealing with both interplant and intraplant labor allocation.[4]

The Kerr Model

In one such institutional model, formulated by Clark Kerr,[5] the labor market is not viewed as operating like an open and competitive bourse, but rather as a series of distinct markets, reminiscent of the 'noncompeting groups' of Cairnes and Mill,[6] each with boundaries determined by geographical, occupational, and most important, institutional factors. While the boundaries of these markets touch or overlap in places, for purposes of labor mobility they are largely separate. The

1. E. H. Chamberlin, *The Theory of Monopolistic Competition*, 8th ed. (Cambridge, Mass., Harvard University Press, 1962).

2. Joan Robinson, *The Economics of Imperfect Competition*, 2nd ed. (Macmillan, 1942).

3. See, for example, Richard A. Lester, 'Shortcomings of Marginal Analysis for Wage-Employment Problems,' *American Economic Review*, Vol. 36, March 1946.

4. Some of the works in this area are John T. Dunlop, 'The Task of Contemporary Wage Theory,' and E. Robert Livernash, 'The Internal Wage Structure,' both of which appear in George W. Taylor and Frank C. Pierson, eds., *New Concepts in Wage Determination* (McGraw-Hill, 1957); J. L. Meij, 'Wage Structure and Organization Structure,' and G. H. Hildebrand, 'External Influences and the Determination of the Internal Wage Structure,' in J. L. Meij, ed., *Internal Wage Structure* (North-Holland Publishing Co., 1963); Clark Kerr, 'The Balkanization of Labor Markets,' in E. Wight Bakke *et al.*, *Labor Mobility and Economic Opportunity* (Cambridge, Mass., Technology Press of M.I.T., 1954); John T. Dunlop, 'Job Vacancy Measures and Economic Analysis,' in National Bureau of Economic Research, *The Measurement and Interpretation of Job Vacancies* (Columbia University Press, 1966), pp. 28–47; and Lloyd Reynolds, *The Structure of Labor Markets: Wages and Labor Mobility in Theory and Practice* (Harper and Brothers, 1951).

5. Kerr, loc. cit.

6. See J. S. Mill, *Principles of Political Economy*, Vol. 1, Book 2, Ch. 14 (Longmans Green, 1909), pp. 480–81; and J. E. Cairnes, *Some Leading Principles of Political Economy Newly Expounded*, Part 1, Ch. 3, Sec. 5 (Harper and Brothers, 1874), pp. 62–5.

existence of these market boundaries creates a distinction, in terms of employment preferences, between workers included within a bounded market and those without. As Kerr describes it,

> Labor markets are of two broad types.
> (1) the Structureless and (2) the Structured. In the structureless market there is no attachment except the wage between the worker and the employer. No worker has any claim on a job and no employer has any hold on any man. Structure enters the market when different treatment is accorded to the 'ins' and to the 'outs.' In the structured market there always exists (1) the *internal market* and (2) the *external market*. The internal market may be the plant or the craft group, and preferment within it may be based on prejudice or merit or equal. y of opportunity or seniority, or some combination of these. The external market consists of clusters of workers actively or passively available for new jobs lying within some meaningful geographical and occupational boundaries, and of the port or *ports of entry* which are open or are potentially open to them.[7]

The theoretical construct of the internal labor market, as introduced by Kerr, may be more precisely defined as an administrative unit within which the market functions of pricing, allocating, and often training labor are performed.[8] It is governed by a set of institutional rules which delineate the boundaries of the internal market and determine its internal structure.[9] These institutional or administrative hiring and work rules define the 'ports of entry' into the internal market, the relationships between jobs for purposes of internal mobility, and the privileges which accrue to workers within the internal market. A single or multiplant enterprise, a union hiring hall providing manpower for a number

7. Kerr, loc. cit., n. on p. 101 (emphasis added).
8. See Dunlop, 'Job Vacancy Measures and Economic Analysis,' loc. cit., pp. 7–15. Dunlop defines the internal labor market as 'the complex of rules which determines the movement of workers among job classifications within administrative units such as enterprises, companies, or hiring halls. These movements may be transfers, promotions, demotions, or layoffs to the exterior labor market. These movements may be temporary or permanent, which may affect the operation of the rules . . .' (ibid. n. on p. 32.)
9. The internal labor market of the manufacturing plant, for example, may be more broadly viewed as a complex equilibrium system composed of the following internal variables which are, at least to some degree, interdependent: (1) the job structure of the plant; (2) the administrative rules defining the patterns and priorities of internal movement; (3) the location of the 'entry ports' and recruitment and selection procedures; (4) training procedures; (5) compensation; and (6) employee pressures and union and employer bargaining objectives.

of different enterprises, and a branch of the military services are all examples of such administrative units. In many instances, these broadly defined internal labor markets are further divided into internal submarkets for different occupational categories, such as managerial, clerical, maintenance, production, and the like, each of which is governed by its own specific set of rules. These may in turn be divided into smaller units for purposes of hiring, upgrading, downgrading, lateral transfer, and layoff. An example of such an internal labor market is shown in Figure 9.1.

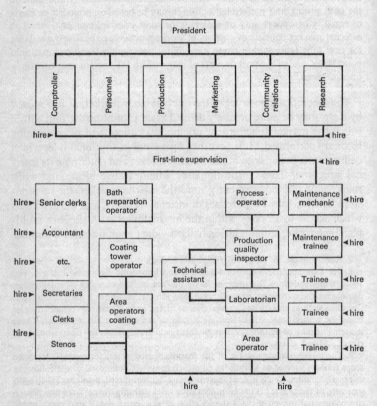

Figure 9.1. Internal Labor Market, Chemical Plant.

Internal labor market structures in manufacturing

This analysis will concentrate upon the allocative mechanism for production and maintenance labor in what is probably the most familiar type of structured internal labor market, the manufacturing plant. The allocative structure found within the internal labor markets of such enterprises may be characterized by a threefold classification scheme: (1) the degree of openness to the external labor market as determined by the number and location of the ports of entry (hiring job classifications); (2) the dimensions, both horizontal and vertical, of the units for internal movement (i.e., upgrading, downgrading, lateral transfer, and layoff); and (3) the rules which determine the priority in which workers will be distributed among the jobs within the internal market.[10]

For purposes of exposition, two polar types of production and maintenance internal submarket structures may be postulated, closed and open. The closed internal submarket has only a single-entry job classification, all other jobs in the plant being filled internally through upgrading. Some plants, notably in steel and petroleum, exhibit such closed structures since they prefer to hire almost exclusively into low-skilled job classifications and to develop most of their blue-collar skills, including maintenance and mechanical skills, internally.[11]

At the opposite end of the classification spectrum is the open internal labor submarket, in which vacancies in all job classifications are filled directly from the external labor market. In men's clothing, for example, a considerable degree of openness is found; vacancies in most stitching and pressing job classifications being typically filled directly from the external market.

In most industrial plants, however, the proportion of job classifications which serve as interfaces between the plant and the external market lies somewhere between those extremes. Typically, the hiring ports into production and maintenance jobs are located at the low-skilled level – such as maintenance trainee, sweeper, machine cleaner,

10. Movement within the internal labor market of the plant is typically of three types: (1) a secular trend as a result of upgrading, (2) vertical and lateral movement in response to output fluctuations, and (3) temporary assignments due to absent employees. This analysis will consider only the first two types which are the most predictable.

11. For a study of an internal labor market which develops all of its operating and maintenance skills through internal training and upgrading, see U.S. Bureau of Labor Statistics, *A Case of a Modernized Petroleum Refinery* (G.P.O., 1957), Report No. 120.

packer, assembler, and the like – and at the high-skilled, journeyman level, while most semiskilled and high-skilled production jobs are closed to the external market.[12]

The entry ports into the internal labor market of the maufacturing plant are typically connected to clusters of jobs within the plant which constitute the districts within which an employee may be upgraded, downgraded, transferred, or laid off.[13] The contours of these districts may vary with the type of movement (i.e., promotion, layoff, and so forth), and are determined by economic variables such as the technology of the production process, predictable fluctuations in product demand, external labor market conditions, and also by such factors as equity and custom. The dimensions of these districts for internal movement are defined by the vertical range of the grades of job content within the district and by the number and the degree of specialization of the job classifications contained within any job grade.[14]

Districts under review

In the study on which this article is based the broadest district for up-grading in the production internal submarket was plantwide. Plantwide districts are typically associated with production job structures with a relatively small range of variation in levels of job content and a low proportion of specialized jobs, such as occurs in food products manu-facturing. A narrower district for upgrading involves the division of production jobs into departments based upon the production process, the nature of the occupations, the product type, or the administrative

12. Formal in-plant training programs may also constitute ports of entry, albeit rather specialized ones. Some companies provide such training entry ports to pre-pare entrants for particular jobs or progression patterns, usually of a skilled nature. Formal production and maintenance training programs of this type, usually for such skills as drafting, production planning, computer programming, and com-puterized equipment maintenance, are designed to (1) provide the plant with the needed skills more quickly and efficiently than through alternative routes in the internal labor market, such as on-the-job training of current employees, and (2) provide a special entry port enabling the plant to hire a select group of employees with higher educational and aptitude qualifications than are required of most unskilled entrants.

13. These forms of internal labor market structuring bear an implicit relationship to the constructs of 'job clusters' used by Dunlop and Livernash (Dunlop, *The Task of Contemporary Wage Theory*, loc. cit., p. 129, and Livernash, loc. cit., pp. 148–9) to describe the process of the determination of the intraplant wage structure.

14. See Sumner H. Slichter, James J. Healy, and E. Robert Livernash, *The Impact of Collective Bargaining Upon Management* (Brookings Institution, 1960), pp. 154–8 for a discussion of the types of seniority districts found in manufacturing.

organization of the plant. In some plants – steel, chemicals, and petroleum, for example – the districts for upgrading are even more narrow, consisting of specific lines of progression within each department. These progression lines may be only one job classification wide or may consist of several branches. When upgrading districts are narrow and interjob mobility linkages are carefully defined, upgrading sequences usually reflect a skill or experience development sequence. The range of job content and the proportion of specialized jobs, moreover, is usually greater in those plants with narrow upgrading districts than in plants with broad districts.

The extreme type of narrow internal labor market district consists of a single job classification and emphasizes the uniqueness or independence of each type of job, in contrast to multiclassification districts which recognize the skill and experience relationships among the jobs in the internal market. These single job classification districts appear when the jobs in the plant are highly specialized, as in the production submarkets in men's garments referred to above – in which, despite the existence of some common skill elements, most pressing and stitching job classifications are not related through internal transfer linkages.

In some plants, the downgrading and layoff districts may be identical with the upgrading districts, but this is not necessarily the case. In a number of plants studied by the author the layoff districts, and often the downgrading districts as well, were broader than the upgrading districts, in order to enhance the employment and earnings security of certain groups of employees. When narrow progression lines were used for upgrading within department districts, for example, surplus employees might be allowed to exercise seniority-based bumping rights into jobs which were within their departments but which lay outside of their specific progression lines. In some plants, surplus employees in job classifications which cut across several departments, such as maintenance mechanics or welders, were allowed to bump laterally, within their classification, into other departments. Other plants may define specific downgrading patterns although upgrading is always intradepartmental.

For layoffs, many plants have also established interdepartmental transfer linkages among low-skilled jobs, in order to permit surplus employees in one department to bump less senior employees in another department, so that employment security is enhanced for senior employees. Presently in the basic steel industry, for example, the interdepartmental linkages in some plants assume the form of a labor pool or 'pan,' containing the bottom three or four job grades, which a number of departments share in common. Workers may exercise their bumping rights within departments until they reach the labor pan, where their bumping and layoff rights become interdepartmental or even plantwide.[15]

Priority of movement

The final dimension of the classification system for industrial type internal labor markets involves the rules governing the priority of movement within the internal market. Relying primarily upon the factors of ability and seniority, these rules define the order in which employees within the relevant internal grouping of job classifications – seniority district, progression ladder, department, or the like – will receive promotions, transfers, downgradings, and layoffs. They may also be supplemented by rules governing bumping rights and the type of choice permitted employees in selecting or accepting internal reassignment.[16]

15. In addition to the broad classifications of the patterns of internal movement within production and maintenance internal submarkets previously described, there are other institutional rules which provide structural variations in the internal allocation process. In some cases in the past, the internal labor market may have been divided along lines of race or sex, so that 'women's' jobs or 'Negro' jobs were separated from the remainder of the production unit, each with its own seniority list. While such forms of structuring appear to be patently illegal under the Civil Rights Act of 1964, it remains to be seen what internal readjustments will be required. Production and maintenance may also be divided among two or more union jurisdictions with the boundaries of the NLRB election units constituting internal barriers to movement. Special internal transfer arrangements may also exist for the staffing of new equipment or new departments. When an entire department is being established, employees performing similar work in older jobs within the plant may be temporarily assigned to the new jobs. Those assignments will usually involve horizontal transfers, and may become permanent once the final manning requirements are determined. Alternatively, new jobs may be opened to the entire production force or to particular departments for bid or assignment, according to priorities. One plant, for example, allows employees displaced by a new facility to have first choice of the new jobs, followed by those employees in similar jobs, and lastly, by other employees in the plant. The attempt here is to maintain job security while utilizing prior job experience effectively.

16. The scope of the district and the rules determining the priority for internal movement are not functionally separable. Especially in the case of layoffs and downgradings, where the equity of employment and earnings security is important, the internal movement district, the rules governing movement priorities, and employees' bumping rights must be viewed simultaneously in order to understand completely the operation of the internal labor market. (See Slichter, Healy, and Livernash, op. cit., pp. 157–8.)

The exclusive reliance upon either seniority or ability for determining all internal movement priorities constitutes the limit of the range of types of movement priority systems. Most plants, however, employ some combination of criteria, although the particular combination will often vary with the type of movement (i.e., promotion, layoff, and so forth).

Twenty-one of the twenty-four manufacturing plants in the present study resorted to the seniority criterion almost exclusively when selecting employees for permanent, and frequently for temporary, layoffs within production and maintenance submarkets. Of the three plants which did not use seniority for layoffs, two had installed employment guarantees for all but temporary employees, while the third used a work-sharing procedure, within limits, followed if necessary by layoffs using inverse seniority.

For promotions, lateral transfers, and occasionally downgradings of employees, however, greater emphasis upon ability factors was encountered. Of the twenty-three plants which promoted from within, only three relied almost exclusively upon seniority as a promotion criterion while only two emphasized merit alone.[17] The remaining plants attached various weights to these factors; some applied both criteria to all types of interjob movement, while others used a 'float-line' system, in which seniority governed movement priorities below a certain job grade and ability governed movement priorities above it.[18]

17. The firms which relied solely on merit criteria for promotion purposes were also unorganized; many unorganized firms, however, were the staunchest adherents to promotion by straight seniority. One non-union company was substantially revising its personnel policies explicitly to define the seniority rights for promotion, downgrading, and layoff, which it would grant to its employees. Coincidentally, this firm was facing an organization drive.

18. The direct impact of seniority as an allocative rule in the industrial internal labor market has been upon the ranking of workers for internal movement, while the indirect influences have been upon criteria and the methods of establishing promotion criteria. Those plants which promote primarily by merit or ability, perhaps with the exception of the smallest plants, usually develop very extensive, and presumably costly, employee appraisal and counseling programs. These programs result from the potential need to justify decisions on internal transfers to a union, in organized plants, and to forestall employee dissatisfaction over the 'arbitrariness' of transfer decisions in unorganized plants. In plants utilizing a seniority criterion the potential costs of the possibility of having to promote a poorly qualified employee on the basis of his seniority may encourage the employer to raise the criteria for entry into the plant in order to screen out applicants with less promotion potential, although this also is not without costs.

All but two plants relied exclusively upon seniority when downgrading employees during reductions in forces.

The rules governing the priorities for internal movement may be supplemented with additional arrangements by which workers may select or accept internal movements and the way in which bumping rights can be exercised during reductions in forces. Job vacancies, for example, may frequently be 'posted' within a particular promotion district. Workers in the district can then express their desire to be assigned to the vacancy by filling out an application or 'bid' for the job. The employer would then fill the vacancy from among these bids on the basis of the criteria described above. An alternative method requires workers to file bids in advance of job vacancies, so that a list of applicants for any job is always available. If no one applies for a vacancy, some plants may expand the area of internal selection to permit a broader group of employees to apply, while other plants might assign the least senior worker in the department or plant to the job or else seek to fill the vacancy from the external market.

During downgrading, an employee's bumping rights also constitute a component of the internal selection process. Within the district in which a surplus employee is allowed to exercise his bumping rights, several types of bumping patterns may occur. Chain bumping, in which a bump by one employee may lead to a number of consecutive bumps before a layoff results, produces the greatest number of moves per surplus employee. Alternatively, rules may exist which curtail the number of bumps by using narrow downgrading districts, by requiring that a surplus employee bump directly into a low-skilled labor pan, or by establishing arbitrary seniority limits upon bumping. Frequently, the scope of the downgrading district is balanced by the rules limiting bumping in order to reduce the costs of the disruptions which accompany the internal movement of workers.[19]

Determinants of the Market Structure

In the manufacturing sector, the types of internal market structures described above occur in an almost bewildering array of combinations. The research suggests, however, that the particular form of internal market structure assumed by a manufacturing plant can be explained

19. See Peter B. Doeringer and Michael J. Piore, 'Labor Market Adjustment and Internal Training,' *Proceedings of the Eighteenth Annual Meeting of the Industrial Relations Research Association*, December 1965, for a discussion of the nature of these costs.

by reference to the operating exigencies and costs created by the economic and social context within which the plant functions.[20]

In a static internal labor market the most important variables shaping its structure, excluding the influence of noneconomic market forces such as custom, are the technology of production and the work methods within the plant. The plant may be perceived as an administrative unit which contains a set of tasks. The technology of the capital equipment and the product mix which must be produced on this equipment define, within certain limits, the skill mix and the proportion of specialized jobs in the plant at any point in time. Whatever flexibility exists in the plant's job structure results from the discretionary fashion in which tasks may be combined to produce broadly or narrowly skilled jobs (i.e., job design) and decisions regarding the division of the work between internal employees and subcontractors. Within the manning range permitted by such flexibility, the technology of the production process establishes a matrix of jobs whose vertical dimension reflects levels of job content. The mobility linkages between the jobs in this matrix and between the matrix and the external labor market are defined by the hiring, promotion, downgrading, transfer, and termination patterns already described.

If the process of filling vacancies in the job structure of the plant, from either internal or external sources of labor, were costless, the employer would be indifferent among the possible combinations of patterns of internal mobility and locations of entry ports. With every new hire, however, there are recruiting costs; and with both new hires and internal reassignments of employees, there are costs of screening and selection. With every new hire or internal reassignment, moreover, some training must occur as the employee becomes acquainted with the duties of his new job; and such training, even when provided on the job as is typically the case with production skills, has certain costs attached to it.

These training costs, often measurable only in terms of reduced productivity, wasted raw materials, damaged machinery, and the like, are a direct function of (1) the content of entry jobs and the differences in content among the job classifications which are grouped together for purposes of internal movement, and (2) the availability of particular

20. See Robert L. Aronson, *Layoff Policies and Practices* (Princeton University, 1950), Research Report No. 82, pp. 15–16, for a discussion of a somewhat similar set of variables governing layoff districts.

labor-force skills or qualities on the external labor market.[21] Given the job structure of the plant, the profit-maximizing employer, excluding questions of equity and employee morale, will presumably attempt to establish a sequence of hiring and internal movement patterns which will permit him to fill vacancies in the job structure at the lowest cost. The process of designing jobs and of determining hiring and internal mobility patterns provides one of the primary mechanisms by which the costs of entry training and internal retraining are controlled within the plant.

Once the content of the jobs contained within the internal labor market is established, some jobs typically will be identified as entry ports because of the minimal entry training associated with them. Many of these entry jobs will necessarily be low-skilled, but more highly skilled jobs may also be entry ports when there is an expectation that workers possessing appropriate skills will be available on the external labor market. The remaining jobs in the internal market will be filled through upgrading, primarily because experience and training acquired elsewhere in the internal job structure can be at least partially transferred to these jobs. The proportion of the jobs opened to the external market, therefore, will be substantially influenced by the skill mix and specificity of the internal job structure and by the relatedness of content among the jobs in that structure.[22]

The dimensions of the patterns of movement within the internal labor market also are largely determined by internal job content relationships. For example, when specific progression ladders defining precise inter-job mobility linkages are established, there is typically a logical relationship between the job progression pattern and the process of incremental skill development through on-the-job training. These lines of progression utilize prior internal training and experience to reduce the amount of additional training which must occur following a promotion. Similarly during downgrading, when internal rules require that an employee bump into a job he has performed previously or which utilizes skills previously learned on other jobs in the plant, the amount of retraining is reduced.

21. See Doeringer and Piore, op. cit.

22. Particular job skills are plant specific when job content is unique to a plant in terms of the high proportion of orientation training to manual skill required, the idiosyncratic content of the job, or the difficulty encountered in adapting work habits acquired elsewhere on similar jobs to job performance in the plant.

If the skill content of most jobs is low, or if the skills are similar or overlapping, narrow patterns of movement do not provide significant training economies, and the likelihood of broad departmental or even plantwide job groupings for purposes of movement is high. When jobs become more specialized and the skill relationships between certain jobs are significantly greater than between others, there is a high probability that narrow districts for internal movement and specific progression ladders will be developed within the internal market, so as to utilize skill relationships effectively and reduce the retraining costs associated with the upgrading of employees. A narrow progression line, such as stamper – utility man – shearman – manipulator – roller, within the blooming mill department of a steel plant, combined with the broad area of transfer permitted within the low-skilled labor 'pan' in steel, is a typical example of such internal structuring forces at work. The scope of the internal movement district, in this case, is narrower among high-skilled and skill-related jobs than among the low-skilled, easily learned jobs.

When jobs in a plant become highly specialized internally, so that skills learned on one job are not significantly transferable to other jobs within the plant, the internal training sequences diminish in importance. This permits the internal labor market considerable flexibility in both the dimensions of the internal patterns of movement and in the number and location of the ports of entry. The extreme example of an internal labor market in which a high degree of job specialization has produced a substantial erosion of internal training sequences and has reduced the cost and earnings incentives for establishing internal interjob mobility linkages, is in the stitching department of the men's garment manufacturing plant, described above. Since skills and experience acquired on any stitching job in the plant contribute little towards reducing the training time required to learn other stitching jobs in the plant, and long training periods are required to achieve full efficiency on these jobs, a high production cost would be incurred if multiple internal moves occurred in filling job vacancies. Temporary earnings penalties, moreover, would be placed upon the workers, since piece-rate wages are paid for stitching. All of the stitching jobs, therefore, represent separate internal submarkets and are connected directly to the external labor market rather than to other jobs within the internal job structure of the plant.

In the static case, a secondary determinant of the structure of the patterns of internal movement, related to the technology of production, is the size of the internal market. While some small internal market units, such as supermarkets, may be highly structured, the plant with a small internal labor force will often have a very informal market structure. The smallest manufacturing plant examined in this study employed sixty workers and exhibited an internal structure; it is therefore difficult to judge, from empirical observation, at what minimum employment level a formal internal market structure is likely to develop. It is intuitively evident, however, that such a structure becomes unnecessary when the internal labor force is small and there is a highly personalized and informal work relationship with the employer.

As the magnitude of plant employment expands, however, the need for formal structuring increases. When management is required, possibly in a decentralized and impersonal fashion, to develop and implement decisions which affect a large group of employees, pressures toward formal promotion, layoff, and transfer policies appear, both to facilitate the administrative process and to establish consistency of industrial relations policies. At some point, however, as the plant increases in size, the administrative difficulties encountered in regulating a large group of employees within a single plant unit or department may encourage the fragmentizing of such a group into more easily managed units.

Technological change

In the dynamic case changes in the technology of production will influence the internal market structure. Technological change may result in increases or decreases in (1) the job content and the proportion of specialized jobs in the plant and (2) the employment opportunities within the plant. Only the effects on the job structure will be considered here, the employment effects being reserved for the discussion of the more general problem of changes in the volume of internal employment later in the article.

When technological change creates a different set of tasks, or produces a shift in the existing job mix, the internal labor market has either to acquire from the external market or to develop from within the labor skills required by the changed job structure. When the new jobs are of a low-skilled nature or are closely related to the job structure of the plant prior to the technological change, they can usually be integrated into the existing internal market structure without much modification of the rules. Otherwise, adjustments in the internal market structure must be made.

If the appropriate internal training sequences for developing the skills required by the new technology do not exist, the plant faces two alternatives: (1) to develop special training programs, either formal or on the job, for the new skills; or (2) to hire pre-trained workers from the external labor market. For new or unique types of equipment, the selection of the former mode of adjustment is frequently dictated by the unavailability of suitably trained employees on the external market.

When the employer chooses to develop the skills for the new jobs largely through internal training programs, a decision must also be made regarding the selection of trainees. For example, in the case of the introduction of numerically controlled lathes into an aircraft engine plant, operator trainees were selected, on the basis of electronics aptitude tests, from among highly skilled mechanical lathe operators within the plant. Another plant, introducing computerized production equipment, chose to man this equipment with electronics technicians who were then trained in machine operation and maintenance, while a third company with similar equipment recruited high school graduates with high electronic and mechanical aptitudes to fill its operator training program. The decision regarding the internal or external selection of trainees seemed to be influenced, at least in part, by the types of skills and abilities within the internal labor force which could be brought to the training program. It appeared that these training programs were destined to be only a transitory phenomenon, moreover, to be replaced at a later date by new on-the-job progression lines.

If job content is altered, the selection standards applied to applicants, both internal and external, for job vacancies in the plant may also change. Rising job content, for example, may result in higher specific or general aptitude and educational hiring criteria, although it appears that such criteria are often more responsive to external labor market conditions than the internal structure of skills.[23] More emphasis may also be applied to ability factors when selecting employees for upgrading or lateral transfer. One petroleum refinery, for example, found that the changing content of its job structure necessitated a transition from a promotion system emphasizing seniority to one stressing ability.[24]

23. This finding is corroborated to some degree by the conclusions of Richard A. Lester in his study of hiring practices in Trenton. See R. A. Lester, *Hiring Practices and Labor Competition* (Princeton University, 1954), Research Report No. 88, and *Adjustment to Labor Shortages* (Princeton University, 1955), Research Report No. 91.

24. See U.S. Bureau of Labor Statistics, *A Case Study of a Modernized Petroleum Refinery* (G.P.O., 1957), Report No. 120, pp. 7 and 26. This change apparently produced some dissatisfaction among employees.

Product market factors

In a dynamic product market environment both qualitative and quantitative shifts in demand often create internal cost and equity stresses which exert equally important influences upon the internal market structure. In plants which produce more than one product, for example, changes in the product mix of production, without any net change in the volume of internal employment, may result in varying degrees of expansion and contraction in different departments within a plant, which may affect the plant's job structure analogously to a change in technology. Under these circumstances, in some industries the desire to provide greater employment security for employees in contracting departments, to retain certain 'key' or skilled employees within the plant, and to utilize some transferable skills, may result in additional interdepartmental transfer linkages beyond those dictated by efficiency criteria in a static internal market.[25] In other industries, where the technology of production permits, these same objectives may encourage work sharing through shorter hours or reduced productivity in the departments with temporarily declining employment, and overtime, increased productivity, the hiring of temporary help, and the like in the departments with increasing employment.[26]

Predictable employment fluctuations in the internal labor market arising from seasonal or cyclical variations in demand introduce a second dynamic product market influence upon the internal labor market structure. For example, a fluctuating output may encourage broader training of employees by enlarging the content of jobs, and perhaps by establishing wider promotion districts, so that the internal labor force will be more adaptable to upgrading and downgrading. Fluctuations in employment will also influence patterns of downward movement within the internal market. Many internal market structures contain rules which are expressly designed to limit the number of bumps which occur

25. The job structure may also be modified as job content is enlarged to facilitate interdepartment transfers and internal training may be increased by making systematic temporary assignments to broaden workers' skills. See Slichter, Healy, and Livernash, op. cit., pp. 144–5 and 160.

26. A somewhat similar situation arises when a plant makes a permanent product shift, such as from mechanical calculators to electro-mechanical computers, or from aircraft to aerospace or electronics production. The internal market structure will undergo significant modifications when the changing job structure requires substantial retraining of the internal work force and the acquisition of certain additional skills from the external labor market.

during reduction in forces. The restriction of bumping rights to low-skilled jobs and to jobs previously performed are examples of such rules. While some of the costs of bumping are of an administrative nature, the costs of retraining and other adjustments associated with internal job changes are also an important factor.[27] Layoff districts may also be broadened to provide greater employment security for some workers.

Seasonal or cyclical fluctuations in demand may also encourage the dichotomization of the internal labor force into permanent and temporary groups of workers. Typically, the permanent core of production and maintenance employees receives broader internal skill development, is afforded greater opportunities for movement within the internal market, and has considerably more employment security than the temporary employees. The size of the permanent internal labor force will usually be determined by the level of work regularly performed within the internal market. When output, and thus employment, is increased, temporary employees are hired with the specific understanding that their internal employment rights are only transitory, although these employees may be granted preferential opportunities for permanent job vacancies as they appear. These temporary employees are usually relegated to the jobs with low content, to minimize training costs. Familiar examples of such temporary jobs are found in supermarkets, the postal service, and department stores during certain holiday periods. Frequently, temporary employees are also hired in light consumer goods industries for special promotional packing operations, which are labor intensive, and to supplement regularly, on a seasonal basis, the permanent internal labor force.

Changes in the employment opportunities within the internal labor market as a result of secular shifts in product demand may also encourage a modification of the structure of the internal market. When internal employment is secularly declining, internal market restructur-

27. Work sharing plans, within limits, may be developed as an alternative to bumping and layoffs, where the production process and the method of wage payment permits.

The feasibility of limiting bumping chains may be reduced by employee opposition to earnings reductions arising from, for example, direct bumping from high-paying jobs into low-skilled jobs with low earnings levels. This problem becomes more serious as the earnings differentials between job grades become wider. During temporary reductions in forces, some employees facing the probability of being downgraded into low-wage jobs may receive earnings or wage-rate guarantees or may be encouraged, perhaps through liberal S U B payments, to accept voluntarily a layoff rather than to initiate a bumping chain.

ing may occur to increase the job security of at least a portion of the internal labor force. The guarantee of employment, as in one sugar refinery studied, or the extension of preferential employment rights to other plants of a multiplant company, and the establishment of retraining programs are examples of such restructuring.

Accompanying guarantees of employment, or as an independent internal reaction to a reduction in the employment and earnings opportunities within the internal market, groupings of job classifications for purposes of internal movement may be expanded. When this form of internal market restructuring occurs, adjustments must also take place in the amount of internal training and often in the selection criteria for hiring or for upgrading and lateral transfer. In one electronics plant with declining internal employment, a regular training program was developed to enable surplus production workers with clerical aptitudes to transfer into clerical jobs. Less dramatically, a sugar refinery permitted surplus employees with high general aptitudes to transfer laterally between production departments. Typically, such transfer rights and retraining opportunities are conditional upon an employee's demonstration of a strong aptitude for acquiring new job skills.

Conversely, if the product market is undergoing secular expansion, a restructuring of the internal market may have to occur to insure that an adequate supply of skills will be available at all levels of the job structure. A chemical plant in this study had a policy of opening temporary transfer linkages between related production departments whenever employment opportunities in one department were expanding faster than they could satisfactorily be filled by upgrading employees within its progression sequence. This procedure raised the cost of training, however, since the prior on-the-job experience of employees upgraded from other departments was not as applicable as that of employees upgraded within the expanding department.

When the internal growth of job vacancies is so rapid that the upgrading or transfer sequences cannot develop skills rapidly enough, workers may be brought into the internal market at all job levels, providing, of course, either that suitable skills are available on the external market, or that the employer is willing to provide the requisite entry training. Under these conditions, both entry and upgrading may operate simultaneously to fill job vacancies throughout the job structure. In terms of the entry port structure, 'there are more ports of entry in a period of prosperity than in a period of depression.'[28]

28. Kerr, loc. cit., p. 102.

Labor market factors

Finally, the characteristics of the labor market in which a plant is situated will also provide an influence upon the location of the ports of entry into the plant's job structure. When the entry ports occur exclusively among job classifications with low content, the external labor market does not significantly affect the internal market structure. Plants which also find it practical, however, in terms of training costs, to hire into skilled maintenance or operating jobs, will find their ability to do so constrained by the external availability of the appropriate skills and experience. This availability is a function of the 'tightness' of the external labor market in which the plant is located. When external shortages of certain types of skill exist, the entry ports of the skills will cease to function, and the required skills will typically be developed internally.[29] One automobile company, for example, activates a transfer linkage between production and maintenance departments to provide an internal training sequence for maintenance craftsmen whenever such skilled workers cannot be hired on the external market. In another case, an electrical equipment manufacturer intermittently institutes an internal on-the-job training program for automatic screw machine operators in response to shortages of this skill on the external market.

Custom, tradition, and employee pressure

The forces of custom, tradition, employee pressure, and in many instances, unionism also impinge upon the operation of the internal market, occasionally to such a degree that the influences of the 'economic' variables upon the structure of the market, described above, may be substantially reduced or even negated. The original causes of the patterns of movement within a plant may later become obscured; the observed structure of the internal market may then be viewed as a holdover from earlier causal economic influences or even historical accident, and so may be unrelated to the strict cost and efficiency requirements of the present internal market. Divergences from the least-cost internal market structures are, however, clearly limited by competitive pressures in the product market.

Employee pressures for employment and earnings security, union and employer bargaining objectives, and considerations of employee morale may also exercise a modifying influence upon the structure of

29. Depending on the production process, it may also be possible to subcontract some of the work performed within the plant to alleviate internal skill shortages.

internal labor markets. The observed grouping of job classifications for purposes of internal movement represents the product of the interests and pressures of the parties to the rules of the internal market. There is no presumption that such pressures, including sometimes even those of the employer, are necessarily related to the least-cost pattern for providing the internal labor market with the appropriate skills required by the job structure of the plant. Nor is there any indication that these pressures of bargaining objectives must reflect an underlying community of worker, union, or employer opinion regarding 'desirable' patterns of internal movement.

To the extent that these non-economic variables modify the internal market structure, it is difficult to predict patterns of internal movement solely from the economic variables. Some of the diversity of hiring, promotion, and transfer patterns, found even among similar plants in this study, is probably attributable in some measure to such factors, since the immediate objectives prescribed by economic variables such as technology, product markets, external labor markets, training ladders, and the like, may be balanced against the non-economic variables by adjusting the amount of internal training.

Summary

The type of structure exhibited by an industrial internal labor market is initially a function of the economic forces of (1) the technology of the production process, (2) the quantitative and qualitative changes in product demand, and (3) the availability of various types and qualities of labor on the external labor market. The influence of these economic forces is frequently modified by non-economic factors such as custom, bargaining objectives, and employment and earnings security.

Since the internal labor market must not only operate efficiently in a static state but must also adjust efficiently to a dynamic economic environment, the influences of the economic determinants upon the internal market structure may be evaluated in terms of their effect upon the costs of obtaining the requisite skills. The costs of recruitment, selection, and skill development associated with various internal market structures are a function of the level, distribution, and plant specificity of the content of the job classifications within the internal job structure, the degree of transferability of skills and experience among these jobs, the amount of labor turnover, and the external availability of workers. These costs must be balanced against the pressures of equity and other non-economic factors in the final determination of the internal market structure. When similar economic costs are associated with alternative internal market structures, considerable latitude is possible in the choice of structure, so that non-economic considerations may be controlling. If significant economic cost differentials exist among alternative internal market structures, however, the competitive product market forces will limit the extent to which the internal market structure can be incompatible with the efficient operation of the plant.

10   A Theory of Labor Market Segmentation

Michael Reich*

Assistant Professor of Economics, Boston University

David M. Gordon*
Richard C. Edwards*

Research Associates, Center for Educational Policy Research,
Harvard University

From: *American Economics Review*, Vol. 63, No. 2, May 1973, pp. 359–65.

A growing body of empirical research has documented persistent divisions among American workers: divisions by race, sex, educational credentials, industry grouping, and so forth (F. B. Weisskoff, B. Bluestone, S. Bowles and H. Gintis, D. Gordon, 1971 and 1972, B. Harrison, M. Reich, H. Wachtel and C. Betsey, and H. Zellner). These groups seem to operate in different *labor markets*, with different working conditions, different promotional opportunities, different wages, and different market institutions.

These continuing labor market divisions pose anomalies for neoclassical economists. Orthodox theory assumes that profit-maximizing employers evaluate workers in terms of their *individual* characteristics and predicts that labor market differences among groups will decline over time because of competitive mechanisms (K. Arrow). But by most measures, the labor market differences among groups have not been disappearing (R. Edwards, M. Reich, and T. Weisskopf, chs. 5, 7, 8). The continuing importance of *groups* in the labor market thus is neither explained nor predicted by orthodox theory.

Why is the labor force in general still so fragmented? Why are group characteristics repeatedly so important in the labor market? In this paper, we summarize an emerging radical theory of labor market segmentation; we develop the full arguments in Reich, Gordon, and Edwards. The theory argues that political and economic forces within

*This research was supported by a grant from the Manpower Administration, U.S. Department of Labor. Needless to say, we alone are responsible for the views expressed in this paper.

American capitalism have given rise to and perpetuated segmented labor markets, and that it is incorrect to view the sources of segmented markets as exogenous to the economic system.

Present labor market segmentation

We define labor market segmentation as the historical process whereby political-economic forces encourage the division of the labor market into separate submarkets, or segments, distinguished by different labor market characteristics and behavioral rules. Segmented labor markets are thus the outcome of a segmentation process. Segments may cut horizontally across the occupational hierarchy as well as vertically. We suggest that present labor market conditions can most usefully be understood as the outcome of four segmentation processes.

1. Segmentation into primary and secondary markets

The primary and secondary segments, to use the terminology of dual labor market theory, are differentiated mainly by stability characteristics. Primary jobs require and develop stable working habits; skills are often acquired on the job; wages are relatively high; and job ladders exist. Secondary jobs do not require and often discourage stable working habits; wages are low; turnover is high; and job ladders are few. Secondary jobs are mainly (though not exclusively) filled by minority workers, women, and youth.

2. Segmentation within the primary sector

Within the primary sector we see a segmentation between what we call 'subordinate' and 'independent' primary jobs. Subordinate primary jobs are routinized and encourage personality characteristics of dependability, discipline, responsiveness to rules and authority, and acceptance of a firm's goals. Both factory and office jobs are present in this segment. In contrast, independent primary jobs encourage and require creative, problem-solving, self-initiating characteristics and often have professional standards for work. Voluntary turnover is high and individual motivation and achievement are highly rewarded.

3. Segmentation by race

While minority workers are present in secondary, subordinate primary and independent primary segments they often face distinct segments within those submarkets. Certain jobs are 'race-typed,' segregated by prejudice and by labor market institutions. Geographic separation plays an important role in maintaining divisions between race segments.

4. Segmentation by sex

Certain jobs have generally been restricted to men; others to women. Wages in the female segment are usually lower than in comparable male jobs; female jobs often require and encourage a 'serving mentality' – an orientation toward providing services to other people and particularly to men. These characteristics are encouraged by family and schooling institutions.

The historical origins of labor market segmentation

The present divisions of the labor market are best understood from an historical analysis of their origins. We argue that segmentation arose during the transition from competitive to monopoly capitalism. Our historical analysis focuses on the era of monopoly capitalism, from roughly 1890 to the present, with special emphasis on the earlier transitional years.

During the preceding period of competitive capitalism, labor market developments pointed toward the progressive *homogenization* of the labor force, not toward segmentation. The factory system eliminated many skilled craft occupations, creating large pools of semiskilled jobs (N. Ware). Production for a mass market and increased mechanization forged standardized work requirements. Large establishments drew greater numbers of workers into common working environments.

The increasingly homogeneous and proletarian character of the work force generated tensions which were manifest in the tremendous upsurge in labor conflict that accompanied the emergence of monopoly capitalism: in railroads dating back to 1877, in steel before 1901 and again in 1919, in coal mining during and after World War I, in textile mills throughout this period, and in countless other plants and industries around the country. The success of the Industrial Workers of the World (IWW), the emergence of a strong Socialist party, the general (as opposed to industry-specific) strikes in Seattle and New Orleans, the mass labor revolts in 1919 and 1920, and the increasingly national character of the labor movement throughout this period indicated a widespread and growing opposition to capitalist hegemony in general. More and more, strikes begun 'simply' over wage issues often escalated to much more general issues (J. Brecher, J. Commons).

At the same time that the work force was becoming more homogenous, those oligopolistic corporations that still dominate the economy today began to emerge and to consolidate their power. The captains of the new monopoly capitalist era, now released from short-run competitive pressures and in search of long-run stability, turned to the capture of strategic *control* over product and factor markets. Their new concerns were the creation and exploitation of monopolistic control, rather than the allocational calculus of short-run profit-maximization. (For examples see A. Chandler, B. Emmet and J. Jeuck, R. Hidy and M. Hidy, and A. Nevins.)

The new needs of monopoly capitalism for control were threatened by the consequences of homogenization and proletarianization of the work force. Evidence abounds that large corporations were painfully aware of the potentially revolutionary character of these movements. As Commons notes, the employers' 'mass offensive' on unions between 1903 and 1908 was more of an ideological crusade than a matter of specific demands. The simultaneous formation of the National Civic Federation (NCF), a group dominated by large 'progressive' capitalists, was another explicit manifestation of the fundamental crises facing the capitalist class (J. Weinstein). The historical analysis which follows suggests that to meet this threat employers actively and consciously fostered labor market segmentation in order to 'divide and conquer' the labor force. Moreover, the efforts of monopolistic corporations to gain greater control of their product markets led to a dichotomization of the industrial structure which had the indirect and unintended, though not undesired, effect of reinforcing their conscious strategies. Thus labor market segmentation arose both from conscious strategies and systemic forces.[1]

Conscious efforts

Monopoly capitalist corporations devised deliberate strategies to resolve the contradictions between the increased proletarianization of the work force and the growth and consolidation of concentrated corporate power. The central thrust of the new strategies was to break down the increasingly unified worker interests that grew out of the proletarianization of work and the concentration of workers in urban areas. As exhibited in several aspects of these large firms' operations, this effort

1. We have paid more attention in this brief summary to employers' conscious efforts because the other papers presented in this session provide a complementary emphasis on systemic forces. We fully develop both explanations in Reich, Gordon, and Edwards.

aimed to divide the labor force into various segments so that the actual experiences of workers were different and the basis of their common opposition to capitalists undermined.[2]

The first element in the new strategy involved the internal relations of the firm. The tremendous growth in the size of monopoly capitalist work forces, along with the demise of craft-governed production, necessitated a change in the authority relations upon which control in the firm rested (R. Edwards). Efforts toward change in this area included Taylorism and Scientific Management, the establishment of personnel departments, experimentation with different organizational structures, the use of industrial psychologists, 'human relations experts' and others to devise appropriate 'motivating' incentives, and so forth (L. Baritz, A. Chandler, S. Marglin and F. Miller and M. Coghill). From this effort emerged the intensification of hierarchical control, particularly the 'bureaucratic form' of modern corporations. In the steel industry, for example, a whole new system of stratified jobs was introduced shortly after the formation of U.S. Steel (K. Stone). The effect of bureaucratization was to establish a rigidly graded hierarchy of jobs and power by which 'top-down' authority could be exercised.

The restructuring of the internal relations of the firm furthered labor market segmentation through the creation of segmented 'internal labor markets.' Job ladders were created, with definite 'entry-level' jobs and patterns of promotion. White-collar workers entered the firm's work force and were promoted within it in different ways from the blue-collar production force. Workers not having the qualifications for particular entry-level jobs were excluded from access to that entire job ladder. In response, unions often sought to gain freedom from the arbitrary discretionary power of supervisors by demanding a seniority criterion for promotion. In such cases, the union essentially took over the management of the internal labor markets: they agreed to allocate workers and discipline recalcitrants, helping legitimize the internal market in return for a degree of control over its operation (P. Doeringer and M. Piore).

One such effort at internal control eventually resulted in segmentation by industry. Firms had initially attempted to raise the cost to workers of leaving individual companies (but not the cost of entering)

2. These efforts were 'conscious' in the following sense. Capitalists faced immediate problems and events and devised strategies to meet them. Successful strategies survived and were copied. These efforts were not 'conscious' in the sense that those who undertook them understood fully the historical forces acting upon them or all the ramifications of their policies. As we argue in the text, in certain cases capitalists acted out of a broader class consciousness.

by restricting certain benefits to continued employment in that company. Part of this strategy was 'welfare capitalism' which emerged from the NCF in particular, and achieved most pronounced form in the advanced industries. At Ford, for example, education for the workers' children, credit, and other benefits were dependent on the workers' continued employment by the firm and therefore tied the worker more securely to the firm. For these workers, the loss of one's job meant a complete disruption in all aspects of the family's life. Likewise, seniority benefits were lost when workers switched companies (Weinstein). As industrial unions gained power, they transformed some of these firm-specific benefits to industry-wide privileges. The net effect was an intensification not only of internal segmentation, but also of segmentation by industry, which, as we discuss in the next section, had other origins as well.

At the same time that firms were segmenting their internal labor markets, similar efforts were under way with respect to the firm's external relations. Employers quite consciously exploited race, ethnic, and sex antagonisms in order to undercut unionism and break strikes. In numerous instances during the consolidation of monopoly capitalism, employers manipulated the mechanisms of labor supply in order to import blacks as strikebreakers, and racial hostility was stirred up to deflect class conflicts into race conflicts. For example, during the steel strike of 1919, one of the critical points in U.S. history, some 30,000 to 40,000 blacks were imported as strikebreakers in a matter of a few weeks. Employers also often transformed jobs into 'female jobs' in order to render those jobs less susceptible to unionization (Brecher, D. Brody, Commons).

Employers also consciously manipulated ethnic antagonisms to achieve segmentation. Employers often hired groups from rival nationalities in the same plant or in different plants. During labor unrest the companies sent spies and rumor mongers to each camp, stirring up fears, hatred, and antagonisms of other groups. The strategy was most successful when many immigrant groups had little command of English (Brecher, Brody).

The manipulation of ethnic differences was, however, subject to two grave limitations as a tool in the strategy of 'divide and conquer.' First, increasing English literacy among immigrants allowed them to communicate more directly with each other; second, mass immigration ended in 1924. Corporations then looked to other segmentations of more lasting significance. Employers also tried to weaken the union movement by favoring the conservative 'business-oriented' craft unions against the newer 'social-oriented' industrial unions. An ideology of corporate liberalism toward labor was articulated around the turn of the century in the NCF. Corporate liberalism recognized the potential gains of legitimizing some unions but not others; the NCF worked jointly with the craft-dominated American Federation of Labor to undermine the more militant industrial unions, the Socialist party, and the IWW (Weinstein).

As the period progressed, employers also turned to a relatively new divisive means, the use of educational 'credentials.' For the first time, educational credentials were used to *regularize* skill requirements for jobs. Employers played an active role in molding educational institutions to serve these channeling functions. The new requirements helped maintain the somewhat artificial distinctions between factory workers and those in routinized office jobs and helped generate some strong divisions within the office between semiskilled white-collar workers and their more highly skilled office mates (Bowles, Bowles and Gintis, Cohen and Lazerson and Edwards).

Systemic forces

The rise of giant corporations and the emergence of a monopolistic core in the economy sharply accentuated some systemic market forces that stimulated and reinforced segmentation. As different firms and industries grew at different rates, a dichotomization of industrial structure developed (R. Averitt, T. Vietorisz and B. Harrison, and J. O'Connor). The larger, more capital-intensive firms were generally sheltered by barriers to entry, enjoyed technological, market power, and financial economies of scale and generated higher rates of profit and growth than their smaller, labor-intensive competitive counterparts. However, it did not turn out that the monopolistic core firms were wholly to swallow up the competitive periphery firms.

Given their large capital investments, the large monopolistic corporations required stable market demand and stable planning horizons in order to insure that their investments would not go unutilized (J. K. Galbraith). Where demand was cyclical, seasonal, or otherwise unstable, production within the monopolistic environment became increasingly unsuitable. More and more, production of certain products was subcontracted or 'exported' to small, more competitive and less capital-intensive firms on the industrial periphery.

Along with the dualism in the industrial structure, there developed a corresponding dualism of working environments, wages, and mobility patterns. Monopoly corporations, with more stable production and sales, developed job structures and internal relations reflecting that stability. For example, the bureaucratization of work rewarded and elicited stable work habits in employees. In peripheral firms, where product demand was unstable, jobs and workers tended to be marked also by instability. The result was the dichotomization of the urban labor market into 'primary' and 'secondary' sectors, as the dual labor market theory has proposed (Gordon, 1972, Piore).

In addition, certain systemic forces intensified segmentation within corporations in the primary sector. As Piore has argued, the evolution of technology within primary work places tended to promote distinctions between jobs requiring general and specific skills. As new technologies emerged which replicated these differential skill requirements, employers found that they could most easily train for particular jobs those workers who had already developed those different kinds of skills. As highly technical jobs evolved in which the application of generalized, problem-solving techniques were required, for instance, employers found that they could get the most out of those who had already developed those traits. Initial differences in productive capacities were inevitably reinforced.

The social functions of labor market segmentation

As the preceding historical analysis has argued, labor market segmentation is intimately related to the dynamics of monopoly capitalism. Understanding its origins, we are now in a position to assess its social importance.

Labor market segmentation arose and is perpetuated because it is *functional* – that is, it facilitates the operation of capitalist institutions. Segmentation is functional primarily because it helps reproduce capitalist hegemony. First, as the historical analysis makes quite clear, segmentation divides workers and forestalls potential movements uniting all workers against employers. (For an interesting analysis, see C. Kerr and A. Siegel). Second, segmentation establishes 'fire trails' across vertical job ladders and, to the extent that workers perceive separate segments with different criteria for access, workers limit their own aspirations for mobility. Less pressure is then placed on other social institutions – the schools and the family, for example – that reproduce the class structure. Third, division of workers into segments legitimizes inequalities in authority and control between superiors and subordinates. For example, institutional sexism and racism reinforce the industrial authority of white male foremen.

Political implications

One of the principal barriers to united anticapitalist opposition among workers has been the evolution and persistence of labor market segmentation. This segmentation underlies the current state of variegation in class consciousness among different groups of workers. A better understanding of the endogenous sources of uneven levels of consciousness helps to explain the difficulties involved in overcoming divisions among workers. Nonetheless, if we more clearly understand the sources of our divisions, we may be able to see more clearly how to overcome them.

References

ARROW, K., 'Some Models of Racial Discrimination in the Labor Force,' in A. Pascal, ed., *The American Economy in Black and White*, Santa Monica, 1971.

AVERITT, R., *The Dual Economy*, New York, 1967.

BARITZ, L., *Servants of Power*, Middletown, Conn., 1964.

BLUESTONE, B., 'Institutional and Industrial Determinants of Wage Differentials,' mimeo, Boston College, 1971.

BOWLES, S., 'Understanding Unequal Economic Opportunity,' *Amer. Econ. Rev., Proc.*, May 1973.

BOWLES, S., and GINTIS, H., 'IQ in the U.S. Social Structure,' *Social Policy*, Jan.–Feb. 1973.

BRECHER, J., *Strike!*, San Francisco, 1972.

BRODY, D., *Steelworkers: The Non-Union Era*, New York, 1965.

CHANDLER, A., *Strategy and Structure*, New York, 1966.

COHEN, D., and LAZERSON, M., 'Education and the Industrial Order,' *Socialist Revolution*, Mar.–Apr. 1972.

COMMONS, J., *History of Labor in the United States*, New York, 1935.

DOERINGER, P., and PIORE, M., *Internal Labor Markets and Manpower Analysis*, Lexington, Mass. 1972.

EDWARDS, R., 'Alienation and Inequality: Capitalist Relations of Production in Bureaucratic Enterprises,' unpublished Ph.D. dissertation, Harvard Univ., 1972.

EDWARDS, R., REICH, M., and WEISSKOPF, T., *The Capitalist System*, Englewood Cliffs, 1972.

EMMET, B., and JEUCK, J., *Catalogues and Counters*, Chicago, 1950.

GALBRAITH, J. K., *The New Industrial State*, Boston, 1967.

GORDON, D., 'Class, Productivity, and the Ghetto: A Study of Labor Market Stratification,' unpublished Ph.D. dissertation, Harvard Univ., 1971.

GORDON, D., *Theories of Poverty and Underemployment*, Lexington, Mass., 1972.

HARRISON, B., *Education, Training and the Urban Ghetto*, Baltimore, 1972.

HIDY, R., and HIDY, M., *Pioneering in Big Business 1882–1911*, New York, 1955.

KERR, C., and SIEGEL, A., 'The Interindustry Propensity to Strike,' in A. Flanders, ed., *Collective Bargaining*, Baltimore, 1969.

MARGLIN, S., 'What Do Bosses Do?', mimeo, Harvard Univ., 1971.

MILLER, F., and COGHILL, M., *The Historical Sources of Personnel Work*, Ithaca, 1961.

NEVINS, A., *Ford: The Times, The Man, The Company*, New York, 1954.

O'CONNOR, J., 'Inflation, Fiscal Crisis, and the American Working Class,' *Socialist Revolution*, Mar.–Apr. 1972.

PIORE, M., 'Notes for Theory of Labor Market Stratification,' Working Paper No. 95, Dept. of Econ., Mass. Instit. of Tech., Oct. 1972.

REICH, M., 'The Economics of Racism,' in D. Gordon, ed., *Problems in Political Economy*, Lexington, Mass., 1971.

REICH, M., GORDON, D., and EDWARDS, R., 'Labor Market Segmentation in American Capitalism,' forthcoming, 1973.

STONE, K., 'Labor Management and the Origin of Job Structures in the Steel Industry,' mimeo, Harvard Univ., 1973.

VIETORISZ, T., and HARRISON, B., 'Labor Market Segmentation: Positive Feedback and Divergent Development,' *Amer. Econ. Rev., Proc.*, May 1973.

WACHTEL, H., and BETSEY, C., 'Low Wage Workers and the Dual Labor Market,' mimeo, American Univ., Apr. 1972.

WARE, N., *The Industrial Worker, 1840–1860*, Chicago, 1964.

WEINSTEIN, J., *The Corporate Ideal in the Liberal State*, Boston, 1967.

WEISSKOFF, F. B., 'Women's Place in the Labor Market,' *Amer. Econ. Rev., Proc.*, Vol. 62, May 1972, pp. 161–6.

ZELLNER, H., 'Discrimination Against Women, Occupational Segregation, and the Relative Wage,' *Amer. Econ. Rev., Proc.*, May 1972.

11　Structured Labour Markets, Worker Organization and Low Pay

Jill Rubery*

Department of Applied Economics, University of Cambridge

From: *Cambridge Journal of Economics*, Vol. 2, No. 1, March 1978, pp. 17–36.

The persistence of low paid sectors in an affluent, advanced capitalist society has been attributed in recent American literature to the emergence of non-competitive, or structured labour markets. Firms operate *internal* labour markets providing high wages and secure employment. This limits the mobility of workers both within the internal or *primary* labour market sector, and between the primary and the residual, competitive *secondary* sector. No competitive equalization of wages takes place, and differences in wage levels may be maintained over the long term if the system of segmentation reduces class consciousness, or if there is divergent development in the economic structure.

Segmentation of the labour market has long been considered a cause of inequality and low wages in the labour market (Mill, 1849; Cairnes, 1874). Recent work in this area, however, effectively divides into two types. The first builds upon the nineteenth-century notion of non-competing groups in the labour market, where social and political inequality is inherited and children are confined to the same segment of the labour market as their parents. Added to this model is the effect of discrimination in setting up further barriers to mobility, barriers which become more resilient in a world of imperfect information, where prejudiced beliefs can become self-justifying (Myrdal, 1944; Akerlof, 1970; Spence, 1973). These theories, often called theories of 'low level equilibrium traps', continue the methodology of orthodox theory, where the origins of inequality are exogenous to the economic system, but add to analysis a process of reinforcement of existing social and political inequality through the operation of the labour market.

The second approach, with which we shall be primarily concerned in

*I am grateful to Frank Wilkinson for his invaluable help and encouragement from the start of my work in this area. I would also like to thank the editors of the *Cambridge Journal of Economics* and Diane Flaherty for their advice during the final stages of preparation of this paper.

this paper, adopts a different methodology and looks at the relationship between the development of the economic structure and the emergence of segmented labour markets. In these models inequality originates within the economic system. Two main sets of theories have been produced using this methodology: dual labour market theories (Doeringer and Piore, 1971) and radical theories (Gordon, 1972; Edwards, Reich and Gordon, 1975). Dual labour market theories look primarily to technological developments under capitalism or to the divergent development of the industrial structure to explain the emergence of labour market segmentation. Radical theories attribute the origins of stratification in the labour market to the capitalists' need to divide and rule the labour force.

Many of the specific elements of the dual labour market and radical approaches can be found in orthodox economics. It has been recognized for some time that labour is often more properly considered as a quasi-fixed factor to the firm rather than variable (Oi, 1962), particularly if there are costs of hiring and firing, and investment in job-specific skills (Marshall, 1920; Becker, 1964). These considerations have led to the development of theories of internal labour markets similar to dual labour market theories. Further, discrimination theories have been used under both approaches to explain the concentration of certain groups in different segments of the labour market. Under the second approach, discrimination only reinforces and does not create inequality. The development of non-competing groups and internal labour markets has seriously reduced the explanatory power of the orthodox theory of wage determination. Dual labour market and radical theories attempt to offer some explanation of the extent of the development of internal labour markets, and its effects on those workers left outside, by relating the analysis to the economic structure.

This important new approach has so far progressed in an *ad hoc* fashion. Dual labour market theory built on theories of internal labour markets, theories of discrimination, and general theories of dualism or divergent development in the economy. The radical approach attempted to place the dual labour market theory in an historical and ideological framework. Each new contribution adopted parts of the previous theories, with no one theory developing its arguments from first principles. The result, we shall argue, is that the analysis as it now stands is more a rationalization of the present structure of the American labour market than an explanation of how this was arrived at from the range of development paths open to it. It is this particular aspect of the American theories which has made them so far so difficult to apply to the analysis of labour market structures outside the U.S. There is evidence that there is some degree of segmentation in the British external labour market, and non-competitive organization of the internal industry or firm labour forces, but the form and nature of this labour market segmentation differs from that found in the U.S. (Mackay *et al.*, 1971).

We shall argue in this paper that the main reason for the lack of general applicability of the American theories arises from the almost exclusive attention paid to the actions and motivations of the capitalists in developing a structured labour market, and the consequent neglect of the role of worker organization in the process. Further inadequacies appear in the theory because the consideration of major change in the economic structure is limited to one historical epoch: the end of the nineteenth and beginning of the twentieth centuries, which saw the development of widespread factory and machine production and the emergence of monopoly capitalism. Change in the economic structure at this time may indeed have been more intensive and extensive than in other eras, but the almost total concentration on this period results in a rather static analysis of present-day labour market structure. Recent work by Braverman (1974) has pointed to the importance of continuing the analysis of the evolution of the employment structure into the period of monopoly capitalism. Significant changes in occupational structure, skills and labour force participation have taken place, changes which may particularly affect the structure and importance of low paid occupations.

If a more general approach to the analysis of labour market segmentation is to be developed which could explain differences between, for instance, the U.K. and U.S. labour market structures, as well as developments within a given labour market, two major changes must be made. First, workers and worker organization must be assigned an active role in the development of labour market structure. Second, changes in the employment structure under monopoly capitalism must be taken into account, and their effects on labour market segmentation examined. This analysis must, we shall argue, be carried out within the context of a continuous struggle between capitalists and workers on the industrial front, over wages and over control of production.

This paper first considers in more detail dual labour market and radical theory, before moving on to a consideration of the evolution of the employment structure under monopoly capitalism. We may then be in a position to analyse the struggle between capitalists and workers, and the role of worker organization in developing labour market segmentation in both internal and external labour markets. This discussion will be illustrated by some examples from the U.K. Finally, we consider how the emergence and persistence of low paid sectors in a capitalist economy could be analysed, comparing our approach both to the dual labour market and radical theories and to a more orthodox perspective.

1. Dual labour market and radical theories

(i) Dual labour market theory

The development of an analysis of low pay, emphasizing the importance of the economic structure, began with dual labour market theory. This built upon the work of Slichter (1950), Lester (1952), Kerr (1954) and others in the 1950s, which pointed to the development of internal, or balkanized, labour markets under modern capitalism. The contribution of dual labour market theory was to consider the effects of the development of internal labour markets not only on those included within them, but also on those excluded from this sheltered sector, and confined to the residual competitive secondary sector.

Internal labour markets develop, according to the theory, because skills are becoming more firm-specific and a worker's productivity is becoming more and more a function of his on-the-job training and experience, and hence of his length of service within a firm. In order to encourage the development of a stable labour force, an employer will pay his workers more than their opportunity wage in the external labour market, thus reducing the incentive to mobility among the workers. With mobility restricted or eliminated, there will be little market influence on the shape of the internal wage structure of the firm, which will come to be determined by custom and by rules. The labour market will thus be divided up into relatively independent sections.

Doeringer and Piore (1971) took up this theory and looked at its implications for the labour market as a whole.[1] In their model the market is divided into primary and secondary sectors. Technology and workers' skills have become less general and more firm-specific and a

1. We are confining our discussion of dual labour market theory to the Doeringer–Piore model. Many other variants of the dualism hypothesis have been presented; for instance, Bluestone (1971) has stressed the importance of industrial structure in determining dualism, and Vietorisz and Harrison (1973) have looked at the problem of divergent technological development in the economy. Many of these other theories are more fruitful than the Doeringer–Piore model, but they are still only partial approaches and not as well known or as often cited.

stable labour force has become more necessary. To induce stability, high wages and prospects of advancement are offered by restricting the number of 'ports of entry', to each of which a promotion ladder is attached, with progress up the ladder determined by seniority. The provision of such employment conditions, however, is costly. The need for a stable labour force applies only to certain types of jobs; where incentives to stability are not necessary, wages remain low, security of employment is not assured, and promotion prospects are few. This type of job forms the secondary sector; the former constitutes the primary sector.

An important aspect of dual labour market analysis is the emphasis on the interaction between developments in the economic structure, developments in technology and the pattern of labour market behaviour. Technological developments required a reduction in labour mobility, but only the development of oligopolistic markets, which allow firms much greater control and certainty in their product and factor markets, permitted the formation of stable, high paid labour forces. The secondary sector, in turn, provides that degree of flexibility still required by the system. Expansion of the primary sector over the trade cycle can be achieved by subcontracting to the secondary sector, or by employing secondary sector workers on a temporary basis. Likewise, the technologically determined division of the labour market is reinforced by the reactions of workers to their position in the market. Workers confined to the secondary sector develop attitudes and modes of behaviour which turn them into inherently unstable workers, unsuitable for employment in the primary sector.[2]

In this theory, all positive developments take place in the primary sector. It is here that technology is changing, that new labour market structures are developed. Changes in the secondary sector serve only to reinforce its already dominant characteristics; that is, its lack of structure, stagnant technology and absence of differentiation between workers.

2. Doeringer and Piore and some radical theorists (Gordon, 1972) argue that secondary workers may become objectively unsuitable for the primary sector. Their proposition of restricted mobility between the two sectors could be maintained under the weaker assumption that secondary sector workers become labelled as unsuitable for the primary sector, a reformulation which would make their analysis more generally applicable. The emphasis in these theories on the development of a subculture in the labour force is probably one example of how this approach has been particularly influenced by the characteristics of the American labour market, where the blacks could be considered to form a lower class (Piore, 1975, p. 114), distinct in attitudes and orientation from the working class.

(ii) The development of the radical approach

Doeringer and Piore emphasized the importance of technology in the development of dualism in the labour market. Control of the labour force enters into the model only in so far as employers cannot expect workers to form a stable labour force unless they are offered advantages over and above the external market wage. Control plays a much more central part in radical theories. These theories developed out of the dual labour market approach in an attempt to incorporate this theory 'into a more general radical framework, convinced that the dual labour market hypotheses can be generated by radical theory and that radical theory provides some important historical foundations for the specific conclusions of dual market analysis' (Gordon, 1972, p. 52). At the outset, the requirement of a stable labour force for the efficient functioning of complex technology was retained, but added to it was another, and complementary, determinant of stratification: the need for capitalists to control the labour force, which, with the development of factory production, was becoming more homogeneous and thus more likely to unite against them. Stratification would allow the capitalists to 'divide and rule' the labour force. Jobs were divided up into grades, or clusters, but within each grade promotion ladders were established. This stratification served to reduce the likelihood of the development of class consciousness between grades in the labour force, but within each grade the promotion ladders provided the incentive necessary to motivate the workers. According to Gordon (1972, p. 77):

employers will seek to develop in the labor force a kind of 'hierarchy fetishism' – a continual craving for more and better job titles and status, the satisfaction of which leads eventually to intensified hunger for still more and better job titles and job status ... And in order to create hierarchical incentives without providing too many mobility opportunities, in order to satisfy 'hierarchy fetishism' without simultaneously establishing a continuum of relationships among workers along which they can develop common class consciousness – employers may find it useful to forge hierarchical ladders within clearly differentiated job clusters.

The capitalists were apparently remarkably successful in their strategy, in as much as they developed 'hierarchy fetishism' among their workers at the same time as they were restricting opportunities for mobility and, indeed, as real skill differences were declining.

Radical theory extends the analysis of stratification to emphasize differentiation between workers within internal labour markets as well as between the secondary and primary sectors. The lowest stratum of workers may either be attached to the bottom of the job hierarchy within a particular firm or industry, or be employed in secondary sector industries or occupations located outside the internal labour market sector. Those groups most subject to discrimination and prejudice would be concentrated in these low paid, menial occupations. This segmentation serves two purposes. First, the existence of a lower stratum increases the status and status orientation of those in the higher strata. Second, workers in the upper strata are unlikely to identify with the interests of the blacks and women concentrated in the menial occupations, and thus low wages can be paid to these workers without risk of class opposition.

Over time, the need to control the labour force has come to be considered the major determinant of stratification in the labour market, and indeed a conflict has been identified between the system of work organization which may be efficient for technology and that which affords capitalists the most 'control' over the labour force (Bowles and Gintis, 1975; Gordon, 1976). Gordon has called these two aspects of efficiency the technological, or quantitative, aspect and the control, or qualitative, aspect, where 'a production process is qualitatively [most] efficient if it maximizes the ability of the ruling class to reproduce its domination of the social process of production and minimizes producers' resistance to ruling-class domination of the production process' (1976, p. 22). Gordon further argues that, as workers' organization becomes stronger, qualitative considerations will become dominant and employers will increasingly make their choice of technique and method of work organization on the basis of the opportunity to control.

(iii) Criticisms of the dual labour market and radical approaches

Our main criticism of both dual labour market and radical theories is that the development of the economic structure is viewed from only one perspective: through the motivations and actions of capitalists. Workers, in these theories, play little part in the formation of structured labour markets. A basic premise of radical theory is that the development of a homogeneous labour force would maximize the benefit to workers and the disadvantage to capitalists. Homogeneity of the labour force would allow workers to develop their organization and carry out their battles over wages and control of production, unhampered by artificial divisions. This proposition, we shall argue, ignores the practical problems for workers of establishing a bargaining position from which to conduct their struggle, a bargaining position which perhaps can only be established and maintained through the development of a structured labour force.

In dual labour market theory, internal labour markets are seen as providing benefits for workers, and, more importantly, costs for employers, particularly as employers must sacrifice flexibility for stability of the labour force. Occasionally, it is acknowledged, unions may force the introduction of internal labour market structures in firms, but technology is seen as the main determinant of the development of the primary sector, unions having only marginal effects on the structure of such markets.

Recently, attempts have been made to incorporate the role of trade unions into the radical theory framework, and even to substitute trade unions for capitalists as the main agent through which structured labour markets are established. Lawrence Kahn has contrasted his view of the development of structured labour markets with that of the radical theorists:

In our view, the day-to-day struggle between unions and employees plays a very important role in the formation of internal labour markets. For Edwards *et al.*, labour unrest serves as a signal to firms to stratify the labour force so as to remove the sources of unrest (Kahn, 1975, p. 15).

However, Kahn's theory suggests that, in the long run, unionization may be of benefit to capitalists, because the high wages associated with unionism may encourage technological change and induce savings in labour productivity within the firm. This would be a long-term process, leading to divergent development in the economy, as unionized firms would expect high wages to persist. It is hard to see in this analysis why capitalists should resist unions, or high wages, if all these high productivity – high wage techniques are open to them. Perhaps the part of the theory that is missing is the role of unions in bargaining over productivity increases and technological changes, at times thwarting the productivity plans of management.[3]

Gordon's (1976) proposition, that as worker organization develops qualitative efficiency considerations will dominate quantitative ones, brings worker organization back into the analysis, but only in a passive

3. Kahn (1975) suggests that management may recoup union losses by increasing the skill mix of the labour force. In section 4 we shall argue that the percentage of skilled labour may well be influenced by unionism, but that the unions will attempt to increase or maintain it while management will attempt to decrease it.

role. It is the threat of worker resistance which determines which system of work organization employers choose. Unions play no active part in the development and organization of the work process.

Worker organization may well have played a more important part in the development of structured labour markets in the U.K. than in the U.S. (see below, section 4). However, Kahn's (1975) evidence of how workers successfully transformed conditions of employment in longshoring in San Francisco, where a system of low wages, unstable earnings and casual employment was overturned, suggests that the role and effectiveness of unions even within the U.S. labour market may have been underestimated.

Radical theory views history not only through the eyes of capitalists, but also through the collective eye of all capitalists, or capitalists as a class. Thus the historical development of a stratified labour market is seen as part of the capitalist class' strategy to divide and rule the labour force.[4] This approach directs attention away from the particular circumstances which induced individual employers to develop internal labour markets where workers earn above the external market wage. Avoidance of imminent industrial action, installation of new technology, or an attempt to gain some competitive advantage over rival firms, are much more likely to underlie a change in wage and employment policy, than some strategy to avoid long-term, widespread class opposition. If one views the process of development of labour market structures at the level of the individual firm, rather than in a class context, it becomes clear that, contrary to Gordon's hypothesis, capitalists may not sacrifice quantitative for qualitative efficiency, but, motivated by competition amongst themselves and forced by opposition from organized labour, may sacrifice some of their qualitative control of the labour force in order to achieve more rapid introduction of new technology (see below, section 4).

The notion of a contradiction between the quantitative and qualitative aspects of efficiency was introduced by radicals in an attempt to integrate recent work on the labour process into their analysis. Braverman

4. Gordon (1972) argues that capitalists share class interests at the same time as being in competition with each other. At times these class interests dominate over competition and the drive for accumulation; 'capitalists may find it in their long-run interest to permit a slight increase in relative wages ... in order to intensify competition among different classes of workers by allowing the relative share of some classes to rise' (p. 65). Indeed, the 'entire set of hypotheses (of radical theory) ... suggests that recent phenomena derive at least partly from a pursuit by the capitalist class of their own collective interests' (p. 80).

(1974) cast doubt on the importance of job-specific skills, thus undermining the Doeringer–Piore theory of dualism, and presenting problems for radicals who had assumed that stratification in the labour market has served two functions for capitalists: providing the stable labour force required by technology and at the same time reducing class cohesion. This proposition was in fact difficult to sustain, for the development of factory production led either to the homogenization of the labour force, or to differentiation of the labour force according to job specific skills. The recognition of this contradiction creates problems for the use of the notion of control. Radicals have continued to define control in a very broad sense, capitalists being deemed to be in control of their labour forces provided they are still in control of the means of production, or provided worker resistance at the industrial level is unlikely to lead to class revolution. However, if capitalists have to sacrifice technological efficiency, and even, according to Bowles and Gintis (1975), worker co-operation and motivation[5] then, we would argue, it is the limitations on capitalists rather than their ability to control that becomes the interesting question.

Braverman's work poses further problems for dual labour market and radical theories, which have so far not been confronted. For instance, his analysis of the development of employment structure under monopoly capitalism suggests that both the characteristics and the importance of secondary sector employment have so far been inadequately analysed. These problems arise because the relationship between the development of the employment structure under monopoly capitalism and the formation and evolution of structured labour markets has yet to be fully explored. Piecemeal adaptation of radical theory is not sufficient; a more thorough analysis of Braverman's work and its implications for labour market structure is necessary. Only then shall we be in a position to return to the first part of our critique and examine the effect of the struggle between capitalists and workers on the development of stratified labour markets.

5. Bowles and Gintis (1975) argue that: 'The lower productivity of the hierarchical division of labour must be ascribed to worker alienation' (p. 23). However, other forms of work organization involving a greater degree of control by workers over the organization of work cannot be risked by capitalists. 'The threat of workers' escalating their demands for control is simply too great, and the usurpation of the prerogatives of hierarchical authority is quickly quashed' (p. 23).

2. Monopoly capitalism and the employment structure

In radical theory, major change in the structure of labour markets was brought about by major change in the economic structure. The late nineteenth and early twentieth centuries saw not only the development of monopoly capitalism and the spread of factory and machine production, but also the destruction of old craft skills and the progressive homogenization of the labour force, a process which was reversed by the introduction of systems of job ladders to provide artificial divisions within it. Braverman has shown the importance of moving on from the changes that took place in the early stages of monopoly capitalism and large-scale factory production to the evolution of employment structure with the spread and development of monopoly capitalism. He suggests that the period of monopoly capitalism has been characterized by a progressive reduction in skills for the mass of workers, a redistribution of employment to those occupations where productivity increases have been lowest, and a growth in the supply of wage labour as capitalism has moved into domestic production and displaced domestic labour. His thesis suggests a progressive reduction in divisions within the mass of the labour force, based on a levelling down of the skilled workers, rather than, as in human capital theorists' analysis, a levelling up as the standards of education and the general productivity level of workers increase.

The implications of Braverman's thesis for the development of stratification have yet to be fully considered. Radical theorists have used the analysis to justify their claim that divisions in the labour market are artificial, imposed by capitalists to counter the homogenization of the labour force and thus prevent the development of class opposition. Braverman himself suggests there may be progressive polarization in the distribution of earnings, with labour piling up in low paid, low productivity occupations (1974, pp. 392–5). These hypotheses may be better considered after a more detailed examination of changes in employment structure, starting with the distribution of employment and moving on to changes in the nature of skills and the composition of the labour force. This discussion will also lead us on from a consideration of specific criticisms of dual labour market and radical theory to the development of a more general approach to the analysis of labour market structure, in which the role of worker organization may be integrated.

(i) Distribution of employment

The process of capitalist development creates new industries, new markets, new technologies, new institutional systems and new concentrations of capital; at the same time it destroys or forces adaptation in existing industries, markets, technologies and institutions. The process of development, therefore, necessarily involves changes in the employment distribution across occupations, industries and sectors.

Within each occupation, industry or sector, the nature and structure of jobs will depend on the scale and technique of production, and the method of work organization. Yet developments in these three directions do not take place at the same rate throughout the economy. Braverman has argued that there will be a tendency for labour to be displaced from those occupations where technological progress is fastest. Displacement through technological progress may or may not be offset by increases in the demand for high productivity industries but, at least within each industry, employment will increase relatively in those occupations least affected by technological change:

labour tends to pile up in the industries and occupations which are less susceptible to engineered improvements in labour productivity ... we see in capitalist industry a secular trend to accumulate labour in those portions of industry and trade which are least affected by the scientific–technical revolution; service work, sales and other forms of marketing, clerical work insofar as it has not yet been mechanized, etc. The paradox that the most rapidly growing mass occupations in an era of scientific–technical revolution are those which have least to do with science and technology need not surprise us. The purpose of machinery is not to increase but to decrease the numbers of workers attached to it (Braverman, 1974, pp. 383–4).

Similarly, capitalist production does not develop in all sectors and industries at the same time, nor at the same rate or on the same scale. Thus, Braverman argues, it is into the service and retail sectors that capitalism has recently expanded fastest, bringing about a change in mode of production, scale of production and method of work organization, as a result of the widespread introduction of scientific management techniques. Likewise, clerical employment has undergone a significant change in technique and method of work organization, associated with an increase in the scale of clerical operations. This can in turn be attributed to changes in techniques in the production process, where mental labour is progressively separated from manual labour, and to the need under monopoly capitalism to devote a growing share of resources to the realization of surplus value, through marketing, sales and accountancy.

Uneven development takes place as much within as between industries and sectors. The existence of relatively obsolete techniques of production, even in industries characterized by rapid rates of technical progress, adds yet another dimension to the complex employment pattern that capitalist development creates. The firms operating on the margin, on the smallest scale, using the oldest techniques, which paradoxically may require the highest skills, may be operating also in the secondary sector, or the lowest part of the labour market. In some sense this employment can be considered 'marginal' or 'peripheral' to the economy. Yet this is only one kind of 'typical' secondary sector employment, which is usually argued to include, for instance, workers in services and retail trade and the lower grades of clerical employment. These occupations do not readily fit the classification 'marginal' or 'peripheral'. Demand for service sector and clerical employment has been generated, at least in part, by the development of the monopoly capitalist sector, the 'core'. At the same time, technological progress in the 'core' may have displaced labour, providing the sources of labour supply for these occupations. Further, some of these occupations have provided new areas for the spread of the capitalist mode of production.

Not all secondary-sector-type employment can thus be said to be characterized by stagnant technology and methods of work organization. Further, the relationship between developments in the two sectors must be carefully analysed. If Braverman's hypothesis is correct, the future development of monopoly capitalism will lead to a relative increase in secondary sector employment. In that case, the interesting question is, of course, how far these currently low paid occupations could be transformed into primary-type occupations; this transformation, we shall argue, must depend on the potential for, and the effect of trade union development.

(ii) Nature of skills

Changes in technology, the scale of production and methods of work organization all necessarily render old skills inappropriate and produce new job structures. The question at issue, however, is whether the process of development, whilst changing the nature of skills, tends to decrease or increase the level of skill for the mass of the working population.

There appears to be a consensus of opinion that the importance of general skills, at least in manual labour, has declined, manufacturing becoming less dependent on the generalized skill of the craft worker, and the relative importance of job-specific, or firm-specific, skills has increased. However, it is not clear that the actual level of job-specific skills has increased, measured by the time it takes to reach maximum efficiency in a job. Arguments presented to support the hypothesis have so far proved unconvincing. For instance, Gordon argues: 'Assembly-line workers can learn quickly how to turn a screw, but it takes time for them to learn enough about the entire process to be able to spot other defects and to identify the sources of defects' (1972, p. 71).

Now, either the development of assembly-line techniques results in the progressive fractionalization of work, reducing workers' understanding of the production process and stifling their initiative, or it demands an extensive understanding of the entire process of production and the use of initiative in detecting defects and their sources. Gordon seems to argue it both ways, but at least a *relative* decline in workers' understanding and scope for initiative is the likely result and, according to Braverman, the purpose of the development of assembly lines. This is not to suggest that on-the-job experience has no effect on relative efficiency, rather that this may be all the special skills that workers have left. These skills are now more obvious, but they are by no means new.

Braverman argues that the development of technology and methods of work organization under capitalism progressively reduces a worker's control over the work process, and thus his skill, where skill is defined as the ability and opportunity to use knowledge and to exercise judgement. In this process, general skills are reduced to job-specific skills, but further developments in technology and work organization in turn reduce job-specific skills. It is interesting to note that, under this hypothesis, the increase in the scale of production and the change in techniques taking place in secondary sector employment would be liable to lead to reductions in skill levels. This trend in skill levels would be in direct contrast to that identified in the dual labour market hypothesis, where the sector with developing technology, the primary sector, increases its job-specific skill level, whilst the stagnant secondary sector remains unskilled.

Under Braverman's hypothesis, mechanization, combined with the introduction of scientific management techniques, has progressively removed from the worker the ability to make decisions over the speed of work, the quality of the product, and the sequence of operations and transferred it to management. Mechanization, by its very nature, replaces the decisions and actions of workers at some stages of the production process, and the study of work organization gives management an understanding of the work process which may be used to control the pace and method of work. If the role of worker organization is brought back into the analysis, one may query how far management is able to obtain full knowledge of the productive potential of the technology, if workers can organize to work at slow rates, using roundabout methods during work-study exercises. However, the significance of this decline in skill, or control over the work process, particularly when associated with a change in technique, depends on its implications for the bargaining position of workers. The decline in skills in Braverman is essentially viewed from a craft perspective: before the advent of mechanization and scientific management, craft workers could control the work process, for knowledge of it was stored in the craftsmen themselves. Braverman extends his analysis to the job content of other types of workers, arguing that most had more opportunity in the past to determine their speed of working and to use judgement and knowledge: for instance he cites the farm labourers, as a group traditionally classed as unskilled but needing a great deal of knowledge and experience to carry out their tasks (p. 434). However, this skill did little to improve their bargaining position. It was the ability of craftsmen in manufacturing industry to use their specialized knowledge as a basis for organization and to control entry into the craft which improved their bargaining position. Their resultant ability to control the work process was both important in maintaining their privileged position in the labour force, and costly for management. What may therefore be crucial for the mass of workers in their relations with their employers is not whether mechanization and scientific management techniques decrease their opportunities to use judgement and knowledge, but how they affect their bargaining opportunities. There may or may not have been more skill, according to the Braverman definition, in pick-and-shovel work than there is in operating a machine, but it is certain that the transformation of many labouring jobs into operating jobs, where workers were in direct contact with machines and thus exercised some control over a greater output than their own unassisted labour could produce, created improved bargaining opportunities for the mass of workers (see below, section 4).

The bargaining position of workers did not enter directly into Braverman's study, because he was deliberately excluding considerations of working-class consciousness and organization in the labour market (pp-26-7). However, because he has no analysis of bargaining he fails to develop a theory of wage determination. Competitive theory, and perhaps an orthodox Marxist approach, would predict a tendency towards equalization of wage levels with the progressive homogenization of labour. Braverman points instead to a progressive polarization of earnings in the U.S. for 'industrial sectors in the United States in which employment is relatively stagnant are the sectors with wage rates above the average, while the sectors in which employment is growing most rapidly are those with lower than average wage rates' (p. 393). Yet it is, in Braverman's analysis, precisely in those industrial sectors that the division of labour and homogenization of the labour force have progressed furthest. In these sectors, too, labour is being displaced and demand for labour is falling, factors which under competitive theory also depress wages. Implicit in Braverman's theory seems to be a belief that workers' wages are determined not by the skill of the worker, but by the productivity of the organization. However, to justify this theory of wage determination it would be necessary to put worker organization back into the centre of the discussion. The omission of trade unions leads Braverman at times to contradictions, when he refers to the 'giant mass of workers who are relatively homogeneous as to lack of developed skill, low pay and interchangeability of persons and function' (p. 359), a mass which includes factory workers along with office and service workers.

The aspect of Braverman's analysis of skill which is important to an understanding of the development of worker organization is the 'relative homogeneity of the workforce' and 'the interchangeability of person and function'. Even if, at present, workers possess special skills that cannot be easily acquired by other workers, these skills may still become obsolete with the progress of technology and work organization. Indeed Braverman argues that management will design their techniques of production in order to de-skill these workers. Thus all workers are threatened by the obsolescence of skills, or by replacement by other equally skilled workers who are in plentiful supply. This threat may induce defensive actions on the part of the workers to stratify the labour force, control entry to occupations and maintain skill status long after these skill divisions have become irrelevant.

Thus the progress of capitalism both destroys old skills and creates new ones, providing new opportunities for organization and control and provoking defensive attempts to maintain old skill divisions in the labour force, with varying degrees of success. The counterpart of this development for capitalists is that new technologies and work organizations provide new opportunities to impose control and also confront capitalists with new problems in obtaining their desired output.

(iii) Composition of the labour force

As capitalism has developed, new groups of labour have been drawn into the wage labour force. When capitalism expands into new sectors, labour is displaced, and forms new supplies of wage labour. Recently, the most important area where labour has been displaced has been domestic production. The spread of capitalist production and state services into this area has 'released' female labour onto the market. Immigration has provided further sources of supply for the labour market in certain periods.

The introduction of new supplies of wage labour in different historical periods may lead to segmentation of the labour market. Those workers previously at the bottom of the structure take advantage of these new supplies to move up the hierarchy, but at the same time protect themselves against the increased competition in the labour market (Baran and Sweezy, 1966, ch. 9). Female workers are still largely confined to certain segments of the labour market, as are Commonwealth immigrants in the U.K., and blacks in the U.S. Their wages tend to be low, and they may be available for work at lower reserve wage levels than the white male majority group. Substitution of women for men may lead to a real decline in relative wages in an occupation, and reduce employment opportunities for men; hence the incentive for males to try to confine women to a different segment of the labour force. It is not our intention here to develop a theory of racism or sexism, only to indicate how the changes in composition of the labour force provide some kind of 'natural' segmentation of the labour force, and further, how the ability of capitalism continuously to generate new supplies of labour forces the existing labour force to organize and protect itself against new competition.

3. The struggle for control under monopoly capitalism

It has been argued that the development and spread of monopoly capitalism have had a much more complex impact on the employment structure than that identified in radical theory. Recognition of this complex development raises the possibility that the analysis of the struggle between capitalists and workers has so far been too simple and too static.

For example, on the one hand it is clear that the development of factory production did reduce the importance of general skills, and thus made it possible for a homogeneous labour force to develop. On the other hand, viewing this development from the Braverman perspective, it is also clear that this process increased the control of capitalists over the speed and method of production; this indicates that the homogenization of the labour force is not the overriding problem for management which radical theory suggests. The establishment of a system of high wages, secure employment and promotion ladders may, from this viewpoint, be thought to indicate workers' success in regaining some of the control lost through the destruction of the craft system, rather than a further increase in capitalists' control.

The development of the employment structure clearly does present capitalists with problems, but of a more complex nature than radical theory has suggested. The problem of control for capitalists is not just one of preventing the development of class consciousness, but of organizing the social relations of production. Introduction of new technology disrupts existing social relations and may meet trade union opposition. This resistance may be more than a bargaining tactic to gain a share in productivity increases, for the new technology may undermine the existing system of worker organization, whose strength is based on workers' knowledge and control of the existing technique. The introduction of new technology may, on the one hand, present management with the opportunity to break down worker organization, yet the very resistance that this induces may limit management's ability to introduce best practice techniques quickly and cheaply. Further regrouping and restructuring of worker organization round new technologies and work organization may present management with similar problems the next time the system of production has to be adapted.

In order to understand the problems for management we must examine further the actions and motivations of workers. Our discussion of the development of monopoly capitalism has pointed to major problems for workers and for workers' organization. Braverman's thesis suggests that there is a continuous threat of displacement of labour, and redundancy of skills. Full employment is in some sense only relative: each new phase of capitalist expansion creates new supplies of labour by displacing labour from production outside the capitalist mode, by displacing labour through the extension and intensification of mechanization, or by drawing in new workers from the international pool of surplus labour. Workers' defence against competition in the labour market is to organize to control the supply of labour. Attempts may be made at the macro level to limit the supply of new types of labour, such as females or immigrants. More importantly, workers will organize to control entry into an occupation, firm or industry. Such control must be to the detriment of groups excluded from the organized sectors, as it reduces their mobility and may even increase competition in the external labour market. The development of worker organization may thus create segmentation in the external labour market.

The establishment and maintenance of bargaining positions within the organized sector may further depend on stratification of the labour force. In so far as workers are acting defensively against the threat of substitution and competition, their most effective tactic is to differentiate themselves from potential competitors. Such protection through differentiation may be provided by various systems, from union organized apprenticeship schemes to promotion lines based on strict seniority provisions. Both types of system provide shelter from labour market competition for the incumbent workforce, although the former offers protection only for one group of workers, whilst the second extends protection down through the whole range of jobs by restricting entry to the bottom of the hierarchy. Clearly both systems also offer various degrees and methods of control for management; this is the point on which the radical theories have focused. On the other hand, in both cases, the existence of a structured labour force, where jobs are strictly defined, and workers are not interchangeable, provides a bargaining base for labour against management's attempts to increase productivity and introduce new technology. Changes in job ladders, skill demarcations and the pace of work become areas for bargaining, whereas a homogeneous labour force, interchangeable in function, would lay itself open not only to competition from the external market but also to further declines in workers' control of production and a continuous undermining of bargaining power. Divisions by custom, rule and status are essential parts of any union's bargaining strategy. Reducing the differentiation between workers and developing job rotation may decrease the monotony of work, increase class cohesiveness, and create opportunities for workers to control the pace and method of work. However, unless they organize to seize these opportunities and to create a bargaining position based on this new organization of work, the development of a more homogeneous labour force may undermine the basis of workers' industrial organization.

The development of capitalism not only presents problems for worker control and organization, inducing defensive tactics on the part of existing trade union organizations, but it also offers new opportunities for organization. Thus the development of machine technology may to some extent have undermined the skilled union's basis for organization and control but, by transforming much unskilled labour into semi-skilled labour or, rather, by increasing the proportion of the labour force directly involved in the mechanized production process, it increased the bargaining power of a large section of the labour force. Semi-skilled workers were now in control of a greater volume of production, and further represented a threat to skilled workers as the real skill differential declined, thus forcing some skilled unions to recruit semi-skilled workers, whilst in other industries organization of semi-skilled workers proceeded independently.

The strategy of worker organization and its effects on the structure of the labour market have so far been discussed only at the general level, and no evidence has yet been presented to back up our line of argument. Full supporting evidence would require detailed study of the development of labour market structures across industries, and preferably across countries. At this stage, it is possible only to cite some examples of how worker organization in the U.K. has been involved in the development of structured labour markets, briefly comparing the U.K. experience with that of the U.S., but also calling into question the radical theorists' contention that even in the U.S. the development of structured labour markets has been both to the disadvantage of workers and independent of worker organization.

4. Worker organization and the development of structured labour markets in the United Kingdom

Worker organization operates to control the supply of labour both at the macro and at the micro level. In the U.K. control of aggregate labour supplies has been attempted at various times by means of a number of different strategies. Recently, the role of the working class family in the nineteenth century in limiting the supply of female labour, and thereby improving the bargaining power of the working class, has been documented (Humphries, 1977 [Reading 6 of this collection]). The unlimited participation of family labour, according to Marx, would not only depress the general wage level by increasing the relative surplus population, but would also reduce the limit below which the wage level could not fall, i.e., the labour-time necessary to maintain the worker and his dependents.

Efforts to control the length of the working day, in particular the campaign to introduce the 10-hour day, were aimed at preventing workers from being forced to work long hours to protect their jobs in the face of competition from the surplus population, and thereby inadvertently increasing competition in the labour market (Marx, 1954, ch. 10). Similarly, the movement to establish legal minimum wages through the trade board system was aimed, in part, at squeezing out the sweater operating with cheap labour, often subsidized family labour, in an attempt to reduce undercutting and competitive pressure on wages, at the possible expense of employment, particularly secondary family employment (Bayliss, 1962, pp. 7–8). A more recent example of control, though one considered less respectable and honourable than the above mentioned campaigns, is provided by the rigid conditions placed on the use of immigrant labour, particularly Polish labour, after World War II (Castles and Kosack, 1973, pp. 29–30).

Most effective efforts to control the labour supply take place at the level of occupation, firm or industry. The technical conditions of production provide the basis for the development of worker organization, but, in the U.K., the system of worker organization has often been strong enough to withstand the obsolescence of the skills on which it has been based. Thus Hinton (1973, pp. 61–2) argues that the engineers in the U.K. successfully maintained their craft demarcations until 1914 despite the fact that 'a substantial proportion of the work performed by craftsmen, at the craft rate, required little of their skill'. Only the 'vast expansion of engineering production required by the war effort revealed the degree to which the genuine skill content of the craftsmen's work had declined'. Indeed, Turner (1962, p. 114) has gone so far as to argue that: 'From the viewpoint of trade union development, at least, workers are thus "skilled" and "unskilled" according to whether or not entry to their organization is deliberately restricted, and not in the first place according to the nature of the occupation itself.'

However, as in the case of the engineering workers, the ability to maintain skill differentials after they have become technologically redundant is limited. Various defensive tactics were available to the skilled unions. In the case of shipbuilding, the craft unions forestalled the threat of dilution (the substitution of unskilled and semi-skilled for skilled workers) by amalgamations with other unions representing 'lesser but possibly competing skills' and later insisted on apprentice-ships as the only means of entry into each organized trade. Thus, 'few new operations were free to be taken up by semi-skilled' (Wilkinson, 1975, Part 2, p. 5). Some cotton craft unions or closed unions, presented with the threat of dilution, opened up their recruitment to those groups of less skilled workers from which the 'skilled' workers were recruited (Turner, 1962). In engineering, Hinton (1973) describes how the shop stewards' movement realized the seriousness of the dilution threat, and attempted not only to preserve craft control, but also to develop organ-ization in all grades, along with an industrial, rather than a craft, policy on wages and labour supply. In the U.K. iron and steel industry, Wilkin-son (1977, p. 103) shows how 'successive groups of less skilled workers established themselves in the formalized industrial relations system and how this modified collective bargaining and redistributed the industry's wage fund in favour of the newly organized groups'. The skilled workers gave way, partly out of altruism, but also because of the increasing im-portance of ancillary grades in the production process.

De-skilling of the labour force in the U.K. thus often led to an ex-tension of organization to semi-skilled and unskilled workers and some reduction in differentials, whilst a structured, sheltered labour market, based on control of entry was still maintained. De-skilling of skilled workers was often matched by an increase in the bargaining position and sometimes the skill of previously unskilled workers. Child (1976, p. 162) documented the technological developments in the printing industry in the late nineteenth and early twentieth centuries which led to a decline in the proportion, though not in numbers, of skilled craftsmen. Techni-cal progress also created a new class of semi-skilled men and 'in many cases the "semi-skilled" machine operators required greater manual dexterity and occupied posts of greater responsibility than many of the "craftsmen" '. The effects of technical progress over the same period on skilled workers in the steel industry may have balanced each other out, increasing responsibility whilst decreasing the need for specialist know-ledge, but it certainly transformed 'the largely unskilled force of "under-hands" into one of semi-skilled operatives', thus improving their bargaining position relative to the skilled workers (Wilkinson, 1974, p. 7).

The introduction of new technology in the U.K. has often required compromise by management with the unions. Management have con-ceded shares in the productivity gains from the new technology in order to allow the smooth and rapid introduction of the new techniques. In the case of printing, management agreed to the first formal collective bargaining agreements to obtain this end (Child, 1967, p. 203). Bargaining over changing the method of work organization, and thus the system of worker control, to suit the new technology, now commonly called 'productivity bargaining', often has not come until later (McKersie and Hunter, 1973, p. 349). Even when the structure of labour force organization has become technologically irrelevant, worker organization has often been sufficiently strong to extract large rewards for relaxing outmoded restrictive practices and skill demarcations. Such has been the case in the shipbuilding industry, where rigid demarcation and expensive demarcation disputes between the numerous skilled unions had clearly damaged the competitive position of the industry. Indeed it was this desperate economic position that forced the skilled unions into conceding some relaxation of demarcation; but in return they have been rewarded with rapidly rising wages (Wilkinson, 1975, Part 6, p. 17).

Trade unions have probably played a more active role in the formation of structured labour markets in the U.K. than in the U.S.[6] The explanation may lie in the different level of maturity of the two economies at the time of the development of large-scale factory production and mechanization. Trade unions were better organized and more established in the U.K. than in the U.S., and capitalists may have been forced to introduce their new technologies through a process of compromise with the unions, rather than through outright suppression.[7] The effect of this different heritage could be that new technologies and scientific management techniques have not been introduced as extensively or intensively in the U.K. as in the U.S., owing to much more effective resistance by the trade union movement (McKersie and Hunter, 1973, p. 372). The reasons for the different historical developments of trade unions and labour market structures in the two countries would no doubt be a fruitful area for research.

6. McKersie and Hunter (1973, p. 370) estimate that 25% of total employment in the U.K. is involved in industries based on the craft system, compared with 10% in the U.S.

7. Hinton (1973, p. 13) argues that the development of working-class consciousness between 1910 and the early 1920s in the U.K. was contained because a 'combination of ruling-class flexibility, reformist initiative within the labour movement and an economic recession which weakened the power and undermined the ambition of ordinary workers, made possible a new and lasting accommodation of organized labour within the capitalist system'. The suppression of unions and the establishment of a bureaucratic system of control were thus not the only tactics open to capitalists.

Nevertheless, there is evidence that the role of unions, or worker resistance, in developing structured labour markets in the U.S. has been underestimated, for instance in the work of Kahn on longshoring in San Francisco. Craft systems of organization have been maintained in some industries in the U.S. or have only recently been broken down (McKersie and Hunter, 1973, p. 370–71). More importantly, there is evidence that the bureaucratic system of control set up in the steel industry, usually taken as the exemplar for radical theory, has not solved all the problems of control for capitalists. Proposed changes to the system of work organization have been successfully resisted by unions over a long period of time (McKersie and Hunter, 1973, pp. 372–3). Clauses in the employment contract resulted in 'unnecessary manpower and prevented flexibility in job assignments'; but the unions succeeded in preventing changes through strike action. Further, there is evidence that the job evaluation scheme introduced into the steel mills has provided almost automatic increases for some workers with changes in technology and increases in productivity (Stieber, 1959, p. 312). These increases result from the weighting given to responsibility for machinery and materials in the job evaluation scheme, a weighting which Katherine Stone (1975) uses as evidence that real skill is not involved in the different job specifications, indicating that the technology would allow the development of systems of job rotation with no differentiation by skill. The high weight for factors likely to lead to wage increases for workers in line with productivity increases at least raises the possibility of direct union or worker involvement in the development of job structures in the industry. Certainly Katherine Stone seems to have played down too far the role of unions in the maintenance and adaptation of the system of job structures, when she identifies the change from promotion on the basis of favouritism to promotion on the basis of seniority as being a change in 'form' but not 'content' of the system of control. The development of a system of promotion by seniority resolves the problem of competition within the plant for the limited number of high paid jobs, and by doing so may even increase the cohesiveness of workers in their struggle over such issues as general pay increases.

While a bureaucratic system of labour force organization, as found in parts of U.S. industry, may serve capitalist interests better than one which has been more influenced by trade union organization, as in many U.K. industries, it is itself likely to cause efficiency losses to capitalists. These losses may increase, for the structure becomes less related to the ideal organization of labour (as technology, scale of production and indeed management techniques develop). They may increase further as workers organize to reap what benefits they can from this particular form of control. Thus the radicals have overstressed the control offered by the bureaucratic division of the labour force, and at the same time underestimated or ignored the benefits for the working class of a sheltered, secure, albeit stratified, labour market.

5. Structured labour markets and the persistence of low pay

It is now time to draw together our discussion, and consider its implications for the analysis of low pay. Stratification of the labour force, in dual labour market and radical theories, and in many orthodox theories (Bergmann, 1971), is identified as an explanation of the development and persistence of low paid sectors in the economy. The major difference between these new approaches and orthodox theory is that now the development of stratification is rooted in the development of the capitalist system. A necessary development of this analysis, we have argued, is to include more fully the effect of worker organization in the development of structured markets. However, trade union development is not to be regarded as an exogenous influence on labour market structure. Rather worker organization attempts to control the competition in the labour market that the capitalist system generates, and, further, adapts and restructures itself in response to developments in the economic structure.

The development of monopoly capitalism continually disrupts industrial organization. Labour is displaced as skills become redundant and as capitalism moves from old into new areas. This process, which destroys both jobs and skills, creates real problems for workers as competition for jobs necessarily reduces their bargaining power. This emphasis on the effects of competition is in direct contrast to the orthodox approach, where workers use a competitive labour market to equalize net benefits between different occupations. Instead, in our analysis, a worker's main concern under competition is to obtain and keep a job.[8] Workers act defensively to protect themselves from the

8. A comparison of Marshall's and Marx's treatment of the length of the working day illustrates this different approach to the effects of competition. Marshall (1920, p. 527) argued that the marginal principle would ensure that labourers must be 'paid for every hour at a rate sufficient to compensate them for the last, and most distressing hour'. Marx (1954, p. 595) argued that competition would force workers to work longer and expend more effort, not for more money but to secure their jobs. 'The overwork of the employed part of the working class swells the ranks of

competition of the external labour market, to obtain job security and higher wages, to the exclusion and possible detriment of those remaining in the unorganized sector.

Our discussion has also indicated how, over time, trade union structure has altered, and how previously unorganized sectors have been drawn in, to the greater or lesser detriment of existing organized groups, and of those left outside. Expansion of trade union organization tends to extend primary-sector-type employment, improving job security and wages. However the effect of this development on the overall shape of the distribution of earnings is not clear. It is possible that the expansion of trade union organization may increase the difficulties of developing organization for those still excluded (Kahn, 1975, p. 13). The barriers to the extension of primary sector employment throughout the job structure may be strong, both for the reasons suggested by radical and dual labour market theorists, and because of the resilient barriers to mobility, or competition, set up by trade union organization. They may be exacerbated if, as Braverman suggests, the share of typically low paying, low productivity occupations is increasing, together with the share in employment of typically low paid labour, such as women, immigrants and part-time labour.

This is no place to predict developments in the shape and composition of the earnings structure, or in the mobility pattern. What is clear, however, is that in contrast to the presumption in orthodox theory, the development of the economic structure cannot be relied upon to extend the share of 'good' jobs requiring high skill and associated with high productivity industries.[9] Monopoly capitalism may create job structures increasingly dominated by low skilled, low productivity occupations, and where the share of labour directly involved in the production process of high productivity industries is likely to decline. The effect of these trends on the position of workers in the labour market will depend on

the reserve, whilst conversely the greater pressure the latter by its competition exerts on the former, forces these to submit to over-work and to subjugation under the dictates of capital.'

9. One orthodox economist, Perlman (1976, pp. 149–50) has recently admitted that 'there will always be bad jobs'. Indeed he argues: 'The dual labour market is here to stay; competitive efficiency in industrial manpower development requires it. Steps to randomize the probability of membership in the secondary sector call for more equality of opportunity. But the pessimistic result of the dual labour market would remain; secondary workers would be poverty prone. The social gain would lie in reducing the disproportionate share of particular demographic groups in dead-end, low-level jobs.'

their ability to maintain, develop, extend and reshape their organization and bargaining power. For instance, Braverman suggests that the pattern of development of the employment structure under monopoly capitalism may result in a polarization of the earnings distribution. This argument is based on an implicit assumption that workers are strong enough to obtain shares in the productivity increase of their own enterprises, but are not strong enough outside the high productivity sectors to ensure a sharing out of the increases in national income across the whole range of occupations. This belief may or may not be correct, but his analysis points to the importance both of the employment structure and of trade union organization in determining the distribution of earnings.

A fuller integration of the effect of worker organization into the study of labour market structure should clearly not be at the expense of an analysis of the relationship between economic structure and labour market inequality. Indeed, we are suggesting that the effects of the dynamics of the economic structure on the labour market are much more important and complex than those that dual labour market and radical theories describe. The development of stratification is clearly a complex process and any analysis must include those determinants already identified in dual labour market and radical theory. The tendency to uneven development in the economy, the development of non-competing groups in the labour force, and the attempts by capitalists to re-establish control over their labour forces will all influence the nature and degree of stratification in the labour market. So far, however, we have argued that the analysis of the development of the employment structure has both been too partial and too static. The spread and development of monopoly capitalism involves much more continuous change in employment structure than that allowed for in dual labour market and radical theory. Trade union organization adds to the complexity of the picture. Worker organization has been shown to have played an important part in developing and shaping structured labour markets, but its own development has been determined, in its turn, by changes in the employment structure. A more evolutionary, dynamic analysis of the development of the labour market structure is thus necessary. Such an analysis would admit the possibility of a whole continuum of shades of segmentation across industries, occupations and sectors, in line with the complex pattern of development of the economic structure and of trade union structure.

References

AKERLOF, G. A., 'Qualitative uncertainty and the market for lemons', *Quarterly Journal of Economics*, August 1970.

BARAN, P., and SWEEZY, P., *Monopoly Capitalism*, Monthly Review Press, 1966.

BAYLISS, F., *British Wages Councils*, Basil Blackwell, 1962.

BECKER, G., *Human Capital*, NBER, 1964.

BERGMANN, B., 'The effect on white incomes of discrimination in employment', *Journal of Political Economy*, March–April, 1971.

BLUESTONE, B., 'The characteristics of marginal industries', in Gordon, D. M., (ed.), *Problems in Political Economy: an Urban Perspective*, D. C. Heath, 1971.

BOWLES, S., and GINTIS, H., 'Class power and alienated labour', *Monthly Review*, March 1975.

BRAVERMAN, H. *Labor and Monopoly Capital*, Monthly Review Press, 1974.

CAIRNES, J. E., *Some Leading Principles of Political Economy*, Macmillan.

CASTLES, S., and KOSACK, G., *Immigrant Workers and Class Structure in Western Europe*, OUP, 1973.

CHILD, J., *Industrial Relations in the British Printing Industry*, Allen and Unwin, 1967.

DOERINGER, P., and PIORE, M., *Internal Labor Markets and Manpower Analysis*, D. C. Heath, 1971.

EDWARDS, R. C., REICH, M., and GORDON, D. M., (eds), *Labor Market Segmentation*, D. C. Heath, 1975.

GORDON, D. M., *Theories of Poverty and Underdevelopment*, D. C. Heath, 1972.

GORDON, D. M., 'Capitalist efficiency and socialist efficiency', *Monthly Review*, July–August 1976.

HINTON, J., *The First Shop Stewards' Movement*, Allen and Unwin, 1973.

HUMPHRIES, J., 'Class struggle and the persistence of the working-class family', *Cambridge Journal of Economics*, September 1977.

KAHN, L., *Unions and Labor Market Segmentation*, Ph.D. thesis, University of California, Berkeley, 1975.

KERR, C., 'The balkanization of labor markets', in Bakke, E. W., and Hauser, P. M., (eds), *Labour Mobility and Economic Opportunity*, MIT Press, 1954.

LESTER, R. A., 'A range theory of wage differentials', *Industrial and Labour Relations Review*, July 1952.

MACKAY, D. I., BODDY, D., BRACK, J., DIACK, J. A., and JONES, N., *Labour Markets under Different Employment Conditions*, Allen and Unwin, 1971.

MARX, K., *Capital*, Vol. 1 (1887 translation), Lawrence and Wishart, 1954.

MARSHALL, A., *Principles of Economics*, 8th ed., Macmillan, 1920.

MCKERSIE, R. B., and HUNTER, L. C., *Pay, Productivity and Collective Bargaining*, Macmillan, 1973.

MILL, J. S., *Principles of Political Economy*, 2nd ed., John W. Parker, 1849.

OI, W., 'Labor as a quasi-fixed factor', *Journal of Political Economy*, December 1962.

PERLMAN, R., *The Economics of Poverty*, McGraw-Hill, 1976.

PIORE, M., 'Notes for a theory of labor market stratification', in Edwards *et al.* (1975).

SLICHTER, S., 'Note on the structure of wages', *Review of Economics and Statistics*, February 1950.

SPENCE, M., 'Job market signalling', *Quarterly Journal of Economics*, August 1973.

STIEBER, J., *The Steel Industry Wage Structure*, Harvard UP, 1959.

STONE, K., 'The origins of job structures in the steel industry', in Edwards *et al.* (1975).

TURNER, H. A., *Trade Union Growth, Structure and Policy*, Allen and Unwin, 1962.

VIETORISZ, T., and HARRISON, B., 'Labor market segmentation: positive feedback and divergent development', *American Economic Review*, May 1973.

WILKINSON, F., *The British Iron and Steel Industry in Historical Perspective*, mimeo, Cambridge, Department of Applied Economics, 1974.

WILKINSON, F., *Demarcation in Shipbuilding*, mimeo, Cambridge, Department of Applied Economics, 1975.

WILKINSON, F., 'Collective bargaining in the steel industry in the 1920s', in Saville, J., (ed.), *Essays in Labour History 1918–39*, Croom Helm, 1977.

12 Occupational Segregation, Wages and Profits When Employers Discriminate by Race or Sex*

Barbara R. Bergmann

Professor of Economics, University of Maryland

From: *Eastern Economic Journal*, Vol. 1, Nos. 2–3, April-July 1974, pp. 103–10.

There are two phenomena associated with employment discrimination against blacks: (1) blacks are distributed among occupations differently from whites, even after differences in education are accounted for; and (2) within occupations, whites earn more than blacks do. The same two phenomena are observed as between men and women. It has been customary to analyze the occupational and wage aspects of discrimination as if they were logically separate and their effects additive.[1] In this paper the two aspects are treated in a unified way, through the development of a model which marries the wage differential approach of Becker (1957) to the approach emphasizing the 'crowding' effects of occupational segregation originally noticed by Edgeworth (1922) and developed by Bergmann (1971). The result allows a clearer view of the distributive effects of employment discrimination.

The Connection Between Wage Differentials and Distribution by Occupation

We shall conduct the analysis initially in terms of a labor market in which there are two occupations and in which all workers have the same degree of skill. Another assumption, which will not significantly affect the results but will make the exposition simpler, is that the marginal productivity of labor in each occupation in each firm is a linear function of the number of workers employed in that occupation and is

*Work for this paper was done in part while the author held a Ford Faculty Research Fellowship in Economics and in part under a grant from the U.S. Office for Economic Opportunity now administered by the U.S. Department of Labor. I would like to thank Martin C. McGuire, Lloyd C. Atkinson and Christopher Clague for suggestions.

1. A leading example is Thurow, 1969, ch. 7.

independent of the number of workers employed in the other occupation. We shall also assume that, although employers in certain situations will hire blacks on some jobs only on condition that they accept a lower wage than the employer would be willing to pay to whites, employers will still arrange matters so as to set the marginal productivity of each man equal to his wage. This amounts to saying that once an employer allows the low wages of Negroes to overcome his aversion to hiring them for a given occupation,[2] he will not deny himself the extra profit he can get by utilizing the labor-intensive methods their low wages make sensible.[3]

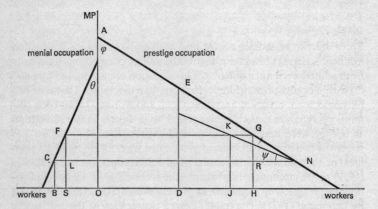

Figure 12.1.

Let us start by assuming that there is perfect segregation by occupation. In Figure 12.1, AE is the marginal productivity curve in one of the occupations, which is assumed initially to be closed to blacks. All of the whites (OD) work in this occupation, and their marginal productivity, and hence their wage, is DE. Similarly, all blacks (OB) work in the other occupation, which has marginal productivity curve FC and they have marginal productivity and wage CB. The result of the segregation of these occupations, given the positions of the marginal productivity

2. The aversion to hiring blacks we cite here may be the result of racial prejudice or, as will be brought out below, may arise out of a loyalty to the employers' group which may be making a good thing financially out of discrimination.

3. This assumption is counter to the one usually made by Becker and most other writers, but it makes the exposition simpler and is probably more realistic. It probably contains the implication of occupational segregation (real or faked by contrived differences in job titles) within firms.

curves and the numbers of blacks and white workers (whose supply of labor we have assumed to be perfectly inelastic) is that the black occupation is overcrowded, in the sense that the marginal productivity of labor is lower in that occupation, and total output could be increased by lowering employment in the black occupation and shifting some of the labor to the other occupation.

Following Becker, we shall assume that there is some crucial differential between white and black wages in each occupation which will make employers indifferent as between white and black workers. For our current purposes it is simplest initially to specify this crucial differential as a fixed money amount which does not differ from one employer to another, although it does differ for each occupation. We would expect it to be high for occupations to which for some reason prestige attaches and low and possibly zero or negative for occupations considered menial.

Segregation of the two occupations is stable if

$$d_m \leq \text{(prestige marginal productivity)}$$
$$- \text{(menial marginal productivity)} \leq d_p$$

where d_m and d_p are the crucial differentials in the menial and prestige occupations respectively. If the difference in the marginal productivities becomes greater than d_p, we would expect some black workers to be able to move to the prestige occupation as shown in Figure 12.1. We may think of certain firms switching from white to black crews in the prestige occupation so as to employ the $BS = JH = KG$ black workers whom we have assumed to have moved over from the menial occupation. As a result of the reduced concentration of blacks in the menial occupation, productivity and the wage level there has risen to SF, and this is the wage we would expect black workers to earn in the prestige occupation, since it is their opportunity cost when leaving the menial occupation.[4]

We may generalize this point by drawing a 'supply curve' (line NK) of black workers to the prestige occupation. It is convenient to draw this curve so that the quantity of black workers supplied to the prestige occupation at each wage is measured leftward from the marginal productivity curve of the prestige occupation. The position of this supply curve (which is linear) depends on the positions of the marginal produc-

4. We are assuming here, of course, that blacks will not be willing to sacrifice income in order to enter the prestige occupation. In the next section, the assumption that whites would not sacrifice income to avoid a move into the menial occupation is made.

tivity curves in the two occupations and on the total number of blacks in the labor market. The wage at point N is that wage below which no black workers will come to work in the prestige occupation and is, of course, that wage which blacks can earn if all of them are crowded into the menial occupation. The slope of the supply curve through N depends on the slopes of the two marginal productivity curves.[5]

How does this assumed move of black workers to the prestige occupation affect white wages? In order to answer this question, we must recall that the marginal productivity curve in any occupation is derived by lateral summation from the marginal productivity curves of each of the firms for this kind of labor. If certain firms swing over to hiring black labor for the prestige occupation, then the new demand curve for white labor in that occupation will be lateral summation of the marginal productivity curves of the remaining firms. In Figure 12.2 this new demand curve has been drawn as AK, on the assumption that KG black workers have entered the prestige occupation and all firms have linear

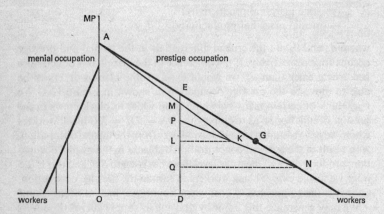

Figure 12.2.

marginal productivity curves which cross the axis at A for the prestige occupation. In this case, the wage rate of white workers must fall from DE to DM. Figure 12.2 displays the range of possibilities when d_p is allowed to vary between zero and plus infinity and d_m is assumed to be zero. As before, the supply curve of Negroes to the prestige occupation

5. Cot $\psi = (JH + RN)/GR = BS/FL + RN/GR = \tan \theta + \tan \varphi$, where ψ, θ and φ are the angles indicated in Figure 1.

is NK, which crosses the total supply curve of white workers at P. This point on the supply curve will be realized if d_p is zero. In that case, wages of white workers and black workers in both occupations will be DP, and the segregation of black workers in the menial occupation will presumably have no further rationale. The other extreme is, of course, the realization of point N, which we have already discussed and which occurs when $d_p \geqslant EQ$. A movement from N to an intermediate position, such as K, means a lowering in d_p from some indeterminably large amount (bounded from below by EQ) to an amount equal to LM. This is accomplished through a rise in the wages of all black workers by an amount QL, and a fall in the wages of white workers by EM.

As we have drawn the curves, the fall in the wages of white workers is smaller in absolute value than the rise in the wages of blacks, but this is clearly not the only possibility. The situation in our diagrams is drawn to represent roughly the racial situation in the United States, where the number of black workers is small relative to the number of whites, and where whites are assigned to a relatively broad range of occupations and blacks to a relatively narrow range, (i.e., where there are many occupations where the d's are positive and large, and few occupations where they are zero). In a country like South Africa, where the discriminated-against races constitute more than 60 per cent of the urban population, and where whites thus have reserved for them a relatively narrower range of occupations, a reduction in the 5-to-1 white to nonwhite income ratio might cause greater wage reduction for whites than wage rise for nonwhites.[6] Similarly if we consider sex discrimination in the United States, where occupational segregation by sex is extreme and the gap in wages between white women and white men is greater than the gap between white men and black men, a reduction in discrimination entailing a desegregation of occupations might very well result in a wage level reduction for men of a larger magnitude than the rise in wage levels for women. This is particularly true if the already large female labor force were to be augmented to any large degree by women who had previously been kept out of the labor market because of discarded notions about women's proper role and because of the low pay and tedious nature of the jobs previously open to women.

We may remark at this point that there may exist crucial differentials which are not expressed in the data for any particular period. For example, where the desegregated occupation has zero crucial differential, whites and blacks will have the same wage in the entire economy, des-

6. See Hutt, 1964.

pite the fact that there is a segregated occupation in which whites may be greatly preferred. Obviously a change in the racial composition of the population or a change in the marginal productivity curves may in such a case create a wage gap between blacks and whites where none existed before without any change in the degree of racism.[7] This consideration would tend to argue that the changes in the distribution of races and the sexes among occupations (correcting for educational differences) is at least as important an indicator of genuine progress towards a color-blind and unisex economy as changes in the black-white or the male-female income gap.

Occupational segregation

The analysis of the last section can be summarized by a simple algorithm for determining the distribution of whites and blacks between the two occupations, given the marginal productivity schedules, the numbers of white and black workers and the value of the crucial differential for each occupation. Initially put all whites into the occupation in which the crucial differential is most in their favor and blacks into the other occupation. We then observe the difference in the marginal productivity of whites and blacks, and depending on what that difference is we re-distribute workers as suggested in Figure 12.3. If desegregation takes

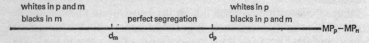

Figure 12.3.

place, the movement of workers will be sufficient to bring the difference in the marginal productivities and the wage rates of the two races into equality with the crucial differential in the desegregated occupation.

In the real world of more than two occupations, there are many occupations which are quite rigidly restricted to one race-sex group, but there will generally be more than one integrated occupation in a typical local labor market. Some occupations will have identical crucial differentials attached to them. Another reason for the multiplication of integrated occupations is that educational and training differences among workers and differing production processes among employers make for a series of labor markets rather than a single market in

7. A similar point was made by Becker, op. cit. This phenomenon may have occurred in Great Britain.

which everybody is a substitute for everyone else in every respect but race and sex. Of course, a factor which cuts the other way is that workers may be forced by discrimination (i.e., by very high d values) out of the market for which they are fitted by education and into a market which includes workers of a lower educational level. Negro high school graduates working as laborers and maids and female college graduates working as typists are the examples which come to mind.

Another reason for occupational integration is the existence of individuals who are highly specialized to particular occupations. Of particular interest is the white person whose talents are such that his natural niche in the economy is in the menial occupations, in which the preference for white workers is nil or small. Paradoxically, such a white is injured by high preference for whites in the occupations for which he is unfit. Such preferences increase the number of blacks in the market to which the low-talented white is restricted and hence lowers both his wage rate and productivity along with theirs. Blacks or women who are very highly specialized to occupations of high prestige (by preference rather than by inability to do anything else) have to put up with lower income than they might make in the lower prestige occupations within which they would face little or no discrimination against them. In any case, specialization to occupations will tend to increase the degree of integration.

It may be remarked here that the disadvantage suffered by the specialized because of discrimination is not restricted to those who cannot escape the occupations to which they are specialized. An interesting case is that of men who by preference and talent would be fitted to do hospital work of a professional or technical nature below the level of physician. Here the field has largely been pre-empted by female nurses, whose number has undoubtedly been swelled by the exclusion of women of energy and intelligence from most managerial posts.

An economy with a high degree of racial or sexual prejudice and a high degree of occupational integration must be one in which each occupation's differentials are distributed over a range and the distributions for many occupations overlap. It is probably correct to throw out the single-value-of-d assumption in occupations where a black clientele is served separately from the white clientele or where some employers are black (teachers, preachers, morticians, etc.). For most other cases, we would argue that employers' ideas concerning the proper occupational spheres for blacks and women (and the financial incentive needed to make employers go against their notions of propriety) are probably not inborn and unalterable. If such attitudes *were* 'biological' in this sense, we might expect considerable variation from one employer to another. What is much more likely is that attitudes concerning which occupations are 'proper' for women and blacks are part of the social system and are learned, and most employers have learned pretty much the same thing.

Measuring the degree of occupational segregation is fraught with difficulties. When we leave the theoretical realm of the simple two-occupation model, the slippery and inexact nature of the concept of 'occupation' begins to give trouble. The measured degree of segregation we find empirically will obviously depend on how we group jobs into occupations and establishments into labor markets. This means that it is more sensible to compare two situations based on comparable occupational classification than to make absolute judgments about the degree of segregation in one place at one time. But even comparisons may be suspect and only the obvious importance of occupational classification in the phenomenon of discrimination makes them worthwhile.

Discrimination and profits

Most previous discussions of discrimination have been in terms of employers who won't hire members of the discriminated-against group. This has meant a general emphasis on the unprofitability of discrimination to the discriminator. The most prejudiced discriminator was pictured as precisely the one who was thought to be missing out on the cheapness of a group of laborers, a cheapness which he was creating by his own behavior. If any employers gained it was thought to be the least prejudiced. Putting the focus on occupational segregation highlights the fact that the discriminating employer does hire black men as janitors and white women in clerical capacities, while his wife hires black women as domestic servants. In fact, one characteristic of the occupations white men have chosen as 'fit' for blacks and white women is that their use is not narrowly restricted to one group of employers. Whatever the profits or losses to employers from discrimination, they are fairly general throughout the system.

As the previous sections will have made clear, when employers discriminate against blacks they lower the wages of blacks and raise the wages of whites. When they discriminate against women they lower the wages of women and raise the wages of men. As a result, employers may on balance gain or lose financially. If gains are possible to employers who discriminate, all sorts of interesting possibilities are raised.

For one, the inclination of employers to restrict blacks and women to jobs for which they are 'fit' may have nothing at all to do with a 'taste for discrimination.'[8] It may instead be adherence to an easily policed gentlemen's agreement on the part of employers whose purpose is the raising of profits. (Note that it is much easier to watch out for and put pressure on violators of 'Thou shalt hire them only as janitors' than violators of 'Thou shalt pay them 80¢ an hour less than whites.') The crucial differential may measure the bribe required to provoke disloyalty to the employers' group on the part of those employers who integrate a prestige occupation rather than the payment for loss of utility from working with blacks or women.[9]

Under what condition will discrimination make for larger profits? As we have seen, discrimination by occupational segregation generally entails differing marginal productivities by occupation. Assuming there are two occupations, and that within each labor will be paid its marginal productivity (this time with no difference in productivity or wages permitted within an occupation by race), profits (Π) depend on the production function (f) and its partial derivatives (f^1, f^2) and on the distribution of the fixed labor force between the two occupations (L_1, L_2):

$$\Pi = f(L_1, L_2) - L_1 f_1(L_1, L_2) - L_2 f_2(L_1, L_2) \tag{1}$$

Then remembering that

$$\frac{dL_1}{dL_2} = -1,$$

a first-order condition for profit maximization is

$$\frac{d\Pi}{dL_1} = -L_1(f_{11} - f_{12}) - L_2(f_{21} - f_{22}) = 0 \tag{2}$$

Now, the marginal productivities do not appear in this condition, so that satisfaction of the condition will not necessarily be consistent with equality of the marginal productivity of labor in both uses.[10]

8. Many readers of *The Economics of Discrimination* have been repelled from Becker's formally correct analysis because of his Chicagoesque use of the non-pejorative word 'taste' to characterize the propensity of discriminators to act in the way they do.

9. Compare Thurow, loc. cit.

10. It turns out that if the production function is homogeneous to any degree, profit maximization and equality of the marginal productivities of the two types of labor are consistent with each other, but this is obviously not the general case.

It must also be noted that each of the two 'occupations' may be a cluster of occupations grouped together, and it is employers who do the grouping. They may be able to do it in such a way as to improve their profits.

Another source of profits to discriminators would lie in racial or sexual differences in the elasticity of the supply of labor. If employers have monopsonistic power, Joan Robinson's (1950) classic discussion of price discrimination would apply. Occupational segregation need not be enforced, but the difficulty of paying people in the same occupation in the same shop different wages may dictate some occupational segregation when employers play this game.

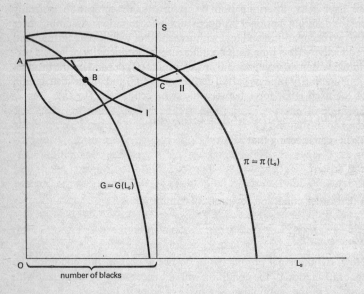

Figure 12.4

Occupational segregation affects relative prices as well as relative wages and the following model demonstrates that even where segregation lowers profits it may at the same time raise the real income of profit-takers. Consider an economy in which there are only two occupations (aside from profit-taking entrepreneur): labor can be employed in manufacturing goods or it can be employed in the form of household servants in the households of the profit-takers. Profits from manufacturing can be expressed as

$$\Pi = f(L_g) - L_g f'(L_g), \tag{3}$$

where Π, f and L_g are profits, the production function for manufactured goods and the amount of labor in manufacturing, respectively. The amount of labor is assumed fixed at

$$L = L_g + L_s.$$

where L_s is the amount of labor in domestic service. It is easy to rewrite (3) so as to make Π a function of L_s. In Figure 12.4, the $\Pi(L_s)$ curve has been graphed, with profits measured on the 'goods' axis. If profit-takers draw their servants from the labor market in the usual competitive way, they must pay them in goods an amount equivalent to the goods value of the marginal productivity of labor in manufacturing. Profit-takers will be able to consume goods (G) equal to profits less wages for servants:

$$G = f(L_g) - L_g f'(L_g) - L_s f'(L_g) \tag{4}$$

Equation (4) can also be rewritten so as to make G a function of L_s, and graphed in Figure 12.4, where it lies inside the Π locus, which it meets at the goods axis where all profits are consumed as goods. The place on the G locus which will be selected under a regime of nondiscrimination depends on the rate of preference substitution between goods and servants; Figure 12.4 shows indifference curve I tangent to the G curve at point B.

The result is different if employers all refrain from hiring some distinguishable portion of the labor force (blacks, women, Catholics) for manufacturing jobs. The supply curve of labor to the domestic service occupation becomes inelastic; we show it in the diagram as vertical line S, whose position depends on the size of the excluded group, here assumed to be blacks. The intersection of this supply curve with the profits curve gives the amount of goods which profit-takers will receive from the manufacturing operation (OA in the diagram). The intersection of the offer curve $O(L_s)$ from point A with the supply curve of servants determines the position of profit-takers under a regime of occupational segregation. In Figure 12.4 this is point C, which may very well be on a higher indifference curve (curve II) than the nondiscriminatory position at B.

The superiority from the point of view of the profit-takers of the discriminatory situation over the nondiscriminatory situation depends on which group the profit-takers have chosen to discriminate against. Consideration of Figure 12.4 shows that picking on too large a group or too small a group as the target for exclusion will mean a failure to improve the position of the profit-takers over the position they could achieve in a nondiscriminatory system. If discrimination had no motive other than increasing the material welfare of the group which sets hiring policy, then whether discrimination in the form of occupational segregation appeared or not would depend on the availability of a well-defined 'target' group of the right size. The fact that the target groups vary greatly throughout the world in the proportion of the labor force which they constitute would argue that a desire to maintain a social system which subordinates women and members of certain racial and religious groups is of more importance in the decision processes which control hiring than a desire for economic advantage.

References

BECKER, G. S., *The Economics of Discrimination*, The University of Chicago Press, 1957.

BERGMANN, B. R., 'The Effect on White Incomes of Discrimination in Employment,' *Journal of Political Economy*, March–April, 1971.

EDGEWORTH, F. Y., 'Equal Pay to Men and Women,' *Economic Journal*, December 1922.

HUTT, W. H., *The Economics of the Colour Bar*, Andre Deutsch, 1964.

ROBINSON, J., *The Economics of Imperfect Competition*, MacMillan & Co., 1950.

Thurow, L. C., *Poverty and Discrimination*, The Brookings Institution, 1969.

13 Sexual Discrimination in the Labour Market *

Brian Chiplin and Peter J. Sloane

Lecturers in Department of Industrial Economics,
University of Nottingham

From: *British Journal of Industrial Relations*, Vol. XII, No. 3, November 1974,
pp. 371–402.

Introduction

In recent years considerable public debate has centred on the question
of unequal treatment between male and female employees in the British
labour force which culminated in the Equal Pay Act 1970 (to take effect
at the end of 1975). More recently, following the introduction of Sex
Discrimination Bills, firstly in the House of Lords and subsequently in
the House of Commons, the Government published a Green Paper,
Equal Opportunities for Men and Women, and announced its intention
to introduce legislation to deal with sex discrimination in the 1973–4
session of Parliament. It is the purpose of this paper to inform the
debate on sexual equality by reference to the economic analysis of discrimination, which has by no means figured prominently in the public
discussion of the issue. This to some extent may be explained by the fact
that no detailed British analysis of the economics of discrimination
exists, despite a mushrooming of the American literature on the subject
(which is mainly but not exclusively devoted to racial discrimination).[1]
The first part of the paper attempts to analyse differences in employment
activity in the labour force between the sexes and to examine how far
these may explain sex wage differentials. This enables us to define more
precisely what constitutes (pure) discrimination in the second section
which surveys various economic models of discrimination, analyses them

*An earlier version of this paper was presented at a seminar of the S.S.R.C.
Labour Economists' Research Study Group. The authors are grateful to the
members of the Group and to an anonymous referee for their comments.

1. The authors have not attempted in this paper to examine directly racial discrimination. This is defended on the grounds that appropriate data is even scarcer
in relation to race than in the case of sex. Further, females are far more important
numerically in the British labour force (though in social terms it could still be argued
that racial discrimination has greater significance).

in terms of their applicability to sexual discrimination, and derives various propositions. In the third section statistical evidence is examined in relation to these propositions in so far as this is possible given the availability of data.[2] Finally, certain implications are drawn from the analysis in comparing the likely effects of equal pay and anti-discrimination legislation on the operation of the labour market.

1. Labour market segmentation and wage differences

The major problem in identifying that component of sexual wage differences which represents discrimination is the fact that male and female labour is not homogeneous. If discrimination is taken to be part of the employer's or employee's utility function one empirical method of identification would be to explain as much as possible of the statistical difference between male and female wages through various labour market and personal characteristics variables and isolate discrimination as a residual. But first, since writers on the subject define discrimination in various ways and look at different aspects of it, we must attempt to identify 'pure' discrimination and compare it with other forms of behaviour in which men and women are treated unequally.

At the outset we may refer to the difference between aggregate male and female earnings in the economy as a whole as 'statistical' discrimination and the figures for recent years reveal that the average weekly earnings of females are about 50 per cent of those for male workers in the case of manual workers and rather less in the case of non-manual workers. However, there is a clear tendency for males to work longer hours, and whilst the provision of overtime opportunities may in itself involve an element of discrimination, it is also appropriate to make comparisons in terms of hourly earnings, especially since shorter hours may reflect a demand for less market work on the part of women. In the case of hourly earnings manual women average approximately 60 per cent of male manual earnings and again the figure is rather less in the case of non-manual women.

In order to clarify the exposition an attempt has been made in Figure 13.1 to classify various forms of 'discrimination'. First, it is important for policy purposes to identify whether the major part of the wage difference is explicable by pre-entry discrimination, that is, discrimination that takes place before the worker has entered the labour force, a

2. It is, however, felt that data limitations preclude the utilization of a detailed cross-section statistical model to explain variations in the extent of discrimination (appropriately defined) among industries and occupations.

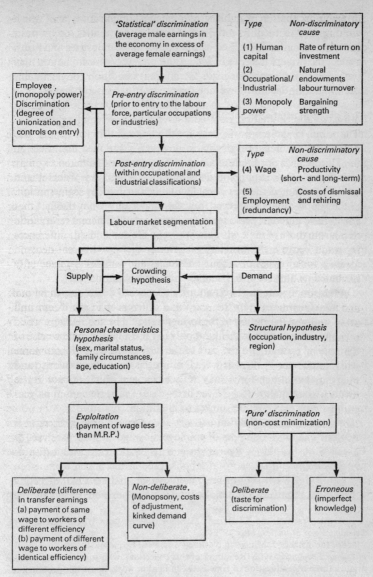

Figure 13.1. Components of Discrimination

particular occupation or industry and the most important type of which would appear to be differential educational opportunities, or by post-entry discrimination, practised within occupations, industries and firms. In effect the two are likely to be linked and pre-entry discrimination may be a necessary though not in itself sufficient condition for post-entry discrimination. Secondly, we must recognize that discrimination may be enforced both by employers and by employees (or trade unions). In both cases discrimination may be analysed as a demand side pheno-menon, but in the employee case it reflects itself through supply side forces (a fuller discussion of this is, however, postponed until Section II). Thirdly, wage differentials and employment differences may result from either supply or demand side factors. As Wachtel and Betsey[3] have noted there is considerable labour market segmentation. On the supply side, differences in wages may result from the fact that females have different personal characteristics (and different reservation prices) from those of male workers, whilst on the demand side differences may result because the structure of industry dictates different demand schedules for all types of labour and males and females are unequally distributed as a result of barriers to entry or lack of mobility.

On the supply side the two major influences are differences in labour force attachment between the sexes and differences in the extent and type of training. In relation to the former it should be noted that married women may leave employment not only to raise a family, but because of geographical mobility on the part of the husband. Female labour force participation must be regarded as a family decision in which entry to and exit from the labour force may reflect changes which do not relate directly to the female herself.[4] Even in the case of single female employees marital status may well be subject to alteration.

Differences in participation between the sexes are clearly discernible when one examines numbers of employees by age. Annual Abstract of Labour Statistics, 1971, figures show that females comprise a dispro-portionate amount of the total labour force in the fifteen to nineteen age group (102.8 per cent of male employment in June 1970) reflecting the fact that relatively more males than females postpone entry into the

3. H. M. Wachtel and C. Betsey, 'Employment at Low Wages', *Review of Economics and Statistics*, May 1972.

4. See for instance J. Mincer in National Bureau of Economic Research, *Aspects of Labour Economics*, 1962 [Reading 1 of this collection], who suggested as appro-priate a three-way allocation of time between market work, household production and leisure.

labour market in order to obtain qualifications, but the female-male employment ratio thereafter is substantially lower. In fact female participation is at its lowest between the ages of twenty-eight and thirty, but rises in the age range forty to fifty-nine, such that it is then above the mean for the whole working population (which is 60.5 per cent of male employment).

The second major area of distinction between males and females concerns the question of training. To the extent that an employer invests in firm specific training the expected length of employment of an individual is important, since it determines the rate of return on the investment. If an employer has the choice of recruiting either a male or a female at the same wage for a job in which an investment in training by the firm is required, other things being equal, the male will be preferred.[5] Therefore, lower wages for women may be seen both as a means of increasing the net rate of return on their training investment and as compensation for the shorter expected duration of employment. Mere differences in rates of pay for men and women in similar occupations do not, therefore, necessarily reflect 'pure' discrimination.[6]

Together these differences suggest that a large number of women may be grouped into a separate labour market from most male employees (as one example of Cairnes' theory of non-competing groups) and may be subject to the influence of a dual labour market. For the situation may be characterized as one in which the primary job market is marked by high levels of skill and wages, employment stability and the prospect of advancement, whilst in the secondary labour market there exist relatively

5. Profit maximizing firms will provide and pay for specific training up to the point where the present value of revenue obtained from it equals expenditure on it. In this respect expected labour turnover becomes a crucial determinant of the investment decision and female turnover rates are significantly higher than those of males. The importance of this variable was particularly well illustrated in one case study of female employees which attempted to estimate the rate of return on training investment in a clothing firm. Whilst 25 per cent of the overall gain was attributed to higher productivity, 75 per cent was attributed to a decrease in labour turnover giving a longer average retention period. Whilst this indicates that female turnover rates are not immutable it also suggests that the rate of return on male workers is likely to be significantly higher than in the case of females to the extent that turnover rates differ. See B. Thomas, J. Moxham and J. A. G. Jones, 'A Cost-Benefit Analysis of Industrial Training', *British Journal of Industrial Relations*, Vol. VII, No. 2, 1969.

6. For an elaboration of these and similar points in relation to equal pay see P. J. Sloane and B. Chiplin, 'The Economic Consequences of the Equal Pay Act, 1970', *Industrial Relations Journal*, Vol. 1, No. 3, December 1970.

low levels of skill and wages, little likelihood of promotion and high labour turnover. To a considerable degree the dual labour market is a function of the development of internal labour markets, noted in several studies,[7] in which favourable treatment is afforded to existing as opposed to potential employees largely by means of promotion ladders internal to the firm and ports of entry limited to low levels of skill. To the extent that women are largely confined to the secondary labour market a vicious circle may operate to perpetuate differences between the male and female wage and occupational structure. For instance, it is suggested that a most important characteristic of the primary labour market is the requirement for employment stability and this will tend to debar not only females who work intermittently but also other females because the probability of employment instability (as assessed by the employer) is greater in their case in comparison to male workers. Furthermore, as workers become confirmed members of the secondary sector they may well adopt behavioural characteristics predominant in that sector. It is also possible that the increasing importance of such factors as on-the-job training will tend to increase the separation between the two markets by making employment stability increasingly significant. In addition the growth of non-wage elements in labour costs implies the need to minimize numbers and maximize hours in order to spread those costs which are fixed in relation to the number of employees. This will tend to raise gross male earnings relative to female, whilst making entry into the primary market even more difficult. The internal labour market will increase the tendency for wages to be a function of age to the extent that seniority provisions prevail, whilst cushioning the firm against supply and demand forces. On the other hand the latter will be more important in determining wage levels for those workers with low separation costs. Therefore, we expect female wages to become a lower ratio of male wages as age increases and to be more closely aligned to the state of the external labour market.

Some evidence of the dual nature of the labour market is provided by age/earnings profiles of male and female employees, data for which were collected in the 1970 New Earnings Survey (though unfortunately not in preceding or subsequent surveys). As shown in Figure 13.2 in the case of weekly earnings, females exhibit flatter earnings profiles than

7. See, for instance, Peter B. Doeringer and Michael J. Piore, *Internal Labour Markets and Manpower Analysis*, D. C. Heath & Co., Lexington, Mass., 1971, and N. Bosanquet and P. B. Doeringer, 'Is there a Dual Labour Market in Great Britain?', *Economic Journal*, June 1973.

males, suggesting perhaps fewer opportunities of advancement to higher graded posts. The female earnings progression tends to flatten out after the twenty-five to twenty-nine age range, whilst male earnings do not reach a peak until the thirty to thirty-nine age range in the case of

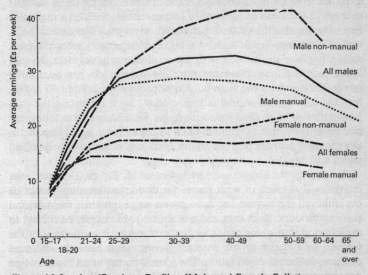

Figure 13.2. Age/Earnings Profiles (Male and Female Full-time Workers, April 1970).

manual workers and the forty to forty-nine age range in the case of non-manual workers.[8] Consistent with the view that investment in human capital is the key factor, manual workers of both sexes earn rather more than their non-manual colleagues until the mid-twenties in the case of males and the early twenties in the case of females. The fact that male earnings in the younger age groups are a relatively lower percentage of the mean compared to females would seem to reflect the greater intensity of training in the former case. It also seems to support the conclusion reached by Bosanquet and Doeringer[9] that women are disproportionately confined to secondary employment – receiving lower wages

8. Non-manual females are exceptional in so far as their earnings peak out in the fifty to fifty-nine age group. This may reflect the importance of incremental pay scales and the fact that those women who return to the labour force possess above-average skills.

9. Op. cit.

and being subject to relatively less upgrading than men. Partly this will reflect the fact that labour turnover is significantly higher in the case of women relative to men.[10] Yet the turnover implied by short job tenure is not reflected in higher recorded unemployment rates for females. In 1970, for instance, male unemployment in Great Britain (total register) averaged 3.6 per cent as opposed to 1.0 per cent for females, and the gap indeed widened in the 1960s. The explanation for the differential (though not its widening) lies in activity rates. Female activity rates exhibit a strong negative association with the level of unemployment, so that lower recorded unemployment rates for women do not necessarily imply that men bear the main burden of unemployment and do not refute the existence of a dual labour market. To some extent the dual labour market may reflect economic forces, but it may also include some components of discrimination in so far as there exist unequal opportunities for entry into the primary labour market between equally qualified males and females.

Finally, on the supply side, as indicated in Figure 13.1, we must recognize that much of what passes for discrimination may in fact be exploitation, the payment to labour of a wage less than the marginal revenue product. Both men and women may, of course, be subject to exploitation, but unionization is likely to reduce it in the case of the former. In a classic article Bloom[11] distinguished between deliberate and non-deliberate exploitation. The former occurs when the employer consciously attempts to pay labour less than the M.R.P., though able to pay the full amount, whilst the latter is traceable to conditions beyond the employer's control (e.g. monopsony, the existence of a kinked demand curve or the fact that the costs of adjustment or search costs do not warrant a change being made). In the case of deliberate discrimination in the hiring of labour perfect discrimination would occur if each

10. For instance Department of Employment Gazette figures show that in 1970 the annual percentage total turnover rate in manufacturing was 49 per cent for females and 30 per cent for males. The NES provides information on the proportion of employees who have been employed by their current employer for less than twelve months, i.e. short-service employees. The figures relating to April 1971, all industries and services, show that no less than 22.8 per cent of all females had been employed less than twelve months compared to 14.5 per cent in the case of males. The difference was more striking in the case of unskilled workers: a slightly higher proportion of men had been with their employer less than twelve months. Therefore it would appear from these figures that the female turnover differential is more marked the greater the level of skill.

11. G. F. Bloom, 'A Reconsideration of the Theory of Exploitation', *Quarterly Journal of Economics*, 1940–41

female were to receive her transfer wage and the total economic rent was retained by the monopsonist. Two less extreme possibilities would be to pay the same wage to workers with different levels of performance, such that each received the M.R.P. of the least proficient worker, as might happen with a time-rate method of payment; and secondly to pay different wages to workers with identical levels of performance. This could occur with two clearly identifiable groups (such as men and women) with different transfer earnings. It seems important to distinguish exploitation from 'pure' discrimination since the policy implications are quite different. The former is a consequence of lack of perfect mobility of labour rather than the utility function of the employer or employee.

To conclude the analysis of the supply side of the market, the above factors will not result in labour market discrimination but may to some extent reflect pre-entry discrimination (e.g. in the family, in the education system, or via the dual labour market). To the extent that females are subject to higher rates of labour turnover (or absenteeism), differences in wages and employment do not suggest discrimination. Indeed, differences in supply functions (or transfer earnings) may indicate that women are *prepared to* work at similar jobs to those of males at lower wages.[12]

When we examine the demand side of the market we see, as in Figure 13.1, that discrimination may take several forms which also may have causes which are 'economic' rather than discriminatory in origin. With respect to pre-entry discrimination employers may refuse to hire females for certain occupations or within particular industries, or at least only hire them when the labour market becomes so tight that male labour is simply not available. In the case of the unequal occupational distribution part of the difference may reflect differences in marginal productivities between the sexes and here lifetime productivities may be just as relevant as short-run ones. In the industrial case one must recognize that natural endowments differ between the sexes and as suggested

12. This accords with the findings of J. Gwartney and R. Stroup, 'Measurement of Employment Discrimination According to Sex', *Southern Economic Journal*, Vol. XXXIV, No. 4, April 1973. They hypothesized that observed income differences between the sexes were primarily the result of variation in employee preferences determined by division of responsibilities within the family unit. Earnings data of groups expected to possess similar and divergent employee preferences were presented according to sex and were found to be consistent with the hypothesis that employee preferences were a more important source of income differences than employment discrimination.

earlier labour turnover is crucial in relation to skill acquisition. A second form of pre-entry discrimination is human capital discrimination – by which female human capital may be reduced by biases in the educational system. As noted by Thurow[13] if sex affects the price of human capital (and individuals are motivated by the potential rate of return to particular occupations) this will in turn affect the human capital decision of both sexes. If female wages are lowered by discrimination females will tend to invest less in their own human capital for this reason. Likewise, if male wages are raised by discrimination men will tend to invest more in their human capital, so that the sex differential will widen even further. Here again, however, one must recognize that firms will be guided by the rate of return on the investment in training and may prefer males simply because the rate of return is higher. Finally, one may distinguish a third form of pre-entry discrimination – monopoly power discrimination – by means of which women are not allowed to enter occupations or industries where monopolistic power results in monopoly factor returns. This differs from occupational discrimination in so far as wages are not directly a function of the level of skill. On the worker side this may be effected by union controls on entry to various occupations, enhanced by the relative unwillingness of women to join trade unions, whilst on the employer side management negotiators may use their bargaining strength to exclude females from high-paying jobs (or, where females are admitted, to pay them lower wages than in the case of males). The most obvious manifestation of post-entry discrimination is wage differentiation, and here also we must recognize that in practice men and women are imperfect substitutes selling their services in imperfect markets, so that wage rates would differ even with zero discrimination. For example, the nature of work may partly explain an unequal sex distribution among occupations, industries and regions because of productive abilities, the physically demanding nature of the work or the necessity for inconvenient hours or shiftwork. We may also identify employment (or redundancy) discrimination by which women suffer more than their proportionate share of unemployment or loss of employment, the latter being particularly apparent where females are the first to be laid off when the market slackens through the adoption by firms of 'last-in, first out' policies,[14] with the result that male incomes

13. Lester C. Thurow, *Poverty and Discrimination*, Washington D.C., Studies in Social Economics, The Brookings Institution, 1969.
14. See L. E. Galloway, *Manpower Economics*, Irwin, Harewood, Illinois (1971) for an elaboration of this point.

are raised by the fact that a greater number of men than usual are employed. This inequality between the sexes, to the extent that it is present, may reflect the relative costs of dismissal and rehiring.

However, given that the above forms of sex differentiation may contain elements of 'pure' discrimination, Thurow[15] has shown which circumstances will optimize the male welfare function. For instance, if both wage discrimination and direction of female labour were possible male incomes would be increased by an optimal allocation of female labour from the resource allocation viewpoint, and the payment to females of subsistence wages (assuming no relationship to exist between the type and size of wage payment and productivity).[16] In the case of occupational/industrial and monopoly power discrimination on the other hand male income gains will accrue as a result of a male occupational/industrial distribution weighted towards high wage occupations/industries and incomes will be higher than if males were distributed across occupations/industries efficiently from the resource allocation viewpoint.[17] In order to maximize male gains from unemployment discrimination females should be distributed occupationally, industrially and geographically, so that their employment is at least equal to the maximum expected unemployment in each situation. Then in theory no males need experience unemployment. Females may suffer high rates of unemployment for two reasons. They may be concentrated in occupations which are relatively prone to unemployment or they may suffer more unemployment than males in each occupation.[18]

15. Op. cit.
16. However, Thurow suggests that it may be wrong to assume that the distribution of male employment and capital is independent of the distribution of female employment. Possible losses may arise from an inefficient distribution of male labour and capital. Whether net gains or losses prevail will be a function of the supply elasticities and marginal productivities of male labour and capital in their new employment.
17. A systematic exclusion of females from particular occupations will, however, lead to a situation in which many of them are overqualified for jobs which they hold whilst some men will be relatively underqualified for their jobs. This misallocation of resources will tend to reduce the average level of productivity. Hence, one must consider the costs of additional investment in training less talented males and the reduced return on capital or labour resulting from the lower average level of performance.
18. On the other hand, if female wage rates were lower than those of males to compensate sufficiently for 'tastes for discrimination' employers would have no incentive to lay off females rather than males. Unemployment discrimination is unlikely in practice to explain a major part of the sex earnings differential.

Finally, a low level of investment in female human capital may increase male incomes. The return to male human capital is likely to increase when the supply of female human capital is reduced, though part of the gain may be eroded by the complementarity of male and female human capital.

This analysis suggests that an attempt to maximize the return to each type of discrimination independently will lead to a conflict among objectives. For instance, if wage discrimination is most effective in skilled occupations, the expropriation of returns to female productivity may require a large investment in female human capital. More generally, maximizing gains for each type of discrimination independently will not result in maximum gains for males as a group. In order to maximize total gains discrimination should be continued up to the point at which the net marginal revenue from it is zero or where it is equal to the loss it causes on the return to other varieties, whichever occurs first.

We must, however, also recognize that discrimination, particularly of the pre-entry variety, may be explained by imperfect knowledge. As McCall[19] has suggested it may pay employers to discriminate rather than engage in search costs in order to identify the productivity level of potential job applicants. Sex is obviously a cheap screening device. Similarly, Zellner[20] argues that there is a need to distinguish between two types of discrimination – deliberate and erroneous. The former indicates a subjective preference for males and has a psychological basis, whilst the latter involves an underestimation of female capacities and is cognitive by nature. In the erroneous case the entry of females into new jobs would presumably remove the discrimination, but in the deliberate case the entry of females might merely reinforce the prejudice.

Thus, whilst each of these forms of discrimination may reflect a taste for discrimination they also illustrate that there are often other economic explanations of inequalities between the sexes. They also point to the fact that the labour market is considerably segmented both on the supply side and on the demand side, which inter-react to provide support for a crowd-hypothesis to explain sex wage differences (referred to in the next section).

19. John J. McCall, 'The Simple Mathematics of Information, Job Search and Prejudice', in A. H. Pascal, ed., *Racial Discrimination in Economic Life*, D. C. Heath & Co., Lexington, Mass., 1972.

20. H. Zellner, 'Discrimination against Women, Occupational Segregation and the Relative Wage', *American Economic Association, Papers and Proceedings*, May 1972.

To conclude, therefore, it would seem that sexual wage differentials within occupations or an unequal sex distribution of manpower do not *necessarily* represent discrimination to any great extent. One must make allowance for the fact that male and female labour is not homogeneous. Further, there is a need to distinguish between equality of activity and equality of opportunity. To quote one observer,[21] 'Only under the circumstances of equal opportunity, identical tastes, abilities, social pressure, psychological and physical attributes would we expect observed behaviour of the sexes to be the same'. Thus, any attempt to achieve proportionate representation for women among occupations would seem to be grounded on an insufficient appreciation of the situation. An optimal allocation of labour may require substantial differences between the male and female occupational structure and might indeed imply a preponderance of women in relatively low-paid occupations, given an unwillingness on the part of both females and firms to invest in female human capital. Alternatively it might imply substantial wage differentials between the sexes in similar jobs.

II A survey of economic models of discrimination

In the light of the analysis contained in Section I and particularly with reference to Figure 13.1 'pure' discrimination may be regarded as a demand side phenomenon in which profits and wages are sacrificed in order to enjoy the commodity of discrimination. Thus we may appropriately define 'pure' labour market discrimination on the part of an employer as any form of unequal treatment between male and female employees which does not *directly* result in cost-minimization in monetary terms in relation to labour utilization.[22] In the case of employee discrimination it is any form of behaviour which does not *directly* result in maximization of the total wage bill (appropriately defined to include male and female earnings). In each case this represents rational behav-

21. See the comments of S. Sandell in the discussion on 'What Economic Equality for Women Requires', *American Economic Association, Papers and Proceedings*, May 1972.

22. This is consistent with a definition of wage discrimination offered by J. E. Stiglitz, 'Approaches to the Economics of Discrimination', *American Economic Review, Papers and Proceedings*, May 1973. He states 'there is wage discrimination if individuals with the same *economic* characteristics receive different wages and the differences are systematically correlated with certain non-economic (racial, religious) characteristics of the individual'. He suggests that an economic characteristic is anything which affects the net marginal productivity of a worker, allowance being made for training and hiring costs.

iour to the extent that the parties are attempting to maximize a utility function including a discrimination coefficient. It should be noted, however, that in all other respects we may regard firms as profit maximizers and workers as maximizers of net economic advantages. Indeed, there may be a fallacy of composition in supposing that the discriminators actually do bear the costs of discrimination. For whilst each entrepreneur loses directly from the refusal to employ females each may gain indirectly from the fact that others are discriminating also. Segregation itself gives rise to the possibility of wage discrimination, which in turn reduces costs, as demonstrated below in the discussion of the employer micro-discrimination model. Similarly in the case of employee discrimination male wages rates may in practice be higher than they would be in its absence. Generally, we may state that the extent and form of discrimination will be a function of the size of the discrimination coefficient (d), representing the taste for discriminatory union policy and the female labour supply function. An alternative definition of discrimination would be a situation in which there exists a departure from Pareto efficiency in the distribution of resources which also results in less inputs for females.[23] This would have the advantage of taking into account social as well as private costs and benefits. However, whilst this approach is obviously appealing from the public policy viewpoint, it is not always clear what the maximization of social benefits will imply in terms of sexual resource allocation, so that the former approach is adopted in this paper.

As noted in Section I discrimination may be enforced both by employers and employees (or trade unions). Examining employee discrimination first and assuming an absence of employer discrimination one might postulate two reasons for such behaviour. First, men may dislike associating with women at work particularly where females gain access to supervisory roles. Secondly, males may oppose entry by females into an occupation because the latter are seen as a threat to job and income security. In a non-discriminatory situation it might be assumed that trade unions would attempt to maximize the welfare function of the total membership irrespective of sex, so that employee (monopoly power) discrimination (possible because males dominate the decision-processes of individual unions) is likely to contain elements of 'pure' discrimination (as defined below). Then we may envisage an employee utility func-

23. For an example of this approach see E. J. Toder, 'The Supply of Public School Teachers to an Urban Metropolitan Area: a Possible Source of Discrimination in Education', *Review of Economics and Statistics*, 1973.

tion in which male workers are prepared to accept lower wages for the privilege of not associating with women at work.[24] In Figure 13.3 below men are prepared to trade wages for a lower female percentage of the labour force.[25] (An alternative would be to measure the absolute

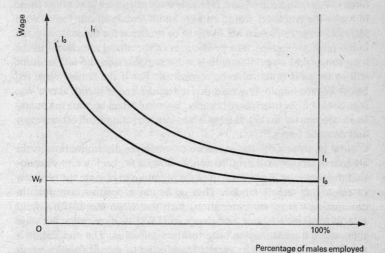

Figure 13.3. Employee Discrimination

number of females on the horizontal axis.) The labour force in this case may be taken to be a particular occupation within a plant (i.e., male employees may not object to the employment of females within a plant in different jobs to their own). Trade unions may, however take a somewhat broader view.

$I_0 I_0$ and $I_1 I_1$ are employee indifference curves for various combinations of wages and percentages of males in the labour force. These, of course, must cease to operate once 100 per cent male employment is achieved. Rising transfer earnings or incomes would cause a movement to a higher indifference curve (e.g. from $I_0 I_0$ to $I_1 I_1$). If males and females are perfect

24. Though this could be construed as *long-run* wage maximizing behaviour on the part of men.

25. This section of the analysis was developed before the authors came across a paper by D. W. Flanders and P. E. Anderson, 'Sex Discrimination in Employment: Theory and Practice', *Industrial and Labor Relations Review*, Vol. 26, No. 3, April 1973. Their analysis is very similar to the above, but they also allow for the possibility that under certain circumstances there may be a preference for females.

substitutes with identical wage rates a decision by the employer to employ females will raise the price he has to pay for male workers and raise the total wage bill. Other things being equal, a rational non-discriminating employer would employ a completely segregated labour force rather than a mixed one. If female wage rates were lower than those of males the employer would employ an all-female labour force. With identical wage rates men are likely to be preferred for the reasons given in the previous section. The predictions of the model are clear – in the long run sexual wage differentials will disappear and the labour force will as far as is practicable be segregated. For if the female wage fell below W_F the employer would prefer females and if it rose above W_F, men could be obtained more cheaply. W_F would then become the operative wage rate for male and female labour abstracting from other supply and demand forces.[26]

Now let us assume the existence of employer discrimination in the absence of employee discrimination. Following Becker[27] we may assume that the employer is prepared to pay a premium to obviate the necessity of employing female labour. That is, he has a positive taste for discrimination ('pure' discrimination) such that when faced with a wage rate W for female labour he behaves *as if* $W(1 + d)$ were the net wage rate, where d measures the taste for discrimination. The implication is that the employer forfeits profits by refusing to recruit females where under competitive conditions the marginal value product is in excess of the marginal cost of hiring an additional unit of labour.[28] We may, therefore, draw an indifference map indicating the employer's tastes for combinations of profits and male employment (Figure 13.4).

Let us assume that male and female wage rates are equated at W_F in Figure 13.3 and that men and women are perfect substitutes. Since pro-

26. For a fuller discussion of the implications of this analysis and related points in relation to racial discrimination see Kenneth J. Arrow, 'Models of Job Discrimination', in Pascal, op. cit.

27. Gary S. Becker, *The Economics of Discrimination*, 2nd edition, the University of Chicago Press, 1971.

28. M. Alexis ('A Theory of Labour Market Discrimination with Independent Utilities', *American Economic Review, Papers and Proceedings*, May 1973) feels that the traditional emphasis on employer discrimination is probably excessive, since much capital is employed in public companies where the owners are not present. He then proceeds to develop a short-run model in which employer discrimination is a function of envy or malice rather than of aversion. We should also note that the above model implicitly assumes that all employers are males. Therefore, the fact that this form of discrimination can take place at all implies that some prior form of discrimination exists (e.g. with respect to access to capital markets).

fits in that case would be independent of the sex distribution of the labour force actual profits would be described by a horizontal line such as $\Pi_0\Pi_0$ and the employer would choose to employ only males in order to move on to the highest indifference curve possible. If, however, female wage rates were below those of male workers the profits would decline as the percentage of males increased. With profits given by $\Pi_1\Pi_1$, $O\,M_0$ percentage male labour force would be engaged at that level of employment at which the profits line is tangential to an indifference

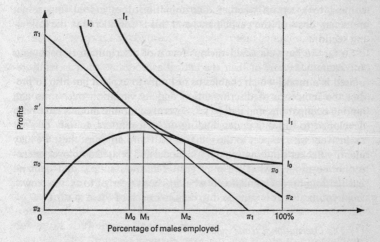

Figure 13.4. Employer Discrimination

curve. Profits in this case would have been maximized by employing all women, so that $\Pi_1\Pi'$ profits have been sacrificed by the employer. Therefore unless there are shortages of male workers sexual wage differentials seem necessary to ensure the employment of women. If, as in practice, men and women are imperfect substitutes the profits curve would reach a maximum at some optimal sex mix such as $O\,M_1$. The employer would, however, maximize his utility function by employing $O\,M_2$ percentage males. The predictions of this model differ from that of employee discrimination in one important respect. In the latter case competitive forces are likely to lead to segregation with equalization of wage rates, whilst in the employer discrimination case in equilibrium wage rates are likely to differ in order to avoid total segregation in so far as women are prepared to accept lower wages than men in order to gain employment.

In practice it could be argued that employers do not have positive tastes for discrimination but merely reflect employee discrimination since non-discriminatory behaviour might adversely affect profits. That, however, would be tantamount to arguing that male employees have different utility functions to those of employers and it is not implausible to suggest that employer and employee discrimination are additive – prejudice is a universal phenomenon. It is necessary, however, in this context to ascertain whether discrimination does indeed impose net monetary costs on the participants and this is considered in the following section.

So far we have classified various forms of discriminatory behaviour and examined some of their theoretical aspects but what is really required is a model which enables us not only to explain but also to predict the incidence of discrimination and its variation over time and among occupations and industries. Several economic models have been developed to aid our understanding of such matters, mainly but not exclusively with respect to the racial issue. From amongst these we may identify Becker's international trade model and related employer microeconomic model, what we may term Thurow's supply and demand elasticities approach and finally what has been referred to as 'the crowding hypothesis'. It is proposed to consider each of these in turn.

(1) *The international trade model*

Becker's model[29] analyses two perfectly competitive societies in which factors of production rather than commodities are traded. Let us suppose that the two groups are men (M) and women (W) and that men are relatively well endowed with capital and women similarly endowed with labour. With free trade each group would export its relatively abundant factor and factor prices would be equalized according to the normal tenets of trade theory. Now, assume that M discriminates and only exports capital subject to the addition of a discrimination coefficient. Becker shows that each group as a whole suffers a monetary loss as a consequence of the reduction in trade, but that M labour and W capitalists gain, and further that it will not pay W to retaliate. This is illustrated in Figure 13.5 which compares the net incomes of the two groups. Income is maximized with free trade at A. As the MDC in-

29. Op. cit.

creases income falls for both groups and reaches a minimum when trade ceases at B. The majority group loses in absolute terms, though it may gain relatively to the other group.

As Thurow[30] and Krueger[31] point out, however, optimal tariff theory would seem to indicate that it is possible for a majority group to gain *absolutely* at the expense of a minority (e.g. as indicated by line AC in

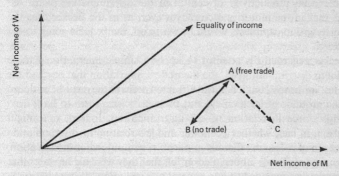

Figure 13.5. The effect of Discrimination on the Incomes of the Parties

Figure 13.5) or for the minority to benefit from retaliation, the success of such policies depending on the relative elasticities of demand for exports. Becker, however, rejected the view that his discrimination coefficient corresponds to a tariff in international trade, claiming that discrimination had more in common with transportation costs than with tariffs.[32] However, in the preface to the second edition of the book he admits that optimal tariff and general monopoly theory 'would become relevant if trade were reduced because of collective action by various members of the majority, to benefit themselves at the expense of

30. Op. cit.

31. Anne O. Krueger, 'The Economics of Discrimination', *Journal of Political Economy*, Vol. 71, 1963.

32. Thus, in footnote 3, p. 21, 2nd edition, Becker states, 'If we compare discrimination with tariffs we find that although some of their effects are similar, other effects are quite different. Discrimination always decreases both societies' net incomes, whilst a tariff of appropriate size can increase the levying societies' net income. A tariff operates by driving a wedge between the price a society pays for imported goods and the price each individual member pays; it does not create any distinction between net incomes and total demand over goods. Discrimination does create such a distinction and does not drive a wedge between private and social prices.'

others including the minority'. Thus, if one regards collective action as a significant element in sexual discrimination, optimal tariff theory is relevant, but much hinges on the question of whether the motive for discrimination is 'economic' or reflects a taste for discrimination. Assuming the former, Krueger develops a model in which the majority group maximizes its real income by imposing an optimal tariff such that the marginal productivity of capital in the discriminating sector exceeds that in the minority sector. However, as in the Becker case the majority group capitalists would be worse off, the benefits going to the workers.

Becker regarded his attempt to apply a simple international trade model to discrimination as 'the theoretical innovation that has had the greatest influence', but it has also attracted perhaps the greatest criticism on the grounds of irrelevancy, and these criticisms seem to have even stronger force in relation to sex discrimination. Indeed, one might question, in fact, whether economic models relating to discrimination by reason of colour are directly applicable, without major modification, to the case of female labour. Becker felt that they were for he states that his model was intended to be a general one including 'discrimination in the market place because of race, sex, colour, personality or other non-pecuniary considerations'.[33] Apart from the fact that there may be an economic justification for 'discriminating' against women in a way which does not apply in the racial case – white and coloured men should exhibit similar participation rates as they both form part of the primary labour force, whilst within an occupation they should not exhibit markedly different turnover rates[34] – it may be suggested (and this to some extent is at variance with the assumption made earlier in this paper also) that male resistance to the entry of females into male preserves (or indeed white resistance to the entry of coloured workers) represents a general fear of a long-run downward pressure on male (white) wage rates rather than a taste for discrimination as such. Indeed, one may note that under certain circumstances males are prepared to pay a premium to associate with females rather than the reverse! On the other hand, it might be held that such an attitude does not hold in relation to contact at work, as evidenced by the apparent unwilling-

33. *The Economics of Discrimination*, op. cit.

34. These differences can be accounted for, however, to the extent that one is able to measure 'pure' rather than 'statistical' discrimination. Other things being equal, it would seem that the discrimination coefficient (d) will be a smaller proportion of the statistical difference between earnings in the case of sex.

ness on the part of males to work in subordinate positions to women. But an even more crucial question is in what sense do males and females represent two independent communities, freely trading with one another? In the case of racial discrimination reality may be represented by a ghetto situation, which may not be totally different from a situation of separate trading entities, but in the case of sex discrimination males and females combine to form family units, so that in Becker's terms the family might be said to be discriminating against itself. This paradox might be explained by the fact that males are in almost permanent employment as members of the primary labour force whilst married females as members of the secondary labour force only participate intermittently. In this situation it is possible that families place a premium on certainty or permanence of income and discriminatory behaviour would be justified in so far as male members of the household manage to appropriate the gains (monopoly profits) resulting from the female losses. Non-discrimination would also tend to lower wages of the male labour force and thus the level of permanent income. (In the case of single female employees this paradox only arises to the extent that they contribute to family income.) Thus, whilst the international trade model may yield some useful observations, its relevance to the analysis of sexual discrimination might be considered to be rather limited.

(2) *Employer (taste for) discrimination model*

So far, we have examined employers' (and employees') behaviour as consumers of discrimination but we must also consider the effect of discrimination on the productive process. In *The Economics of Discrimination* Becker suggests that discrimination will not alter the individual firm's criterion for minimizing costs, but will cause actual factor proportions to differ in such a way that there will be a smaller demand for those factors against which the employer discriminates and, secondly, that the money cost at each output will be greater than minimum cost without discrimination. However, an extension of the figure on page 42 of the above suggests that neither of these results is inevitable. In Figure 13.6 AB represents the relative costs of male and female labour without discrimination. If, however, the employer has a taste for discrimination he will act as if AB^1 represents the true relative costs of the two types of labour;[35] I_0 is an isoquant representing the desired level of

35. The distance B^1B will of course be determined by the size of the discrimination coefficient (d). If men and women were perfect substitutes with identical supply conditions AB would be a 45° line.

output for the firm and its slope suggests that male and female labour is imperfectly substitutable. We may conceive of an occupation which involves elements of both heavy work and dexterity and in which labour is flexible. (As Becker suggests, if men and women were perfect substi-

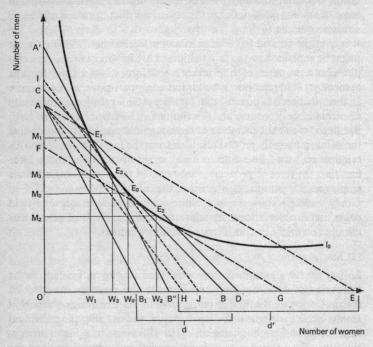

E_0 = zero discrimination equilibrium
E_1 = occupational/employment discrimination equilibrium
E_2 = wage discrimination equilibrium
E_3 = wage and occupational/employment discrimination

Figure 13.6. Employer Discrimination in Production

tutes the isoquant would be represented by a straight line and with discrimination no women would be employed.) In the case presented the employer desires to produce I_0 and acts as if the relative price line is A^1B^{11} reaching equilibrium at E_1. In the Becker model only perceived relative costs of the two types of labour alter, actual relative costs remaining the same as represented by CD, so that the costs of producing

I_0 have risen from OA to OC, and the employment of women falls from OW_0 to OW_1. Becker assumes therefore that relative wage rates do not alter, in which case it would appear that there can be no wage discrimination, merely employment discrimination or segregation. This assumption is surprising in view of the fact that he places considerable emphasis on the market discrimination coefficient (d) which relates to differences in wages.[36]

Indeed, in this case it is hardly likely that discrimination will have no effect on relative wage rates, since the females who are unemployed $(OW_0 - OW_1)$ will exert a downward pressure on wage rates in their occupation (and presumably to a lesser extent on those males who are close substitutes). Let us make the other extreme assumption that wage discrimination alone takes place, such that female wage rates are reduced, but employers are willing to employ women at lower wage rates. In this case let us assume that AE is the relevant price line. Then, the employer can now produce I_0 at a lower level of costs OF (suggesting that capitalists *can* gain from wage discrimination).[37] Further in this example the employment of women increases and that of males declines.

A more likely situation than either of the above extremes is one in which wage and occupational/employment discrimination occur jointly. This will yield a new discrimination coefficient such as d′ which may be taken to be proportional to the wage and will tend to offset the effects of lower wages. In this case both female wages and female employment at E_3 are lower than in the zero discrimination case. But it can easily be demonstrated that an alternative result is possible in which female employment is higher than in the zero discrimination case.[38] If female employment does, indeed, increase in total, general equilibrium can only be achieved by an increase in the size of the female labour force. But, with the existence of wage discrimination, costs of producing a

36. He also goes to great pains to distinguish between market discrimination and segregation. Thus, referring to the two coefficients in the conclusion (p. 157) he states, 'it is easy to confuse these two concepts, and yet a careful distinction between market segregation and market discrimination is essential for a clear understanding of the observable consequences of tastes for discrimination'.

37. This still leaves to be explained how employers are able to enforce the lower wage. Presumably supply conditions must be favourable to this result. Since we have previously defined discrimination as a non-cost minimizing form of behaviour it is perhaps better to refer to this case as one of exploitation.

38. Female employment will in fact be a negative function of the size of the discrimination coefficient and a positive function of the marginal rate of substitution between male and female labour.

given output will be lower than in the zero discrimination case. The above analysis suggests that a combination of wage and employment discrimination is compatible with

(a) Increased employer costs, reduced employment for the minority (e.g. females) and increased employment for the majority (e.g. males). This is the Becker result.

(b) Reduced employer costs, decreased employment for the minority and increased employment for the majority.

(c) Reduced employer costs, increased employment for the minority and decreased employment for the majority.

The second and third follow from the existence of wage discrimination (i.e., the fact that employers will be prepared to employ women if the latter will accept a sufficiently low wage). More women may be employed (though fewer than if there had been no taste for discrimination) and costs will be lower. Becker, thus, considers the reducement effect (d) to the neglect of the inducement effect (lower wages) and to some extent the use of the *as if* curve is misleading. For when the employer acts as if $W(1 + d)$ is the net wage rate rather than W, this may well tend to reduce the actual wage rate.

One problem with the above analysis is to explain how discrimination can persist under competitive conditions.[39] As Becker suggests, given a dispersion of discrimination coefficients and identical production functions, an employer with a smaller discrimination coefficient will have lower costs, so that under competitive conditions the lowest coefficient must prevail. Throughout monopolistic industries, however, the median coefficient will not be subject to downward pressures. Thus, Becker's model predicts that monopolistic enterprises will discriminate more than competitive ones. In relation to the female labour market, however, one must note the fact that monopolistic enterprises may be more heavily unionized and wage discrimination at least may be resisted by the unions, whilst in competitive industries with high costs of membership recruitment union protection may not be present.

Another important question is whether discrimination is likely to increase or decrease as the relative size of the minority grows. Here Becker finds that discrimination against Negroes is positively related to their relative number. However, the relationship is stronger in the case

39. For a detailed discussion of this issue see Stiglitz, op. cit. Besides the existence of monopoly he suggests that disequilibrium in the labour market (i.e. the existence of queues) and differences in information about jobs on the part of job seekers may be important contributory factors.

of discrimination prior to entry into the labour force (as illustrated by opportunities for formal education) than for discrimination in the labour market. In relation to female labour in Britain we observe a substantial growth in the size of the minority group relative to the total workforce and this provides the possibility of testing this hypothesis.

(3) Thurow's supply and demand elasticities approach

The major weakness of the above two models stems largely from their failure to take sufficiently into account differences in supply conditions between the two types of labour. Thurow attempts to rectify this by using simple supply and demand analysis as follows:

Discrimination may be represented as a downward shift in the demand curve for labour, the vertical distance representing the size of the discrimination coefficient. The effect on male and female incomes will not only depend on the size of the downward shift but also on the supply elasticity of female labour and the male demand elasticity for female labour.

The demand curve D_1 in Figure 13.7 represents the economic value of employing an extra man (marginal productivity) whilst demand

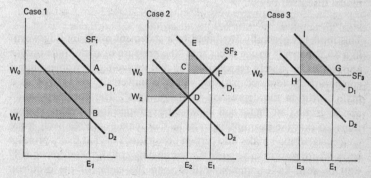

Figure 13.7. Supply and Demand under a Situation of Discrimination

curve D_2 represents the actual valuation or social valuation of utilizing additional units of female labour (i.e., the demand curve after discrimination). In Case 1 with a perfectly inelastic female labour supply curve the whole of the surplus represented by $W_0 W_1 AB$ will be appropriated by the employer, but if the male unions are strong it may be shared with male workers. There is an unambiguous gain to the male sector. In Case 2 with a positively sloped female supply curve, there is a loss to the community represented by DEF but males may still gain provided the area of rectangle W_0W_2CD exceeds the area of triangle CEF. Where the female labour supply curve is perfectly elastic, there is an analogous loss represented by GHI, since in this case women cannot be paid less than their MRP.

In this model discrimination bears a close affinity to exploitation, since female labour is paid less than the true value of its MRP, and male workers gain either through collusion with the employer or because a downward shift in the demand curve for females may lead to an upward shift in the demand curve for males. Also, it emphasizes the importance of supply conditions, for when the elasticity of female supply is zero male losses are zero, whilst in the other limiting case where the elasticity of female supply is infinite male gains are zero. Generally male losses do not exceed male gains unless both the elasticities of supply and demand are large. This, therefore, also contradicts the predictions of the Becker model. Further the emphasis Thurow's analysis places on the supply side makes it particularly relevant to the female labour market. Indeed, it is broad in scope and can be taken to encompass the final model discussed below.

(4) *The crowding hypothesis*

This model is generally attributed to a statement made by Edgeworth in a 1922 paper[40] to the effect that 'the pressure of male trade unions appears to be largely responsible for that crowding of women into a comparatively few occupations, which is universally recognized as a main factor in the depression of their wages'. The corollary would appear to be that males will likewise be crowded into certain occupations, so that the assumption must be that females are relatively more concentrated than males into certain occupations or that males prohibit entry where returns are higher. Overcrowding could, therefore, equally well be seen as a symptom rather than the cause of the problem. Crowding must include elements of occupational and monopoly power discrimination if it is to be a meaningful model. The hypothesis was first applied to the problem of racial discrimination by Barbara R. Bergmann.[41] As she states, the enforced abundance of supply will

40. F. Y. Edgeworth, 'Equal Pay to Men and Women for Equal Work', *Economic Journal*, Vol. 31, 1922.

41. Barbara R. Bergmann, 'The Effect on White Incomes of Discrimination in Employment', *Journal of Political Economy*, Vol. 79, 1971.

lower marginal productivity in certain occupations, whilst maintaining it at a higher level in the male sector. If an overcrowded market is to be cleared marginal productivity must be pushed to a relatively low level and even in the absence of exploitation women would receive a wage below that received by males for similar levels of skill. The relationship to the analysis of the dual labour market is clear, but the crucial factor here is the size of the female labour force relative to restrictions on the hiring of females. We must recognize further that this situation is likely to lower the earnings also of those who are employed in predominantly male occupations, since their transfer earnings will be correspondingly reduced.

We may list the propositions derived from this analysis of economic models of discrimination as follows:

(a) To the extent that employee discrimination dominates we expect considerable employment segregation between the sexes.

(b) To the extent that employer discrimination dominates sexual wage differentials will be important.

(c) Becker's international trade model suggests that both parties lose from discrimination, but the adapted micro model and the supply and demand elasticities approach suggest that it is possible for males to gain as a group to the extent that wage discrimination predominates. The latter suggests it may be difficult to persuade the relevant parties to abandon discrimination.

(d) The taste for discrimination model suggests that the extent of discrimination will be negatively related to the degree of competition and possibly positively related to the relative size of the female labour force.

(e) To the extent that females are subject to wage discrimination their employment prospects are increased.

(f) The crowding hypothesis suggests, however, that it is segregation that causes low wages.

The subsequent section attempts to clarify some of these issues in relation to the British labour market.

III Empirical evidence on sex discrimination in Great Britain

The first necessity is to establish whether female employment is unfavourably distributed both by occupation and by industry. The only source of earnings by occupation for a wide range of activities and covering both males and females is that collected on a sample basis for the New Earnings Survey. Female employment as a percentage of total employment for each broad occupational group is shown in Table 13.1. There is ample evidence here that women are unequally distributed between occupations. In order to ascertain whether those occupations which employ a low proportion of women are also those which are characterized by high male earnings (a variant of the crowding hypothesis) the Spearman's Rank Correlation coefficient was calculated. For this test two alternative measures of female intensity were utilized: first, the actual female employment as a proportion of total employment and, secondly, actual female employment as a proportion of expected female employment in each occupational group. Expected employment was calculated on the basis that, for the manual and non-manual occupations *separately*, women would form the same proportion of employment as they did in the labour force as a whole. From Table 13.1 it can be seen that both measures provide the expected negative coefficient but only in the case of the actual employment as a proportion of expected employment is this result significant.

In Table 13.2 the relationship between female employment intensity among industries and earnings ranking is examined separately for manual and non-manual employees. In the case of the former there is a negative relationship which is significant at the 5 per cent level, but in the case of the latter the results are insignificant. Therefore, in general, it would appear that females are not quite so unfavourably distributed occupationally and industrially as is sometimes alleged by the anti-discrimination lobby.[42]

Given, however, the fact that there is an unequal sex distribution both occupationally and industrially it is interesting from the policy viewpoint to ascertain the relative importance of unequal payment and unequal employment distribution.

The relative importance of unequal earnings opportunities (the male/female earnings differential) and unequal opportunity (differential

42. However, a further calculation was made for total employees in employment at October 1972 (Department of Employment Gazette figures). The percentage of females was again ranked with male earnings and yielded a significant result at the 1 per cent level ($r = -0.58$). Since this series includes part-time workers the implication would seem to be that part-time females are relatively unfavourably distributed industrially in comparison with full-time females.

A further possible explanation of the gross earnings differential could lie in an unequal regional sex distribution of employment. For this reason a separate exercise was carried out, again using N.E.S. estimates for 1971, to ascertain whether or not females were more than proportionately employed in low paying regions. No significant relationship emerged.

Table 13.1 **Male earnings by occupation and female employment, April 1971, Great Britain**

Occupational group	(1) Average male weekly earnings[1] £	(2) Female employment as a percentage of total employment %	(3) Actual female employment as percentage of expected number %
Managers	51.8	8.4	19.6
Supervisors, foremen, forewomen	35.6	15.3	55.1
Engineers, scientists, technologists	44.1	1.7	4.1
Technicians	34.5	12.5	29.0
Academic and teaching	41.4	48.4	112.5
Other professional and technical	45.7	9.5	22.0
Office and communications	28.1	63.0	151.6
Sales	30.2	41.3	103.1
Security	31.4	4.7	14.6
Catering, domestic and service	22.5	69.7	379.7
Farming, forestry and horticultural	21.0	6.5	35.3
Transport	30.2	3.1	16.8
Building, engineering, etc.	30.7	7.4	40.4
Textile, clothing and footwear	26.4	62.4	339.8
Other occupations	28.5	18.4	100.2

Spearman's Rank Correlation Coefficient:
between (1) and (2) $r = -0.26$
between (1) and (3) $r = -0.57$[2]

N.B. The medical, dental, nursing and welfare occupational group has been omitted because no male earnings data are available in the sample.
 1. Excluding those where pay was affected by absence.
 2. Significant at the 5 per cent level.
 Source: N.E.S. 1971

Table 13.2(a) **Male earnings by industry and female employment, manual workers, April 1971, Great Britain**

Industry group	(1) Average male weekly earnings[1] £	(2) Female employment as a percentage of total employment %
Vehicles	34.9	7.1
Paper, printing and publishing	34.1	20.6
Coal and petroleum products	33.7	6.6
Shipbuilding and marine engineering	33.5	2.5
Bricks, pottery, glass, cement, etc.	31.3	15.9
Metal manufacture	31.3	5.3
Transport and communication	31.2	5.1
Chemicals and allied industries	31.0	17.4
Mechanical engineering	30.8	9.4
Other manufacturing industries	30.4	27.9
Food, drink and tobacco	30.0	28.2
Electrical engineering	29.9	35.2
Metal goods n.e.s.	29.9	21.6
Mining and quarrying	29.6	0.5
Gas, electricity and water	29.6	2.5
Instrument engineering	28.7	31.5
Construction	28.5	0.6
Timber, furniture, etc.	28.2	13.0
Insurance, banking, finance, etc.	28.0	14.7
Textiles	27.4	41.3
Clothing and footwear	25.9	71.9
Distributive trades	25.6	18.9
Professional and scientific services	25.0	50.6
Public administration	24.5	15.0
Miscellaneous services	23.8	36.7
Agriculture, forestry and fishing	23.0	8.9

Spearman's Rank Correlation Coefficient:
between (1) and (2)   r = −0.37[2]

1. Excluding those whose pay was affected by absence.
2. Significant at the 5 per cent level.
Source: N.E.S. 1971. Office of Manpower Economics, Equal Pay, First Report on the Implementation of the Equal Pay Act 1970. H.M.S.O. 1972.

occupational and industrial distributions between sexes) may be crudely assessed by two procedures (both assuming levels of employment remain unaltered).

Table 13.2(b) **Male earnings by industry and female employment, non-manual workers, April 1971, Great Britain**

Industry group	(1) Average male weekly earnings[1] £	(2) Female employment as a percentage of total employment %
Insurance, banking and finance, etc.	43.5	46.1
Chemical and allied industries	42.9	31.4
Paper, printing and publishing	41.3	40.7
Professional and scientific services	40.9	58.4
Electrical engineering	39.8	27.7
Construction	39.7	22.2
Transport and communication	39.4	36.3
Gas, electricity and water	38.9	20.1
Metal manufacture	38.8	27.7
Vehicles	38.6	21.5
Public administration	38.1	35.7
Mechanical engineering	37.9	25.6
Miscellaneous services	35.3	49.0
Distributive trades	33.0	55.5

Spearman's Rank Correlation Coefficient:
between (1) and (2) $r = -0.06$

1. Excluding those whose pay was affected by absence.
Source: N.E.S. O.M.E. Report.

(a) Granting females the male mean earnings within each occupation (industry), leaving the occupational (industrial) distribution unaltered.
(b) Redistributing females to accord with the 'expected' occupational (industrial) distribution on the basis of the proportion of the sexes in the total labour force. This estimate can be made separately for the manual

and non-manual labour forces.[43] The results of the exercise are contained in Table 13.3.

The calculations are based on the published results of the 1971 New Earnings Survey.[44] The data are incomplete because results are given only for those occupations (industries) represented by at least 100 in the sample and for which the estimate of average weekly earnings has a standard error of not more than 2 per cent of the mean.[45] To estimate the expected number of women for the occupational re-distribution, manual and non-manual occupations were considered separately. For these two categories women were re-allocated so that they formed the same proportion in each occupation as they did in the sample as a

43. Weighted averages of female earnings may be computed as follows:
(1) current average female earnings by occupation (industry) are given by

$$W_1 = \frac{\sum_{j=1}^{n} a_j e_j}{\sum_{j=1}^{n} a_j}$$

where a_j = actual no. of females in occupation (industry) j. e_j = average female earnings. (2) the payment of male average earnings, given the current occupational (industrial) distribution, is given by

$$W_2 = \frac{\sum_{j=1}^{n} a_j e'_j}{\sum_{j=1}^{n} a_j}$$

where e'_j = average male earnings.

(3) The payment of male average earnings, given the 'expected' female occupational (industrial) distribution, is given by

$$W_3 = \frac{\sum_{j=1}^{n} b_j e'_j}{\sum_{j=1}^{n} b_j}$$

where b_j = expected no. of females in occupation (industry) j or total no. of employees in occupation (industry) j × proportion of females in the total labour force (manual or non-manual).

44. The reclassification by industry cannot be done from the Department of Employment's October Earnings survey because this covers manual women only and the full-time female labour force by industry cannot be calculated since figures on part-time women are not separated into manual and non-manual.

45. Additional information was obtained from the Department of Employment covering occupations (industries) where the sample size was fifty or more and when the estimate of average weekly earnings had a standard error of not more than 4 per cent of the mean. Recalculating some of the results for which the coverage was weakest made little difference and therefore estimates using the published figure were adhered to.

Table 13.3

---

(1) *Occupational redistribution*

(a) All occupational groups (excluding medical, dental, nursing and welfare for which no male earnings data are available in aggregate)

W_1 = £18.3   (proportion of sample covered – actual   = 92.3 per cent)
W_2 = £29.4   – expected = 95.9 per cent)
W_3 = £32.9

(b) Broad occupational groups where female earnings data are available

W_1 = £17.5   (proportion of sample covered – actual   = 88.2 per cent)
W_2 = £28.9   – expected = 78.4 per cent)
W_3 = £30.5

(c) Occupational categories where male earnings data are available

W_1 not available (but average for sample as whole = £18.3)
W_2 = £28.0   (proportion of sample covered – actual   = 61.6 per cent)
W_3 = £31.1   – expected = 78.1 per cent)

(d) Occupational categories where both male and female earnings data are available

W_1 = £15.2   (proportion of sample covered – actual   = 55.7 per cent)
W_2 = £25.8   – expected = 41.3 per cent)
W_3 = £28.5

(e) Occupational categories in office and communications where both male and female earnings data are available

W_1 = £17.9   (proportion of sample covered = 100 per cent)
W_2 = £25.9
W_3 = £26.9

(2) *Industrial redistribution*

(a) non-manual women for whom data are available

W_1 = £20.1   (proportion of sample covered – actual   = 88.9 per cent)
W_2 = £38.8   – expected = 86.6 per cent)
W_3 = £37.6

(b) manual women for whom data are available

W_1 = £15.3   (proportion of sample covered – actual   = 94.5 per cent)
W_2 = £27.9   – expected = 74.3 per cent)
W_3 = £29.2

Source: New Earnings Survey 1971. All figures relate to gross weekly earnings and exclude those workers whose pay was affected by absence. Part-time women are excluded from the analysis.

whole. The preferred method of re-allocation was to use the actual numbers of women for whom earnings results were given. However, since the coverage for male earnings was generally better, the number of females was frequently estimated using the total in the whole sample.

Thus in the N.E.S. there are two sample sizes – the whole sample and the total for whom earnings data are given. The difference between the two reflects the fact that certain workers receive no earnings during the sample period for reasons of sickness, etc. As between the two samples there is a slight difference in the female proportion of the manual and non-manual labour force. For the sample as a whole the proportions are 18.36 per cent manual and 43.00 per cent non-manual; for the earnings sample the figures are 18.63 per cent and 42.55 per cent respectively.

The procedure adopted is likely to be the most favourable for women since it assumes that they achieve the same representation in all occupations including those involving high investment in human capital. However, the manual and non-manual occupations were considered separately since the difference might to some extent represent differences in education levels.

The re-allocation on an industrial basis was done for all those industries where both male and female earnings were available and the female workers were reclassified according to the proportions in the sample for whom earnings were given.

Much stress has been put on the importance of removing the inequality of occupational distribution (via anti-discrimination legislation as opposed to inequality of payment (via equal pay legislation). The results of the exercise strongly suggest in fact that the redistribution of females, keeping earnings constant, makes little difference to average earnings in comparison to granting females the male earnings' levels (and hours) in their existing occuptions.[46] A corresponding exercise for American Negroes by S. Michelson[47] gave very similar results. He found using 1960 Census data that the effect on the difference in average incomes between white and non-white of correcting the occupational male-distribution of Negroes, but keeping Negro earnings in each occupation constant, was small compared with the effect of assigning to Negroes white earnings in their occupations, but keeping their occupational distribution unchanged.

One explanation for these results may be that redistributing occupationally only affects a proportion of the minority labour force, whilst all would benefit in the higher earnings case, but this also reflects the im-

46. Part of the difference can, of course, be explained by the fact that men and women work different hours. This explains relatively little of the difference in the case of non-manual workers, but is more important in the case of manual workers.

47. 'Incomes of Racial Minorities', mimeographed, Brookings Institute, Washington D.C., 1968.

portance of the existing pay differential within occupations. The relative unimportance of occupational redistribution might seem to imply that the overcrowding hypothesis is not a major explanation of earnings differences. The problem, however, is one of general equilibrium since any redistribution would in practice affect wage rates. Bergmann[48] for instance, finds that this result is not inconsistent with the crowding hypothesis, but indeed is mildly favourable to it. Crowding in the female occupations may lower earning of females in other occupations and hence make the wage gap between males and females larger in those occupations. This is one example of the failure of the crowding hypothesis to provide unambiguous predictions.

As stated above crowding may result from the exercise of monopoly power and reflect the ability of the employer to indulge his taste for discrimination as in the Becker model. To test whether statistical discrimination (in wages or employment) was in fact related to the degree of monopoly three-firm concentration ratios for 1958 (the last year for which concentration data in the Census of Production were available on a comparable basis to earnings) were used as a proxy for monopoly power. A simple least squares regression analysis failed to provide much support for this hypothesis on either a wage or employment discrimination basis.[49] Possibly this may be the result of a failure to use a 'pure' discrimination variable or the fact that conventional measures of monopoly power are inadequate but at least any such relationship, if it exists, does not appear to be a simple one.

The second suggestion of Becker that discrimination increases as the

48. Op. cit.
49. Three separate measures of concentration were in fact used, namely sales, output and employment, each of which provided almost identical results. The use of the employment concentration measure, for instance, gave the following result for employment discrimination:

$$F = 43.12 - 0.23C \qquad \bar{R}^2 = 0.06$$
$$(2.71)$$

where F = percentage of females in industry
and   C = three firm employment concentration ratio
(figure in parenthesis is the T statistic)

The coefficient is, in fact, significantly different from zero at the 1 per cent level. Even poorer results were obtained in the case of wage discrimination. Thus

$$W = 0.53 + 0.00007C$$
$$(0.37) \qquad \bar{R}^2 = 0.0009$$
where W = female/male earnings ratio.

relative size of the minority grows is more straightforward. However, despite substantial changes in the labour force the male/female gross earnings differential has remained remarkably constant over a very long period of time (the female weekly earnings being 50.2 per cent of males in 1906 and 50 per cent in 1970 with only minor variations in between). The growth of female employment has been particularly marked in the period since World War II. In 1951 females comprised 30.8 per cent of total employees in employment. By 1961 this had risen to 32.4 per cent and by 1971 to 38.5 per cent. Clearly, therefore, to the extent that 'pure' discrimination is reflected in the total male/female earnings differential, the size of the female working population relative to the male does not appear to have been a major influence on the degree of discrimination.

As outlined earlier in this paper in order to isolate the 'pure' discrimination component, one must allow for differences in productivity and human capital between men and women. Conceptually it would then be possible to explain and predict the incidence of discrimination on a cross-section industrial basis. Here a fruitful area of inquiry is the extension and application of the human capital approach to the question of male/female wage differentials. A number of American studies have used this method in an attempt to isolate the discrimination component,[50] but similar work for the United Kingdom is frustrated by the lack of published data on human capital. An alternative possibility would be to apply the model to an individual firm on the lines of the Malkiels' study. For the United Kingdom, therefore, the measurement of the residual, pure discrimination, remains a most difficult task worthy of further research.

IV Conclusions and policy implications

The above analysis suggests that discrimination may most usefully be regarded as a demand side phenomenon in which employers (and employees) obtain satisfaction from various types of exclusion and wage discrimination. Several economic analyses have been examined each of which to some extent aids our understanding of such behaviour, particularly in drawing the distinction between wage discrimination and

50. See for instance, R. L. Oaxaca, *Male-Female Wage Differentials in Urban Labour Markets*, Ph.D., Princeton, 1971; Burton G. Malkiel and Judith A. Malkiel, 'Male-Female Pay Differentials in Professional Employment', *American Economic Review*, Vol. LXII, No. 4, September 1973. For a somewhat different approach see L. E. Galloway and G. W. Scully, 'An Economic Analysis of Minority Group Discrimination in the United States', *Mid-West Economic Association*, Chicago, April 1969.

segregation. The statistical evidence reveals the extent to which men and women are subject to unequal treatment, but we are not in a position to measure precisely the extent to which 'pure' as opposed to 'statistical' discrimination is present.

In terms of policy the evidence for the United Kingdom would seem to indicate that inequality of wages is more crucial than the unequal occupational and industrial distribution of manpower by sex, thus perhaps implying that the Equal Pay Act 1970 has more potential than an Anti-Discrimination Act in closing the statistical earnings gap between men and women. However, to the extent that females have lower productivity levels than males, granting them equal wages (without allowing adequately for the difference in performance) will tend to lead to some female unemployment, other things being equal, and presumably even more overcrowding in female-dominated activities. This points to one reason why legislation may be needed on both fronts of equal pay and equal opportunity.

Any economic analysis of discrimination must acknowledge the fact that social and historical factors play a key role particularly in relation to pre-entry discrimination, which itself is likely to perpetuate differences in the treatment of each sex within the labour market. A recent study in the United States by Freeman[51] has shown that there has been a rapid decline in the 1960s in the degree of discrimination against Negro workers, particularly women, at least in so far as this is reflected in the gross earnings differential between white and Negro workers. The reasons for this sudden change are not altogether clear, but it is possible that tastes for discrimination may not be constant over time, or may be highly influenced by exogenous factors (one example of which would be legislation).

On the other hand it is also clear that employers must take into account lifetime earnings and productivities in determining their employment decisions. Costs of training must be compared with expected duration of employment. Neither the Equal Pay Act 1970 nor the Green Paper on Discrimination have explicitly taken into account the long-run costs of employing particular categories of labour. If legislation has harmful economic consequences, employers are likely to take evasive action unless they obtain a positive utility from its implementation, and one is faced with the problem of enforcement. In the case of the anti-discrimination legislation it will indeed be difficult to prove that a

51. Richard B. Freeman, 'Decline of Labour Market Discrimination and Economic Analysis', *American Economic Review, Papers and Proceedings,* May 1973.

female is not employed on account of her sex, and it seems that no attempt will be made to enforce quota regulations on the employers. (An alternative to the latter would be to require women to guarantee potential employers that they will remain in employment equally as long as the average male.)

The Green Paper in fact proposes that men and women should receive equal treatment from employers, which is taken to imply:

(a) Equal access to potential benefits, including opportunities for recruitment, training, upgrading and promotion, and also opportunities to earn more (e.g. via overtime and shift work);

(b) Equal protection against acts to their detriment (e.g. in relation to questions of discipline and dismissal).

Since the Government feels that all exceptions weaken the principle of non-discrimination it aims to limit the exceptions to the minimum necessary to make the Bill workable or more specifically to manifest absurdities relating to occupations such as acting and lavatory attendants. Consequently according to the Green Paper the following do *not* justify a general exception:

(a) Where the employment of both sexes indiscriminately will be more costly to the employer than the employment of one sex only;

(b) Where it can be shown that a male (or female) is statistically more likely to perform a task more satisfactorily or show more satisfactory employment behaviour (e.g. because of lower rates of absenteeism or turnover);

(c) Where the work would expose women to physical danger or adverse working conditions.

Aggrieved individuals are to have the right of complaint to an industrial tribunal (with appeal to the National Industrial Relations Court), though Department of Employment Conciliation Officers will attempt to obtain a settlement at an early stage, thus avoiding the necessity of resort to the legal apparatus. In addition an Equal Opportunities Commission would conduct wide-ranging inquiries and in particular examine the situation of women in the professions. Special attention is also to be given to the question of discrimination in education.

The major weakness of the document is its failure clearly to define discrimination, which in places seems to be equated implicitly with 'statistical' discrimination and as a consequence rejects the possibility that an optimal allocation of labour may call for an unequal sex distribution of manpower. Indeed, if the legislation goes through in its present form cost minimization appears to be forbidden where this implies differentiating between the sexes. Such an Act would, therefore, appear to encourage one form of inefficiency.

The conclusions of our analysis would seem to be that three necessary (though perhaps not sufficient) conditions exist for sex equality in the labour market, namely no occupational segregation by sex, equal pay for equal work and equal unpaid work in the home by men and women. However, given that there are natural constraints, one must allow that an optimal allocation of manpower between household and non-household jobs may require that males occupy relatively more skilled jobs with high training costs. In a free market we cannot be certain that women will invest in themselves to equate their human capital with that of males.

Part Three
Women's Employment and the Economy

14 The Female-Male Differential in Unemployment Rates*

Beth Niemi

Assistant Professor of Economics, Newark College of Arts and Sciences, Rutgers University

From: *Industrial and Labor Relations Review*, Vol. 27, No. 3, April 1974, pp. 331–50.

This study attempts to explain why women have had a higher unemployment rate than men in the United States throughout the postwar period. It can be seen in Figure 14.1 that the female unemployment rate has exceeded the male rate since 1948 and that this differential between the two rates has been greatest at business cycle peaks.

The three factors most likely to be responsible for the relatively high unemployment rate of women are: a high level of frictional unemployment because of movement in and out of the labor force; a relative lack of training, particularly specific training, and consequently a susceptibility to cyclical layoffs and unemployment; and occupational and geographic immobility, resulting in a high level of structural unemployment. A fourth factor, the differing industrial distribution of the male and female labor forces, with women tending to be concentrated in less cyclically volatile sectors, works in the opposite direction, lowering the unemployment rate of women relative to that of men.

The causal chain for the first three factors tends to run in both directions, so that the female worker is to some extent caught up in a vicious

*This study tests the effect of three factors often cited to explain the fact that the rate of unemployment is higher for women than for men. The most significant cause of this differential is shown by several measures to be the high rate of movement by women into and out of the labor force. Also of some importance is the lower rate of occupational mobility and of economically purposeful geographic mobility among women, which, the author argues, results in a higher level of structural unemployment among women. On the other hand, only a minor effect is traceable to the relative lack of specific training among women.

This paper is based on Beth Niemi's doctoral dissertation, 'Sex Differentials in Unemployment in the U.S. and Canada' (Columbia University, 1970). She wishes to express her appreciation to Jacob Mincer for his most helpful comments at every stage of this project, which was supported in part by a grant from the Rutgers Research Council.

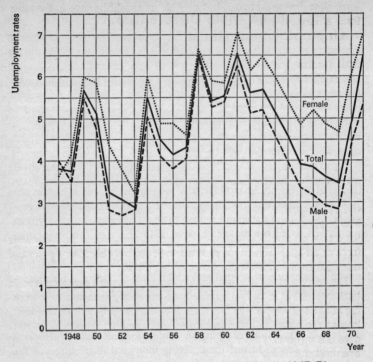

Figure 14.1. Unemployment Rates in the United States, 1947–71.
Source: *Manpower Report of the President* (Washington, D.C.: G.P.O., March 1972), Table A-14, p. 175.

circle. Basically, high labor force turnover, lack of specific training, and geographic immobility are interrelated, for all result from the fact that a female growing up in this society is conditioned to expect that she will spend a substantial proportion of her adult life outside the labor force. Discrimination against women in the labor market reinforces this expectation, thus creating the effect of a self-fulfilling prophecy.

Frictional unemployment

The high frictional unemployment rate of women can best be understood by examining their high rate of inter-labor force mobility. Over half the women in the United States in 1968 were in the labor force at some time during that year, but only about two-fifths were in the labor force at any one point in time.

A woman's shift from housework to market work or vice versa can be viewed as an interindustry shift. The family's income affects a woman's total consumption of leisure and thus her total hours of work in home and market combined. The market wage rate W_m and the imputed wage for work in the home W_h, which is derived from the family demand for home goods and services and the availability of substitutes for the wife in home production, affect the allocation of time among market work, work at home, and leisure. The relative values of W_m and W_h will determine whether a woman will be in the labor force at a given time.

A job shift from home to market differs from a job shift within the market sector, however, in that the former is more likely to involve unemployment as currently defined by the Bureau of Labor Statistics (BLS). There are two possible ways of making either type of job shift. The first is to leave one's present job and devote one's time to the search for a new job until a satisfactory one is obtained. Either an intra-labor force or an inter-labor force shift made in this way involves a period of unemployment while the search is taking place.

The second method of job mobility, and the more common one in both inter-labor force and intra-labor force shifts, is to continue working at one's present job and to search for a better job in one's free time, leaving the old job only after a new one is secured. This type of shift does not involve transitional unemployment in the case of a shift from one market job to another, for having a job takes precedence over seeking work, according to the BLS definitions of employment and unemployment. On the other hand, a housewife who is seeking employment in the market is defined as unemployed, with her search for a job taking precedence over her nonmarket work. Thus, with the exception of the case in which an individual is offered a job without seeking one and moves directly from outside the labor force into employment, inter-labor force mobility necessarily involves transitional unemployment, and this difference by sex in the type of job mobility is one factor contributing to the higher unemployment rate of women.

The fact that men make more intra-labor force moves and women make more inter-labor force moves has been established in several studies,[1] but there has been no previous attempt to combine data on

1. For example, see Donald J. Bogue, *A Methodological Study of Migration and Labor Mobility in Michigan and Ohio in 1947*, No. 4 (Oxford, Ohio: Scripps Foundation Studies in Population, 1952); Robert L. Bunting, 'Labor Mobility:

inter- and intra-labor force mobility to arrive at a single measure of total mobility. In order to provide such a measure in Table 14.1, it was necessary to draw on different sources for estimates of the number of job shifts of both types made by men and women in the course of a year.

It was expected that the total number of shifts per capita would be roughly the same for men and women but would be made up of proportionately more inter-labor force shifts among women and proportionately more intra-labor force shifts among men.[2] Actually, the data in Table 14.1 show that, although men are more mobile within the labor force than women, the great amount of inter-labor force movement of women results in a rate of total mobility that is almost twice as high for women as for men.[3]

Since women clearly exhibit more inter-labor force mobility, and, as a result, more mobility in general than do men, it would be expected that their unemployment rate would be higher. Transitional unemployment occurs most frequently when a job shift is made from non-market work to the labor force, and this type of shift seems to account for close to half the total mobility of women.

Turnover and frictional unemployment

The actual effect of inter-labor force mobility on unemployment can be observed in six surveys dealing with the sources of unemployment (job loss, quitting, labor force entry and re-entry for both males and females), taken at various times throughout 1964, 1965, 1966, and 1968, which reveal that 37 to 47 per cent of the unemployment of females over twenty years of age was a result of entry or re-entry into the labor

Sex, Race and Age,' *The Review of Economics and Statistics*, Vol. 42, No. 2 (May 1960), pp. 229–31; R. L. Bunting, Lowell D. Ashby, and Peter A. Prosper, Jr., 'Labor Mobility in Three Southern States,' *Industrial and Labor Relations Review*, Vol. 14, No. 3 (April 1961), pp. 432–45; Paul Eldridge and Irwin Wolkstein, 'Incidence of Employer Change,' *Industrial and Labor Relations Review*, Vol. 10, No. 1 (October 1956), pp. 101–7; and University of Minnesota Industrial Relations Center, *Minnesota Manpower Mobilities* (Minneapolis, Minn., 1950).

2. Suggested by a comment by Jacob Mincer in Mark Perlman, ed., *Human Resources in the Urban Economy* (Baltimore: Johns Hopkins Press, 1963), p. 116.

3. The greater total mobility rates of women may be a result of the second factor that will be considered here – the fact that men receive much more on-the-job training than women, and thus more training with some element of specificity. Since one effect of specific training is to reduce turnover, it is possible that total mobility rates would be approximately the same for men and women if the groups could be standardized for amount of on-the-job training.

Table 14.1 **Inter- and intra-labor force mobility for men and women**

Labor force mobility	Men	Women
	Married Men, 1960 (in thousands)	Married Women, 1960 (in thousands)
Inter-labor force mobility		
Labor force additions during year	3,156	12,360
Labor force withdrawals during year	3,912	11,856
Total inter-labor force shifts	7,068	24,216
Total married population	40,205	40,205
	(in percentages)	(in percentages)
Inter-labor force mobility rate *	17.6	60.2
	All men 1955 (in thousands)	All women 1955 (in thousands)
Intra-labor force mobility		
Number of job shifts made during year	8,332	3,163
Total population of adults	55,122	57,610
	(in percentages)	(in percentages)
Intra-labor force mobility rate**	15.1	5.5

*These mobility rates indicate the average number of inter-labor force shifts made by married men and women in 1960. The average married man moved into or out of the labor force 0.176 times in 1960; the average married woman moved into or out of the labor force 0.602 times.

**These mobility rates represent the average number of intra-labor force shifts made by men and women in 1955. The average man changed jobs 0.15 times; the average woman changed jobs 0.055 times.

Sources: Data on additions to and withdrawals from the labor force of married men and women in 1960 were obtained from Stuart H. Altman, 'Factors Affecting the Unemployment of Married Women' (Ph.D. diss., University of California, Los Angeles, 1964), pp. 128–9 and 233–4. Bureau of the Census, 'Job Mobility of Workers in 1955,' No. 70 in Current Population Reports Series P–50 (Washington, D.C., 1955), Table 8, p. 20 provided data on the total number of job shifts (from one market job to another) made by all men and women in 1955. The population figures by which I divided the number of shifts in order to arrive at mobility rates were obtained from *Statistics on Manpower*, a supplement to the *Manpower Report of the President* (Washington, D.C.: G.P.O., March 1969), Table A-1, p. 1 and Table B-1, p. 28.

force.[4] Table 14.2 shows total unemployment rates and the division of the total rates into job loser rates, job leaver rates, and entry and re-entry rates for adult males and females.

The total unemployment rate is consistently higher for females, and their high entry and re-entry rates, from two to four times as great as those for males, account for much of this difference. Even if the rate

Table 14.2 **Rates for different sources of unemployment for men and women.***

Date	Males, 20+				Females, 20+			
	Total	Job Loser†	Job Leaver‡	Entry	Total	Job Loser	Job Leaver	Entry
June 1964	3.6	2.3	0.5	0.8	5.2	2.2	0.9	2.0
Dec. 1964	3.8	2.5	0.4	0.8	4.1	1.7	0.8	1.6
June 1965	2.9	1.8	0.4	0.7	4.8	2.1	0.9	1.8
Nov. 1965	2.5	1.6	0.4	0.5	4.3	1.4	0.9	2.0
Jan. 1966	3.4	2.3	0.5	0.6	4.2	1.7	0.8	1.7
June 1966	2.3	1.2	0.4	0.7	3.9	1.1	1.0	1.8
Aug. 1968	2.2	1.3	0.4	0.5	3.8	1.3	0.6	1.8

*Rates rounded to the nearest tenth.

†One who was laid off or fired, remains in the labor force, and has not yet found another job.

‡One who quits his or her job, remains in the labor force, and has not yet found another job.

Source: Kathryn D. Hoyle, 'Why the Unemployed Look for Work,' *Monthly Labor Review*, Vol. 90, No. 2 (February 1967), p. 35.

of unemployment resulting from labor force entry had been as low for women as for men, the female unemployment rate would have still exceeded the male rate on five of the seven survey dates. Job leaver rates tended to be at least twice as high for women as for men, whereas the female job loser rate was higher than the male loser rate for only one of the seven survey dates.

Recent research has shown that the net effect of the unemployment rate on the labor force participation rate is a negative one.[5] Workers, especially those, such as women and young people, who do not devote

4. Kathryn D. Hoyle, 'Why the Unemployed Look for Work,' *Monthly Labor Review*, Vol. 90, No. 2 (February 1967), p. 34.

5. See Jacob Mincer, 'Labor-Force Participation and Unemployment: A Review of Recent Evidence,' in Robert A. Gordon and Margaret S. Gordon, eds., *Prosperity and Unemployment* (New York: John Wiley and Sons, 1966), pp. 73–112 for a summary.

their time exclusively to labor market activities, tend to time their participation in the labor force to coincide with the peaks of business cycles, when their chances of finding employment are best and wage rates and general conditions of employment are most favorable.

A lower rate of labor force participation has generally been accompanied by greater labor force turnover and therefore by a higher rate of frictional unemployment. In the case of women, in fact, their greater labor force turnover is a major *reason* for their higher unemployment rate.

In order to examine more closely the relationship between labor force participation and inter-labor force turnover, it will be assumed that there are two groups in the population – Group A, which has a labor force participation rate of 90 percent, and Group B, which has a labor force participation rate of 25 percent. One would reasonably expect that Group A would have low labor force turnover and Group B would have high labor force turnover, but only the first expectation is logically necessary. If 90 percent of a population group is always in the labor force, this group simply does not have much leeway for inter-labor force mobility. On the other hand, Group B, with a labor force participation rate of only 25 percent, has the potential for high inter-labor force mobility. It is also logically possible, however, for such a group to be characterized by the complete absence of labor force turnover. This would be the extreme case of complete specialization, with 25 percent of Group B – always the same 25 percent – remaining in the labor force continuously and the other three-quarters of Group B never entering the labor force. Such complete specialization in either market or nonmarket activity, however, does not describe the actual behavior patterns of groups such as married women and young people, whose labor force participation rates are well below 100 percent.

Assuming that some degree of labor force turnover rather than complete specialization is the characteristic pattern, the labor force participation rate can be interpreted as approximately the proportion of an 'average' person's working life that is spent in the labor force. Thus, the average individual in Group A will be in the labor force almost continuously throughout his working life, whereas the average individual in Group B will spend a total of about 25 percent of his working life in typically intermittent labor market activities. This way of looking at labor force participation makes it clearer why high labor force participation tends to be associated with low labor force turnover and vice versa.

One good measure of labor force turnover is the ratio of the proportion of any group in the labor force at any time during the year (which will be called the labor force experience rate) to the average labor force participation rate of that group for the entire year – the higher this ratio, the greater the labor force turnover for the group. One would expect this turnover index to be negatively correlated with the labor force participation rate. This index cannot be less than 1 nor greater than the quotient obtained by dividing 100 by the labor force participation rate. A value of 1 would occur if the labor force participation rate were equal to the labor force experience rate – that is, if the same people were always in the labor force, and there were no labor force turnover.

For example, the labor force experience rate would equal 100, and the index of labor force turnover for the year would equal 100/labor force participation rate, if everyone in the population in question were in the labor force at some time during that year. The upper limit on the value of the index of labor force turnover would be 1.11 if the labor force participation rate were 90 percent, 2 if the labor force participation rate were 50 percent, and 4 if the labor force participation rate were 25 percent. Thus, labor force turnover is necessarily low for a group with a high labor force participation rate and is probably, but not necessarily, high for a group with a low labor force participation rate.

Table 14.3 presents actual labor force participation rates, labor force experience rates, and labor force turnover indices for men and women in the United States for the years 1959 (the first year for which data are available on experience rates) through 1969.

These data appear to confirm the generally inverse relationship between labor force participation and labor force turnover, but data for the 1959–69 period cannot tell the whole story. If data were available for earlier years, they would undoubtedly show that rates of labor force turnover and of unemployment of women were lower in the past, even though female labor force participation rates were much lower than they are today. This is because there has been some decrease in specialization, with more women dividing their working time between home and the labor market.

Tables 14.1–14.3 nevertheless have demonstrated that women have a much greater rate of inter-labor force mobility than do men and that this high rate of labor force turnover does contribute to raising the unemployment rate of women relative to men. The other two hypotheses

Table 14.3 Labor force participation rates, labor force experience rates, and labor force turnover indices, for married and single men and women in the U.S., 1959–69

Year	Married men			Married women		
	Labor force partici-pation	Labor force experience	Labor force turnover	Labor force partici-pation	Labor force experience	Labor force turnover
1959	89.6	93.5	104.3	30.9	43.6	141.3
1960	88.9	93.1	104.7	30.5	45.2	148.2
1961	89.3	92.2	103.2	32.7	45.1	137.6
1962	88.3	91.9	104.1	32.7	45.7	139.8
1963	88.1	91.3	103.6	33.7	46.9	139.0
1964	87.8	91.7	104.5	34.4	47.1	136.9
1965	87.7	91.8	104.7	34.7	47.2	135.9
1966	87.2	91.3	104.7	35.4	48.9	138.1
1967	87.0	91.1	104.7	36.8	50.4	137.0
1968	87.0	90.1	103.5	38.3	51.5	134.5
1969	86.9	90.9	104.6	39.6	52.0	131.4
	Single men			Single women		
1959	57.0	67.7	118.8	43.3	59.9	137.9
1960	55.5	69.8	125.8	44.1	64.0	145.2
1961	55.6	66.1	118.9	44.4	56.6	127.5
1962	51.7	68.7	132.8	41.7	58.2	139.5
1963	50.5	66.8	132.3	41.0	56.1	136.9
1964	50.8	66.7	131.3	40.9	58.7	143.4
1965	50.3	66.5	132.3	40.5	57.3	141.7
1966	58.5	74.4	127.2	60.0	70.4	140.6
1967	59.7	76.0	127.7	50.7	72.7	143.3
1968	59.6	76.5	128.5	51.8	69.7	135.8
1969	59.1	77.1	130.4	51.2	69.8	136.3

Note: The figures for 1959–65 refer to married and single men and women, age fourteen and over; the 1966–9 figures refer to married and single men and women, age sixteen and over.

Sources: Labor force and population figures are taken from the *Manpower Report of the President* (Washington, D.C.: G.P.O., March 1972), Table B-1, p. 192. Labor force experience figures are taken from BLS Special Labor Force Reports, Nos. 11, 19, 25, 38, 48, 62, 76, 91, 107, 115, and 127 (Washington, D.C., various years).

The Female-Male Differential in Unemployment Rates 333

to be investigated with respect to the female unemployment rate derive from the theory of investment in human capital.[6]

Specific training and cyclical unemployment

Although expenditures on formal education are not much smaller for females than for males, investments in on-the-job training are substantially smaller for females than for males.[7] This is not unexpected in light of investment theory. The fact that the average woman expects to spend less than half her working life in the labor force lowers the expected return on any investment in training that she may make. Since her labor force participation is also likely to be intermittent, specific training will be even less attractive than general training. On the other hand, a woman who plans on permanent labor force attachment and seeks to invest in herself may find that her chances of receiving on-the-job training with any element of specificity are small. Employers will develop their hiring policies on the basis of their experience with group averages, and, believing that the average woman is more subject to turnover than the average man, they will prefer to invest in male training.[8]

The specifically trained have lower quit rates and layoff rates than the untrained or the generally trained and should be less susceptible to disemployment and therefore to cyclical and random or sectoral unemployment. Thus, one would expect the relatively small amount of on-the-job training (and consequently specific training) received by women to be a contributing factor to the high female unemployment rate.

Because several other factors affect cyclical unemployment among men and women, some effort must be made to isolate the effects of specific training. The absence of direct data on amounts of specific training, which could be correlated with the incidence of unemployment, makes it necessary to test the effect of this factor in an indirect

6. As developed by Gary S. Becker in 'Investment in Human Capital: A Theoretical Analysis,' *Journal of Political Economy*, Vol. 70, No. 5, Part 2 (October 1962, Supplement), pp. 9–49.

7. Jacob Mincer, 'On-the-Job Training: Costs, Returns, and Some Implications,' *Journal of Political Economy*, Vol. 70, No. 5, Part 2 (October 1962, Supplement), p. 67.

8. 'The employer who seeks to maximize expected profit will discriminate against . . . women if he believes them to be less qualified, reliable, long-term, etc. on the average than . . . men, . . . and if the cost of gaining information about the individual applicants is excessive.' Edmund S. Phelps, 'The Statistical Theory of Racism and Sexism,' (see above, p. 206).

fashion. If other things were equal, it would be expected that, if women really do receive significantly less specific training than do men, the female unemployment rate would be more volatile over the course of the business cycle than the male unemployment rate. Figure 14.1 shows, however, that the male unemployment rate is more sensitive to cyclical fluctuations than the female rate.

This in itself, however, does not constitute evidence that the specific-training hypothesis is incorrect. Two factors work in the direction of damping cyclical fluctuations in the female unemployment rate: the cyclically oriented timing of female labor force participation and the concentration of women workers in industries and occupations that are less affected by cyclical fluctuations. It may well be that women are penalized by lack of specific training, but this effect is outweighed by the combined effect of the other two factors.

The effects of female labor force turnover can be eliminated by looking at cyclical changes in *employment*, rather than unemployment, for men and women. The figures in Table 14.4 represent the 'cycles' in total employment for both men and women, adjusted for the trend of secular growth during the period 1947–68. These data show that female employment has exhibited greater variability over the course of the business cycle than male employment. All the percentage deviations from trend – and often the absolute size of the deviations – were larger for female employment. This greater cyclical variability of female employment during the postwar period tends to support the hypothesis that women workers receive less specific training than their male counterparts.[9]

Education, training and unemployment

The interrelationships among education, specific training, and unemployment among men and women are further illuminated by data on unemployment rates by sex and educational attainment from the 1960 Census. For both men and women age twenty-five and over, unemployment rates in that year showed a consistently negative relation to educational levels. (See Figure 14.2.) Female unemployment rates neverthe-

9. In an attempt to achieve still more complete standardization and to eliminate the effect of the different industrial distributions of the male and female labor force, I applied the procedure used in Table 14.4 to the employment data for the service industry alone, for the period 1958–68, but no clear pattern emerged. This is probably the result of the fact that information on service employment by sex was available only for the years since 1958, and thus the number of observations was only half as large as that for total employment.

Table 14.4 Cyclical changes in employment of females and males, 1947–68.[a]

Year	Deviations of actual employment from secular trend $(A - T)$ (in thousands)		'Cycles' in employment $\dfrac{A - T}{T} \times 100$	
	Female	Male	Female	Male
1947	+291.6	−107.4	+1.8	−0.2
1948	+404.6	−8.2	+2.4	−0.01
1949	+304.6	−12.0	+1.7	−0.02
1950	+355.6	−34.8	+2.0	−0.1
1951	+442.6	+210.4	+2.4	+0.5
1952	+147.6	+191.6	+0.8	+0.4
1953	−292.4	+534.8	−1.5	−1.1
1954	−558.4	+307.0	−2.8	+0.7
1955	−247.4	+148.2	−1.2	+0.3
1956	+108.6	+202.4	+0.5	+0.4
1957	−176.4	−119.4	−0.8	−0.2
1958	−347.4	−329.2	−1.5	−0.7
1959	−535.4	−422.0	−2.3	−0.9
1960	−334.4	−328.8	−1.4	−0.7
1961	−323.4	−377.6	−1.3	−0.8
1962	−669.4	−547.5	−2.7	−1.1
1963	−535.4	−479.2	−2.1	−1.0
1964	−383.4	−299.0	−1.5	−0.6
1965	−149.4	−111.8	−0.6	−0.2
1966	+396.6	+130.4	+1.5	+0.3
1967	+903.6	+596.6	+3.3	−1.2
1968	+1095.6	+856.8	+3.9	−1.6

a. The technique of least squares was used here to fit straight line trends to the female and male employment figures. The trend values were then computed from the equations thus derived. The trend equation was $T = 16{,}391.4 + 555t$ for female employment and $T = 44{,}365.4 + 371.8t$ for male employment, with t taking the following values: 1947 = 0, 1948 = 1, 1949 = 2, etc. These trend values (T) thus derived were then subtracted from actual employment (A) in each year, to determine the deviation of actual from predicted employment ($A - T$) for each year from 1947 to 1968. The column, 'Cycles' in employment, converts these absolute deviations from the trend into percentage deviations.

Source: Employment figures taken from *Statistics on Manpower*, a supplement to the *Manpower Report of the President* (Washington, D.C.: G.P.O., March 1969), Table A–1, p. 1.

less exceeded those for males within each educational attainment category, and the female-male unemployment differential was greatest at the levels of education located in the middle of the distribution – those covering from eight to twelve years of schooling.[10]

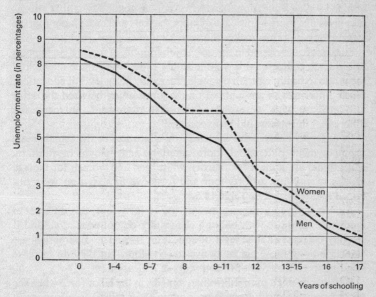

Figure 14.2. Unemployment Rates by Sex and Years of Schooling, United States in April 1960 for Persons Twenty-five and Over.
Source: 1960 Census 1 : 1,000 Sample.

Three factors are probably responsible for the inverse relationship between educational level and unemployment rate. The first of these is the difference in the industrial and occupational distribution of workers at varying levels of education; the more educated are more concentrated in such cyclically insensitive industries and occupations as finance, education, public administration, management, and the professions. In

10. Unemployment rates by sex and educational attainment in 1950, although inversely related to years of schooling for both men and women, do not display any consistent pattern with respect to female-male differentials. The female unemployment rate exceeded that for males in only half of the educational attainment classifications, and the differences between the rates by sex were small and apparently random.

The Female-Male Differential in Unemployment Rates 337

addition, to the extent that formal and specific training are complements, those with more education will receive more specific training and thus will be less susceptible to cyclical unemployment. Mincer found that more on-the-job training is received by workers who had attained higher educational levels.[11] Another possibility is that education gives one more knowledge of labor markets and more labor market information and thus makes job search more efficient.

Since more is invested in the on-the-job training of males than females at the same educational level, one would expect the female unemployment rate to be higher than the male rate at any given level of education. Since differences in amounts of on-the-job training between the sexes also increase with increasing educational attainment, an increasing differential in rates would be expected.[12]

In order to analyze the variation by education in the female-male unemployment differential more carefully, unemployment rates by educational attainment for married white men and women for the age groups twenty-five to forty-four and forty-five to sixty-four were obtained and recorded in Table 14.5.

Among married whites age twenty-five to forty-four, this differential is highest for those with only an elementary school education, and it steadily decreases as the level of education rises. The differentials are smaller among those age forty-five to sixty-four, but they do increase steadily up to the level of fifteen years of education.[13]

Whether or not a married woman remains in the labor force when she becomes unemployed depends on, among other things, family income; those whose family income is low are more likely to remain in the labor force when they become unemployed. In general, one finds that the wife's educational level is positively correlated with her husband's income. Thus, one would expect the duration of unemployment to decrease for married women as the level of education rises. Also, the

11. Mincer, 'On-the-Job Training: Costs, Returns, and Some Implications,' Table 1, p. 55.

12. Ibid., p. 71.

13. Similar information on unemployment rates by sex and educational attainment was available from a special survey made in April 1962 by the Bureau of Labor Statistics. The completed survey included 3,013 individuals, of whom 2,068, or nearly 70 percent, were men. The relatively small number of observations in each sex-and-education classification made it practically impossible to observe any consistent pattern among the BLS group, although there appeared to be some tendency for female-male unemployment differentials to increase with rising levels of educational attainment.

income effect on the labor force participation of married women works in the direction of decreasing labor force participation at higher levels of education. The actual relationship between educational attainment and labor force participation among married women, however, is a positive one in the aggregate. This can be explained in terms of a rising differential $W_m - W_h$ as education increases, assuming that education yields a greater increase in market productivity than in home productivity.

Table 14.5 **April 1960 unemployment rates for white married men and women by age and educational attainment**

Age category, sex, and differential	Years of schooling				
	≤ 8	9–11	12	13–15	16+
Ages 25–44	5.3	3.5	2.0	1.1	0.7
Married men					
Married women	9.1	6.2	4.5	2.8	1.9
Female-male differential	3.8	2.7	2.5	1.7	1.2
Ages 45–64					
Married men	5.3	3.6	2.0	2.0	0.6
Married women	5.6	4.4	2.9	3.0	0.3
Female-male differential	0.3	0.8	0.9	1.0	−0.3

Source: 1960 Census   1 : 1,000 Sample.

Labor force participation does not vary much with education for married white women in the twenty-five to forty-four age group, but it rises significantly with education for those aged forty-five to sixty-four. Married women age twenty-five to forty-four are more likely to have small children than are those age forty-five to sixty-four. About half the white married women between twenty-five and forty-four years of age in the 1:1000 Sample had at least one child younger than six years of age. (This compares to only 2 percent of the forty-five to sixty-four age group.) It is harder to find good substitutes for the wife's time in child care than in other forms of household production, and education may increase productivity in child care more than it increases productivity in other areas of home production.

A look at labor force participation rates of married white women age twenty-five to sixty-four by education, from the 1:1000 Sample of the 1960 Census, should help to resolve the effects of these various forces.

The labor force participation rates and the unemployment differentials appear to be consistent with each other. For the forty-five to sixty-four age group, female labor force participation rises with education as market productivity is increased relative to home productivity; and the female-male unemployment differential increases as the educational level rises. Although the rate of unemployment is inversely related to educational attainment for both men and women, it falls relatively faster for men than for women, because – it is hypothesized here – men at the higher educational levels obtain more specific training than women receive.

The pattern displayed by the twenty-five to forty-four age group, on the other hand, appears puzzling at first, but it can be explained by the effect of family income on female labor force participation and the fact that labor force turnover decreases as the level of education rises. Female labor force participation does not vary much for this group, since the increase of market relative to home productivity with education is less when there are small children in the home. These variables counteract the effects of specific training, and, overall, one finds decreasing female-male unemployment differentials with rising educational levels.

Table 14.6 Labor force participation rates of married white women, Age 25–64, by years of schooling. (*in percentages*)

| Age category | Years of schooling | | | | |
	≤8	9–11	12	13–15	≥16
Age 25–44	30.1	32.7	31.9	30.6	34.2
Age 45–64	26.2	33.5	38.5	41.4	51.1

In summary, differences in specific training probably make little quantitative contribution to the observed female-male differential in unemployment rates. Although women do tend to receive less specific training than men, and there is some evidence in Table 14.4 that they are therefore more susceptible to cyclical layoffs and unemployment, most of the effect of this factor is apparently offset by the two factors previously noted: the concentration of the female labor force in industries and occupations less vulnerable than most to cyclical fluctuations and the extent to which the labor force participation of the secondary labor force is procyclically timed, which has a damping effect on cyclical variations in female unemployment.

Intra-labor force immobility

Geographic migration and occupational mobility, which usually involves training or retraining, are two forms of investment in human capital that may be undertaken in response to changing wage prospects. (The 'wage' in this case includes nonpecuniary aspects of the job that have utility or disutility for the worker.) The individual must decide whether to move from Job A to Job B, which is in another geographic area or occupation. An inability or unwillingness to make such moves increases a person's vulnerability to unemployment.

Investment in geographic or occupational mobility is more likely the larger the average differential (D), the larger the relevant time period over which the individual expects to receive the earnings differential (N), the smaller the discount rate (R), and the smaller the total cost of the move (C). Because of systematic differences by sex in N and C, women will make such investments less readily than men. Whereas the average adult male remains in the labor force throughout his working life, the average woman is in the labor force for only approximately two-fifths of this period. Thus, the relevant time period N is much shorter for a woman than for a man, and the expected gain from a given investment is correspondingly reduced. Female labor force participation also tends to be intermittent; this further lowers the relevant N for a particular move.

In the case of geographic movement for married women, there is an additional element in C, the total cost of moving, which one would expect to be large enough in many cases to outweigh the gains of the move. This item is the opportunity cost incurred by the primary earner. It includes his foregone earnings while moving, his opportunity and other costs of job search in the new location, and the difference between his old and new wage in each time period, if he has to work at a lower wage in the new location. In effect, the geographic location of a married woman tends to be more dependent on her husband's than on her own economic opportunities. Geographic immobility may therefore involve either inability to move in response to a personal employment opportunity or geographic movement that is random in relation to personal economic opportunity, when a job shift involving migration is made by the primary earner. This second case involves an involuntary shift – analogous to a layoff.

These factors would be expected to have their strongest effect on the geographic mobility of married women. The opportunity cost to be incurred by the primary earner is not relevant to the consideration of purely occupational mobility (a change of occupation that may involve retraining but may not require migration), although the shorter relevant time period N would still be a consideration for the female worker. If occupational changes and migration were two independent types of moves within the labor force, one might not expect women to display much more immobility with respect to occupational changes than men. Occupational mobility and migration, however, may go together – a change to a new occupation may involve moving to a new location. Thus, women might tend to be even more immobile occupationally as a result of their geographic immobility. This lack of intra-labor force mobility, if it exists, will increase the rate and duration of female unemployment, but it might also lead to withdrawal from the labor force, which would tend to decrease the observed duration of unemployment.

Potential Mobility of Men and Women

These speculations can be tested in part by data gathered by the Bureau of Labor Statistics in a detailed survey in April 1962 of a sample of persons who had experienced five or more weeks of unemployment in 1961.[14] Particularly interesting for this study are the answers of those within the sample who were still (or again) unemployed in April 1962 to questions regarding their interest in training (or retraining) and in relocation. Table 14.7 gives the percentage distribution of the answers of that group to the question, 'Would you accept a job in another area?'; Table 14.8 gives the distribution of their responses to a query phrased to determine interest in a hypothetical training program, which would not require geographic movement and would provide for some payment to the trainees.

With respect to geographic movement, the unemployed in this sample were asked if they would accept a job in another area at the same wage as they had received at their last job. In this case, expected wage (income) differentials between areas would reflect only the probability of obtaining employment in the new area versus no employment in the old area. Training, on the other hand, can be assumed to affect both the actual wage and the probability of obtaining it.

It appears in Table 14.7 that the unemployed, even the long-term un-

14. Data on potential occupational and geographic mobility were collected for that subgroup of the BLS sample who were unemployed at the time of the survey in April 1962. These individuals were asked about their willingness to take a job in another area of the country and their interest in retraining.

Table 14.7 **Distribution of answers, by sex, to the question, 'Would you accept a job in another area?'** [1] (*in percentages*)

Sample group	Males			Females		
	Yes	It depends	No	Yes	It depends	No
White	32.5	24.5	43.0	10.6	10.3	79.1
Nonwhite	43.3	25.4	31.3	19.4	13.9	66.7
Married	29.9	29.9	40.2	8.2	9.8	82.0
Single	41.9	12.8	45.3	21.3	18.0	60.7
Other	48.1	16.9	35.0	19.0	10.5	70.5
18–24	41.3	16.7	42.0	11.8	11.8	76.4
25–54	36.0	36.5	37.5	12.6	11.1	76.3
55+	26.1	26.7	47.2	15.6	10.9	73.5
Average	34.6	24.7	40.7	12.9	11.2	75.9

1. All male-female differences were significant at the 0·01 level.

Note: The survey included persons unemployed five weeks or more in 1961 who were eighteen years of age or older and unemployed in April 1962, able to work, not in school, and who had some prior work experience.

Source: From BLS Survey of Unemployment in 1961. For a more detailed account of this survey, see U.S. Bureau of Labor Statistics, 'Survey of the Work History of the Unemployed', *Monthly Report on the Labor Force*, March, May, and August 1963, pp. xiv-xxi, 16–24, and 15–27, respectively; or Robert L. Stein, 'Work History, Attitudes, and Income of the Unemployed,' *Monthly Labor Review*, Vol. 86, No. 12 (December 1963), pp. 1405–13.

employed, are reluctant to migrate in order to obtain employment, and, as predicted, women are significantly less interested than men in investing in such a move. On the other hand, Table 14.8 shows that a great proportion of both men and women expressed an interest in training, indicating that many more people are interested in being trained than in moving to another area. Also, as expected, the male-female differentials are smaller in Table 14.8 than in Table 14.7, and in fact none in Table 14.8 are statistically significant.

It appears that the expected wage differential, moving costs, and time period involved would all explain why both men and women find a greater incentive to invest in training than in relocation. As previously noted, migration, under the conditions assumed, would raise only the probability of being employed at a given wage or skill level, whereas

The Female-Male Differential in Unemployment Rates 343

Table 14.8 **Distribution of answers, by sex, to question of interest in training program in same geographic area.**[a] (*in percentages*)

Sample group	Males			Females		
	Yes	It depends	No	Yes	It depends	No
White	76.8	7.5	15.7	71.7	7.3	21.0
Nonwhite	89.8	2.3	7.9	91.0	3.0	6.0
Married	78.6	7.7	13.7	73.6	7.8	18.6
Single	83.4	4.6	11.9	88.1	0.0	11.9
Other	74.7	4.0	21.3	77.1	6.2	16.7
18–24	86.7	5.5	7.8	80.3	4.9	14.8
25–54	82.4	6.4	11.2	79.5	6.4	14.1
55+	65.8	7.7	26.5	58.9	7.2	33.9
Average	79.3	6.5	14.2	76.7	6.2	17.1

a. None of the male-female differences were significant at the 0.10 level.

Note: The survey included persons unemployed five weeks or more in 1961 who were eighteen years of age or older and unemployed in April 1962, able to work, not in school, and who had some prior work experience.

Source: From BLS Survey of Unemployment in 1961. For a more detailed account of this survey, see U.S. Bureau of Labor Statistics, 'Survey of the Work History of the Unemployed,' *Monthly Report on the Labor Force*, March, May, and August 1963, pp. xiv–xxi, 16–24, and 15–27, respectively; or Robert L. Stein, 'Work History, Attitudes, and Income of the Unemployed,' *Monthly Labor Review*, Vol. 86, No. 12 (December 1963), pp. 1405–13.

training would raise both the skill level (and thus the wage) and the probability of employment. Thus, one would expect the average differential in earnings to be greater after retraining than migration. Second, migration would incur moving and psychic costs that training (in the same location) would not. Finally, gains from training would be seen, by both men and women, as not only greater but also more permanent than gains from migration. Thus, even though a woman may expect to spend less time in the labor force than the average man does, training is more likely to continue to be of some value to her, if she leaves and re-enters the labor force, than would previous migration in response to a specific job offer.

Actual mobility of men and women

The 1962 BLS survey indicates only that women show less interest than men in occupational and geographical mobility, not that women *are* actually less mobile within the labor force. Data are available, however, on the incidence of intra-labor force mobility and are presented in Tables 14.9 through 14.12.

Table 14.9 **Job changes by men and women in the United States, 1955 and 1961.** (numbers in thousands)

| | 1955 | | | 1961 | | |
| | | Changing jobs | | | Changing jobs | |
Sex	Total working	Number	Percentage	Total working	Number	Percentage
Total	75,353	8,366	11.1	80,287	8,121	10.1
Men	47,624	5,940	12.5	49,854	5,509	11.0
Women	27,729	2,426	8.7	30,433	2,612	8.6

Sources: Bureau of the Census, 'Job Mobility of Workers in 1955,' Current Population Reports Series P-50, No. 7 (Washington, D.C.), p. 27; and Gertrude Bancroft and Stuart Garfinkle, 'Job Mobility in 1961,' *Monthly Labor Review*, Vol. 86, No. 8 (August 1963), pp. 898 and 905.

Table 14.9 shows that *total* intra-labor force mobility, measured as the proportion of workers who change jobs at least once in a year, was lower for women than for men in both 1955 and 1961, the only years for which such data are available. Tables 14.10 and 14.11 show that in those years the *occupational* mobility of women was lower than that of men. In 1955, for example, among those workers who shifted from one job to another (that is, ignoring the last line of data in Table 14.10), about one-half of the women stayed in the same occupation but less than one-half of the men did so. In 1961, among job changers as defined in Table 14.11, 56 percent of women stayed in the same occupation, compared to 51 percent of men. These differences do not appear to be substantial, but when coupled with the fact that total intra-labor force mobility is less for women than for men, they show that the overall sex differential in occupational mobility – that is, the proportion of all employed women who change occupations in a year, compared to the proportion of all employed men who change occupations – is clear and striking.

The measurement of differences in the *geographic* mobility of men and women presents difficulties. For the reasons described previously, the geographic immobility of women, as the concept is used in this

Table 14.10 **Job changes by men and women in the United States, 1955.**

Job changes	Number (in thousands)			Percentage		
	Total	Men	Women	Total	Men	Women
Total job changes	13,324	9,448	3,876	100	100	100
Same occupation	5,417	3,832	1,585	41	41	41
Different occupation	6,087	4,519	1,568	46	48	40
Job left, no other started	1,820	1,097	723	13	11	19

Source: Bureau of the Census, 'Job Mobility of Workers in 1955,' Current Population Reports Series P-50, No. 70 (Washington, D.C.), Table 15, p. 27.

study, may involve either the conventional inability or unwillingness to move in response to a job opportunity *or* (particularly for married women) geographic movement that is random in relation to personal

Table 14.11 **Industry and occupation patterns of job changes by men and women in the United States, 1961.***

Sex	Number (in thousands)	Distribution of each type of shift (in percentages)				
		Total	SS	SD	DS	DD
Men	7539	100	33.5	17.6	10.0	38.9
Women	3329	100	34.7	21.3	9.9	34.2

*Persons making four or more job changes during 1961.

  SS = same occupation and industry.

  SD = same occupation, different industry.

  DS = same industry, different occupation.

  DD = different occupation and industry.

  Source: Gertrude Bancroft and Stuart Garfinkle, 'Job Mobility in 1961,' *Monthly Labor Review*, Vol. 86, No. 8 (August 1963), pp. 898 and 905.

economic opportunity. Census data do not show any systematic differences between men and women with respect to geographic moves, but Table 14.12 suggests the large element of randomness in such moves for women workers. Whereas interstate mobility in the period studied was

Table 14.12 Unemployment rates in April 1960 for men and women age fourteen and over, by extent of geographic mobility, 1955–60.

Sex	Nonmobile	Mobile*	
		Within State	Interstate
Men	4.6	5.1	4.4
Women	4.5	6.3	7.1

* Mobile refers to anyone who changed addresses between 1955 and 1960.

Source: Computed from U.S. Census of Population, 1960, Final Report PC (2)-2B, *Mobility for States and State Economic Areas*, Table 9, pp. 23–9.

associated with a decreasing unemployment rate for male workers (or, at the very least, with no worsening of that rate, compared to that for nonmobile males), the unemployment rate of women actually increased with geographic mobility, indicating that such migration was often in response to factors other than personal economic opportunity.

Table 14.13 Long-term unemployment for men and women, in selected years. (in percentages of total unemployed)

Year	Men		Women	
	More than 15 weeks	More than 27 weeks	More than 15 weeks	More than 27 weeks
1957	20.4	8.9	16.7	6.7
1958	33.5	15.6	26.0	11.5
1961	34.7	18.6	26.9	13.5
1964	26.7	13.7	22.9	10.6
1968	16.0	6.7	13.2	4.2

Source: Computed from *Statistics on Manpower*, a supplement to the *Manpower Report of the President* (Washington, D.C.: G.P.O., March 1969), Table A–19, pp. 20–21.

The Duration of Unemployment

Other things being equal, one would expect the geographic immobility of women to raise their duration and rate of unemployment relative to that of men. On the other hand, more viable alternatives to labor force participation are available for women than for men, and this will tend

Table 14.14 **Distribution of unemployed persons age twenty and over, by sex, reason for unemployment, and duration, 1968 annual averages.**

Reason for unemployment	Number of unemployed (thousands)	Percentage of unemployed				
		<5 wks.	5–14 wks.	15–26 wks.	27+ wks.	Average weeks
Male						
Job losers	599	46.6	32.4	12.2	8.8	11.3
Job leavers	167	56.3	26.3	9.0	7.8	9.8
Entrants	227	52.9	31.3	7.9	7.9	10.0
Reentrants	205	53.2	30.7	7.8	7.8	9.9
New workers	22	na	na	na	na	na
Total or average	993	49.6	30.9	10.8	8.6	10.9
Female						
Job losers	341	48.4	31.7	13.5	6.2	10.2
Job leavers	167	57.5	26.3	9.6	6.6	9.3
Entrants	477	65.2	24.1	6.9	3.8	7.3
Reentrants	422	66.1	24.2	6.4	3.3	7.0
New workers	55	58.2	23.6	10.9	5.5	8.8
Total or average	985	58.2	27.0	9.7	5.1	8.7

Source: Kathryn D. Hoyle, *Job Losers, and Entrants – A Report on the Unemployed*, Bureau of Labor Statistics, Special Labor Force Report No. 106 (Washington, D.C.: G.P.O., 1969), Table 7, p. A-1.

to cut down the duration of female unemployment. In fact, the data on long-term unemployment by sex presented in Table 14.13 indicate that the duration of unemployment is longer for men than for women.

Raw duration data are not terribly useful, however, in ascertaining whether unemployed women will have more difficulty than unemployed men in finding new jobs or whether women tend to be less mobile than men, either geographically or occupationally. The total duration data include many women whose attachment to the labor force is only marginal and who leave the labor force after a short period of unemployment. In order to test the hypothesis that relative immobility within the labor force raises female unemployment, those women who enter the labor force, seek work for a short period, and leave the labor force without becoming employed must be eliminated from the data on the duration of unemployment.

One way to partially eliminate the effect of the high labor force turnover of marginal female labor force participants would be to look at the duration of unemployment for men and women classified by reason for unemployment, particularly the duration of unemployment for male and female job losers. Such information for the year 1968 is given in Table 14.14.

Unemployed men average a longer duration of unemployment than unemployed women, regardless of source of unemployment. The difference in duration of unemployment by sex is greatest among labor force entrants. On the other hand, the duration of unemployment among women who lost or left a job and stayed in the labor force approaches that of their male counterparts. This might represent the effect of unemployment insurance on female job losers and job leavers. In both these categories, a greater proportion of women than men experienced unemployment of fifteen to twenty-six weeks, but a higher proportion of men were unemployed more than twenty-six weeks. Evidently women who are eligible for unemployment insurance remain in the labor force as long as they can collect such benefits but tend to drop out of the labor force if they fail to become employed within a short time after the exhaustion of benefits.

In summary, women are less mobile than men within the labor force, occupationally and geographically, because of systematic differences by sex in the profitability of a given move and the expected period over which returns will be reaped. This factor raises the female unemployment rate. When women are faced with the prospect of very long-term unemployment, however, and the expected gain from continued labor force participation falls quite low, they are more likely than men to leave the labor force, because more valuable nonmarket uses for time tend to be available to women.

Conclusion

The most important reason for the relatively high rate of female unemployment is the extensive movement of women into and out of the labor force. Women clearly exhibit more inter-labor force mobility, and consequently more total mobility, than men, and the effect of this is to increase their unemployment rate. Second, intra-labor force immobility makes it harder for women to find jobs and also accounts for some of the female-male unemployment differential. Finally, women do tend to receive less specific training than men, but the effects of factors acting in the opposite direction make the net effect of lack of specific training on the female unemployment rate quite small.

15 Curing High Unemployment Rates Among Blacks and Women *

Barbara R. Bergmann
Professor of Economics, University of Maryland

From: *Joint Economic Committee, Congress of the United States*, 17 October 1972 pp. 41–9 (excerpts).

We will not begin to take the monetary and fiscal steps necessary to reduce the unemployment rate in the United States toward levels considered respectable in most other developed countries – in the neighborhood of two percent – unless and until progress is made in solving the problem of high unemployment of blacks and women, who now together constitute 44 percent of the labor force. Women's unemployment rates are currently running 64 percent higher than men's and black rates are running 110 percent higher than white rates. Even in times (unlike the present) when the labor market for white prime-age males is tight, and further expansion via monetary and fiscal policy threatens highly inflationary consequences, high unemployment among blacks and women as well as among youths keeps the size of the total group of unemployed people very large.

I will argue that we can bring down the pathologically high unemployment rates among blacks and women by policies which encourage employers to treat members of these groups more as white males are now treated. I will further argue that such policies would not merely have the effect of spreading the misery around more evenly, but would enable us to move to an era in which unemployment rates could be lower for all groups, without inflationary consequences.

Martin Feldstein[1] has brought together in a very helpful way the evidence on unemployment by race, sex and age. He shows that women, blacks and youth tend to have high unemployment rates whether the rate for white males is high or whether it is low. Improvement in the

* Research for this paper was supported by a grant to the Project on the Economics of Discrimination by the Office of Economic Opportunity. I would like to thank Clair Vickery, Bradley Schiller, Henry Aaron, and Robert Hartman for helpful comments.

1. 'Lowering the Permanent Rate of Unemployment,' a report to the Joint Economic Committee, 17 October, 1972.

state of aggregate demand changes the unemployment rates for women and young blacks very little.[2] Rates for black men and women and white male youth are reduced by improvement in aggregate demand, but even in the best of times their rates are high.

In explaining this phenomenon of high unemployment rates for blacks, women and youth, Feldstein attributes great importance to high labor turnover among these groups – to a tendency to leave jobs. Speaking of young workers he says, 'Why is employment so unstable and labor force attachment so weak in this age range? Why do young American workers experience so much higher unemployment rates than their British counterparts? I believe that *a fundamental reason is the types of jobs that are available and the lack of adequate reward for stable employment.*'[3] [Emphasis supplied.]

While I believe that shortage of demand is even more important than high turnover in causing high unemployment, I do believe high turnover deserves more attention than we have given it. Moreover, I believe Feldstein is right on target in his diagnosis of the cause of high turnover among youths.

The very same diagnosis is to a great degree applicable in the case of high turnover among women and blacks. Women and blacks also suffer from 'the types of jobs that are available and the lack of adequate rewards for stable employment.' Robert E. Hall put the matter very strikingly when he said, '. . . the whole notion of a career with steady advancement is relevant only for white males . . . Blacks and women seem to be excluded from work that offers an incentive to stay with a job permanently . . .'[4]

The lack of careers leads to drift from one job to another and to drift into and out of the labor force. It is these drifting people who create the high labor turnover statistics and contribute, along with deficient demand, to the high unemployment rates that Feldstein documents . . .

The occupational segregation of women from men is even more

2. We must be careful not to interpret an unchanging rate of unemployment over the cycle as an unchanging degree of hardship in these groups. The unchanging rate of unemployment is probably due to a reduction in the rate of quitting jobs in bad times, which balances out the reduction in opportunities to leave the state of unemployment through finding a job. In bad times, the average length of unemployment rises in these groups, and hence the hardship of finding oneself unemployed rises also.

3. Op. cit., pp. 34–5.

4. Robert E. Hall, 'Why Is The Unemployment Rate So High At Full Employment?' *Brookings Papers on Economic Activity, 3: 1970,* pp. 393, 396.

extreme than the occupational segregation by race.[5] Its extent has been documented by Harriet Zellner, to whom is owed the figures in Table 15.1.[6] Zellner has grouped detailed occupations by the extent to which they were segregated by sex. She found that 47 percent of all women

Table 15.1 Distribution of women and men amongst occupations grouped by segregation level, private sector, 1960[1]

	Females	Males	Percent distribution		Females as percent of total
			Females	Males	
Total employed	16,370,285	36,708,583	100	100	31
Occupation group:					
1. Occupations with 80 to 100 percent women	7,673,389	578,057	47	2	93
2. Occupations with 50 to 79 percent women	3,664,547	1,730,629	22	5	68
3. Occupations with 33 to 49 percent women	1,731,389	2,320,730	11	6	43
4. Occupations with 0 to 33 percent women	3,300,960	32,080,166	20	87	9

1. Based on data from the U.S. Bureau of the Census, '1960 Census of Population,' PC(2) 7A, occupational characteristics, Table 21.

worked in occupations which were almost entirely female, while 87 percent of all men worked in occupations where women were grossly under-represented. Only 11 percent of women and six percent of men work in occupations where women have fair representation. The lack of a meaningful career for most women which occupational segregation entails is well illustrated by the familiar figures of the young executive trainee (male) and his secretary (female) both of whom may have gone to the same college, taken the same courses, and achieved identical grades.

5. See Victor R. Fuchs, 'Male-Female Differentials in Hourly Earnings,' National Bureau of Economic Research, 1970, p. 12.

6. Harriet Zellner, 'Discrimination Against Women, Occupational Segregation and the Relative Wage.' Paper delivered at the Meetings of the American Economic Association, New Orleans, December, 1971. A condensed version of this paper appeared in the *American Economic Review*, May 1972.

The kinds of jobs to which most women and blacks are consigned tend to be repetitive, boring, and without interesting human contact. These kinds of jobs may be tolerated by the less talented or imaginative. Even those of ability may tolerate such jobs if they are seen as possible stepping stones to higher things. But where these jobs are dead ends, as they are for most blacks and most women, incentive to stay in any particular job is low. To go in exasperation from one boring job to another, even at the cost of a spell of unemployment, may be better than staying on one particular boring job, especially if nothing is to be gained by staying in terms of salary, responsibilities and advancement. An occasional retreat from a boring job into unpaid household work is undoubtedly refreshing for women who can afford such a luxury.[7] I would conjecture that much of the job leaving is done – and therefore much of the associated unemployment is suffered by – those blacks and female workers with the most ability, to whom the system of occupational segregation is least tolerable and most galling.

I know there is a great temptation in some quarters to attribute the poor labor market position of blacks and women and their high unemployment to the inferior characteristics of the sufferers rather than to the discriminatory action of employers in restricting access to certain jobs to white males. Blacks, it is said, lack aptitude, and women lack labor force attachment. Whatever truth there is to these assertions will not be uncovered until employers begin giving a square deal to those blacks *with* aptitude and those women *with* labor force attachment. Only then will we begin to see whether the present labor force behavior of blacks and women, particularly their higher turnover rate, is not merely a reaction to employer discrimination.

There is considerable evidence already which implicates discrimination as the reason for higher turnover rates for women and blacks. Relative labor turnover rates by occupation, based on unpublished data of the Bureau of Labor Statistics are shown in Table 15.2. The rates of turnover for laborers, service workers and clerical workers are two to three times as high as turnover rates among professionals, technical workers and craftsmen. But where is cause and effect here? Are rates for blacks and women high because they are over-represented in high turnover occupations, or do these occupations have high turnover because they are peopled by blacks and women? I have made calculations which indicate that a considerable part of the large difference in job

7. Of course, millions of working women are in families with no working man, or a working man with low earnings.

leaving between blacks and whites is due to the fact that blacks tend to have jobs in occupations in which both blacks and whites leave jobs relatively frequently.[8] A calculation by Isabel Sawhill indicates that about one-half of the 18 percent difference in turnover between men

Table 15.2 **Estimated index of turnover rates by occupation, for the period 1967–70**

[*Professionals, technical workers, managers* = 1]	
Professionals, technical workers, managers	1.00
Sales workers	2.36
Clerical workers	1.83
Craftsmen and foremen	1.16
Operatives	1.80
Service workers	3.14
Laborers	3.86

Source: Unpublished data of the U.S. Department of Labor.

and women can be accounted for by the fact that women tend to be employed in industries and occupations in which both men and women leave jobs frequently.[9]

What this means is that the reduction of occupational segregation would tend to reduce the difference in the turnover and unemployment rates of whites and blacks and reduce the difference in the turnover and unemployment rates of men and women. But would such a development – justified on equity grounds alone – leave the total rate of turnover and unemployment as high as ever? I believe that the effect of lower rates of turnover for women and blacks would not be cancelled out by higher turnover for white males. There are four reasons for this: (1) Labor would be better distributed across occupations according to aptitude. Many women and blacks of above average ability find themselves, because of race and sex discrimination, in jobs in which their full talents are not utilized. These people are surely major contributors to the turnover statistics. If nondiscriminatory hiring were the rule, fewer individuals would find themselves mismatched in their job.

8. Barbara R. Bergmann and William R. Krause, 'Evaluating and Forecasting Progress in Racial Integration of Employment,' *Industrial and Labor Relations Review*, April 1972.

9. Isabel V. Sawhill, 'The Economics of Discrimination Against Women: Some New Findings,' *Journal of Human Resources*, Vol. 8, No. 3.

(2) A higher proportion of the total workforce would realistically consider themselves in the running for promotions in their current places of work. Here the analogy of a sweepstakes is useful. By cutting discrimination, the number of tickets in the promotion sweepstakes would be increased, although the chance of any ticket paying off would be reduced. A disproportionate amount of the turnover comes from those who have no ticket in the promotion sweepstakes whatever. Therefore, increasing the number of tickets, even while somewhat debasing their value, should reduce total turnover.

(3) Certain types of occupations – laborers, service occupations, some clerical occupations – which now contribute disproportionately to the turnover statistics, would tend to fall in size. These occupations are now overcrowded and hence underpaid because they have a 'captive' labor supply – women and blacks who because of discrimination have no place else to go. If discrimination were eased, part of this labor supply would go to other occupations.

(4) In all probability the laborer, clerical and service occupations would improve in terms of pay and working conditions, just to meet the competition for labor. This might in turn reduce turnover in these occupations, even as they were falling in size.

Let me emphasize again that I do not believe that relatively high turnover is the entire explanation for relatively high unemployment among women and blacks, or even the most important reason. These groups have been growing in size relative to the size of the group of white prime-age males. Yet women and blacks continue by and large to be restricted to the same occupations they were restricted to twenty or thirty years ago. As a result these occupations have tended to become overcrowded. This overcrowding, which accounts for the low wage levels[10] in the occupations given over to women and blacks also is a cause of high unemployment for these groups.

I have attempted in a very simple way to estimate the amount of unemployment which can be attributed to turnover and the amount which must be ascribed to deficient demand. These estimates appear in Table 15.3. While estimated unemployment among black men due to turnover (1.1 percent of the labor force) is higher than the amount of unemployment due to turnover among white men (0.6 percent), most of the difference in the white and black rates seem attributable to a lower demand for black men as compared with white men. About 15 percent of the

10. See Barbara R. Bergmann, 'The Effects of White Incomes on Discrimination in Employment,' *Journal of Political Economy*, March–April 1971.

difference in the two rates is due to differences in turnover between blacks and whites. Similarly, about four percent of the difference in unemployment rates among men and women is due to differences in turnover. Thus, while the high turnover of women and blacks does contribute to their higher unemployment rate, the most important source of high unemployment for these groups is deficient demand due to occupational crowding and generally slack conditions.

Table 15.3 Part A. Unemployment estimated as due to turnover (Percent of the labor force)

	Male		Female	
Age	White	Black	White	Black
16 to 19	0.8	1.3	0.9	1.6
20 and over	0.6	1.1	0.7	1.2
Part B. Unemployment rates – August 1972				
16 to 19	13.0	22.4	13.4	31.2
20 and over	3.2	6.5	5.6	8.8
Part C. – Residual unemployment estimated as due to deficient demand				
16 to 19	12.2	21.2	12.5	29.6
20 and over	2.6	5.4	4.9	7.6

Source: See text and 'Employment and Earnings.'

Feldstein, Hall and others trace high unemployment rates back to high labor turnover in youth, blacks, women. We have traced the chain of causation back another step, from high turnover rates to occupational discrimination and have added another factor which seems considerably more important – occupational overcrowding. Only a great curtailment in occupational discrimination will bring down the turnover, reduce the overcrowding and hence the unemployment rates of these groups. There is good cause to believe that such a curtailment would also bring down total turnover and would permit total unemployment to be reduced safely by increases in aggregate demand.

Is progress being made?

It would be pleasant to report that the problems of women and blacks with unemployment and occupational segregation are being relieved at a respectable pace, but I believe the evidence now available points the other way.

Our research group is planning an extensive study of the results of the 1970 Census focused on just this question. The evidence we have now, based on older data, seems to indicate that progress for blacks is quite slow and that women may be going backwards rather than forwards . . .

When we turn to the developments for women, we see a retrogression. In the period between 1950 and 1970, women in the labor force increased by 70 percent, as compared with a 15 percent increase for men. Largely because of employer discrimination, vast numbers of these women crowded into the already overcrowded clerical occupations, which more than doubled in size. Women in these occupations lost ground relative to the rest of the economy in terms of salary, which is a way of saying that the price the economy paid for increasing the size of clerical occupations was to put these women to lower priority (and no doubt more alienating) tasks. It is no wonder that such a situation should lead to high turnover and high unemployment among women.

What policies for reducing turnover and unemployment?

Martin Feldstein has proposed that we set up a Youth Employment Service and Youth Employment Scholarships which would have the effect of getting more on-the-job training for youth, and encouraging young people to stay on in particular jobs.[11] I would wholeheartedly endorse that suggestion, but only on condition that care be taken to ensure that young people have access to the federally subsidized jobs without regard to race or sex. The Federal record in ensuring nondiscriminatory entry to its youth programs is quite poor, the most shameful case being the programs of the Bureau of Apprenticeship. I think that a federal youth program which would help to perpetuate present occupational segregation by race and sex would do more harm than good. After all, the labor market problems of young white males very soon solve themselves through the process of aging – the employment problems of young black women and men and of young white women are not so easily conquered.

To a nondiscriminatory youth program, I would add two other programs as essential: an expanded program of public service jobs and a

11. Op. cit., p. 38 ff.

strengthened program of affirmative action by nondiscriminatory hiring by private employers, enforced by the Federal Government.

Public service employment is a necessary tool for breaking down patterns which have led to high turnover and high unemployment for youth, blacks and women, simply because it is too much to expect the private economy to solve this problem all by itself. The public service already plays a role in giving blacks and women a better deal than does the private labor market. Its role must be expanded and whatever patterns of discrimination remain within the government service must be broken up. Naturally, a public service employment program which was ill paid, offered no training, offered no future and segregated women and blacks would not be much help. But a greatly expanded and improved public service jobs program could have a significant effect on current unemployment problems. Although I realize the idea has little political appeal, I would urge experimentation on a small scale with public construction in which the usual market for construction labor organized by contractors was bypassed, and the work done and supervised by employees on the public payroll, chosen in a nondiscriminatory way. There is a precedent for this in the way the city of Minneapolis operates its construction projects, a method initiated by Hubert H. Humphrey when he was mayor.

I believe that vigorous affirmative action programs in private industry are also a necessary ingredient to success in reducing occupational segregation, and thus in reducing excessive rates of turnover and unemployment for women and blacks. A lot of opposition to such programs has been generated by exaggerated notions about what such programs entail. They do not entail firing any person currently on any job, and they do not entail hiring masses of unqualified people. Our research group has computed the share which blacks would have to be of all persons hired to fill job openings in manufacturing if the targeted share for black employment were to be reached in ten years. For example, blacks now are about 1.7 percent of all persons hired for professional and technical jobs in printing and publishing. That share needs to be raised to 5.2, if blacks are eventually to have their fair share of such jobs in that industry. There is a great deal of difference in 1.7 and 5.2, but it is hard to see a great menace to whites or to competence in printing and publishing if the hiring rate is so changed.

16 The 1974–1975 Recession and the Employment of Women *

Organisation for Economic Co-operation and Development, 1976, pp. 7–32 (slightly abridged).

I. Introduction

This paper examines the effects of the 1974–5 recession on the labour market experience of women in selected OECD Member countries. The analysis is based to a large extent on data supplied by Member countries participating in the Working Party on the Role of Women in the Economy. Countries were requested to supply information for two comparative periods, a recent period of low unemployment and their most recent period of high unemployment. Most typically the low unemployment period was in 1973 or 1974 and the high unemployment period in 1975. Information was most commonly available on male and female unemployment, labour force participation and employment in the aggregate, as well as by industry. The analysis focuses on these basic statistics. Only very limited data were available on involuntary part-time employment, labour force discouragement, reason for un-employment and long-term unemployment.

Before reporting the results of the study, some methodological issues should be discussed. These relate both to problems in measuring the overall impact on employment and unemployment of a recession and to problems in measuring the effects on women in particular.

The labour market effects of the recession cannot be determined by looking simply at changes in unemployment. A reduction in job oppor-

*The data for this study were supplied to the Secretariat by the Member countries through the Working Party on the Role of Women in the Economy. Members of the Working Party also contributed their comments and suggestions. The original analysis of data was conducted by Dr June O'Neill, U.S. Council of Economic Advisers and Dr Ralph Smith, Urban Institute, who acted as consultants to the project. The organizations with which Dr O'Neill and Dr Smith are affiliated are, of course, not responsible for any of the descriptive material or views expressed in this report. Revisions of the original analysis and the final report were prepared by the Secretariat. The results, of course, only apply to the countries which partici-pated in the survey.

tunities may lead to withdrawal from the labour force or may discourage people from entering the labour force in the first place. The OECD countries generally define unemployment to include only those who are registered as unemployed or who have made a specific effort to find work in a recent period (usually the past four weeks). It is difficult to identify precisely those who would in fact be seeking work if opportunities were better. Only a few countries include a question relating to discouragement from seeking work and the group counted in this category is classified as 'out of the labour force'. Women are more likely to be out of the labour force than men and their labour force behaviour seems to be more sensitive to changes in economic conditions. For this reason comparison of movements in unemployment levels could understate the impact of the recession on women relatively more than on men.

Changes in each group's *employment* levels over the course of the recession may also understate the impact of the recession, and relatively more for women. The working-age population in some OECD countries has been increasing and total employment opportunities must expand simply to keep pace with this increase. In addition, in most Member countries there has been a secular rise in the proportion of working-age women participating in the paid labour market. Thus, it is quite possible, because of this secular trend, for employment to increase during a recession and to increase more for women than for men. However, these increases may be below the trend rate of increase. Thus, employment changes should be adjusted to take account of the trend in the period before the recession if the true effect of the recession is to be isolated.

This report contains an analysis of the pattern of labour market experience of women during the recent recession in some 16 OECD countries, followed by an attempt to identify the main factors affecting the impact of the recession on women by comparing the employment trends and distribution of employment by sector in some 13 OECD countries.

II. Pattern in the labour market experience of women

Table 16.1 shows the levels and changes for both sexes in the unemployment rate, employment and labour force participation in 16 OECD countries during their most recent business downturn, usually from 1974 to 1975. In examining the Table it should be noted that the levels of unemployment, employment and labour force participation are not truly comparable across countries. The definitions and the manner of data collection vary from country to country and this affects the measured statistics. For example, some countries rely mainly on a count of the unemployed from the offices that register the unemployed for unemployment compensation or other employment services. Thus, those unemployed who do not register, perhaps because they are new entrants to the labour force, would not be counted as unemployed. Even among countries which have regular surveys of households to derive their labour force statistics, variation can occur. While the concept of unemployment is rather clear for those who are laid off from work and begin to look for another job, it is much less clear for those who have been out of the labour force. The wording of the household survey can in this case affect the count of the unemployed. For example, Canada changed its labour force survey in 1975 and simultaneously took two household samples – one using the new survey and one using the old. Under the new survey (see Table 16.1) the unemployment rate for women is 2 percentage points higher than under the old.[1] One can only speculate how differences in surveys between the OECD countries may affect their measured unemployment rates.

The point of this digression on the data is that the country to country differences in the way the statistics are developed make it difficult to determine actual differences in the level of unemployment, etc., between countries. However, in this study we are looking mainly at the *changes* in unemployment, employment and labour force and these changes are probably less affected by differences in concept.[2]

As was to be expected the labour market impact of the recent recession on women was not the same in all countries. However, the present statistical material suggests that there are significant similarities in country experience.

One of the important issues to be raised in assessing the impact on employment opportunities is whether or not during the recent economic

1. The change that seems to have had the most effect on the female unemployment rate is the introduction of a series of probing questions including whether the individual had done something specific to find a job in the last four weeks. Before 1975 the questionnaire was more vague, asking generally, 'What did the person do last week?' Looking for work was often not reported by women who were mostly occupied with housework.

2. For an extensive analysis of the concepts of unemployment and the reasons why unemployment rates differ among countries see Constance Sorrentino, *Methodological and Conceptual Problems of Measuring Unemployment in OECD Countries*, (mimeograph) OECD, Paris, 1976.

Table 16.1 Change in unemployment rate, employment and labour force participation from period of low to high unemployment, by sex, 16 OECD countries

	Unemployment rate			Number employed (thous.)			Labour force participation rate		
	Period Low (1)	High (2)	Change (2)–(1) % chg.	Period Low (1)	High (2)	Change (2)–(1) % chg.	Period Low (1)	High (2)	Change (2)–(1) % chg.
Country									
Australia* (May '74–May '75)									
Men	1.1	3.2	2.1 109	3,805	3,772	–33 –0.9	81.8	81.1	–0.7 –0.9
Women	2.4	5.0	2.6 108	1,945	1,939	–6 –0.3	41.4	41.7	0.3 0.7
Austria* (July '74–July '75)									
Men	0.3	0.8	0.5 167	1,651[a]	1,640[a]	–11 –0.7	76.1[b]	75.2[b]	–0.4 –0.5
Women	1.9	2.2	0.3 16	1,025[a]	1,036[a]	11 1.1	42.6[b]	43.1[b]	0.5 1.2
Canada* – New Survey (seasonally adjusted) (June '74–Aug. '75)									
Men	4.4	6.6	2.2 50	5,873	5,956	83 1.4	77.9	78.4	0.5 0.6
Women	6.2	8.6	2.4 38	3,264	3,425	161 4.9	42.8	44.7	1.9 4.4
Canada* – Old Survey (seasonally adjusted) (June '74 – Aug. '75)									
Men	5.1	7.7	2.6 50	5,942	6,010	68 1.1	76.5	76.8	0.3 0.4
Women	4.5	6.6	2.1 47	3,155	3,287	132 4.2	39.6	41.0	1.4 3.5

Data are not seasonally adjusted unless noted otherwise; * Household survey data.

[a] Employed and labour-force excludes the military, unpaid family workers and the self-employed.

[b] Working age population figures are assumed to represent the same proportion of total population (by sex) as they did in 1971.

Table 16.1 (continued)

Country	Unemployment rate				Number employed (thous.)				Labour force participation rate			
	Period		Change (low to high)		Period		Change (low to high)		Period		Change (low to high)	
	Low	High	(2)-(1)	% chg.	Low	High	(2)-(1)	% chg.	Low	High	(2)-(1)	% chg.
	(1)	(2)			(1)	(2)			(1)	(2)		
Denmark* (Nov. '73–Oct. '74)												
Men	0.6	3.5	2.9	483	1,445	1,412	-33	-2.3	80.5	80.5	0.0	0.0
Women	1.1	3.7	2.6	236	981	977	-4	-0.4	54.2	55.2	1.0	1.8
Finland* (74:3–75:3)												
Men	1.1	1.9	0.8	73	1,243	1,219	-24	-1.9	75.4	74.3	-1.1	-1.5
Women	2.0	2.2	0.2	10	1,066	1,065	-1	-0.1	60.0	59.8	-0.2	-0.3
France*e) (Mar. '74 – Apr. '75)												
Men	1.9	3.5	1.6	84	13,019	13,291	272	2.1	73.0	73.7	0.7	1.0
Women	6.1	7.9	1.8	30	8,100	8,174	74	0.9	42.5	43.6	1.1	2.6
Germany** (Apr. '74 – Apr. '75)d)												
Men	1.9	4.5	2.6	137	16,471	15,886	-585	-3.6	73.8e)	71.9e)	-1.9	-2.6
Women	2.9	5.2	2.3	79	9,735	9,522	-213	-2.2	38.7e)	38.3e)	-0.4	-1.0

Data are not seasonally adjusted unless noted otherwise.

* Household survey data.

** Unemployed based on registration data. Consequently, these data may underestimate the extent of unemployment especially among women.

c) Unemployed, employed and labour force data include the 'marginally active'.

d) 73 : 4 to 74 : 4 for employment and labour force participation. e) Labour force participation rates are quarterly labour force figures divided by working age population figures which are annual averages.

Table 16.1 (continued)

Italy*												
(Apr. '74 – Apr. '75)												
Men	2.2	2.9	0.7	32	13,635	13,585	−50	−0.4	69.6[f]	69.9[f]	0.3	0.4
Women	3.2	4.9	1.7	53	5,127	5,184	−57	1.1	24.4[f]	25.1[f]	0.7	2.9
Japan* – Unemployment rates only, seasonally adjusted												
(Oct. '73 – Sept. '75)												
Men	0.9	2.0	1.1	122	32,234[g]	32,146[g]	−88	−0.3	82.3	81.3	−1.0	−1.2
Women	1.1	1.6	0.5	45	19,884[g]	19,325[g]	−599	−2.8	50.7	46.8	−3.9	−7.7
Netherlands**												
(Apr. '74 – Apr. '75)[b]												
Men	2.7	4.1	1.4	52	3,503	3,452	−51	−1.4	80.9	80.0	−0.9	−1.1
Women	1.9	3.1	1.2	63	1,114	1,098	−16	−1.4	26.1	25.7	−1.4	−1.6

Data are not seasonally adjusted unless noted otherwise. * Household survey data. ** Unemployed based on registration data. Consequently, these data may underestimate the extent of unemployment especially among women.

[f] Labour force participation rates are monthly labour force figures divided by CEA-estimated annual figures for working age population.

[g] Employment figures include armed forces and are averages for the periods 73 : 4, 74 : 1 and 74 : 2; and 74 : 4, 75 : 1, and 75 : 2, respectively.

[b] Calculation of participation rates includes an adjustment for changes in hours worked.

Table 16.1 (continued)

New Zealand**												
(Apr. '74 – Apr. '75)												
Men	0.05	0.2	0.15	300	824	831	7.4	0.9	N.A.	N.A.	N.A.	N.A.
Women	0.08	0.3	0.22	275	356	362	6.5	1.8	N.A.	N.A.	N.A.	N.A.
Norway*												
(Nov. '74 – Nov. '75)												
Men	1.1	2.5	1.4	127	1,058[1]	1,050[1]	−8	−0.8	77.6	77.5	−0.1	−0.1
Women	1.6	2.8	1.2	75	625[1]	649[1]	24	3.8	45.7	47.8	2.1	4.6
Spain*												
(2nd ½ '73 – 2nd ½ '74)												
Men	2.3	2.8	0.5	21	9,630	9,611	−20	−0.2	78.1	77.4	−0.7	−0.9
Women	2.4	3.1	0.7	29	3,851	3,910	59	1.5	28.3	28.8	0.5	1.8
Sweden*												
(70 : 2 – 72 : 1)												
Men	1.3	3.2	1.9	146	2,336	2,262	−74	−3.2	80.7	79.1	−1.6	−2.0
Women	1.4	3.0	1.6	114	1,522	1,546	24	1.6	52.8	54.1	1.3	2.5

Data are not seasonally adjusted unless noted otherwise.
* Household survey data; ** Unemployed based on registration data. Consequently, these data may underestimate the extent of unemployment especially among women.
1) Employment figures include permanent members of the armed forces.

Table 16.1 (continued)

United Kingdom**												
(74 : 1 – 75 : 1)												
Men	3.3	4.1	0.8	24	15,224	15,080	−144	−0.9	79.6[1]	78.7[1]	−0.9	−1.1
Women	1.0	1.5	0.5	50	9,371	9,454	83	0.9	43.7[1]	44.0[1]	0.3	0.7
United States* – (Seasonally adjusted)												
(73 : 4 – 75 : 4)												
Men	4.1	8.0	3.9	95	52,450	51,339	−1,111	−2.1	79.0	77.6	−1.4	−1.8
Women	5.9	9.2	3.3	56	32,978	33,903	925	2.8	45.1	46.4	1.3	2.8

Data are not seasonally adjusted unless noted otherwise.

* Household survey data.

** Unemployed based on registration data. Consequently, these data may underestimate the extent of unemployment especially among women.

[1] Quarterly data for civilian labour force divided by annual data for working age population.

downturn the burden of the increase in unemployment was borne more by women workers than by men. The answer to this question is of considerable importance to policymakers since many Member governments have adopted policies to increase employment opportunities for women. It is important to know if short-run economic fluctuations are likely to affect the position women have gained in the labour market over period of many years. As is shown in Table 16.1, before the recession, the unemployment rate was higher for women in all but two countries. If the burden of the recession fell disproportionately on women, then their unemployment rate might have risen more than the male rate. This in fact occurred in six of the countries (Australia, Canada,[3] France, Italy, New Zealand and Spain). In the remaining 10 countries, however, the rate for men increased at the same rate or more rapidly than the rate for women.[4] If change in unemployment rate is used as an indicator of the impact of the recession on women's employment it therefore appears that for most countries the unemployment situation of women deteriorated less than that of men during the recession. In order to assess the impact of the recession other indicators must also be examined.

As already discussed, it is quite possible for countries to experience a rising unemployment rate and at the same time have an increasing level of employment. The growth of population, and/or rising labour force participation rates, will result in an increase of persons in the labour market. Consequently, unless a recession is extremely severe, it is quite possible that the level of employment will increase at the same time as the number and rate of unemployment is rising. Table 16.1 shows that for many countries employment increased in absolute terms even though unemployment was also rising. A significant indication of the position of women as a labour force group is, therefore, whether the employment gains for women were absolutely and relatively greater or less than for men.

The results of the employment analysis show that during the recession 12 of the countries experienced an absolute decline in the number of

3. When the absolute change in unemployment rate is based on the New Survey method of measuring unemployment.

4. The absolute change in the unemployment rate is used here rather than the percentage change in order to reflect the actual increases in unemployment. The percentage change would show relatively smaller changes in the unemployment rate for women because the latter starts from a higher base. Thus the percentage change in the unemployment rate for women was higher in only three of the 16 countries.

males employed, while female employment declined in only five countries. Relatively, the change in the employment situation was generally more favourable for women than for men. In seven of the countries (Austria, Italy, Norway, Spain, Sweden, the United Kingdom and the United States) female employment increased while male employment declined; in two countries (Canada and New Zealand) both male and female employment expanded but in each case the total employment of women increased proportionately more than that of men. In five countries (Australia, Denmark, Finland, Germany and the Netherlands) employment declined for both men and women but in each case the absolute and proportionate decline was less for women than for men.

There were, in fact, only two countries in which women's share of total employment declined. In France both male and female employment improved with male employment rising proportionately more than for women. Finally, in Japan both employment of women and men declined with women accounting for a substantial share in the total drop in employment.

The pattern of net change in the level of employment therefore does vary considerably among countries. Despite these variations in the pattern and amount of change in employment the general finding is that during the recession in most countries in the study, the employment opportunities for women as a group were less severely affected when compared to the changing employment opportunities for men.

Changes in the labour force participation rate will also affect the employment situation of both men and women. *Short-term* changes in this rate are related to the business cycle with changes in the demand for labour being the dominant influence. As it becomes more difficult to find or keep a job, entry to the labour force may decline as some persons decide to leave the labour force rather than remain unemployed. Therefore, as the economy moves into a recession it is likely that the labour force participation rate will decline slightly and rise again with the recovery.[5] The data for this study cover mainly the change from the period of low unemployment in 1973–4 to the period of highest unemployment in 1975. Since these periods do not include the upswing of the economy in any country, rapid increases in the participation rates cannot be expected. Quite the contrary, any short-term changes are likely to be either a drop in the rate or a levelling off for those groups,

5. Additional family workers may also enter the labour force when other family members become unemployed. However, empirically the dominant effect of a cyclical increase in unemployment seems to be a slow-down in labour force growth.

such as women, whose rate has been increasing over the past decade or so.

The results of changes in the labour force participation rates in Table 16.1 show that for some 10 of 15 countries the rate for men actually declined. These small declines are likely to be in part a continuation of the gradual long-term decline which has occurred in the male rate in most countries. For the remainder of the countries the rate either remained stable or increased very slightly. For women, however, the reverse was the case. During the recession the rate for women increased in 11 of the 15 countries and declined somewhat for the others. The precise reason for the strength of the trend towards increased participation of women in the labour market cannot be determined with the available data. It is possible that the rate of change for women was moderated by the recession. This is certainly the case for Finland, Germany and Japan which experienced a decline in the participation rate for women. For other countries, however, the growth of employment opportunities for women was strong enough to offset at least some of the impact the recession was bound to have on women's participation in the labour market.

III. Trends and distribution of employment

Any explanation of the relative change in women's and men's employment and unemployment in each country is likely to be quite complex. Differences among countries are likely to be partially attributable to institutional practices which are unique to each country. For example, the social attitude of employers, existing programmes and public policies aimed at assisting the unemployed, the existing job security provisions which have been negotiated between labour and management, and the extent to which employers find it desirable to 'hoard' labour during a recession, are factors which will affect changes in the employment situation of men and women during a recession. There is, however, one factor that could have an important effect on the relative change in women's and men's employment and unemployment. Business downturns tend to be more severe in manufacturing and construction industries (the 'industry sector') than in the service industries. Since working women are, in many countries, relatively more concentrated in the service industries than men, their overall employment may be relatively less affected during recessions. The strength of the sectoral distribution of female employment in explaining the impact of the recession is not likely to be the same in all countries because of different institutional practices, but it is nevertheless important. Thus, an analysis of the relative impact of the recession should include an examination of the change on a sector by sector basis, in order to interpret the aggregate effects properly.

Data restrictions prohibit a *detailed* sector by sector analysis of all countries included in the study. The remainder of the report will therefore first present some analysis which has been done for the United States and finally present a broad comparative sectoral analysis for selected OECD countries. The United States experience is not applicable to all countries, although it may be relevant to many, since in about one-half of the countries reviewed (including the United States) the employment impact was similar, with female employment expanding and male employment declining during the recession.

a) Trends and distribution of employment in the United States

The recession in the United States began in the fourth quarter of 1973 (1973:4). Employment continued to rise, but at a slow rate, through 1974:3 and then fell by about 2 million workers by 1975:1. Throughout most of 1975 employment growth was sluggish.

Table 16.2 provides seasonally adjusted labour force, employment and unemployment levels by sex, and the corresponding unemployment and civilian labour force participation rates in 1973:4 and 1975:4. The data are derived from the Current Population Survey, a national sample survey of households conducted for the United States Bureau of Labor Statistics by the Bureau of the Census.[6] These data suggest that over this two-year period working women in the United States were not as severely affected by the recession as men. The female unemployment rate rose by 3.3 percentage points, while that of males rose by 3.9 percentage points; female employment rose by 925,000, while male employment fell by 1,111,000; and the female labour force participation rate rose by 1.3 percentage points, while that of males declined 1.5 points.

i) The Influence of Trends in Employment

For the reasons discussed earlier, however, these comparisons are not only the result of short-term changes in demand but may also reflect underlying long-term patterns rather than simply the impact of the

6. These data reflect the seasonal adjustment revisions made in 1976, as reported in *Employment and Earnings*, Vol. 22, Department of Labor, Bureau of Labor Statistics (February 1976).

recession. In the United States, for example, there has been a trend over a number of years of declining male labour force participation rates (largely because of increases in early retirements) and of rising female labour force participation rates. Thus, in order to evaluate the cyclical changes for men and women it would be useful to estimate for women and men what employment would have been if the recession had not occurred. A recent study developed statistical techniques for making such estimates using historical data series.[7]

Table 16.2 presents data on *potential* labour over the period of the recession and compares them with the *actual* labour force data during the recession in the United States. The *potential* labour force is an estimate based on past patterns of population growth and labour force participation. The difference between the potential and actual labour force is a measure of 'discouraged workers'. It is estimated that as a result of the recession, the number of discouraged female workers increased by 431,000 and the number of male discouraged workers by a similar amount – 458,000 (Table 16.2).[8] However, because the female labour force is smaller (two-thirds of the male labour force), these increases in discouraged workers represent a larger proportion of the female than of the male labour force and if counted as unemployed would also add relatively more to the female unemployed.

Table 16.2 also estimates the 'labour loss' (unemployed plus discouraged workers) due to the recession. Because discouraged workers are relatively more important among women than among men, the female share of aggregate increase in total labour loss is somewhat greater than if only the rise in unemployment is considered. Since labour force participation rates have been rising in most of the OECD countries included in the study, it is clear that the impact of the recession is

7. R. E. Smith, 'Has the Recession Been an Equal Opportunity Dis-Employer?', Urban Institute Working Paper 876–01, 1976.

8. Survey data in the United States are also collected on those who report that they want to work but are not actively searching because they think they cannot get a job. These data show that the number of male discouraged workers increased by 123,000, while that of females increased by 178,000. The survey measure of discouragement is conceptually quite different from the potential labour force measurement used in the text. The survey provides an indication of the state of mind of some of the people not in the labour force, but provides no indication of the kind of economic environment required to induce the non-participant to enter (or re-enter) the labour market. Nevertheless, both techniques show that labour force discouragement was relatively larger among women but increased during the recession by similar amounts.

Table 16.2 **Labour market impacts of the recession in the United States, by sex, selected quarters** (in thousands, except as indicated)

Female	1973:4	1975:4	Change 1973:4 to 1975:4
Actual data			
Labour force	35,057	37,338	2,281
Employment	32,978	33,903	925
Unemployment	2,079	3,435	1,356
Unemployment rate (%)	5.9	9.2	3.3
Civilian labour force participation rate (%)	45.1	46.4	1.3
Estimated data			
Potential labour force	35,880	38,592	2,712
Discouraged workers (potential minus actual labour force)	823	1,254	431
Labour loss (discouraged workers plus unemployed)	2,902	4,689	1,787
Labour loss rate (% of potential labour force)	8.1	12.2	4.1
Potential employment	34,086	36,662	2,576
Male			
Actual data			
Labour force	54,689	55,815	1,126
Employment	52,450	51,339	−1,111
Unemployment	2,239	4,476	−2,237
Unemployment rate (%)	4.1	8.0	3.9
Civilian labour force participation rate (%)	79.0	77.6	−1.4
Estimated data			
Potential labour force	54,836	56,420	1,584
Discouraged workers (potential minus actual labour force)	147	605	458
Labour loss (discouraged workers plus unemployed)	2,386	5,081	2,695
Labour loss rate (% of potential labour force)	4.4	9.0	4.6
Potential employment	53,026	54,558	1,532

Table 16.2 (*continued*)

	1973:4	1975:4	Change 1973:4 to 1975:4
Female share of aggregate			
Labour force	39.1%	40.1%	67.0%
Employment	38.6	39.8	—
Unemployment	48.1	43.4	37.7
Potential labour force	39.6	40.6	63.1
Labour loss			
(discouraged workers plus unemployed) 54.9		48.0	39.9

Source: Derived from R. E. Smith, 'Has the Recession Been an Equal Opportunity Dis-Employer?', Urban Institute Working Paper 876–01, 1976.

larger for both sexes than the changes in the unemployment rate would suggest.

Estimates of what the male and female employment would have been in the absence of the recession (i.e., potential employment) are also given in Table 16.2. It is estimated that in the United States female employment would have risen by about 2.5 million and male employment by about 1.5 million. The actual employment changes during the recession were, of course, much less, with women's employment increasing by a little less than 1 million and male employment declining by a little over 1 million.

This more detailed analysis of employment trends in the United States may well apply to other countries, especially those which have also experienced a strong secular rising trend in the labour force participation rate for women and where women outnumber men among new labour force entrants. For countries with secularly rising participation rates changes in the unemployment rate and in actual employment underestimate the impact of the recession for both men and women. In addition, in those countries where the female unemployment rate increased proportionately less than the rate for men, one must be careful to take into account the impact of the recession on the long-run secular rise in the participation rate of women. In a sense such an interruption is a reduction in the potential employment opportunities for women which, if data were available, might show up in some measure of 'discouraged' workers. Consequently, while in most of the OECD countries women's share of employment increased, in another respect women were affected more adversely than men because the recession interrupted the strong underlying trend in labour force growth of women.

ii) *The influence of the Sectoral Distribution of Employment*

The various sectors of the economy are affected unevenly during a recessionary period. The most severely affected industries are typically construction and the durable goods sector of manufacturing. The service sector, especially wholesale and retail trade, may also be affected but generally to a much lesser extent than manufacturing and construction.

In the United States, although a little more than four out of every ten workers are women, they account for only 6 per cent of construction employment and only 22 per cent in the durable goods sector of manufacturing. Since women are heavily represented in retail services (48 per cent) and other services (58 per cent) it is therefore not surprising that they were relatively insulated from the impact of the recession.

The question of the extent to which women's employment experience during the recession is attributable to the pattern of female employment, combined with the uneven sectoral impact of the recession, was analysed for the United States and the results shown in Table 16.3.[9]

The basic technique is to estimate what the impact on women would have been if the recession had affected all industries equally. The first two columns of Table 16.3 provide an indication of the impact of the recession on 12 sectors of the United States economy. (The data are annual averages from the Current Population Survey of households and therefore do not precisely correspond to the period used in the preceding analysis.) The next two columns provide female employment levels in each industry in both periods.

Column (5) shows the number of people who would have been employed by each industry in 1975 if employment in each had decreased by the same percentage. The final column (6) indicates the number of women who would have been employed in each industry if it had experienced the hypothetical employment loss; this was computed by multiplying the sector employment in column (5) by women's actual proportion of employment in that sector in 1975.

It is estimated that if the 12 industries had experienced proportionate losses, 33.1 million women would have held jobs in 1975, about 500,000 fewer women than were actually employed. That is, because the actual employment losses in 1975 were smaller in industries such as retail trade

9. Data from R. E. Smith, op. cit.

Table 16.3 Impact of a shift in industrial structure of female employment (annual averages, in thousands)

Industry	(1) Total employment[a] 1974	(2) Total employment[b] 1975	(3) Female employment[a] 1974	(4) Female employment[b] 1975	(5) Hypothetical total employment[c] 1975	(6) Hypothetical female employment[a] 1975
Agriculture	3,492	3,381	592	579	3,445	589
Mining	655	732	61	70	646	62
Construction	5,454	5,015	323	311	5,381	334
Manufacturing, durables	12,523	11,441	2,800	2,479	12,355	2,681
Manufacturing, nondurables	8,356	7,834	3,225	3,031	8,244	3,190
Transportation, public utilities	5,716	5,623	1,203	1,231	5,639	1,235
Wholesale trade	3,323	3,333	753	760	3,278	747
Retail trade	13,930	14,137	6,726	6,844	13,743	6,652
Finance, insurance, real estate	4,697	4,665	2,431	2,396	4,634	2,382
Private household services	1,430	1,378	1,261	1,213	1,411	1,242
Other services	21,706	22,477	12,663	13,162	21,415	12,549
Public administration	4,654	4,770	1,379	1,477	4,592	1,423
Total	85,936	84,786	33,417	33,553	84,783	33,086

Notes: (a) G. P. Green, 'Publication of Industry Employment Estimates from the Current Population Survey,' Employment and Earnings, Vol. 22 (February 1976), p. 18.

(b) Ibid., p. 19.

(c) See text for calculation method. Hypothetical total employment should equal actual total employment, except for rounding error.

(d) See text for calculation method.

Source: R. E. Smith, op. cit.

and services in which women were concentrated, they lost 500,000 fewer jobs and men lost 500,000 more jobs. A similar analysis using changes in employment between 1973 and 1975 produced similar results.

The sectoral analysis indicates that the employment of women in the United States was less adversely affected by the recession than men's because women happened to be in the least cyclically sensitive sectors. Examination of women's share of employment within each sector suggests that there was very little change in their representation within most sectors. An exception was the durable goods manufacturing sector where their employment share fell from 22.4 per cent to 21.7 per cent (about 100,000 jobs). Because women in this sector are less likely to have been employed at the same job for as many years as men, they are probably more likely to be laid off as a result of the operation of seniority rules.

Overall, the analysis of the impact of the recession on working women in the United States indicates that the effect on women was largely to slow down their rate of employment increase. However, women were somewhat sheltered from the full effect of the recession because of their low representation in the industrial sector where the recession hit hardest.

b) Trends and distribution of employment for selected OECD countries

Data on the broad distribution of employment by sector were collected for the period of 'low' unemployment at the outset of the recession and the 'high' period during the recession. These data, presented in Table 16.4, permit a comparative review of some issues which are of importance in assessing the labour market experience of women during the recession.

In most countries there has been a substantial increase in the labour force participation of women. Since a high proportion of the new entrants into employment have been women, there would be more women than men with shorter length of service and it is expected that women would be a significant group among workers who lost their jobs during the economic downturn. Although macro data presented in Table 16.4 do not permit this 'last in, first out' hypothesis to be tested in a rigorous manner, the available data do provide an insight into the issue. It is quite clear that, in the service sector, employment for women expanded during the recession in all countries except Germany. In addition, in all countries except Finland, France and Japan, employment in the service sector expanded more rapidly for women than for men. Consequently, while some women *may* have lost their jobs in the service sector due to the 'last in, first out' practice, in most countries the growth of employment was strong enough substantially to overcome any disadvantage that women as a group may have experienced because of shorter average length of service than men.

The employment situation for women in the industry sector (manufacturing and construction) in almost all countries deteriorated substantially during the recession. Employment for men in this sector also declined but in most countries the decline in female employment was proportionately greater than for men. In Australia and Japan the drop in female employment was almost 10 per cent and in the United States it was 8 per cent. There were a few exceptions to this general pattern. In Germany the decline for males in industry was proportionately slightly larger than for women. In Italy and Norway employment for women in industry actually expanded during the recession and women had a more favourable industrial employment experience than men. In both these latter exceptions to the typical pattern, however, women account for a very small proportion of the total employment in industry compared to other countries. In addition, in these countries women may have fared much better since aggregate industrial employment did not appear to be seriously affected by the recession.

These findings, along with the fact that the trend in labour force participation rate has been rising in most countries, suggest that in the industrial sector in most countries women may have been more adversely affected than men because of their shorter length of service. The 'last in, first out' practice may therefore in this instance have been operating to the disadvantage of women.

The results presented in Table 16.4 also show the very high concentration of women in the service sector. In more than half the countries, over 70 per cent of female employment was in services. Clearly, as has already been demonstrated, this was an important factor in protecting women from the worst effects of the recession. It is, however, not possible to generalize about the precise relationship between relative changes in unemployment rates, employment and labour force participation rates, and the degree of female concentration in service employment. Nevertheless, the aggregate data on sectoral distribution of employment provide some indication of the impact of service employment on these indicators of women's labour market experience.

In most countries the labour force participation rate of women con-

Table 16.4 Employment by sector[1] and sex in recent periods of high and low unemployment, 13 OECD countries (thousands)

Country	Agriculture			Industry			Services and other activities			Employment in services and other activities as % of total employment (low period)
	Low	High	% change	Low	High	% change	Low	High	% change	
Australia (May '74 – May '75)										
Men	327	318	−2.8	1,642	1,585	−3.5	1,836	1,868	1.7	48.3
Women	61	63	3.3	403	363	−9.9	1,481	1,513	2.2	76.1
Austria[2] (July '74 – July '75)										
Men	33	32	−3.7	917	891	−2.8	707	722	2.1	42.7
Women	17	16	−7.3	367	350	−4.7	646	675	4.5	62.7
Canada (74:3 – 75:3)										
Men	561	561	0.0	2,449	2,403	−1.9	3,276	3,343	2.0	52.1
Women	105	117	11.4	575	537	−6.6	2,566	2,711	5.7	79.0
Denmark (Nov. '73 – Oct. '74)										
Men	167	166	−0.6	666	655	−0.2	631	643	1.9	43.4
Women	65	62	−3.1	199	192	−3.5	728	761	4.5	73.4

[1] 'Agriculture' includes hunting, forestry, and fishing, and agriculture. 'Industry' includes mining and quarrying, manufacturing, electricity, gas and water, and construction. 'Services and Other Activities' include trade, restaurants and hotels, transportation and communication, finance, insurance and real estate, community, social and personal services, and activities not adequately defined.
[2] Salaried employees and wage earners only. Excludes self-employed and unpaid family workers.

Table 16.4 (continued)

Finland (Sept. '74 – Sept. '75)										
Men	217	185	−14.7	592	582	−1.7	434	452	4.1	34.9
Women	165	150	−9.1	241	235	−2.5	660	680	3.0	61.9
France[3] (March '74 – April '75)										
Men	1,348	1,332	−1.2	6,055	6,147	1.5	5,455	5,637	3.3	42.4
Women	755	685	−9.3	2,047	2,022	1.2	5,100	5,238	2.7	64.5
Germany (73:4 – 74:4)										
Men	904	868	−4.0	9,439	8,937	−5.3	6,127	6,081	−0.8	37.2
Women	1,032	990	−4.1	3,261	3,150	−3.4	5,443	5,382	−1.1	55.9
Italy (April '74 – April '75)										
Men	2,147	1,994	−7.1	6,543	6,572	0.4	4,945	5,019	1.5	35.4
Women	974	949	−2.6	1,646	1,664	1.1	2,507	2,571	2.6	48.9
Japan (73:4 – 74:2 74:4 – 75:2)										
Men	3,327	3,263	−1.9	13,434	13,250	−1.4	15,473	15,633	1.0	48.0
Women	3,258	3,199	−1.8	6,037	5,491	−9.0	10,589	10,635	0.4	53.3
New Zealand (April '74 – April '75)										
Men	125.0	125.7	0.6	326.0	327.3	0.4	372.6	378.0	1.4	45.2
Women	15.8	15.8	0.0	83.7	81.9	−2.2	256.6	264.9	3.2	72.1

[3] Data for France in this table exclude the 'marginally active'.

Table 16.4 (continued)

Country	Agriculture			Industry			Services and other activities			Employment in services and other activities as % of total employment (low period)
	Low	High	% change	Low	High	% change	Low	High	% change	
Norway (Nov. '74 – Nov. '75)										
Men	121	121	0.0	480	471	−1.9	456	458	0.4	43.1
Women	44	42	−4.5	96	105	−9.4	486	502	3.3	77.6
United Kingdom (March '74 – March '75)										
Men	569	549	−3.5	7,853	7,725	−1.6	6,802	6,806	0.1	44.7
Women	142	117	−17.6	2,595	2,514	−3.1	6,634	6,822	2.8	70.8
United States (1974–1975)										
Men	2,900	2,802	−3.3	20,579	19,131	−7.0	29,040	29,300	0.9	55.0
Women	592	579	−2.2	6,409	5,891	−8.1	26,416	27,083	2.5	79.0

Source: Country reports and *Labour Force Statistics*, OECD.

tinued to rise while the rate for men either remained stable or declined slightly. There is no doubt that this result reflects the impact of a long-term structural change in the supply of labour. At the same time, however, the data clearly show that for those countries where the female rate increased there was also over this short period a shift in the demand for labour to the sector in which women were highly concentrated. Consequently, despite the recession, this demand was strong enough to continue to pull new female entrants into the labour market, though perhaps at a reduced rate. The female participation rate in Japan was opposite from the majority of countries and the demand pull conclusion is not as relevant. The rate fell by about 4 per cent despite a small rise in service employment but only a little over half the female labour force is employed in services. Clearly, the demand pull in the service sector was not strong enough to offset the decline in the labour demand in agriculture and especially in the industry sector.

Changes in the male/female employment also appear to be affected by the male/female sectoral composition of employment. As previously discussed, for the vast majority of countries the employment situation for women was less adversely affected than for men. In most cases these countries had a high proportion of women workers in services. In France and Japan, however, women's employment was more adversely affected than the male employment situation. In Japan, women did not have the protection generally offered by the service sector. In France, a high proportion (65 per cent) of women workers are in services and employment in this sector expanded, but there was a substantial decline in female employment in agriculture and industry.

The importance of the service sector to the employment situation of women in 13 OECD countries is shown in Table 16.5. Utilizing the same approach as was used in the more detailed analysis of the United States, an estimate was made of what the male/female change in employment would have been if the recession had affected the three major sectors (Agriculture, Industry and Services) equally.

In Table 16.5, columns (1) and (2) provide a rough measure of the pre-recession trend rate of the growth in employment. In most of the countries studied employment among women had been growing substantially faster than for men. This labour market phenomenon is attributable to a number of factors including structural changes in the supply of labour and changing distribution of the sectoral demand for labour. The strength of this long-term trend was likely to carry over into the relatively short period of the recession. It is therefore not sur-

Table 16.5 Comparison of the trend growth with the actual and hypothetical (sector adjusted) change in employment during the recent economic downturn: 13 OECD countries

Country	Average annual rate of increase in employment (1970–74)		Actual (annualized) rate of change in employment during recession[1]		Hypothetical annual rate of change in employment during recession assuming all sectors equivalently affected[1]	
	Male	Female	Male	Female	Male	Female
Australia	1.3	3.5	−0.9	3.6	0.9	2.6
Austria	2.1	3.7	−0.7	1.1	−0.2	0.2
Canada	3.0	5.4	0.3	3.6	0.9	2.6
Denmark	(1.0)[2]		0.7	2.3	1.2	1.5
Finland	0.5	2.1	−1.9	−0.1	−1.2	−0.9
France	0.3	1.9	2.0	0.5	2.2	0.2
Germany	0.0	1.0	−3.6	−2.2	−3.3	−2.7
Italy	0.0	1.0	−0.4	1.1	−0.4	1.2
Japan	1.1	0.0	−0.3	−2.8	−0.1	−3.1
New Zealand	2.5	3.0	0.9	1.8	1.1	1.4
Norway	0.5	6.9	−0.7	3.7	−0.4	3.2
United Kingdom	−0.4	1.8	−0.9	0.9	−0.5	0.2
United States	1.8	3.0	−2.4	0.4	−1.6	−0.9

1. For recession dates see Table 16.4.

2. Employment increase for men and women together.

Note: Hypothetical employment in the high unemployment period was estimated by a) taking the actual aggregate rate of change in all sectors (for men and women together), b) multiplying the individual pre-recession industry totals (men and women together) by that rate, and c) multiplying the individual sector totals derived for the high period by women's actual proportion of employment in that sector.

Source: Cols. 1 and 2 – *Labour Force Statistics*, OECD and country reports.
Cols. 3–6 – Derived from data in Table 16.4.

prising that during the recession in all countries (except Japan and France) women's employment increased faster (or declined less) than men's, as indicated in a comparison of columns (3) and (4).

An additional result of the findings presented in Table 16.5 is that for most countries women do not appear to have fallen away from their pre-recessionary growth in employment as did men. As has been clearly suggested this is in most countries in part attributable to the demand pull for labour in the service sector. The importance of the relative strength of the service sector compared with other sectors and the concentration of women in services is also shown in Table 16.5. Columns (5) and (6) show what the change in employment during the recession would have been if each sector had experienced the same rate of growth (or decline) as the rate for all sectors. Thus, in the calculation of this hypothetical employment change from the low to the high unemployment period, services would be given the same rate of growth as industry and agriculture. In this hypothetical situation, it is estimated that male employment in all countries would not have declined as much (or would have grown faster) than it actually did over the cycle. But female employment in all countries would have declined more (or have grown more slowly). Thus, the fact that the recession was not evenly spread over all sectors but hit industry disproportionately had particularly adverse effects on male employment, since men are more likely to work in industry. On the other hand, female employment was relatively less affected because women are less likely to work in industry and because of the relative strength of demand in the service sector.

IV. Conclusions and implications

Most of the analysis in this report has focused on the recession's impact on employment, unemployment and labour force participation. The full effects of the recession are likely to reach well beyond these statistics. Those who remained employed throughout the recession (as well as those who were employed discontinuously) may have experienced lower wage rate increases than would have been the case in a period of prosperity. Hours worked per week may have been involuntarily reduced. Opportunities for job changes also may have been restricted. These effects are potentially important although lack of data prevented any exploration of these issues.

In overall terms the study shows that women workers were affected differently than male workers. Women, because of their disproportionate concentration in the service sector were insulated from the harshest effects of the recession which had its greatest impact in the industrial sector. However, those women who did hold industrial jobs experienced greater employment losses than men.

The effect of the recession on the employment of women has therefore been to slow down the growth of their employment in those industries in which they have been traditionally under-represented. To the extent that jobs in these industries have higher wage structures and represent the areas of employment which women have recently sought to penetrate, the recession has restricted the opportunities for women. Data limitations make it difficult to explain why employment for women declined more than for men. It is possible that the high concentration of women in sectors of 'industry' which are highly sensitive to the business cycle and the 'last in, first out' practice may have both operated to the disadvantage of women. This experience, especially when compared to their relatively favourable experience in the service sector, raises the possibility that the recession may have reduced the incentive for women to enter the industrial sector.

It is, of course, difficult to speculate about the future sectoral distribution of employment for women. In many OECD countries the goal of public policy, even if sometimes only implicitly stated, is to improve the opportunities for women to work in all parts of the occupational structure. There are obviously many occupations in which the sex of the worker is related to the performance of the job and men and women will have different occupational preferences. Nevertheless, the existence of some form of equal employment opportunity policy in many countries, along with the differential structures of wages among industries, is likely eventually to encourage the participation of women in some of the industries in which they have traditionally been underrepresented. If this occurs then the effect of the recent recession in the employment of women in industry will prove to have been a short-run phenomenon.

During the past 20 years, women in OECD countries have been making the major occupational change from work in the home to work in the labour market. An effect of the recession has been to slow down their labour force growth. Nevertheless, in those sectors of the economy where the demand for labour remained strong, employment of women actually expanded. The aggregate data presented in this study demonstrated that the female rate of participation is still rising and it is therefore expected that, as the economies of the OECD countries begin to expand during the post-recessionary period, there will be a renewed surge of women into the labour market. This prediction of a continued increase in participation rates is also justified by the changing structure of labour supply in some countries.

The structural characteristics of demand during the post-recessionary period will also affect the rate of future labour force growth of women. If, as appears to be the case in some countries, there is a major shift in the structure of demand towards more services this will result in an autonomous expansion of employment opportunities for women.

The prediction of a continued increase in women's labour force participation is probably also supported by the changing structure of labour supply in some countries. The tendency towards smaller families and the growing acceptance of working wives are factors which will contribute to the continuing increase in the participation of married women. In some countries there has been an increasing number of single-parent families headed by women who have very high levels of labour force participation rates. If this trend continues it will affect the structure of labour supply. In addition, in many countries there are a great number of social and labour market governmental policies which will influence women's participation in the labour market. Government policy in the area of child care and early education, access to educational and training opportunities and the implementation of equal employment opportunity policy will in time change the labour market behaviour of women. The expected future upward trend in the supply of female labour will therefore be a dominant influence on the structural labour market situation in many countries in the years ahead.

17 Wives' Labor Force Behavior and Family Consumption Patterns *

Myra H. Strober*
Director, Center for Research on Women, Stanford University

From: *American Economic Review*, Vol. 67, No. 1, February 1977, pp. 410–17.

In 1940 the labor force participation rate for married women, husband present, was 14 percent. By 1970 it had increased 26 percentage points to 40 percent. The supply and demand variables associated with this increase have been widely investigated. However, there has been very little research on the economic *effects* of wives' labor force participation. (See R. Agarwala and J. Drinkwater, Margaret Carroll, Robert Holbrook and Frank Stafford, Lucy Mallan and Jacob Mincer.) This paper analyzes two economic effects: the effect on the ratio of consumption to income (C/Y) and the effect on the ratio of durable goods purchases to income (Dur/Y). The primary question addressed is: Controlling for total family income and several other variables, what are the differences (if any) in the ratios of C/Y and Dur/Y for working-wife $(W\text{-}W)$ and nonworking wife $(N\text{-}W\text{-}W)$ families? Looked at in another way, the question may be rephrased: How do $W\text{-}W$ families use wives' income?

I. A theoretical framework and two hypotheses

Although based on quite different assumptions and paradigms, the two theories extant in the literature which deal with the relationship between wives' labor force behavior and family consumption patterns both postulate that, total family income held constant, the C/Y ratio will be lower in $W\text{-}W$ than in $N\text{-}W\text{-}W$ families. John Kenneth Galbraith's conclusion flows from combining the observation that family

* The research on which this paper is based was supported in part by the Stanford University Research and Development Fund and in part by a grant from the E. I. du Pont de Nemours Co. to the Stanford Graduate School of Business. I wish to thank Alice Amsden, Michael Cummins, William Dunkelberg, Robert Flanagan, Martin Rein, Robert Michael, Frank Stafford, Charlotte Stiglitz and Robert Willis for helpful discussions and Lynn Rosener for research assistance.

consumption requires highly labor-intensive consumption administration with the suggestion that working wives have less time for (and possibly less interest in) such administration. Jacob Mincer's deduction, on the other hand, is reached by incorporating into Milton Friedman's permanent income theory the assumption that wives' earnings have a large transitory component.

While Galbraith and Mincer reach the same conclusion with respect to the C/Y ratio, they propose opposite hypotheses with respect to the Dur/Y ratio. Galbraith posits a lower Dur/Y ratio for W-W, as compared with N-W-W families. However, since Mincer regards the purchase of durables as a form of saving, he hypothesizes that, holding total family income constant, the Dur/Y ratio will be higher for W-W families.

Neither of these theories is sufficient to fully explain relationships between wives' labor force behavior and family consumption patterns. Galbraith's theory ignores the important fact that some durables can save time and effort even after consumption administration requirements are accounted for. Mincer's thesis, because it relies on the assumption that families treat wives' earnings as transitory income, also seems somewhat narrow. It appears to me that the following theoretical framework, which builds upon the work of James Duesenberry, provides a more useful approach to explaining the relationship between wives' labor force behavior and family consumption.

For most wives, the economic motivation to work is closely associated with husbands' earnings. Most families have a life-cycle reference group with whom they compare themselves. This reference group tends to be similar in age, education level, geographic region, etc. When a N-W-W family finds a gap between its income and consumption levels and those of its reference group, the wife in that family is likely to work some number of hours so that, at the relevant wage rate, sufficient income to close the income-consumption gap is obtained.

In families where wives have very low market wage rates, wives' labor supply may not be forthcoming even though there exists an income-consumption gap with respect to life-cycle reference groups. In such situations, the effort required by the wife to eliminate or significantly reduce the gap is deemed too arduous and/or not worthwhile in terms of lost home production. On the other side of the income distribution, among wives with high levels of education and hence relatively high earning ability and 'tastes' for work, the level of husbands' earnings or the concept of an income-consumption gap may play only a minor role in determining labor supply. However, for the vast majority of families, wives work in order to raise their family incomes to those of their life-cycle reference group.

In an effort to become like their friends and neighbors, W-W families by and large plan to use wives' incomes to purchase durables, non-durables and services and to save in approximately the same propor-tions as N-W-W families with the same total income. However, once the wife is in the workforce, W-W families find that although they may have the same aggregate income as their N-W-W family counterparts, they are in fact quite different in several respects from these other families. These differences cause W-W families to have a higher C/Y ratio than N-W-W families, but to maintain parity with respect to the Dur/Y ratio.

What are the key differences between W-W and N-W-W families? First, and foremost, because W-Ws perform considerable amounts of housework in addition to their market work, their total work week, market plus nonmarket work, is significantly longer than that of N-W-Ws (about 11 hours longer for women employed full-time. See Joann Vanek [Reading 3 in this collection]). Thus, for a given vector of prices facing consumers, W-Ws should find it more profitable to sub-stitute time-saving (and probably also fatigue-saving) goods and services for home production. However, most families already own such time-saving durables as refrigerators and stoves and many also own washers, dryers and dishwashers. Moreover, time and effort-saving durables purchases, while expensive, tend to be nonrecurring. Thus, although initial labor force participation by wives may be associated with an increase in the Dur/ratios, after wives have been at work for a few years, most of the substitution out of home-production is likely to be into time-saving non-durables (e.g., convenience foods) and services (laundries, restaurants, etc.).

The second major difference between W-W and N-W-W families is that W-Ws incur work-related expenses (transportation, clothing, child-care, etc.). Thus, total work related expenditure, and, therefore, total consumption, is likely to be greater in W-W than in N-W-W families with comparable incomes.

The final difference between the two types of families concerns the motivation to save. Having a working wife may well diminish a family's motive to save as a hedge against husband's job loss. Each earner tends to lessen the need for reliance on savings should the other become un-employed or disabled. Moreover, if a working wife is covered by a pension plan, which is in part employer financed, the family's motive to save for retirement may also be lessened. The strength of the relationship between wife's employment and reduction in family motivation to save is likely to be a positive function of the proportion of total family income earned by the wife.

In summary, the theory proposed here leads to the following two hypotheses: total family income held constant, (1) the C/Y ratio will be higher in W-W families than in N-W-W families but (2) the Dur/Y ratio will not differ across the two types of families.

2. Data and models

The data for this study are panel data from the Michigan Survey Research Center 1967–70 Survey of Consumer Finances. I concentrate here on the data for 1968 for families with husbands between the ages of 25 and 64. In order to test more accurately the two hypotheses, the sample excludes non-husband-wife households; farmers and farm managers; families where the husband was retired, permanently disabled, or a student and families who received inheritances in 1968.

Total consumption (C) was not directly measured in the survey; it is derived, as noted in equation (1), by adding to 1968 total family income (Y) the change in debt from 1967 to 1968 and then subtracting the change in savings (S) from 1967 to 1968 as well as 80 percent of expenditures on mortgages ($Mortg$), net outlay on durables (Dur) and net outlay on automobiles ($Cars$). Durables are defined as furniture, refrigerators, washing machines, stoves, television sets, household appliances and air conditioners.[1]

$$C_{68} = Y_{68} + (Debt_{68} - Debt_{67}) \qquad (1)$$
$$- (S_{68} - S_{67}) - 0.8(Mortg_{68}$$
$$+ Dur_{68} + Cars_{68})$$

Consumption is hypothesized to be a function of current family income (Y), human and nonhuman wealth, life-cycle stage, expectations about future income, and wife's labor force behavior. Net assets ($NASTS$), assets minus debt, measures nonhuman wealth, where assets

1. Total family income (Y) excludes both realized and nonrealized capital gains. Debt is defined as the sum of mortgage debt, installment debt, amount owed on stocks and real estate and miscellaneous debt. Savings is defined as the sum of amounts in checking and savings accounts, certificates of deposit, and the value of stocks, bonds and real estate. Expenditures on mortgages ($Mortg$) is the annual mortgage payment. Net outlay on durables (Dur) and net outlay on automobiles ($Cars$) are exclusive of finance charges and are defined as the price of durables (or autos) minus the value of any trade-in.

equal total savings in 1968 plus the undepreciated value of cars and durables in 1968. A variable created by adding husband's and wife's levels of education (HWEDUC) measures both taste for current vs. future consumption and human wealth. For each spouse the variable is scaled as follows: $1 = 0$–5 grades; $2 = 6$–8 grades; $3 = 9$–11 grades; $4 = 12$ grades; $5 = 12$ grades plus other noncollege training; $6 =$ some college, no degree; $7 =$ college, Bachelor's degree; $8 =$ college, advanced or professional degree. Thus, HWEDUC ranges from 2–16. Life-cycle stage is measured by three dummy variables (H35–44, H45–54, and H55–64), each taking on a value of 1 if the husband is respectively 35–44, 45–54, or 55–64. Expectations about future income is measured by a dummy (EXHIEARNS) which takes on a value of 1 if the husband is less than 45 and in a professional or managerial occupation. Thus, the basic consumption regression equation is:

$$C = a + b_1 Y + b_2 NASTS + b_3 HWEDUC$$
$$+ b_4 H35 - 44 + b_5 H45 - 54$$
$$+ b_6 H55 - 64 + b_7 EXHIEARNS \qquad (2)$$

where b_1, b_2, and b_7 are expected to be positive, b_3, b_4, b_5 and b_6 to be negative.

The significance of wife's labor force behavior on consumption is measured in four ways. First, I add to (2) a dummy (WDIN68) which is equal to 1 if the wife worked at least one hour during 1968. If this dummy is positive and significant and does not change the coefficient on Y, then I conclude that, cet. par., W-W families have a higher C/Y ratio than N-W-W families. A second test is performed by substituting the continuous variable, hours worked in 1968 (HRSYR), for WDIN68 and applying the same test to that variable. It is important that b_1 not change when WDIN68 or HRSYR are entered in order to be somewhat assured of the lack of collinearity between either of these variables and Y. (The correlation between Y and WDIN68 is 0.006; between Y and HRSYR, 0.08.)

The third and fourth methods of testing the significance of wife's labor force behavior on consumption are quite similar. The third method consists of substituting two separate income variables for Y in equation (2), one equal to $Y \times WWF$ and one equal to $Y \times NWWF$, where WWF is equal to 1 if the wife worked in 1968 and NWWF is equal to 1 if the wife did not work in 1968. The regression using these two income variables is then compared with (2) by means of a Chow test and the resultant F is tested for significance. Test four involves substituting three variables for Y in equation (2): wife's earnings (Y_W); total family income minus wife's earnings, called other family income (Y_{OF}); and an interaction term ($Y_W \times Y_{OF}$). The regression using these three income variables is then again compared with (2) by means of a Chow test and examined for significance.

The regression with net outlay on durables as the dependent variable contains the seven independent variables in the consumption regression plus one additional variable. On the assumption that a recent change of residence is highly positively related to the purchase of durables, I create a dummy, $MOVHSREC$ which is equal to 1 if the family moved into a different apartment or home in 1967 or 1968. Precisely the same four procedures as those described above are applied to test the significance of wife's labor force behavior on net outlay on durables.

An alternative two-stage specification of the consumption and durables regression was also attempted. However, in the stage-one regression estimating wife's hours worked, the R^2 was so low (0.06) that the attempt was abandoned.

3. Results

(a) t-tests

Table 17.1 presents data for 433 W-W and 379 N-W-W families with husbands 25–64 and for four life-cycle subgroups, based on husband's age. Student t-tests are employed to test the significance of differences in means between W-W and N-W-W families. The most striking aspect of the table is that, while in the aggregate and for each life-cycle group, the means of other family income (Y_{OF}) are significantly higher for N-W-W families, the means of total family income (Y) and also of disposable family income (Y_D) are the same for the two family groups. (Y_D was not directly measured by the Michigan Survey, but was estimated for each family by the Center staff.) As hypothesized, wives' earnings tend, on the average, to equalize the incomes of W-W and $N.W.W.$ families.[2]

The second interesting finding is that the means of the variables C/Y

2. If reference groups are defined by husbands' education level rather than husbands' age, the hypothesis that wives' earnings equalize family income within a reference group is substantiated only for middle and higher education groups (where husbands' education is $\geq$ twelve years). In the reference group where husbands have less than twelve years of schooling, there is a significant difference in mean total family income but no significant difference in other family income. Thus, for this education group wives' earnings improve rather than equalize family income.

Table 17.1 Variable means for *W-W* and *N-W-W* Families

	I H25-34 W-W (N = 122)	I H25-34 N-W-W (N = 103)	II H35-44 W-W (N = 136)	II H35-44 N-W-W (N = 102)	III H45-54 W-W (N = 125)	III H45-54 N-W-W (N = 117)	IV H55-64 W-W (N = 50)	IV H55-64 N-W-W (N = 57)	Total H25-64 W-W (N = 433)	Total H25-64 N-W-W (N = 379)
Other Family Income (Y_{OF}) (total income less wives' earnings)	$8,236 (330)[a]	10,328* (540)	10,611 (453)	13,064* (882)	10,333 (692)	14,344* (962)	8,556 (624)	11,802* (1,090)	9,624 (276)	12,527* (445)
Total family income (Y)	$10,581 (365)	10,328 (540)	13,603 (510)	13,064 (882)	13,873 (879)	14,344 (962)	11,927 (744)	11,802 (1,090)	12,636 (335)	12,527 (445)
Disposable income (Y_D)	$9,401 (296)	9,191 (427)	11,854 (402)	11,339 (623)	11,888 (593)	12,220 (709)	10,307 (602)	10,106 (830)	10,994 (244)	10,842 (329)
Consumption/income (C/Y)[b]	0.72 (0.047)	0.56 (0.145)	0.81 (0.074)	0.45** (0.148)	0.73 (0.068)	0.64 (0.115)	0.89 (0.083)	0.77 (0.279)	0.77 (0.035)	0.59** (0.078)
Consumption/disposable income (C/Y_D)[e]	0.69 (0.053)	0.51 (0.158)	0.79 (0.085)	0.41** (0.154)	0.69 (0.079)	0.60 (0.138)	0.87 (0.095)	0.73 (0.322)	0.74 (0.039)	0.54** (0.088)
Durables/disposable income (Dur/Y_D)	0.0382 (0.005)	0.0332 (0.003)	0.0309 (0.004)	0.0240 (0.003)	0.0202 (0.003)	0.0226 (0.003)	0.0205 (0.005)	0.0124 (0.003)	0.0287 (0.002)	0.0243 (0.002)
Durables/disposable income (Dur/Y_D); $Dur > 0$[d]	0.0598 (0.006)	0.0496 (0.004)	0.0489 (0.005)	0.0437 (0.004)	0.0382 (0.004)	0.0433 (0.004)	0.0411 (0.007)	0.0371 (0.005)	0.0487 (0.003)	0.0449 (0.002)
Net assets	$8,196 (627)	10,026 (1,222)	18,878 (2,392)	23,567 (2,945)	19,214 (1,821)	37,595* (7,224)	25,501 (3,402)	41,796 (9,133)	16,730 (1,046)	26,959* (2,816)

Debt	$9,321	9,565	13,128	11,370	7,882	10,088	5,816	2,570	9,697	9,160
	(810)	(898)	(1,749)	(1,675)	(922)	(2,074)	(1,410)	(687)	(681)	(836)
Number of cars	1.42	1.22*	1.55	1.46	1.63	1.52	1.52	1.35	1.533	1.398*
	(0.053)	(0.058)	(0.057)	(0.065)	(0.069)	(0.073)	(0.071)	(0.099)	(0.032)	(0.036)
Net outlay on cars/disposable income (Car/Y)	0.0741	0.0635	0.0621	0.0705	0.0770	0.0617	0.0536	0.0838	0.0688	0.0679
	(0.011)	(0.011)	(0.009)	(0.011)	(0.010)	(0.010)	(0.013)	(0.018)	(0.005)	(0.006)
Vacation/disposable income (V/Y_D)	0.0118	0.0122	0.0149	0.0083	0.0137	0.018	0.0152	0.0154	0.0137	0.0161
	(0.002)	(0.002)	(0.002)	(0.004)	(0.002)	(0.003)	(0.003)	(0.003)	(0.001)	(0.002)
Hobby and recreation items/ disposable income $(H\&R/Y_D)$	0.0048	0.0083	0.0135	0.0096	0.0089	0.0064	0.0040	0.0053	0.0086	0.0076
	(0.001)	(0.002)	(0.006)	(0.003)	(0.003)	(0.002)	(0.002)	(0.003)	(0.002)	(0.001)
Expenditures on college education/ disposable income $(Educ/Y_D)$; $Educ > 0$	—	—	—	—	—	—	—	—	0.1372e	0.1299
									(0.013)	(0.013)

* Indicates difference in means is significant at the 1% level.

** Indicates difference in means is significant at the 5% level.

a Numbers in parentheses are standard errors of the means.

b Mean consumption/income is not the average propensity to consume (APC). $APC = C/\bar{Y}$. Mean consumption/income = $\dfrac{\sum_{i=1}^{n} C/Y}{N}$

c Consumption here is $= C' = Y_D + \Delta Debt - (\Delta S + \Delta Debt - (Mortg + Dur + Cars))$.

d The sample sizes for this variable are as follows: I W-W = 78; I N-W-W = 69; II W-W = 86, II N-W-W = 56; III W-W = 66, III N-W-W = 61; IV W-W = 25, IV N-W-W = 19; Total W-W = 255; Total N-W-W = 205.

e $N = 54$.

f $N = 33$.

Table 17.2 Coefficients for independent

Consumption[b]

Regression	Sample size	$\bar{R}^2$	a (constant)	b_1 (Y)	b_2 (NASTS)	b_3 (HWEDUC)	b_4 (H35–44)	b_5 (H45–54)	b_6 (H55–64)
A	808	0.148	6,515.94	0.437* (0.109)	0.148* (0.019)	−725.71* (263.27)	−1,034.99 (1,765.01)	−1,206.84 (1,854.64)	−2,565.18 (2,282.58)
B	802	0.154	4,811.76	0.409* (0.110)	0.156* (0.020)	−744.86* (264.81)	−1,176.08 (1,768.88)	−1,062.94 (1,858.20)	−2,274.24 (2,296.51)
C	795	0.179	6,143.18	0.431* (0.107)	0.162* (0.019)	−857.61* (255.20)	−1,414.56 (1,715.37)	−813.51 (1,797.29)	−2,996.34 (2,210.06)
D	802	0.162	6,668.68	—	0.169* (0.020)	−763.14* (263.58)	−1,425.84 (1,762.32)	−1,233.47 (1,858.21)	−2,555.53 (2,283.95)
E	808	0.165	7,905.14	—	0.174* (0.020)	−730.04* (261.83)	−1,131.32 (1,751.53)	−1,262.90 (1,838.02)	−2,953.11 (2,262.73)

Net outlay on

Regression	Sample size	$\bar{R}^2$	a (constant)	b_1 (Y)	b_2 (NASTS)	b_3 (HWEDUC)	b_4 (H35–44)	b_5 (H45–54)	b_6 (H55–64)
A'	886	0.159	80.24	0.01336* (0.00019)	−0.00007 (0.00018)	6.26 (5.24)	−15.75 (35.63)	−99.37* (36.88)	−122.62* (44.90)
B'	880	0.159	69.10	0.01328* (0.00201)	−0.00005 (0.00018)	6.15 (5.29)	−18.33 (35.82)	−97.89* (37.11)	−120.67* (45.33)
C'	871	0.164	65.49	0.01314* (0.00201)	−0.00004 (0.00018)	6.99 (5.27)	−14.20 (37.89)	−102.46* (37.09)	−119.91* (45.17)
D'	880	0.159	79.81	—	−0.00004 (0.00018)	6.04 (5.29)	−19.19 (35.82)	−98.26* (37.06)	−121.04* (45.28)
E'	886	0.162	81.31	—	−0.00002 (0.00018)	5.70 (5.24	−17.96 (35.60)	−99.70* (36.84)	−125.06* (44.86)

*Indicates significances at 1 percent level.
**At 5 percent level.
a Numbers in parentheses are standard errors.

and C'/Y_D (where, in calculating C', Y_D replaces Y in (1)) are higher in W-W than in N-W-W families in every life-cycle group. In the aggregate and for the group 35–44 this difference in means is significant at the 5 percent level. The means of the variables Dur/Y_D and Dur/Y_D where $Dur > 0$ are, on the other hand, not significantly different either in the aggregate or in any of the life-cycle groups.

Several other differences and non-differences between the two sets of families are also noteworthy. N-W-W families have significantly greater mean net assets than W-W families, while W-W families have more cars and spend more on cars. On the other hand, between W-W and N-W-W

Regressions

b_7 (EXHIEARNS)	WDIN68	HRSYR	Y × WWF	Y × NWWF	Y_W	Y_{OF}	$Y_W × Y_{FO}$	b_8 (MOVHSREC)
3,270.29	—	—	—	—	—	—	—	
(2,033.79)								
3,784.53	3597.77*	—	—	—	—	—	—	
(2,052.38)	(1,333.67)							
4,038.47*	—	2.08*	—	—	—	—	—	
(1,976.99)		(0.778)						
3,889.18	—	—	0.582*	0.233	—	—	—	
(2,039.93)			(0.116)	(0.122)				
4,002.55**	—	—	—	—	0.795**	0.160	0.00003*	
(2,020.89)					(0.362)	(0.128)	(0.00001)	
durables[c] regressions								
10.27	—	—	—	—	—	—	—	437.20*
(40.89)								(52.32)
13.79	23.57	—	—	—	—	—	—	435.80*
(41.44)	(26.55)							(52.50)
10.68	—	0.01471	—	—	—	—	—	441.99*
(41.27)		(0.01607)						(52.63)
14.22	—	—	0.01447*	0.01236*	—	—	—	436.45*
(41.37)			(0.00223)	(0.00218)				(52.47)
16.71	—	—	—	—	0.02259*	0.01229*	—	423.38*
(41.00)					(0.00552)	(0.00208)		(42.32)

[b] See (1) in text for definition of consumption.
[c] Durables are defined as furniture, refrigerators, washing machines, stoves, television sets, household appliances, and air conditioners.

families, there are virtually no differences in mean debt, the mean ratios of vacation expenditures/Y_D, hobby expenditures/Y_D, or college education expenditures/Y_D.

(b) Consumption regressions

The results for the consumption regressions are presented in the top half of Table 17.2. In regression A, b_1, the marginal propensity to consume, all else being constant, is low, 0.437, and is significant at the 1 percent level. The marginal propensity to consume (MPC) out of net assets all else constant is 0.148 and is also significant at the 1 percent level. The only other significant variable is *HWEDUC*. The mean education level for the sample is 8.5, about 12 years of education for each spouse. All else constant, an additional 'unit' of education for either spouse (units having been defined in Section II) decreases consumption by about $725. (Mean consumption was $8,787.) This may be the result of more patience on the part of more educated persons or of a difference in tastes (e.g., college education for children) which requires higher savings rates. The adjusted R^2 $(\bar{R}^2)$ for regression *A* is 0.148.

I also examined possible effects on consumption of number and age of children,[3] race, husband's unemployment, and having a large decrease or increase in income in 1968 as compared with 1967. None of these variables was significantly related to consumption or to net outlay on durables and none increased $\bar{R}^2$. Nor did adding 23 families with heads under the age of 25 significantly affect the regression coefficients. Changing the definition of consumption to include as saving 20 percent of mortgage payments, net outlay on durables and net outlay on cars (rather than 80 percent) raised the *MPC* to 0.468 but otherwise did not affect any of the regression coefficients.

In regression *B* (Table 17.2) the dummy variable, *WDIN68*, which is equal to 1 if the wife was employed in 1968, is significant at the 1 percent level and indicates that, all else constant, having a working wife in 1968 raised total consumption by $3,600. The coefficient on *Y* changes slightly, to 0.409, when the dummy is introduced. In regression *C*, the variable *HRSYR* is significant at the 1 percent level and indicates that, all else constant, an additional hour of work above the mean (659 hours) increases consumption by $2.08. The coefficient on *Y* is virtually the same as in *A*. It is not clear whether the small change in b_1 in regression *B* meets the test that coefficients not change when *WDIN68* is introduced. I am inclined to accept the significance of both the dummy and the *HRSYR* variables but to be cautious about placing credence in their size.

When regressions *D* and *E* are compared with regression *A* by means of Chow tests, the hypothesis that either *D* or *E* is the same as *A* may be rejected at the 1 percent level (for *D*, $F_{2,798} = 9.3$; for *E*, $F_{3,797} = 5.2$.)

3. In regressions substituting age-of-children dummy variables for life-cycle dummy variables, the results were quite similar to those reported in Table 17.2. Age-of-children dummies were insignificant.

(c) Durables regressions

In the durable regression A' (see bottom part of Table 17.2), $\bar{R}^2 = 0.159$. The sample sizes for the durables regressions are slightly larger than those for the consumption regressions because there were about 80 families with missing observations on the consumption variable. The most significant variable in regression A' is the dummy, $MOVHSREC$, which indicates that, all else constant, the 7 percent of all families who changed their place of residence in 1967 or 1968 spent an additional $437 on durables in 1968. The mean outlay on durables for the sample was $280. Size of income is also a significant determinant of durables expenditure; the marginal propensity to consume durables, all else constant, is 0.013. $NASTS$, $HWEDUC$, $H34$–44 and $EXHIEARNS$ are not significant. However, $H45$–54 has a significant negative coefficient of $99 and $H55$–64 a significant negative coefficient of $123. Thus, while life-cycle group does not appear to be negatively related to consumption expenditure *in toto*, it is significantly negatively related to durables expenditures.[4]

In regressions B' and C' respectively, neither $WDIN68$ nor $HRSYR$ is significant. Moreover, when regression D' and E' are compared with regression A', the Chow tests indicate that we cannot reject the null hypotheses that the two regressions are structurally the same ($F_{2,800} = 0.99$; $F_{1,800} = 1.4$). (The interaction term $Y_W \times Y_{OF}$ is excluded from E' because it was found to be insignificant.)

Durables regressions were also run for only those 489 families who made durables purchases in 1968. In these regressions, as expected, the coefficient on Y increased somewhat, to about 0.018, while the coefficient on $MOVHSREC$ fell to about $360. (Mean net outlay on durables was about $500 for these families.) The coefficients on $H45$–54 and $H55$–64 also fell and became insignificant. However, there were no changes with respect to the insignificance of wives' work on durables expenditures, once total family income was taken into account.

4. Conclusions

Wives' earnings tend, on the average, to raise W-W family incomes to the level of N-W-W family incomes in the same life-cycle group. Total

4. In regressions substituting age-of-children dummy variables for life-cycle dummy variables, none of the age-of-children dummies were significant. Nor was number of children significantly related to durables expenditures.

family income held constant, the Dur/Y ratio is the same for W-W and N-W-W families; however, the C/Y ratio is higher for W-W families. Given the increasing labor force participation (LFP) among wives, these findings have important implications for employment, price stability and economic growth. However, space constraints permit only a cursory examination of these implications.

A higher C/Y ratio for W-W families may help to create employment and/or increase pressure on prices. The effects on employment and prices depend upon exactly which goods and services are demanded and on the relative degree of tightness and monopoly and monopsony power in the relevant goods and labor markets. For example, if highly labor-intensive child care services are demanded and the labor and product markets associated with these services are rather loose and competitive, then at least in the 'first round', an increased demand for child care is likely to have substantial employment effects and few price effects. To the extent, on the other hand, that increased automobile-associated goods (e.g. gasoline) are demanded, there may be substantial price effects but few employment effects.

Possible effects on growth are even more complicated to assess. Generally, higher savings rates are associated with a more rapid rate of economic growth. However, productivity and the rate of growth of labor input (population and labor force) also affect economic growth. Before we can begin to measure the overall relationship between wives' employment and economic growth, considerable further investigation is required with respect to the effects of wives' employment on productivity and the birth rate.

References

AGARWALA, R., and DRINKWATER, J., 'Consumption Functions With Shifting Parameters Due to Socio-Economic Factors,' *Rev. Econ. Statist.*, Vol. 54, pp. 89–96, Feb. 1972.

CARROLL, M. S., 'The Working Wife and Her Family's Economic Position,' *Mon. Lab. Rev.*, Vol. 85, pp. 366–74, April 1962.

DUESENBERRY, JAMES S., *Income, Saving and the Theory of Consumer Behavior*, Cambridge, Mass., 1949.

FRIEDMAN, MILTON, *A Theory of The Consumption Function*, Princeton, 1957.

GALBRAITH, JOHN K., *Economics and The Public Purpose*, Boston, 1973.

HOLBROOK, ROBERT, and STAFFORD, FRANK, 'The Propensity To Consume Separate Types of Income: A Generalized Permanent Income Hypothesis,' *Econometrica*, Vol. 39, pp. 1–21, Jan. 1971.

MALLAN, LUCY, 'Financial Patterns in Households with Working Wives,' unpublished Ph.D. Dissertation, Northwestern University, 1968.

MINCER, JACOB, 'Employment and Consumption,' *Rev. Econ. Statist.*, Vol. 42, pp. 20–26, Feb. 1960.

MINCER, JACOB, 'Labor Supply, Family Income and Consumption,' *Amer. Econ. Rev. Proc.*, Vol. 50, pp. 574–83, May 1960.

VANEK, JOANN, 'Time Spent in Housework, see above,' p. 82.

18 The Employment of Wives and the Inequality of Family Income *

James A. Sweet

Center for Demography and Ecology, and Institute for Research on Poverty, University of Wisconsin

From: *Proceedings of the American Statistical Association, Social Statistics Section*, 1971, pp. 1–5.

In his 1960 Census Monograph, *Income Distribution in the United States*, Herman Miller reports that the incomes of families in which the wife is in the labor force are more evenly distributed than those of families in which the wife is not in the labor force.

Table 18.1

	Wife Works	Wife Does Not Work
Percent of Aggregate Money Income Received by Highest:		
5% of families	13%	19%
20% of families	37%	43%
Gini ratio	.29	.38

Miller suggests that since the proportion of wives who are working has increased considerably in recent years, the effect has been to reduce family income inequality.[1] In discussion of the income inequality within

*The research reported here was supported by funds granted to the Institute for Research on Poverty at the University of Wisconsin by the Office of Economic Opportunity pursuant to the provisions of the Economic Opportunity Act of 1964. The conclusions are the sole responsibility of the author. Certain data used in this analysis were derived by the author from a computer tape file furnished under the joint project sponsored by the U.S. Bureau of the Census and the Population Council and containing selected 1960 Census information for a 0.1 percent sample of the population of the United States. Neither the Census Bureau nor the Population Council assumes any responsibility for the validity of any of the figures or interpretations of the figures presented herein or based on this material.

1. Herman Miller, *Income Distribution in the United States*, U.S. Bureau of the Census, 1960 Census Monograph (Washington, D.C.: U.S. Government Printing Office, 1966), p. 22.

urban areas, Wilber Thompson asserts, 'The existence of jobs for women acts to reduce inequality (of family income) in that working wives come more proportionately from the lower income groups.'[2]

In this paper we will describe the effects of the employment of wives on the distribution of family income in the United States, and the possible reasons for the observed effects. We will then look at the trend in family income inequality in relation to the trend in labor force participation of wives, and finally at the effect of the employment of wives on the inequality of income between blacks and whites.

As a statement of logical necessity, Miller's argument supposes that the dispersion of two combined samples is some sort of a weighted average of their separate dispersions. Thus as more wives enter the labor force, their relative weight increases and the dispersion tends to move toward the within class dispersion of families of working wives – i.e., the dispersion tends to become less. A simple example will demonstrate that this is clearly not necessarily the case. If one combines two samples each with a different mean and zero dispersion, the dispersion of the combined sample is clearly non-zero and may be considerable depending on the difference in means.

Although Miller does not assert that the lower income inequality of families in which the wife is employed is caused by the employment of the wife, it seems to be implicit in his discussion. It is equally plausible to hypothesize that among families in which the wife is employed there is initially less inequality in husband's income, and for that reason, less inequality in family income. Comparisons of the inequality of family income by themselves tell us nothing about the effect of wife's employment on the degree of family income inequality, unless we can demonstrate that there is a comparable degree of inequality to start with before adding in wife's income.

Since the employment of wives is related to a great variety of factors including age, education, color, husband's income, type of residence, and family composition, it is difficult to determine a priori how husband's income inequality would be related to wife's employment. To the extent that the employment of wives is inversely correlated with husband's income, we would expect that husband's income inequality

2. Wilber Thompson, 'Internal and External Factors in the Development of Urban Economics,' in Harvey Perloff and Lowden Wingo, Jr., (eds.), *Issues in Urban Economics* (Baltimore: Johns Hopkins University Press, 1968). See also, Wilber Thompson, *A Preface to Urban Economics*, (Baltimore: Johns Hopkins University Press, 1965), pp. 106 ff.

would be less for working wives, simply on the basis of the systematic under-representation of families with high income husbands.

On the other hand, the association of wife's employment with the absence of young children in the family has an effect working in the opposite direction. Wives of young men are more likely to have young children, and are thus less likely to work than are wives of older men. Young men are more likely to have low incomes, and less dispersion in income because they consist disproportionately both of men in dead-end jobs and of men at the beginning of careers. As these latter men age, they will experience relatively rapid income increases, while the men in dead-end jobs will have smaller income increases. Thus dispersion in husband's income ought to be related positively to age. Data from the 1960 Census indicate that older married men have greater income dispersion than younger men (Table 18.2).

Table 18.2 **Income inequality of married men living in urbanized areas, by age (1959 income as enumerated in 1960 census)**

Age of husband	Gini coefficients	
	Total	Nonwhite
Less than 18	47.2	44.7
18 – 24	28.8	31.1
25 – 34	26.6	27.4
35 – 44	28.2	29.1
45 – 54	30.9	30.9
55 – 64	35.0	35.6
65 – 74	45.8	44.3
75 and over	53.0	47.7
Total	33.1	32.3

Source: Derived from data in 1960 United States Census, 'Persons by Family Characteristics,' Subject Report PC(2) 4B, Table 10b.

In Table 18.3 we present Gini coefficients computed on each of three income measures: family income, husband's income, and family income minus wife's earnings. Our sample consists of 32,521 nonfarm married couples in which the wife is under the age of 60. It was drawn from the 1/1000 sample of the 1960 United States Census. Data are shown separately by color, and by presence or absence of children under 18. In each case the degree of inequality of non-Negro families is very little different for husband's income and family income minus wife's earnings. For Negro families, the contribution of family members other than the wife and husband tends to *increase* income inequality over the inequality of husband's income alone. This pattern is particularly pronounced for families with no children under 18. For non-

Table 18.3 **Gini coefficients on three income measures: husband-wife families, wife under age 60, nonfarm**

	Husband's income	Family income minus wife's earnings	Family income
Total	35.6	35.8	33.7
Negro	33.5	35.3	35.1
Non-Negro	34.7	35.1	32.9
Families with no children	39.2	39.7	36.0
Families with children	33.6	33.8	32.4
Families with children under 18			
Negro	31.9	32.5	32.9
Non-Negro	32.8	33.1	31.7
Families with no children under 18			
Negro	36.2	39.5	38.3
Non-Negro	38.5	39.0	35.1

Incomes of $25,000 and over are coded as $44,000.
   Source: 1/1,000 Sample.

Negro families, the effect of the employment of wives is to decrease income inequality somewhat (from 32.9 to 30.9). For the Negro population, the employment of wives has almost no effect on income inequality. The effect of wife's employment on income inequality is greater for families with no children under 18 than for families with children. In the case of the Negro population, the employment of wives with no children under 18 *reduces* the degree of income inequality from 39.0 to 37.9, while the employment of Negro mothers *raises* the degree of inequality. Clearly the effect of employment of wives on income inequality is rather small and not invariant in direction.

In Table 18.4 we show Gini coefficients for the same three income variables computed separately for families in which the wife earned income in 1959 and for those in which she did not. Again the population is disaggregated by color and child status. Among non-Negro families there is less inequality in husband's income and family income minus wife's earnings in families in which the wife is employed (had income in 1959) than in those in which she is not. For the Negro population, the reverse tends to be true – the husband's income inequality tends to be greater for families in which the wife is employed. Miller's comparisons, then, are clearly distorted by systematic differences in dispersion of husband's income between men whose wives are in and those whose wives are not in the labor force.

Table 18.4 Gini coefficients computed on three income measures: husband–wife families, wife under age 60, nonfarm, by color, family status, and whether or not wife received income

	Husband's income		Family income minus wife's earnings		Family income	
	Wife with income	Wife without income	Wife with income	Wife without income	Wife with income	Wife without income
Total	32.6	36.6	33.3	36.0	30.2	36.0
Negro	34.1	32.8	36.3	34.0	34.6	34.0
Non-Negro	31.6	35.8	32.4	35.3	29.1	35.3

Incomes of $25,000 and over are coded as $44,000.
Source: 1/1,000 Sample.

Thompson argues that income inequality is reduced when the wife works because wives of low income husbands are more likely to work – i.e., the bottom end of the distributions of families in terms of husband's income are more likely to have their incomes incremented than the upper end of the distribution. Thompson's argument would be logically valid if there were no variation among working wives in the amount earned. However, working wives of high income husbands tend to receive more income than working wives of low income husbands (see Table 18.5). The combination of a strong negative relationship between employment and husband's income and positive relationship between the earnings of employed women and husband's income results in only a small differential in the average amount of income per family (irrespective of whether or not the wife is employed) among various levels of husband's income. This means that while families toward the lower end of the husband's income distribution are being disproportionately moved upward in the distribution, the amount by which they move is relatively less than the movements achieved by families with employed wives in the middle and upper end of the husband's income distribution.

Trends

Figure 18.1 plots the time series of labor force participation rates of married women and Gini coefficients for various income measures as published in the U.S. Census Report, 'Trends in the Income of Families and Persons in the United States, 1947–1964.'[3] The labor force participation rate has risen rapidly and regularly by almost one percentage point per year. The income inequality measures show little evidence of trend. To the extent that there is a trend of decline in the inequality of family income, it appears to be matched by a similar decline in the inequality of husband's income. It does not appear that the increase in labor force participation of wives that has been occurring over the past two or three decades has had any impact on the level of income inequality.

The effect on family income inequality of any increase in the employment of wives depends on at least three things: (1) The pattern of change in labor force participation of wives in relation to husband's income; (2) The pattern of change in both the mean and the dispersion of wife's earnings in relation to husband's income; and, (3) The change in the shape of the distribution of husbands among income levels. Without attempting to specify exactly what has happened in recent history to each of these relationships, it does appear that the outcome of these changes has been neutral with respect to income inequality.

Income Inequality Between Black and White Families

Negro wives have considerably higher rates of employment than do white wives. A Negro husband-wife family is considerably more likely to have its total income result from the contributions of more than one earner than a white family, but the size of the Negro wife's contribution is on average considerably smaller than that of the white wife's. What effect do these differences have on the inequality of family income between the races?

3. U.S. Bureau of the Census, 'Trends in the Income of Families and Persons in the United States: 1947–1964,' Technical Paper #17, 1967, Tables 12 and 37; U.S. Bureau of Labor Statistics, Statistics on Manpower: A Supplement to the Manpower Report of the President (1969), Table B-1.

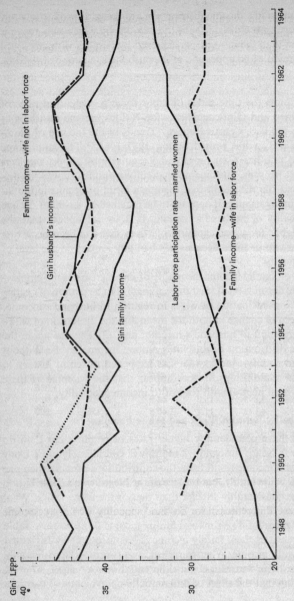

Figure 18.1. Recent Trend in Income Inequality and Labor Force Participation Rates of Married Women

Source: U.S. Bureau of the Census, Trends in the Income of Families and Persons in the United States: 1947–1964. Technical Paper 17, 1967. Tables 2 and 37; U.S. Bureau of Labor Statistics, Statistics on Manpower: A Supplement to the Manpower Report of the President (1969) Table 3.1.

To summarize the overall effect of differential employment and differential earnings of wives on the inequality or dissimilarity of the income distributions of the Negro and white populations, we have again used the Gini coefficient. Here, rather than comparing the cumulative distributions of families and money income, we are comparing the cumulative distributions of black and white families ordered with respect to incomes. In these comparisons a value of $35,000 was used for the category $25,000 and over. Other reasonable values were tried and produced no major change in results. Again, three separate income measures were used: (1) husband's income, (2) family income minus wife's earnings, and (3) total family income. Differences between (2) and (3) reflect the effect of differential contributions of other income recipients (and wife's nonearnings income) on income inequality between Negroes and non-Negroes.

Table 18.5 Wife's contribution to family income by husband's income and age

Husband's income	N	Percent	Proportion of wives with income	Wife's average income per recipient	Wife's average income per family
None	614	1.6	44.8	2,424	1,085
Less than $1,000	1,941	5.2	51.0	1,542	787
$1,000 – $1,999	2,736	7.3	50.3	1,625	818
$2,000 – $2,999	3,463	9.3	49.5	1,752	868
$3,000 – $3,999	4,493	12.0	48.7	1,994	972
$4,000 – $4,999	5,471	14.6	47.3	2,192	1,036
$5,000 – $5,999	5,895	15.8	44.3	2,312	1,024
$6,000 – $6,999	4,192	11.2	40.8	2,356	960
$7,000 – $9,999	5,350	14.3	35.9	2,365	850
$10,000 – $14,999	2,006	5.4	31.2	2,412	754
$15,000 +	1,245	3.3	32.1	2,613	838
Total	37,406	100.0	43.8	2,112	925

Source: 1960 U.S. Census, *Sources and Structure of Family Income*, Table 17.

Overall, the Gini coefficient for husband's income is 54.3 in comparison to a coefficient of 47.3 for total family income (bottom row, Table 18.5). Quite clearly, then, family income is less inequitably distributed than is husband's income. When family income is compared with family income minus wife's earnings, the differential is very small, 47·3 vs. 47.4, indicating that the effect of differential employment and earnings patterns of wives makes an insignificant difference to the inequality of distribution of income.

The differential in inequality between the total family income and husband's income results from the much greater incidence of earnings of adult family members other than the husband and wife, and may have nothing to do with family economic welfare. There are more earners, who may or may not pool their resources with those of other family members, and there are more adult consumers.

The employment rates of black wives are especially high relative to those of whites in the case of women with young children. Black mothers of children under six are 66 percent more likely to be working than their white counterparts. For mothers with children 6–11 and 12–17, the differentials are 45 and 5 percent respectively. Married Negro women without children have employment rates that are not much greater than those of white women, and in the case of women 14–29

Table 18.6 Negro-white income inequality by family status for three income measures (Gini coefficients)

Family status	Husband's income	Family income minus wife's earnings	Family income
Husband-wife families with one or more children under 18			
Youngest 0–2	56.2	48.8	45.9
3–5	61.6	55.7	50.2
6–11	60.4	56.1	51.4
12–17	54.0	49.2	50.9
Total	58.2	52.3	49.6
Husband-wife families with no children under 18			
Wife 14–29	38.1	26.2	36.9
30–44	49.2	41.0	44.8
45–59	50.0	46.2	47.6
Total	46.0	40.5	43.5
Husband-wife families, wife under age 60			
	54.3	47.4	47.3

Source: 1/1,000 Tabulations.

with no children, the black employment rate is considerably lower than the white rate.

If we disaggregate the population into two categories, those couples with children and those with none, and examine the separate Gini coefficients, we discover that the aggregate pattern presented above results from differential patterns within these two groups. For both categories income inequality is substantially reduced by virtue of the greater contribution of other family members. For childless couples (i.e., those with no children present), the racial inequality *increases* as a result of contributions by wives to family income, while for couples with children, inequality *decreases* somewhat. The effect of income of other relatives is greater, however, than that of income of wives.

Further disaggregation of couples in relation to age of youngest own child reveals that the wife's contribution in the case of couples with youngest own child age 12–17 tend to slightly increase inequality, just as it does for childless couples. Thus in those groups with very much higher employment rates, the degree of racial inequality is slightly reduced by virtue of the income of wives. In groups where the black employment rates are only slightly higher, the degree of racial inequality of income is unaffected, or in some cases increased.

The effect of wife's earnings on the inequality of family income between the races is small because, despite the higher rate of employment of Negro wives, their earnings are on the average considerably lower. Thus, a higher proportion of Negro families move up in the income distribution from where they would be in the absence of wife's income. The distance which they move in the distribution, however, is smaller, on average, than is the distance moved by white families with employed wives.

More About Penguins
and Pelicans

Penguinews, which appears every month, contains details of all the new books issued by Penguins as they are published. It is supplemented by our stocklist, which includes almost 5,000 titles.

A specimen copy of *Penguinews* will be sent to you free on request. Please write to Dept EP, Penguin Books Ltd, Harmondsworth, Middlesex, for your copy.

In the U.S.A.: For a complete list of books available from Penguins in the United States write to Dept CS, Penguin Books, 625 Madison Avenue, New York, New York 10022.

In Canada: For a complete list of books available from Penguins in Canada write to Penguin Books Canada Ltd, 2801 John Street, Markham, Ontario L3R 1B4.

In Australia: For a complete list of books available from Penguins in Australia write to the Marketing Department, Penguin Books Australia Ltd, P.O. Box 257, Ringwood, Victoria 3134.

Dutiful Daughters
Women talk about their lives

Edited by Jean McCrindle and Sheila Rowbotham

'As remarkable and immediate as Oscar Lewis's *Children of Sànchez*
... an extraordinary compilation of the voices and memoirs of
women over the past half century' – Emma Tennant in the
Guardian

The Wise Wound
Menstruation & Everywoman

Penelope Shuttle and Peter Redgrove

'An important, brave and exciting exploration into territory that
belongs to all of us, and nobody could read it without a sense of
discovery' – Margaret Drabble in the *Listener*

The Ambivalence of Abortion
Linda Bird Francke

In interviews with men and women of all ages and social groups,
Linda Bird Francke describes the human experience of abortion,
and in doing so casts new light on one of the most controversial
and complicated issues of our time.

Against Our Will
Men, Women and Rape

Susan Brownmiller

'Rape is nothing more or less than a conscious process of
intimidation by which *all men* keep *all women* in a state of fear.'

Opening her book with this explosive statement Susan Brownmiller goes on to show why she considers rape to be not just a
brutal crime but a reflection of how our society is conditioned.
Tracing the sociological, psychological and legal history of rape,
she sheds new and disturbing light on the tensions that exist
between men and women.

Words and Women
Language and the sexes

Casey Miller and Kate Swift

'Dear God', wrote one little girl, 'Are boys better than girls? I know you are one but try to be fair.'

George Orwell was right when he talked about the prefabricated words and metaphors – 'bitch-goddesses', 'the man-in-the-street' – that litter our everyday speech. We use them because they are convenient and easy: here the authors consider just how they affect our moral values, our religious beliefs and our attitudes towards the sexes.

Scream Quietly or the Neighbours Will Hear

Erin Pizzey

Erin Pizzey's struggle to open, and keep open, her refuge for battered wives in Chiswick has become a national issue, opening up to public scrutiny a problem that has been, hitherto, conveniently swept under the carpet.

The Captive Wife

Hannah Gavron

'A perceptive and telling account of the lives and difficulties of some young mothers' – *The Times Literary Supplement*

and a Penguin Special

Who Cares?
A New Deal for Mothers and Their Small Children

Penelope Leach

After many years of working with young families, Penelope Leach – author of *Babyhood* and *Baby and Child* – is convinced that we are giving them a raw deal. The pleasure and responsibility of childbearing is ceasing to be a personal and individual matter: it is becoming a matter for professionals running day-care facilities. As well as detailing a long-term programme aimed at changing society's attitudes to parents and their young children, Dr Leach offers many practical suggestions which could be implemented right now – if we care enough.

Recently published in Penguin

Modern Economics

J. Pen

Professor Pen, the well-known Dutch economist, is a sceptic, but one who has not lost his faith in a free enterprise economy – provided that the business community, trade unions and governments behave in a sensible way. His optimism is reflected in this new edition of *Modern Economics*: an invaluable analysis of the Keynesian revolution for the general reader.

Geographical Economics

Patrick O'Sullivan

A lucid introduction to geographical economics. Devoting separate chapters to the theory of location, agglomeration economies, travel, trade and transport facilities, Professor O'Sullivan builds up an equilibrium model of the geographical economy. He then examines the geographical aspects of economic growth, in an analysis which provokes questions of equity and efficiency, and their implications for regional policy, and for political decision-making at regional and national level.

Social Goals and Economic Perspectives

G. P. Marshall

Some of the most pressing areas of social concern are explored here through a broad economic perspective. The main body of this study is devoted to considering inequality and income maintenance: the author analyses the changing distribution of income and wealth in Britain since the war, and assesses the arguments for a State run scheme to provide a guaranteed minimum living standard. The problems of defining and measuring poverty are examined in detail, as are the aims and achievements of the private charities and Britain's social security system. The final chapter discusses the contribution of women in the mixed economy, and its effect on their choice and decisions.

The World of Goods
Towards an anthropology of consumption
Mary Douglas and Baron Isherwood

Cast as a debate between anthropology and economics on the
question of why people want goods, this book argues that we can
better understand our own demand for material possessions if
we know what they mean for other peoples outside the
industrial system and beyond the ingenious chicanery of advertising.
Anthropology suggests that we use goods to build a communication
system – a code of transactions. Nobody denies that food is for
nourishment, housing for shelter, clothes for comfort. But if that
were all, our choice of products would be selective in very different
ways.

Education and Equality
Edited by David Rubinstein

Black children are forced to adopt the viewpoint of the White
Anglo-Saxon Protestant; girls are discouraged from doing
certain subjects and are allowed day-release facilities far less often
than are boys; working-class children and children who are more
'practical' than 'academic' suffer from lack of educational resources
and lack of interest from their educators; primary schools and
further education establishments receive less prestige and funding
than universities and secondary schools.

In this pertinent and provocative collection the contributors look
at the way these inequalities and others pervade the English
education system, and suggest ways in which we can achieve true
equality of education.